Sci ✓

Celestial Delights

The Best Astronomical Events through 2010

Celestial Delights

The Best Astronomical Events through 2010

Francis Reddy
and
Greg Walz-Chojnacki

CELESTIAL ARTS
Berkeley, California

Celestial Arts
P.O. Box 7123
Berkeley, California 94707
www.tenspeed.com

Distributed in Australia by Simon & Schuster Australia, in Canada by Ten Speed Press Canada, in New Zealand by Southern Publishers Group, in South Africa by Real Books, in Southeast Asia by Berkeley Books, and in the United Kingdom and Europe by Airlift Book Company.

Copyediting by Kristi Hein
Cover design by Toni Tajima
Interior design by Jeff Brandenburg, ImageComp

Cover photo: Curtains of red and green aurora—also known as the Northern Lights—dance above Hatcher Pass in Alaska's Talkeetna Mountains. On October 25, 2001, twisted magnetic fields on the sun suddenly released their energy and sent an enormous bubble of solar material racing toward our planet. The cloud swept past us on October 28, disrupting the Earth's magnetic environment and triggering vivid auroral displays from Alaska to areas as far south as North Carolina. (Photo by Wayne Johnson)

Library of Congress Cataloging-in-Publication Data
Reddy, Francis, 1959–
Celestial delights : the best astronomical events through 2010 /
Francis Reddy and Greg Walz-Chojnacki.
p. cm.
Rev. ed. of: c1992.
Includes bibliographical references and index.
ISBN 1-58761-157-0 (alk. paper)
1. Astronomy—Observers' manuals. 2. Astronomy—Amateurs' manuals.
I. Walz-Chojnacki, Greg, 1954– II. Title.
QB63 .R33 2002
520—dc21 2002008711

Printed in the United States
First printing, 2002

1 2 3 4 5 6 7 8 9 10 — 06 05 04 03 02

Contents

To my parents, Elizabeth and Francis,
who introduced me to the Cape Cod sky.

—FR

To my mother, whose love has been a
guiding star to all her children.

—GWC

Preface

There is a widespread impression that the scientific appreciation of the universe must be left wholly to those who have had years of formal training or who devote a large part of their free time to science as a hobby. Everyone takes a moment to sky-gaze now and then—admiring the colors of a sunset, noticing the Man in the Moon, or playing connect-the-dots with the Big Dipper—but there is a sense that astronomy is best left to those with expensive equipment and lots of time for observing the heavens.

That's far from the truth. Although the skies under which most of us live are awash with the tawny glow of city lights, they are surprisingly well suited for observing the motions and arrangements of the solar system's brightest members—the sun, moon, and planets. Their ever-changing configurations fascinated and puzzled skywatchers for the first few thousand years of human civilization, a time when the human eye was the primary observing tool. Tracking their wanderings through the sky requires nothing more than good weather and some guidance on when and where to look.

This book is designed both as an introduction to astronomy and as a calendar of upcoming celestial events. Our first aim is to share the simple beauties of the sky as seen by our ancestors. By using the moon and brighter planets as celestial signposts, the tables and charts in this book serve as a guide to every planet that can be seen with the unaided eye. Separate chapters detail upcoming eclipses, introduce the major constellations, describe the best meteor showers, and explore other more challenging, if less predictable, phenomena. Appendix A provides an almanac of easy-to-see astronomical events from 2003 through 2010, all organized by date and time and cross-referenced with diagrams and tables found elsewhere in the book. For convenience, we have also collected some of this information in additional appendices.

Our secondary goal is to explore how we see the sky from the perspective of our spacefaring culture—which has literally touched some of the worlds that humankind has watched, prayed to, and feared for ages. An exciting burst of planetary exploration is currently under way—plans include spacecraft visits to Mercury, Saturn, Mars, and a couple of comets—and with the unprecedented communications ability afforded us by the World Wide Web, the discoveries of such missions have become more quickly and completely available than ever before. We also have attempted to share something of the excitement felt and the challenges faced by those who continue to delve into the long-observed phenomena that this book describes.

Observant readers will notice that in some diagrams the labels for east and west are reversed from their expected placement on a map of the Earth. Terrestrial maps plot the world as if we are looking down on the Earth from above, but in charting the sky we're looking in the opposite direction. The east-west reversal occurs in our illustrations of the paths of Venus across the sun (chapter 3), the path of the moon through the Earth's shadow in lunar eclipses (chapter 4), and the star charts (chapter 7).

It's our hope that you will come to enjoy the beauty of the heavens that is everyone's heritage, and we encourage you to participate in this centuries-old delight. All we ask is that you occasionally look up and wonder, "What is that bright star?"

This book would not be possible without the assistance of many others. Our own eclipse maps are based on data made available by Fred (Mr. Eclipse) Espenak of NASA's Goddard Space Flight Center. Our friend Robert Miller graciously created custom software for us, and for this new edition he also offered to improve on our maps illustrating the Mars, Jupiter, and Saturn retrograde loops. The wonderful photographs of António Cidadão, Robert Miller, and Bill Sterne enhance the book; we thank them for their help. Geoff Chester, Doug Caswell, Bill Cooke, Audouin Dollfus, Michael Rappenglück, David Pankenier, Peter Schultz, Ewen Whitaker, and Donald Yeomans were all generous with their time and knowledge. Judith Heymann translated the writings of eighteenth-century astronomer J. J. Lalande for us. Of course, the authors alone are responsible for any errors in the text and illustrations.

Judy Young, director of The Sunwheel Project at the University of Massachusetts, gave us encouragement from an unexpected quarter. We thank Ken Crossen of TechView Corp. in Carrboro, North Carolina, for our long and productive relationship with the technical drawing program TechEdit. We also thank Paul Wessel and Walter Smith, University of Hawaii, for the Generic Mapping Tools (GMT) software package and Alan Cogbill of Los Alamos National Laboratory for his continued ports of GMT. Other software we found helpful includes Dance of the Planets 2.71, from ARC Science Simulation Software; Project Pluto's Guide 7.0; and Shinobu Takesako's EmapWin 1.21 eclipse simulator. NASA's ADS Abstract Service, the Jet Propulsion Laboratory's Horizons ephemeris computation service, and the supportive staff of the Newberry County Library in Newberry, South Carolina, all proved immensely helpful. And we gratefully acknowledge the Rector and Visitors of the University of Virginia for permission to use excerpts from their electronic text collection.

Last but not least, we are grateful to our copyeditor, Kristi Hein, and the folks at Celestial Arts for their support in creating this new edition: Joann Deck, publisher; our editors, Brie Mazurek and Justin Wells; and designers Toni Tajima and Jeff Brandenburg.

1 The Meaning of the Sky

> The movements of the heavenly bodies are an admirable thing, well known and manifest to all peoples. There are no people, no matter how barbaric and primitive, that do not raise up their eyes, take note, and observe with some care and admiration the continuous and uniform course of the heavenly bodies.
>
> —Bernabé Cobo, *History of the New World,* 1653

The heavens were once seen as the exclusive domain of supernatural beings, but over the past two generations we mortals have moved in. We have created machines that enable astronauts, albeit briefly, to take up residence in orbit around our world. Hundreds of miles above us, construction proceeds on the third major space station, a growing research laboratory that is sometimes plainly visible to the unaided eye. The space near Earth has become a valued resource: the "high ground" for global communications, military reconnaissance, and the scientific study of the Earth itself. From this increasingly crowded realm we can view the sun, the planets, and the wider universe unfiltered by Earth's atmosphere and unaffected by weather. Beyond it lies the moon, where footprints still attest to brief human visits, and the planets, asteroids, and comets that to date have been explored only by our mechanical surrogates. Farther still, and for now beyond our immediate technological grasp, shine the nearest stars and the vast interstellar frontier of the Milky Way galaxy. With vision extended by telescopes in low earth orbit and on mountaintop observatories, astronomers now catalogue the alien worlds that circle some of the nearest stars. We have taken millennia to unravel the basic structure of our own planetary system. Now we begin the task of comparing it to others, probing for clues that will tell us, among other things, whether our home planet is as unique as we suppose.

As citizens of the twenty-first century, nearly all of us are somewhat familiar with the basic layout of our solar system and the physical laws that govern the universe. But knowing that the planets circle the sun is one thing—recognizing how that movement expresses itself in the sky above us can be quite another. Our ancient forebears may not have understood why the sky worked the way it did, but they certainly knew it better. We have the advantage, though, because the basic motions that beguiled and bewildered our ancestors remain on display. The enjoyment of seeing becomes the deeper pleasure of understanding what we see.

Skywatching and Skywatchers

The single most striking observation of the sky is one so obvious we might at first overlook it entirely. It is that of the daily motion of the sun, moon, planets, and stars as they appear to rise in the eastern sky and set in the west. Extended, methodical observation reveals other motions superimposed on this basic east-to-west movement.

The sun has always been recognized as vitally important and was viewed by many ancient cultures as the greatest deity. Even the most primitive peoples appreciated the life-giving powers of what we now regard as our star. The reverence shown to the sun was reflected by the astronomical functions adopted by ancient priests. The diurnal cycle is even more basic than the motion of the sun, yet even the most casual observers are aware that the length of our days and nights varies as the year passes. The first astronomers noticed that these variations were linked to annual variations in the sun's position throughout the year. The changing apparent position of the rising or setting sun stops and reverses course at two extremes, called solstices, that occur in summer (near June 21) and winter (near December 21). (Note: Unless specified otherwise, all references to seasons and corresponding months apply to the northern hemisphere; they are, of course, reversed in the southern hemisphere.) The longest day occurs at the summer solstice, the date on which the sun rises and sets at its northernmost point and makes its highest arc through the sky. The days then slowly grow shorter until the sun reaches its winter solstice position, when it rises and sets at its southernmost point and traces its lowest arc through the sky. The daylight hours then gradually increase again until they reach another maximum at the following summer solstice. As the sun oscillates from one solstice (literally "standing sun") position to the next, it passes through the point midway between them twice each year. This point is called the equinox ("equal night"), the date on which the hours of daylight equal the hours of darkness. The sun's spring, or vernal, passing of the equinox occurs about March 21; it returns to this point in autumn around September 23. The appearance of the sun at a solstice or an equinox defines the formal start of that season. With this fundamental knowledge, ancient sunwatchers could track the march of the seasons and guide essential activities, such as planting and harvesting, and the festivals and other cultural activities that became associated with them.

We can track this motion easily at sunset (or, for early risers, sunrise). The sun's apparent motion is fastest in spring and fall so the changes are most easily seen then, but the starting date doesn't really matter, as the motion itself is continuous. A few observations of the setting sun's place on the western horizon, spaced over a few weeks, reveals the trend. The direction of sunset creeps along the horizon: southward from July to December, northward the other half of the year. The farthest positions north and south correspond to the summer and winter solstices, respectively, and the point midway between them marks the sun's position at the equinox.

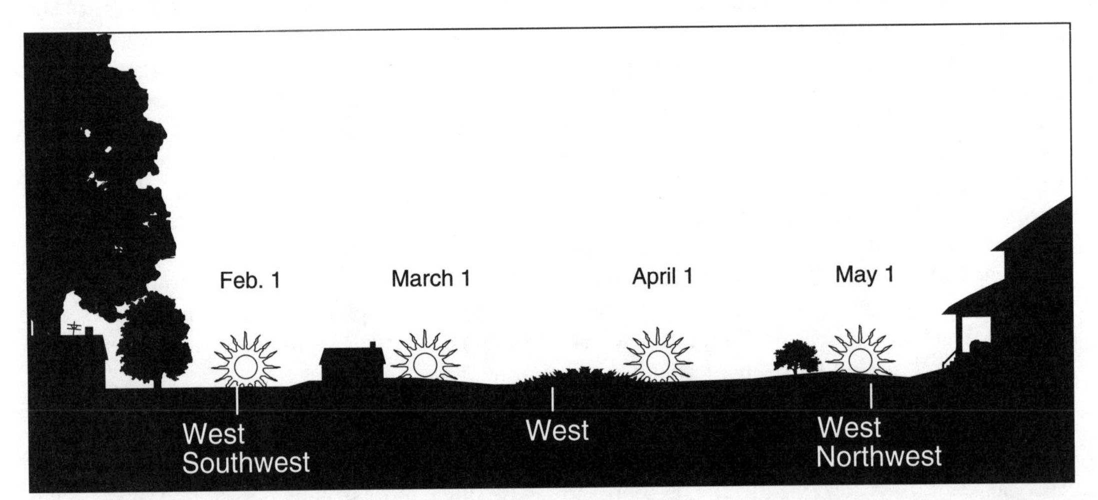

Figure 1-1. Track the setting sun for a few weeks and you'll see the location of sunset move along the horizon. The sun slides northward from late December to late June, then reverses direction and heads south for the rest of the year. This diagram shows how the sunset point travels between February and May for observers in middle northern latitudes.

Timeworn structures—from England's Stonehenge, to the passage tombs of Ireland, to the pyramids of Mexico—incorporate clear knowledge of the sun's movements. These were sacred places consecrated by the astronomical alignments that connected them to the seasonal signposts in the sky.

Even today, many of our holidays and holy days reflect the seasons. The dates of Easter and Passover, for example, are tied explicitly to the spring equinox. Scholars tell us Christ was born in the spring, yet Christmas falls near the winter solstice—that hopeful date after which the days begin to lengthen, promising greater warmth and sunshine to come. The date of the winter solstice was set at December 25 on the calendar reformed by Julius Caesar in 46 B.C. This was also the date for the festival of Sol Invictus (the Unconquerable Sun), a sun cult introduced to Rome in the first century A.D. that became the state religion in A.D. 274. The sun was seen as the divine source of light and order for the universe; the emperor, as the font of Roman civilization, fulfilled a complementary role on earth. Sol Invictus was also associated with Mithras, central god of a mysterious cult that was especially popular among soldiers. There is no date recorded for Christ's birth, but December 25 was selected by the early Church in part for the ease with which it meshed with long-established customs. The Roman world was already celebrating on that date, and the underlying symbolism of the Unconquerable Sun could be suffused with a new Christian meaning.

It's worth noting that the sun's solstice and equinox positions could just as easily be reckoned as marking the height of each season, rather than its start, and there are cultural traditions that acknowledge this. The European holiday of Midsummer in fact falls near the summer solstice. Many observances occur midway between solstice and equinox, an echo of the ancient importance of these midseason dates that reverberates even today. February opens with Candlemas and Groundhog Day, derived from the Celtic festival of Imbolc. May brings us both the bonfire festival of Beltane and its descendant May Day, as well as the witch-vigil of Walpurgisnacht in Bavaria. The Irish feast of Lammas and the Celtic festival of Lughnasa occur at the start of August. The end of October sees the Celtic new year's festival of Samhain and its descendant Halloween, as well as All Saint's Day and the Mexican celebration of Dia de los Muertos. These examples come from Euro-American culture, but independent traditions also acknowledge the dual approach. What ties them together is recognition of the sun's continued journey as vital to the maintenance of the natural order and as something in which humankind must participate, either by encouraging the sun—like spectators cheering on a marathon runner—as it treks through times of special risk, or by celebrating the sun's victorious arrival at its annual stations.

Seen from the tropics, the sun attains another position of importance easily overlooked by those located elsewhere on the globe. Within the band of latitudes bounded by the Tropic of Cancer and the Tropic of Capricorn, the sun passes through the zenith—the point directly overhead—at noon

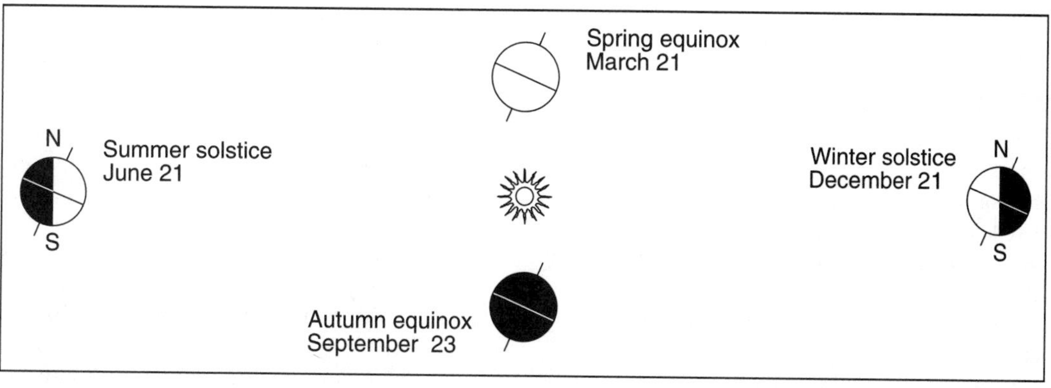

Figure 1-2. Earth's tilt with respect to its orbit (23.45°) creates the seasons. On June 21, the start of northern summer, the northern hemisphere angles into the sun most directly and the sun arcs highest in the sky, rising and setting at its northernmost points. Six months later, on December 21, northern observers see the sun make its lowest track through the sky, rising and setting at its southernmost points.

on certain dates. Each zenith passage occurs on well-defined dates for any particular location. Historical and archaeological evidence from Mexico to South America shows that many peoples observed and celebrated one of the sun's zenith passages as the start of the new year.

Today, the moon, a lesser light, is what first draws our attention to the night sky. Early calendars were based on the motions of the moon, mainly because its cycle is shorter, more obvious, and therefore more accessible than that of the sun. The priest-astronomers of ancient Mesopotamia and Greece determined the start of a new lunar month by watching for the first appearance of the moon's slender crescent in the evening twilight. In Egypt the month began with the disappearance of the waning crescent moon from the predawn sky. The system of marking time by the moon doubtless goes back millennia. Suggestions of some sort of lunar time-reckoning can be found among the 17,500-year-old cave paintings of Lascaux in France, and Paleolithic bone artifacts found throughout Europe bear carved tally marks that may represent even older lunar scorecards. But the moon's convenience as a short-term timekeeper is offset by the unpleasant mathematical problem of reconciling its cycle with that of the sun and the seasons. The solar year cannot be reduced to a whole number of lunar months. Ancient calendar-keepers thus needed some way to recalibrate the two cycles if a lunar calendar was to stay in step with the seasons. They did this either mathematically, by inserting days at culturally acceptable times, or empirically, by observing the sun and stars and synchronizing the cycles anew each year.

The Lure of the Planets

Long before skywatching became part of a formalized time-keeping system, ancient observers must have realized that the sun and moon weren't the only objects moving through the heavens. Unlike most moderns, the diligent starwatchers of ancient times also noticed five peculiar "stars" that wander independently among the constellations, each moving at a different speed. Like the sun and moon, they follow roughly the same path through the sky and usually move eastward relative to the stars. But now and then these wanderers slow down, stop, loop west for a time, stop again, and then resume their eastward journey. Today we know these objects as the planets, a word that derives from the literal Greek description of their peculiar astronomical behavior (*planetes*, "wanderers"). Ancient astronomers knew of only five planets: Mercury, Venus, Mars, Jupiter, and Saturn. Although under ideal conditions Uranus can be seen without some sort of optical aid, evidently it didn't catch the attention of early skywatchers; like the still fainter Neptune and Pluto, Uranus remained undiscovered until long after the invention of the telescope.

In their wanderings through the sky, one or more planets may appear to pass close to another, forming captivating and sometimes striking arrangements. The diagrams in this book illustrate many of these through 2010. The greater the number of planets involved, the greater the time between successive displays, so gatherings of all five visible planets are the least common. These events were characteristically regarded as messages from the heavens—blessings or warnings for the state and its ruler. Nowhere was this more true than in early China. There the planets were viewed as the ministers of Shangdi, the Lord on High, and their gatherings were seen as a congress of sky spirits called only when the celestial realm was deliberating major changes in policy. The emperor was the chief shaman, his role on earth a heavenly appointment, and early in the second millennium B.C. observation of the heavens became his greatest responsibility. It was the emperor's divine obligation to ensure that all human activity conformed as closely as possible to Shangdi's desires. This precept, which became more formalized over time and was first explicitly stated in early writings of the Zhou Dynasty (1046–256 B.C.), is referred to as the "Mandate of Heaven" *(tian ming)*. Chinese rulers believed that the will of Shangdi could be determined by detailed skywatching, with particular importance given to rare and unusual happenings. Astronomical or meteorological events could indicate displeasure with the way affairs on earth were being conducted.

David Pankenier of Lehigh University has shown that tight five-planet clusters are closely associated with dynastic transitions and with the development of the Mandate of Heaven in ancient China. A deliberation of Shangdi's ministers suggested that the current ruler had fallen out of favor and sent a signal throughout the land to would-be political challengers. Official records credit close planetary groupings as heralds of the Zhou, Han, and Song dynasties; astronomical and historical evidence suggest that the Shang and Xia dynasties also began with tight conjunctions. Driven by their heavenly mandate, Chinese rulers created the world's longest continuous record of astronomical observation, one that remains an important source of historical data today.

Belief in planet power is persistent. Jupiter and Saturn appear close together about every twenty years, infrequently enough that their conjunctions were regarded as particularly ominous. In 1348, King Philip VI of France asked physicians at the University of Paris to report on the origin of the terrible plague then sweeping across Europe. Their *Paris Consilium* proposed that the Black Death was in part the result of the conjunction of Jupiter, Saturn, and Mars in Aquarius three years earlier. Most of the Jupiter-Saturn pairings between 1345 and 1538 occurred within astrological signs connected with water. Broadsheets and pamphlets circulated throughout Europe as each conjunction approached, their authors warning of poor harvests and terrible weather culminating in horrific, even biblical, floods.

There is a long and singularly unsuccessful record of apocalyptic predictions associated with planetary groupings, and the phenomenon is still with us. In the past few decades, several planetary gatherings made headlines as mystics and doomsayers foretold of approaching disaster. Mixing such well-worn topics as Nostradamus, pyramid mysteries, and lost continents, as well as a pinch of science here and there, with each event doomsayers concocted a recipe of coming chaos, economic ruin, and geological upheaval. As of this writing, our most recent appointment with doom by planetary alignment was one scheduled for May 2000; just as with similar gatherings in 1962 and 1982, nothing extraordinary happened.

The earth-shattering interpretation of planetary conjunctions reaches back at least to the writings of Berosus, a Babylonian astrologer who brought the astrology and mythology of his homeland to the Greek world around 300 B.C. As transmitted to us through much later writings, he believed that the world is alternately destroyed and recreated—first by fire, then by water—and that the planets hold the key to the timetable. Seneca, in his *Natural History*, summed it up this way:

> For all earthly things will burn, he contends, when all the planets which now maintain different orbits come together in the sign of Cancer and are so arranged in the same path that a straight line can pass through the spheres of all of them. The deluge will occur when the same group of planets meets in the sign of Capricorn.

It's remarkable to us that anyone would look upon a gathering of planets as a harbinger of anything, good or ill. Yet we can sympathize with

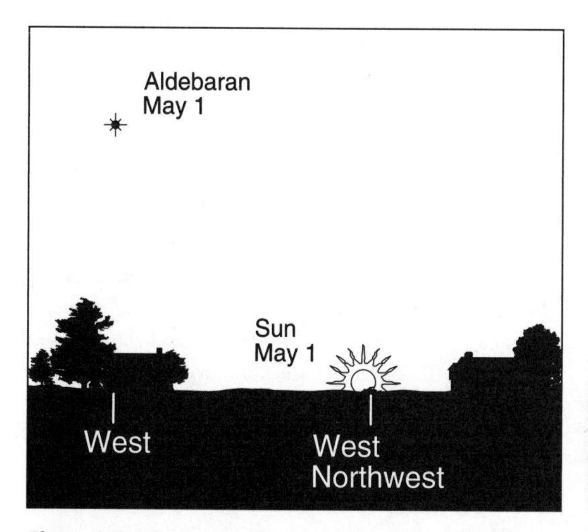

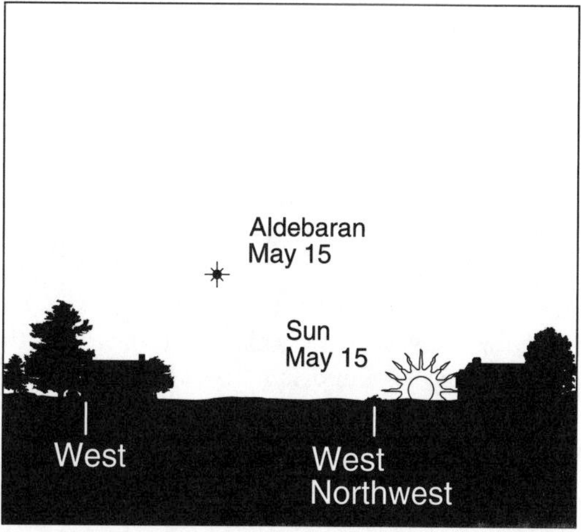

Figure 1-3. The sun appears to drift eastward among the stars, making one complete circuit through the sky each year. Throughout May, for example, the setting sun creeps ever closer to the bright star Aldebaran.

both the impulse to discern order in the universe and the yearning to achieve some of that predictability in the often tumultuous human experience. So perhaps it was natural for our ancestors to attempt to glimpse some guidance in celestial rhythms.

Astronomy and astrology began to part company in the seventeenth century. A continuing thread of late-twentieth-century science is the recognition that other bodies in the solar system truly can affect life on Earth—by impacts or through the long-distance interactions of gravity—in ways explainable by physical laws determined from observation and mathematics. Ancient observers, whose motivations were very different from those of modern scientists, nevertheless recorded data that provide important insights in many astronomical investigations today. Their interpretations, however, have been left behind in the rise of science.

Or so astronomers would like to think. A 1998 Harris poll found that 37 percent of adult Americans professed a belief in astrology; the figure rose to 41 percent in 2000. Gallup polls over the last decade show somewhat lower numbers but a similar trend of an increase of a few percentage points, with 28 percent of American adults agreeing in 2001 that "the position of the stars and planets can affect people's lives." Unfortunately, these surveys provide no measure of the depth of astrological belief.

In 1999, Michael De Robertis and Paul Delaney attempted to fill this void by surveying first-year students at York University in North York, Ontario, about their attitudes toward astrology and astronomy. Over 51 percent of both science majors and other students indicated that they subscribed at least somewhat to astrological principles. Still, only about 15 percent of both groups indicated that they made "many conscious decisions" based on horoscopes. The authors conclude, as have others, that the widening acceptance of astrology is part of a larger problem with the development of critical thinking skills in schools. They also recognize that the need to believe plays an important role in forming and maintaining the very attitudes such surveys measure. And there's the difficulty, for it means that changes to the curriculum that address only science literacy and critical-thinking skills cannot resolve the problem.

Star Light, Star Bright

We see the travels of the sun, moon, and planets against the backdrop of the starry sky, so it should not be surprising that some of the world's oldest surviving literature contains references to the same conspicuous objects and patterns we see there today. Homer's *Iliad,* the epic Greek poem about the Trojan War, can be traced back to at least 700 B.C. In Book 18, Hephaestus fashions and decorates the shield of Achilles with emblems of our winter sky:

> And first Hephaestus makes a great and
> massive shield . . .
> There he made the earth and there the sky
> and the sea
> and the inexhaustible blazing sun and the
> moon rounding full
> and there the constellations, all that crown
> the heavens,
> the Pleiades and the Hyades, Orion in all
> his power too
> and the Great Bear that mankind calls the
> Wagon:
> she wheels on her axis always fixed,
> watching the Hunter,
> and she alone is denied a plunge in the
> Ocean's baths.

The inspirations for these adornments are still in our night sky: the familiar stars of Orion the Hunter, the bright clusters of the Pleiades and the Hyades in Taurus and Ursa Major (the Great Bear, whose brightest stars form the Big Dipper). Homer's observation that the Great Bear "wheels on her axis always fixed" and is "denied a plunge in the Ocean's baths," is a clear reference to the fact that these stars circled about the northern sky and never set below the horizon—a fact of the middle northern latitudes that is as true for us today as it was for the ancient Greeks.

A few generations later, the Greek poet Hesiod wrote *Works and Days.* A kind of *Farmer's Almanac* from 650 B.C., *Works and Days* is a poem about peasant life that weaves an astro-agricultural calendar into a framework of mythology and the virtues of labor. The key dates for the calendar were determined by the rising and setting of certain stars just before sunrise or just after sunset.

When the Pleiades, daughters of Atlas,
are rising,
begin the harvest, the plowing when they set.
Forty nights and days they are hidden
and appear again as the year moves round,
when first you sharpen your sickle.

The Pleiades rose just before the sun in May, heralding the proper time to begin the harvest of what we call winter wheat. In November these stars slipped beneath the western horizon as the sun rose, the signal for farmers to prepare their fields and sow their grain. Five months later the stars were lost in the sun's glare, but they returned the following May, just preceding the dawn and commencing another yearly cycle.

Hesiod relates other aspects of everyday life to the schedules of the stars. The first appearance of Arcturus in the evening, together with certain animal signs, announces the coming of spring. Sirius rising just before dawn is a sign of midsummer, when "goats are plumpest and wine sweetest," while the morning rising of Arcturus signals the best time for picking grapes.

We can watch the motion of the sun among the stars Hesiod describes by locating a bright star in the south or west as evening twilight fades. A good example is Aldebaran, the brightest star in the winter constellation of Taurus the Bull, gleaming low in the western sky in late spring. If we check on the star after a week or two, we'll see that it has drifted slowly westward from its original position, gradually appearing lower in the sky. Continued observation reveals that it moves ever closer to the sun, sliding westward until it is eventually lost in the glow of evening twilight. This westward drift of the stars can be interpreted in another way: as an eastward drift of the sun through the starry background. Figure 1-4 illustrates how the movement of the Earth along its yearly orbit places the sun closer to our line of sight with Aldebaran. Eventually both sun and star lie roughly along the same line of sight and the star is lost in the sun's brilliant glare. When Aldebaran emerges from twilight on the opposite side of the sun, it will be visible just before sunrise.

As Hesiod's descriptions of the Pleiades bear out, ancient observers had noticed that the sun makes a complete circuit through the stars once each year. The path traveled by the sun through the stars became known as the ecliptic; the twelve constellations along the ecliptic gave rise to the famous astrological "signs of the zodiac."

While there can be no question that the sky played an important role in the great cultures of the past, we take for granted the vestiges of its significance remaining in today's societies. Our week has seven days—the time it takes the moon to go through one-fourth of its phases. Seven is also the number of seemingly independent lights known to wander through the sky—the sun, moon, and five planets—and we have given their names to the days of the week. Sunday derives from the Roman *dies Solis,* "day of the sun"; Monday comes from *dies Lunae,* "day of the moon"; Saturday is Saturn's Day. The remaining celestial connections come to us obscured by the names of figures from the Nordic pantheon. For now, it's enough to realize that Tuesday is named for Mars, Wednesday for Mercury, Thursday for Jupiter, and Friday for Venus. We'll have more to say about the mythology associated with each planet later on.

The objects in the sky have one more obvious attribute that we have not yet discussed: brightness. The maps and diagrams throughout this book indicate the brightness of the stars and planets by the size of the dots that represent them. This follows a numerical scale of brightness that owes its essential form to the Greek astronomer Hipparchus. Chief among his contributions is a catalog of stars visible from his home, with notes on their position and brightness (129 B.C.). His notation was a model of clarity: the brightest stars were of the first magnitude, the next brightest were second magnitude, and so on, down to sixth magnitude, into which he grouped the faintest stars visible to the unaided eye. Although the brightness scheme makes sense when described this way, those new to astronomy are often puzzled to learn that a star with a higher magnitude number is actually fainter than one with a lower value. It helps to think of the word "magnitude" as meaning "class": "first-class" (first magnitude) stars are brighter than "second-class" (second magnitude) stars, and so on.

When the brightness scale was later precisely codified, it became clear that some of the stars Hipparchus had classified as first magnitude were in fact considerably brighter than others. Astronomers therefore found it necessary to extend the magnitude scale down to zero and lower. Sirius, the brightest star, has a magnitude

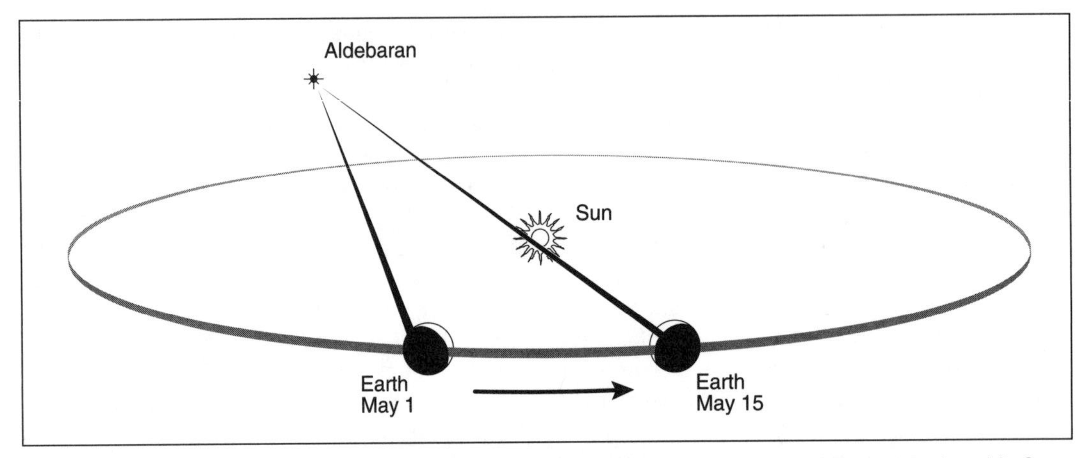

Figure 1-4. The sun's apparent eastward drift among the stars reflects the movement of Earth along its orbit. Once each year, for instance, Earth's motion in space brings the sun close to our line of sight with distant Aldebaran.

of –1.4. And when we apply this scale to objects within the solar system, the numbers look peculiar indeed. Mars can attain a brightness of –2.9, Venus at its brightest is magnitude –4.7, the full moon ranks as –12.7, and the sun naturally tops the scale at –26.8.

Loss of the Night

For about two-thirds of the world's population, the night sky isn't what it used to be—namely, darker—since, out of economic necessity, we moderns spend much of our lives deep within the artificial skyglow of major cities. This was part of our motivation in writing *Celestial Delights:* we chose to examine astronomy using the brightest objects in the sky because they are still available to everyone, even most city-dwellers.

Thanks to the dramatic increase in skyglow over the past decade, it's a challenge to view even Mars and Saturn when they are not at their brightest. Anyone who has taken an evening flight from a large city airport has seen the lattice of orange and green streetlights and the gleam of decorative lighting on buildings far below. Our artificial constellations far outshine the stars. The fact that we can see these lights from high overhead underscores the problem. Most streetlights are intended to illuminate the ground directly below, but a considerable amount of their light spills sideways and upward. Light going where it is neither useful nor wanted creates the washed-out sky of the city and the suburbs—a phenomenon that astronomers refer to as "light pollution."

Light pollution is only beginning to be recognized as a serious environmental problem. Setting aside the aesthetic, ecological, and astronomical concerns, consider the problem from a purely economic perspective. A portion of the energy required to operate a streetlight is wasted if part of that light is thrown directly into the sky. Greater energy demand requires more electrical power and, in turn, the burning of more oil and coal to generate it. Energy use translates to energy cost—wasted light burns money. In 2001 the International Dark Sky Association, a group that supports legislative efforts to limit light pollution, estimated the cost of wasted light at $1.5 billion per year in the United States alone.

The extent of the problem can be seen from the orbital perch of satellites. Pierantonio Cinzano and Fabio Falchi of the University of Padova in Italy and Chris Elvidge of the U.S. National Oceanic and Atmospheric Administration have produced the first world atlas of artificial night sky brightness, using images from the Defense Meteorological Satellite Program. The atlas reveals that 99 percent of the U.S. population and two-thirds of the world's population live in areas where the night sky can be considered polluted. For about half of the world's population, including all but a few percent of U.S. residents, artificial light pollution makes the sky brighter on a clear moonless night than the sky at the darkest observatory sites when illuminated by a first quarter moon. For two-thirds of the United States and one-fifth of the world population, the faint band of the Milky Way is lost in the skyglow. More troubling still, the night sky is now so bright for one-sixth of the world's people that their eyes cannot complete the dark adaptation required for full night vision. "Mankind is proceeding to envelop itself in a luminous fog," the study's authors conclude.

Californians in the Los Angeles area experienced their darkest sky in decades with the power outages that followed the 1994 Northridge earthquake. The city's Griffith Observatory logged hundreds of calls from people wondering why the stars were so bright and concerned over the nature of the unusual "silver cloud" (the Milky Way).

Our loss of the night denies us a wellspring of human inspiration. It disconnects us from a natural resource that binds cultures of the past to cultures of the present. It reinforces the thoroughly modern illusion that we are somehow apart from nature.

There is cause for encouragement. The sky-brightness atlas revealed Venice as the only city in Italy with a population greater than 250,000 from which observers in the city's center could see the Milky Way's subtle glow. The reason? Venice strives for a romantic image and preserves its ambiance by using unobtrusive outdoor lighting, providing an example in which an emphasis on quality, rather than quantity, meets public needs without excising the stars. Solutions that work do exist and cities all over the world are beginning to address the issue. In February 2002, the Czech Republic became the first country to enact a national light-pollution law. It obligates citizens to "take measures to prevent the occurrence of light pollution," which it defines as "every form of illumination by artificial light which is dispersed outside the areas it is dedicated to, particularly if directed above the level of the horizon."

All ancient peoples made some sort of connection with the sky. To them, it was a place where powerful beings worked and played—at times helping, at others hindering humanity. To us today, it is important as a new frontier, a place where a few of us now live and work and which all our minds can explore. We'll conclude this chapter by amending the epigram we began with: There are no people, no matter how sophisticated and technological, who do not profit from observing the night sky.

2 Moon Dance

Well it's a marvelous night for a moondance
With the stars up above in your eyes.
A fantabulous night to make romance
'Neath the cover of October skies.

—Van Morrison, "Moondance," 1970

The moon is our nearest neighbor in space, Earth's partner in a never-ending dance around the sun. For much of each month, it's also the most prominent object in the nighttime sky. The moon whirls around the celestial vault in just over 27 days, and each day throughout its cycle it appears slightly different—a sliver of light at the beginning and end, a brilliant silvery disk in between. Compared to every other object in the sky, the moon is a flagrant show-off. Its regular cycle of waxing and waning is so obvious that it formed the basis of early calendars, providing a convenient interval of time intermediate between the day and the more subtle annual cycle of the sun and seasons.

While there is only one purely lunar calendar in wide use today, the moon remains an important cultural symbol. The flags of more than half a dozen nations feature its crescent, and some of the world's most important religious festivals are tied to its phases. As both a signpost of the cosmic and a symbol of inaccessibility, the moon has been a source of inspiration and mystery throughout the ages.

Today, however, the moon also serves to remind us of a remarkable technological milestone. A dozen men have walked on its dusty gray surface, placing scientific instruments, retrieving rock samples, taking photographs—and in one case even hitting a golf ball. The moon remains the first and only alien world that humanity has visited in person. It's fitting, then, that this stepping-stone of the Space Age also should serve as the starting point for our explorations of the solar system.

By the Light of the Moon

The moon attracts our gaze—a pale silver night-light washing out all but the brightest stars. As the Roman naturalist Pliny the Elder observed, "She, like the rest of the planets, is ruled by the sun's brilliance, in that she shines with a light completely borrowed from the sun." The moon does in fact shine by reflecting the sun's light back to us, albeit only a relatively small fraction thereof. The darkest parts of the lunar surface reflect just 5 percent of the sunlight they receive—equivalent to newly paved asphalt—while the brightest regions reflect about three times more. Our impression of the moon as a brilliant object stems in part from the contrast between its sunlit disk

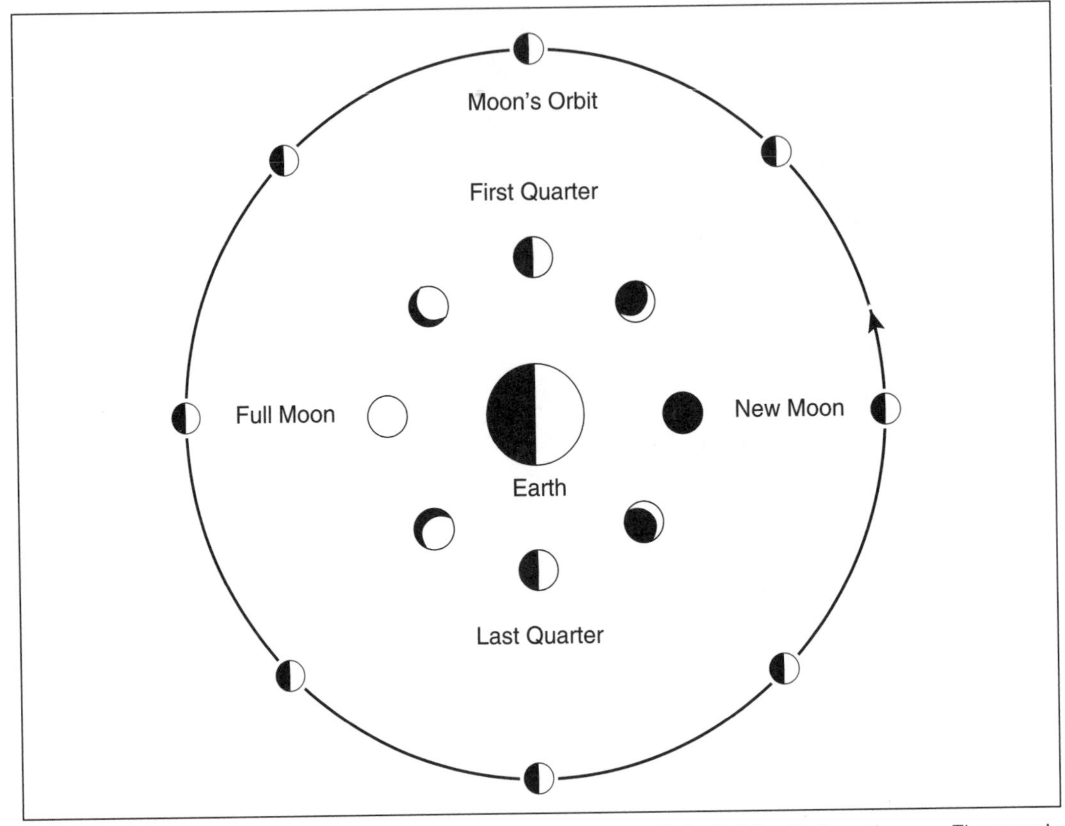

Figure 2-1. Sunlight streaming from the right always illuminates exactly half of the Earth and moon. The moon's motion along its orbit (outer circle) allows us to see different fractions of its sunlit hemisphere, resulting in the familiar lunar phases (inner circle).

and the dark night sky, and in part from the sensitivity of the human eye once it adapts to darkness. The ghostly daytime moon, faintly visible in the bright blue sky, gives a far more representative picture of our satellite's intrinsic brightness.

Another of the moon's more distinctive qualities is its rapid motion through the sky. It completes one orbit around the Earth every 27.32 days, on average. This period, called the sidereal month, represents the time it takes the moon to make one full pass through the sky with respect to the stars. If on some night we find the moon in the vicinity of a bright star, a sidereal month must pass before the moon returns to that area of the sky. The moon's orbital motion carries it from west to east by about thirteen degrees per day, a distance slightly greater than the apparent width of a fist held at arm's length. On occasions when the moon lies near a bright star or planet, its eastward motion may be apparent even in the course of an hour. As a result of this rapid eastward motion, the Earth must spin us about fifty minutes longer every day before we're turned toward the moon's new position. As a result, the moon rises an average of fifty minutes later each day.

More noticeable than the moon's changing place in the sky is its changing appearance, which goes through a cyclic sequence of phases. Astronomers refer to each complete cycle of phases as a lunation. Though the moon can appear to us as a slender crescent or a fully lit disk, half of the moon is always in sunlight. We see the moon go through phases because the portion of its sunlit hemisphere that faces Earth changes daily as the moon courses along its orbit (fig. 2-1).

Each lunation begins at new moon, when the moon is positioned roughly between Earth and the sun. Since the side facing away from Earth receives all of the sunlight, the new moon cannot be seen unless it passes directly in front of the sun and produces a solar eclipse. Usually within about twenty-five hours, but sometimes in less

Figure 2-2. As the moon orbits the Earth, we see the fraction of its illuminated surface change in a regular pattern known as lunar phases. This montage of images acquired over the course of single lunation illustrates how the moon's appearance changes daily throughout the cycle. From a slender crescent (top row) visible in the western sky at dusk, the moon waxes through first quarter (second row) and gibbous phases (third row) as its angle from the sun increases. When opposite the sun, the moon is full (fourth row) and rises at sunset. It then wanes with each day that follows, eventually becoming a thin crescent that gleams in the predawn sky (bottom row). A few days later it appears again in the evening twilight. (Photo by António Cidadão)

than fifteen, the moon's motion carries it far enough east of the sun that attentive observers can find its hair-thin crescent low in the west just after sunset. As the moon moves farther east, it rises and sets progressively later than the sun and also shows us a greater portion of its daylight side. After about a week that slim crescent has grown to a half-lit disk, the phase somewhat confusingly known as first quarter because it occurs one-quarter of the way through the monthly cycle. The first quarter moon rises around noon, sets near midnight, and is highest in the sky at sunset. Between the quarter and full phases, in which the moon is more than half but less than fully illuminated, the moon is said to be gibbous. A week after first quarter the Earth, moon, and sun again align—but this time the Earth lies roughly in the middle. The full moon, now opposite the sun in the sky, rises in the east as the sun sets in the west and is visible all night long. Up to this point the moon is said to be waxing, but after full moon it begins to wane. After a week the moon shrinks back to a half-disk—the last quarter phase—at which point it rises around midnight, stands highest in the sky at dawn, and sets at noon. Throughout the last week of a lunation the moon becomes an ever thinner crescent and closes on the sun. The cycle begins anew when Earth, moon, and sun realign for another new moon. Figure 2-2 illustrates the moon's changing appearance over a single lunation; the dates and times of lunar phases are provided in appendix B.

Take another look at figure 2-1. In this diagram, the sun lies to the right and the Earth's orbital motion carries it downward. So when we gaze at the first quarter moon at sunset, or at the last quarter moon at dawn, we are looking approximately in the direction of the Earth's motion around the sun. The first quarter moon marks the position in space that we occupied about three and a half hours earlier, while the last quarter moon marks Earth's location at roughly the same time in the future.

We noted above that the moon takes 27.32 days to circle the Earth, but each lunation cycle takes an average of 29.53 days. Why the discrepancy? The moon completes an orbit in one sidereal month, but during that time the Earth and moon together have moved about one-twelfth of the way around their yearly orbit of the sun. Relative to the background stars, the sun appears to have moved about twenty-seven degrees east of where it was at the start of each lunation. Before new moon can occur again, the moon must travel a bit farther in its orbit to line up with the Earth and sun. Since it takes the moon a couple of days to make up the difference, the lunation cycle takes that much more time. This longer period, called the synodic month, forms the basis of most lunar calendars.

The moon's crescent phases offer another treat for the careful observer. For a few days at the start and end of each lunation, we can see more of the moon than its thin, sunlit crescent—the remainder of the disk also glows faintly. Sometimes called "the old moon in the new moon's arms" when seen in the evening, this secondary illumination is caused by the gleam of our own planet reflected back to us. Leonardo da Vinci (1452–1519), the Italian artist and engineer, seems to have been the first to offer a correct explanation for the phenomenon. Our oceans and seas, he concluded, are "illuminated by the sun which is already setting in such a way that the sea then fulfills the same function to the dark side of the moon as the moon at its fifteenth day does to us when the sun is set." Thanks to clouds, ice caps, and oceans, Earth reflects nearly three times the sunlight of the moon. From the lunar surface, our world appears as a brilliant bluish disk almost four times larger and thirty times brighter than the full moon we see. In addition, the phases of Earth and moon are complementary—when we see the young crescent moon, a lunar astronaut would see a gibbous Earth. Earth's reflected light, called earthshine, is most noticeable when the ecliptic cuts the horizon most steeply and the moon stands high, which occurs on spring evenings for the young crescent and autumn mornings as the moon approaches new (fig. 2-3).

Earthshine is far from being a purely aesthetic phenomenon, however. Scientists have realized that reflected earthlight provides them with a means of probing changes in the Earth's atmosphere. An important quantity in climate studies is the Earth's albedo—the fraction of sunlight that the Earth reflects. In 1991, Steven Koonin of the California Institute of Technology argued that monitoring earthshine could be an effective and inexpensive complement to satellite data.

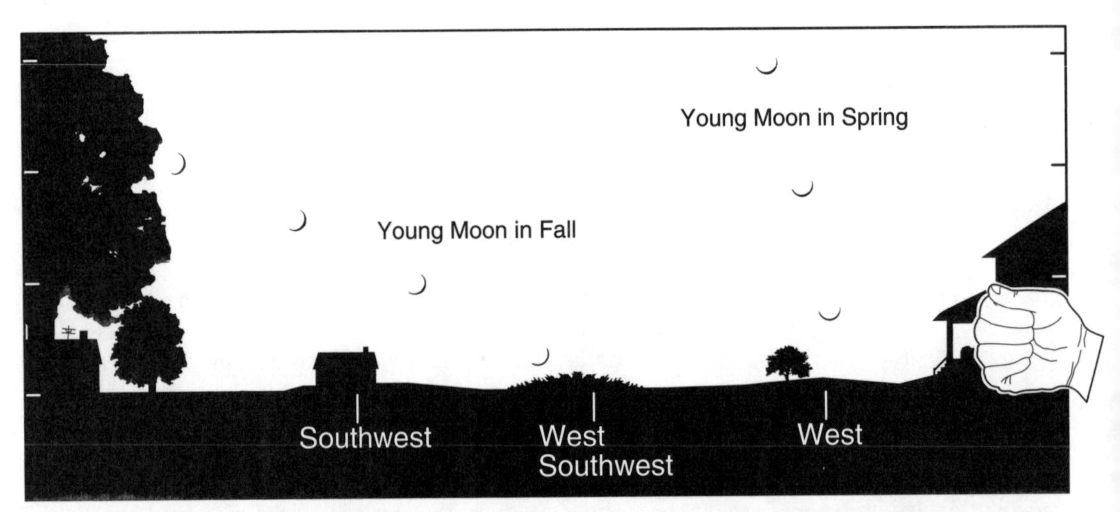

Figure 2-3. The angle of the moon's path to the horizon changes throughout the year. The young moon can be seen more easily in spring evenings than in the fall; the reverse is true for the waning crescent seen in the mornings. For clarity, the moon is enlarged four times. Horizon scenes like these occur throughout the book. Tick marks along the bottom mark off the directions, and those along the sides represent altitude intervals of ten degrees—equal to the width of your fist at arm's length.

"Earthshine observations are ideally suited to this," Koonin says, "because, in contrast to satellite determinations of the albedo, they are self-calibrating, easily and inexpensively performed from the ground, and instantaneously cover a significant fraction of the globe." Earthshine observations can, over long periods, provide measures of variations in cloud cover or in the density of atmospheric particles known as aerosols that play a role in climate change.

A group led by Philip Goode of Big Bear Solar Observatory in California reported the first results from a modern study of earthshine in 2000. Using this technique to determine Earth's albedo requires large numbers of observations in order to smooth out nightly variations due to shifting weather patterns and seasonal changes due to snow and ice cover. Their data even detect the increase in earthshine as the sun rises over Asia and the huge land mass rotates into daylight.

"We have found surprisingly large—up to 20 percent—seasonal variations in Earth's reflectance," Goode says. Based on 270 observations, the study found Earth's albedo to be 0.297; in comparison, the moon's albedo is 0.11. The group also found a possible 2.5-percent decrease in Earth's albedo over the previous five years, a result perhaps linked to the rise in solar activity occurring over the same period.

Goode hopes to increase the precision of observations by monitoring earthshine around the clock with a worldwide network. "That precision," he notes, "will also make it possible to test connections between solar activity and Earth's climate." By reflecting the glow of its partner in space, the moon takes on an additional role as a sort of natural weather satellite.

A phenomenon with a more elusive explanation is more noticeable a little farther along in the lunar cycle. The full moon, low in the east at dusk, looms especially large as it rises into the darkening sky. In fact, most people judge the rising moon to be about twice as large as the elevated moon just a few hours later. Yet, regardless of its height in the sky, the moon's physical size and distance from us are essentially the same—the moon's disk subtends an angle of about 0.5 degree no matter where it is located. Photographs of the rising moon and the elevated moon, for instance, show that the lunar disk is the same size in both cases. This paradox, called the "moon illusion," has been known since antiquity and as yet there is no complete explanation for it. Like any optical illusion, it represents a breakdown between what we consciously expect to see and the way in which the human perceptual system actually responds to the outside world. Despite its name, the moon illusion also enhances sunrise and sunset and inflates the appearance of constellations near the horizon. For most people, all it takes to break the illusion is to view the enlarged moon upside-down or between pinched fingers, thereby jumbling the visual cues that lead to the misperception.

Of Time and Tide

Humans have been using the moon as a timekeeper for millennia. The first hints of lunar records can be found among Upper Paleolithic carvings and cave paintings in Europe and Asia. Many stone and bone artifacts from this time are carved with circular or serpentine designs. The meaning of the designs is unknown, but guesses range from the practical—such as tallies of kills in a given hunt—to the purely artistic. In the 1970s, Alexander Marshack of the Peabody Museum of Archaeology and Ethnology found intriguing evidence that some of these designs were indeed practical in nature. He proposed that they represented the oldest human records of the passage of time and involved lunar phases. For example, a 30,000-year-old bone plate from Dordogne, France, seems to show a two-month-long record of lunar phases, each turn in a serpentine design representing a new or full moon. Michael Rappenglück of Volkshochschule Gilching in Germany finds similar meaning in sequences of dots that appear in the Paleolithic paintings that adorn the walls of the Lascaux and La Tête du Lion caves in France. While we may never know if these interpretations are correct, it's worth noting that similar lunar tallies have been documented among other peoples, such as Native American groups and the Nicobar Islanders of the Indian Ocean.

Civilization first arose in the valleys fertilized by major rivers—the Indus, the Nile, and the Tigris and Euphrates. The land between these last two rivers, Mesopotamia, saw the rise of the earliest Sumerian cities sometime in the fourth millennium B.C. The Mesopotamian calendar, based on the phases of the moon, took shape by the second millennium B.C. Each month had either 29 or 30 days, alternating irregularly—the basis of the month in today's Western calendar. Days began at sunset, and religious authorities declared a new month to have begun when they first saw the young crescent moon low in the evening twilight. If weather interfered and the length of the month exceeded thirty days without a sighting of the moon, a new month was declared anyway. By the fifth century B.C., the start of the month was determined by computation and the calendar lost its reliance on observation.

While the moon served as a convenient timepiece, there are built-in problems with any purely lunar calendar. Twelve complete cycles of the moon typically take 354 days—eleven days short of the seasonal year. Left to itself, this mismatch would cause each calendar year to begin about eleven days earlier in the solar year, with the years slowly drifting back through the seasons. This is exactly the case with the Islamic calendar, the only true lunar calendar still in wide use. The beginning of each calendar year slides through the seasons for about thirty-three years, after which things are back where they started.

The Western calendar, established by Pope Gregory XIII in 1582, abandons the moon altogether. We ensure that the calendar stays in sync with the seasons by adding (intercalating) one day every few years according to some relatively straightforward rules. We add a 366th day (February 29) to every year that is exactly divisible by four, except in century years, but if a century year is evenly divisible by 400 then it too becomes a leap year.

Calendars are complicated because the relevant cycles—the day, the lunar month, the seasonal year—do not mesh perfectly together and even change over time themselves. Most cultures found the drift of a lunar calendar through the seasons hard to live with because the seasonal, or solar, year controlled agricultural activities. Early astronomers spent considerable effort devising methods of intercalation to pad out a lunar calendar for a better fit with the average solar year. A calendar that takes into account both lunar and solar cycles is called lunisolar.

In Egypt, no fewer than three calendars were in use by the fourth century B.C. The survival of Egypt depended on the annual flood of the Nile, and Egyptian astronomer-priests noticed early on that the first appearance of the star Serpet (known to us as Sirius) in the eastern sky just before dawn coincided with the flood season. By 3500 B.C. they had devised a lunisolar calendar kept in step with the seasons by intercalating a month whenever Serpet's appearance occurred on certain days. This calendar was used in timing religious events related to agricultural and seasonal activities. But the inconvenience of a year with either twelve or thirteen months was not lost on the Egyptians, and by 2800 B.C. a civil calendar appeared for governmental and administrative purposes. The months were fixed at 30 days each, resulting in a year 360 days long: 5 days and a fraction short of the seasonal year. The five extra days, tacked on at year's end, were considered very unlucky.

The Egyptians made no attempt to keep this calendar in step with either the seasons or the moon—the whole point was to strip out natural cycles that could not be made to agree and so avoid the need to intercalate. Each year contained exactly the same number of days. Administrators and businessmen alike could perform calculations over several years without having to determine when intercalations had occurred. For the same reason, the Egyptian civil calendar also found a home with astronomers—including Nicolaus Copernicus—even into the 1500s. When it became apparent that their original lunar calendar was drifting with respect to the civil calendar, Egypt devised a second lunar calendar to be used for scheduling festivities tied to the moon. Whenever the first day of the new lunar calendar fell before the first day of the civil calendar, religious authorities inserted a month to bring the two back into agreement.

Corrections to the earliest lunar calendars were probably first made simply by watching the harvest or other natural indicators and then adding whatever length of time seemed necessary. Over time, and with continued observation and record keeping, other cycles were recognized that could facilitate the process. After eight years, the same lunar phase recurs on nearly the same day in a solar year—for instance, full moons occur on July 12 in 1995, July 13 in 2003, and July 15 in 2011. This pattern, known as the octaeteris and recognized in the sixth century B.C., formed the basis of early Greek calendars but, as is evident above, it loses step with the moon by about a day and a half per cycle. Despite this error, and the additional confusion caused by a determined Athenian misapplication of calendar rules, the octaeteris came to be considered an important time unit. The Olympic Games were held every four years, or half an octaeteris, as are their modern counterparts. A more rigorous lunar cycle was recognized by Meton and Euctemon of Athens in 432 B.C. This same cycle had already been discovered and put to use in Mesopotamia and was recognized in India and China as well, although we do not know whether this occurred through a general diffusion of knowledge or by independent discovery. In any case, Meton and Euctemon recognized that 235 synodic months occurred in almost exactly nineteen seasonal years—the error is less than two hours per cycle. This means that lunar phases recur on essentially the same date every nineteen years. For example, full moons occur on July 13 in 1908, 1965, 1984, 2003, 2022, and 2041, and on July 14 in 1927 and 1946. The Earth's annual motion around the sun gives rise to the seasons; the monthly relationship between the sun and moon causes phases—and since the Metonic cycle relates one to the other, it could be used to keep a lunar calendar in sync with the seasons.

Not everyone based their month on lunar phases, though. In India, an early calendar gave more importance to the moon's motion through the stars (its sidereal period); accordingly, the months had 27 or 28 days. The Inca civilization of South America also worked the sidereal month into its calendar. The Maya of Mesoamerica perfected a unique calendar system inspired by astronomical cycles but, like the Egyptian civil year, never referenced to them, so intercalation was not required.

Vestiges of the moon's importance as a timekeeper survive in the timing of religious festivals. Rosh Hashanah, the first day of the Jewish calendar, falls on the new moon after the September equinox, although calendar rules may cause it to be postponed for a couple of days. The Christian festival of Easter falls on the first Sunday following the first full moon that falls on or after the vernal equinox, which ecclesiastical rules fix as March 21; thus, Easter can occur as early as March 22 and as late as April 25. In truth, neither the Jewish calendar nor the Christian calculation of Easter actually refer to the *real* moon, employing instead an abstraction that behaves with much greater consistency. The Koran, however, does specifically instruct Muslims to see the crescent moon before beginning and ending the daylight fast of Ramadan. Some U.S. Muslims argue that, for social convenience in countries where Islam is not the dominant religion, scholars should be permitted to declare the start of the most important holy days by mathematical calculation, a proposition that echoes the movement from observation to theory seen in other major calendars.

Nearly everywhere the moon was correctly linked to a primary natural rhythm—the ebb and flow of the ocean tides. Among the Maori of New Zealand, the moon's responsibility for the tides became a part of its name: *Rona-whakamau-tai,* Rona the Tide Controller. Along the southeast coast of what is now Alaska, the Tlingit, Haida, and Tsimshian tribes imagined the moon as an old woman who governed the tides. They tell the story of how Raven and Mink tricked the old woman into making the sea flood and ebb twice each day, thereby providing people with seafood at every low tide.

Even into the seventeenth century, the link between the moon and the tides was not fully accepted. Galileo Galilei, whose observations revolutionized knowledge about the moon, sharply criticized his contemporary Johannes Kepler for suggesting a lunar influence on the oceans. Galileo instead proposed that the tides were proof of the Earth's motion. Just as water in a vase sloshes when the vase is moved, he posited, so the tides resulted from the Earth's combined rotation and motion around the sun.

The issue was finally settled in 1687, the year English physicist Isaac Newton (1642–1727) published what is considered to be one of the greatest works in the history of science. In his *Mathematical Principles of Natural Philosophy*—better known as the *Principia,* from a short form of its Latin title—Newton describes the theory of universal gravitation that allowed him to "deduce the motions of the planets, the comets, the moon, and the sea." Just as the gravitational attraction of the sun prevents the planets from flying off into space, so the gravity of the Earth keeps the moon in its orbit. But gravity is a mutual attraction—the moon also pulls back on the Earth—and its strength changes over distance, which means that the force of the moon's pull varies slightly across the Earth's diameter. This differential force leads to one bulge of matter directly beneath the moon and another, counterintuitively, on the opposite side of the Earth. Think of these tidal bulges as the crests of a giant wave, low in height—only a couple of feet on the open ocean—but half of the Earth's circumference in length. The wave crests move slowly over the Earth's surface as the moon proceeds in its monthly orbit and the Earth spins daily beneath them. A given location passes under each tidal bulge once every twenty-four hours and fifty minutes. Since there are two bulges, a high tide recurs every twelve hours and twenty-five minutes. This idealized picture is greatly complicated by the positions of continents, friction, the irregular shapes of ocean basins, and the fact that the moon's orbit is not in the same plane as the Earth's equator—all of which conspire to alter the timing and the water range between high and low tide. The greatest tidal ranges occur where tidal periods closely match the natural frequency of the regional topography. One such place is the Bay of Fundy in Nova Scotia, where the tidal range averages fifty feet (fifteen meters).

The sun also raises tides—less than half the height of those caused by the moon—and the two sets of tidal bulges interact with one another. When the Earth, sun, and moon are aligned during full and new moon, a higher-than-normal high tide (called a spring tide) occurs as the crests of the solar and lunar tidal bulges coincide. At the moon's quarter phases, solar tides instead interfere with lunar tides and a lower-than-normal high tide (neap tide) results. These extreme tides may change the water level by up to 20 percent above or below the normal tidal limits.

The sun and moon also produce tides in the atmosphere and, more surprising, in the solid body of the Earth. The rocks of the Earth rise and fall less than a foot under tidal influences, an oscillation that goes unnoticed because it occurs over enormous horizontal distances. A popular notion attributes the occurrence of earthquakes to the periodic stresses induced in geologic faults by Earth tides. Various studies have shown that any tidal influence on earthquakes is both barely detectable and, more importantly, of absolutely no predictive value.

Just the opposite, however, is true of the moon. Seismometers placed on the lunar surface during the Apollo era transmitted information on the depth, energy, and frequency of moonquakes for six years. Most of the seismic energy released on the moon comes from a few modest quakes each year that occur at random times and locations in the upper 185 miles (300 kilometers) of the lunar crust. A more numerous but much weaker type of moonquake occurs in about eighty discrete locations at depths greater than 500 miles (800 kilometers) and recurs at these locations every twenty-seven days. The Earth's tidal force drives the moon's deep quakes, but internal heat drives the temblors of our world.

The tides raised on Earth require an enormous continuing energy input of about three terawatts—slightly less than the estimated total electrical generating capacity of the world. There has been interest in putting a fraction of this energy to our own use for decades and various designs have been proposed for tidal turbines. A tidal generating plant has been operating at the mouth of the Rance River in France since the 1960s. One proposed large-scale plant would link the Samar and Dalupiri islands in the Philippines and produce an average of over one gigawatt of power from the tidal cycle; nearby islands offer the possibility of expansion. But since the power input to the tidal system is continuous, there must be forces that work to dissipate it. About one-third of the energy is lost deep in the ocean basins, where undersea topography impedes tidal currents and creates large-scale turbulent water motion. Some scientists suggest that this energy may be the power source for the thermohaline circulation, a worldwide ocean current considered important to the Earth's climate. The remaining tidal energy, about two terawatts, is lost by friction between the sloshing oceans and the continental margins.

All of this tidal friction between Earth and sea has astronomical consequences. The long-term effect on the Earth is a slowdown in the Earth's spin and a gradual increase in the length of the day. Modern calculations indicate that the tides should lengthen the day by about 2.3 milliseconds every 100 years; over historical time, additional factors have retarded the slowdown to about 1.7 milliseconds per century. Investigations by paleontologists confirm that the Earth day was indeed shorter in the past. Fossil coral and other invertebrates show daily and annual growth patterns that can be counted to estimate the number of days in their year and, since the length of the year is taken to be constant, the number of hours in their day. Such studies point to a day about twenty-two hours long some 400 million years ago; this correlates well with the estimate based on tidal friction.

Tides raised by the Earth have had a similar effect on the moon, slowing its rotation until its spin became synchronous, or locked, to its orbital period. The moon spins once on its rotational axis every sidereal month; this is why the moon always shows us the same features no matter when we look at it. (Over time, both the tilt of the moon's orbit and slight variations in its motion allow us to see about 7 percent more than half of the moon from Earth.) People who speak of the "dark side" of the moon are really referring to its farside, the side we never see from Earth, since every part of the moon is illuminated by the sun for half the lunar month. As shown in figure 2-1, the farside of the moon is in daylight at new moon, but the side facing Earth is dark.

Tens of billions of years hence, the moon's tidal brake on the Earth's spin will slow it until both Earth and moon make a single rotation in the time it takes the moon to complete one orbit—both worlds will perpetually keep the same face to one another. Long before the time needed to reach this state, however, the sun will have gone through physical changes that will greatly alter the inner solar system—the boiling off of our oceans is one of the lesser effects—and will complicate forecasts of the decelerating dance of Earth and moon.

We've described one of the tidal bulges raised by the moon as lying underneath it, but this is not quite true. As the Earth rotates beneath the tidal bulge, friction tends to drive it forward ahead of the moon. This offset allows the mass of the bulge to pull on the moon, which very slightly speeds it up in its orbit. According to the dictates of celestial mechanics, the accelerated moon must then increase its distance from the Earth. Reflectors placed on the moon by Apollo astronauts enable astronomers to bounce laser beams off of the moon and regularly measure its changing distance. The result: the moon currently retreats from us by 1.5 inches (3.8 centimeters) per year.

Moon Lore

If the moon has influence over the vastness of the sea, might it also have power over life on Earth? This idea, central to many occult themes, is reflected in folk tales of mythical creatures such as werewolves. But many animals that live in or near the ocean do exhibit cycles of activity patterned by the rhythm of the tides and the phases of the moon. During the spring and early summer, for example, a few days after each full and new moon a small coastal fish called the grunion spawns by the thousands on the beaches of southern California. The palolo worms *(Palolo siciliensis)* of Fiji and Samoa swarm as part of their reproductive cycle during the moon's last quarter in October and November. Under laboratory conditions simulating the day/night and seasonal cycle, the brown algae *Dictyota dichotoma* failed to release gametes as part of its summer reproductive activities—until researchers left the lights on for just one night to simulate a full moon.

At each low tide, fiddler crabs emerge from their burrows to roam the mudflats, then return to sit out the incoming tide. In the laboratory, with no cues from water movements or light from the sun or moon, they retain this decidedly lunar activity cycle—two active and two inactive periods every 24.8 hours—for several days. Rhythmic changes—in the color of some crab species and in the opening and closing of bivalve shells—similarly coincide with the tides and the moon's period.

These are but a few examples of biological clocks—internal programming that benefits an organism by, for example, inducing activity during the best times to feed. For many organisms, these clocks initiate the physiological changes required for breeding when triggered by environmental cues that occur in the proper season and month. Scientists believe that these cycles are "hard-wired" into the genome of organisms. Indeed, genes that can modify or eliminate biological cycles have been identified in bread mold, fruit flies, and mice. Reset by environmental cues—the diurnal, seasonal, and monthly variations of sunlight and moonlight, for instance—the clock maintains its relationship with the organism's surroundings.

Our own biological clocks are synchronized by the day/night cycle. Jet lag, a familiar complaint of long-distance travelers, occurs because our internal clocks are set for our own time zone and need a period of adjustment to sync up with the new one. The internal clocks of organisms living in the tide-washed coastal environment are reset by water pressure, salinity, and temperature changes.

Could the moon create a "biological tide" affecting people? That the moon should affect us is an age-old notion echoed in such words as *moonstruck, moon-eyed, moony, lunacy,* and *lunatic.* But gravity is the weakest of the fundamental forces in nature. Ocean tides are dramatic because the moon's tidal force acts across the entire diameter of the Earth, whereas tides acting across a single human body are insignificant. "A book that you hold in your hand exerts a tidal force thousands of times greater than that of the moon," noted University of California astronomer George O. Abell.

The moon's long association with fertility stems from a tantalizing coincidence between the cycle of lunar phases—the synodic month—and the length of the human menstrual cycle, which on average lasts between twenty-eight and twenty-nine days. It is a widely held belief that the two cycles are related, but if there were a true causal connection, we would expect to see a clear lunar influence in the reproductive cycles of other primates. The average cycles of gorillas and orangutans agree with the synodic month within a day or so, but the cycles of chimpanzees and bonobos—the two apes biologists identify as our closest relatives—are much longer (thirty-six and forty-two days, respectively). Cycle length varies considerably among the primates. Ultimately, there is no evidence that the correspondence between the lunar and human reproductive cycles is anything but a coincidence; we'll take a look at another lunar coincidence in chapter 4.

Many believe that the moon influences human behavior. Surveys of personnel at various emergency services show that most of them routinely credit full moons for keeping them busier than usual, yet numerous statistical studies have shown that this association is far more imagined than real. In 1996, James Rotton of Florida International University and Ivan Kelly of the University of Saskatchewan combined data from 37 published and unpublished studies of a "lunar effect" and used a statistical technique called meta-analysis to examine all of the data. They show that lunar phases "accounted for no more than 3/100 of 1 percent of the variability" in the number of crimes, crisis calls, psychiatric admissions, and other activities supposedly modulated by the moon. They found that inappropriate analytical techniques and failure to properly account for other cycles—such as the recurrence of weekends—can create the appearance of a relationship between behavior and lunar phase where in fact none exists.

Why, then, does the belief persist? Sensational media reports play a role, but there is more to it. It's human nature to seek patterns, especially when we find one that helps us make sense of emotionally demanding situations. It's also our nature to forget occasions when the patterns we think we recognize fail and to remember the times when they behave as we expect. A few people may notice a full moon during an unusually eventful day, which validates their expectation. But studies show that most people are completely unaware of the phase of the moon when they blame it for a busy day: "There must be a full moon tonight!" That allows the lunar effect myth to survive by consensus, as received wisdom passed down and uncritically accepted. It becomes common knowledge—another one of those things "everybody knows" that simply isn't true.

The moon has been worshipped and personified in many different ways, although it was rarely made a chief deity. Among the Fon people of Benin, the sun and moon form a powerful pair of twins that express the dualistic aspects of nature. Mawu holds the female principle: earth, moon, coolness, fertility; Liza holds the male principle: sky, sun, warmth, power. Together they created the universe, and their perfectly balanced union suffuses it with order.

The moon's role in Egyptian mythology is more diffuse. In Thebes, it was known as Khonsu, a god with healing powers; in Hermopolis, it was worshipped as Thoth, the god of wisdom, inventor of writing and language, the one who recorded the verdict as the dead were tried before Osiris in the afterlife. As god of the dead, vegetation, and fertility, Osiris is himself associated with the moon in the late period of Egyptian history.

Osiris and his sister-wife Isis reigned with great wisdom and passion, helping humanity by sharing knowledge of agriculture and the arts. Set, the brother of Osiris, seethed with jealousy over their success. He murdered Osiris, suffocating him in a box and disposing of the evidence in the river. On hearing of the treachery, Isis quickly tracked down the body and arranged to have it returned to her, keeping it hidden in the marshes of the Nile delta. Despite her secrecy, Set came across the body one day, cut it into fourteen pieces, and scattered the remains along the river. Isis searched for the pieces and found all but one. She embalmed Osiris, creating the first mummy, and through these rites she gave him everlasting life in the underworld. The fourteen pieces of Osiris represent the fading moon of the last half of the lunar cycle, dwindling and then disappearing from the morning sky—but like Osiris the moon is resurrected. The Nile withdrew after each life-giving flood, but the waters would return and the parched lands of Egypt would sprout crops again because the river itself contained a part of Osiris. His resolute wife Isis manifested herself as the star Serpet that proclaimed the yearly floods and seemingly stirred the Nile to swell its banks.

To be fair to the Egyptians, it should be noted that this story dates from the period of heavy Greek and Roman influence. The Egyptians were eminently practical, and although the foundations of their religion were inspired by the sky, they showed little interest in actual observation beyond the needs of reckoning time and orienting structures. There is nothing in purely Egyptian records that reveals any interest in detailed observation of lunar and solar eclipses or planetary movement.

The Babylonian moon god was Sin, controller of the night and of the calendar; his earlier Sumerian counterpart was Nanna. He was a wise and generous god who marked off time and whose advice was sought by other deities each month. His bright light kept evil forces at bay during the night, but he was attacked by these creatures when they conspired with Sin's daughter Ishtar to extinguish his light. Marduk, the chief Babylonian deity, fought them off and restored Sin's light.

In ancient Greece, Artemis ruled the moon, the hunt, and all nature, brought fair weather for travelers, and protected young girls. She later became identified with Selene, who fell in love with the sleeping shepherd Endymion and stopped in her passage through the sky to visit him nightly. She bore him fifty daughters, representing the fifty synodic months between the Olympic Games. The Roman moon goddess Diana, identified with Artemis, became the patroness of witches in medieval Europe.

In the surviving books of the Maya, the moon was Ix Chel, Lady Rainbow, sometimes depicted as an old, toothless woman sitting in the glyph representing the moon sign and holding a rabbit. She was the patron of childbirth, healing, and the art of weaving, and there was a popular shrine to her on the island of Cozumel.

Various stories have arisen to explain the moon's movements and appearance. A Scandinavian tale about a boy and girl, Hjúki and Bil, who were swept up by the moon as they carried water from a well may have been the basis of the nursery rhyme of Jack and Jill. Some scholars believe the story represents an illustration of the moon's ups and downs over the course of its cycle: climbing the dome of the sky when waxing, reaching the top when full, and then "tumbling down" to the invisibility of new moon.

We often picture the moon's dark markings as forming the Man in the Moon. According to one story, he was caught working on Sunday and cast onto the moon—perhaps that accounts for his expression of surprise. Other commonly recognized figures include the profile of a girl or old woman, a rabbit, and a toad. The prolific rabbit, typically associated with fertility, was a symbol for the moon in Europe, China, and the ancient Americas (fig. 2-4).

Moon Science

By the fifth century B.C., Greek astronomy and mathematics had become sophisticated enough for some imaginative scientists to explore the moon's true nature. Anaxagoras (ca. 500–428 B.C.) correctly explained the causes of eclipses and was banished for considering that the moon was at least partly made of the same material as the Earth. Both he and the influential philosopher Aristotle (384–322 B.C.) said that the moon was a solid sphere illuminated by sunlight, and they explained its phases. Using simple geometry, Aristarchus (ca. 320–250 B.C.) showed that the moon was much closer than the sun, and Hipparchus (ca. 190–125 B.C.) later determined the moon's distance within 10 percent of the correct value. Despite these pioneering efforts, the moon came to be regarded as a sphere of crystalline smoothness and perfection, a member of the flawless realm beyond the mundane one.

Leonardo da Vinci is generally credited as being the first to attempt to portray the markings on the moon realistically, although some small moon images appear in several of the works of Jan van Eyck (1390–1440). Da Vinci's chalk drawings, only one of which is known today, were made between 1505 and 1514—surprisingly recent for a depiction of an object so easily visible. Apart from these efforts, all known previous depictions of the moon appear to be symbolic rather than representational.

In 1994, Philip Stooke of the University of Western Ontario described a contender for the oldest lunar map, one that would extend the history of lunar mapmaking back to the same period as the earliest maps of the Earth and sky. It appears on a stone that archaeologists have dubbed Orthostat 47, inside the passage tomb of

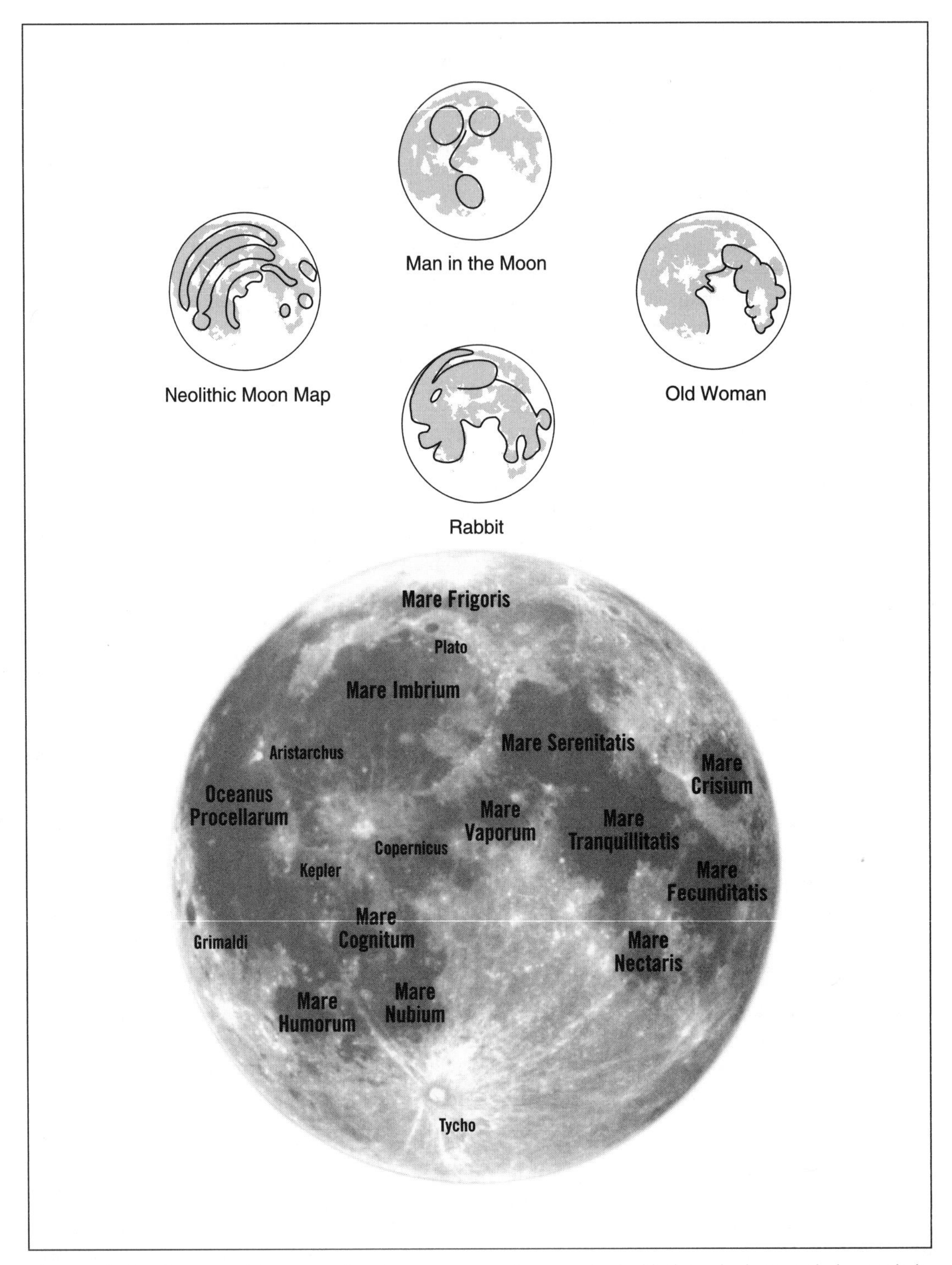

Figure 2-4. Top: The moon's largest surface features are easily recognized with the naked eye and play a role in lunar folk tales. The popular Man in the Moon is most obvious when the moon rises early in the evening. The markings resemble the profile of an old woman when the moon is highest in the sky, and the Rabbit adorns the setting moon. The arced bands pecked onto the "moon stone" in the Irish passage tomb of Knowth may be the earliest representation of lunar markings (after Stooke). Below: A photograph of the moon illustrates the location of selected visible features. The craters Tycho and Copernicus are two of the moon's newest. (Photo by Bill Sterne)

Knowth, located in the Boyne Valley of Ireland. Constructed some 5,000 years ago—predating Stonehenge in England and the great pyramids of Giza—the Irish passage tombs are places in which Neolithic peoples placed the cremated remains of their dead so that their spirits could be reborn in the afterlife.

The "moon stone" of Knowth occupies the center recess at the end of the tomb's eastern passage. Pecked onto the stone are three long arcs, a short arc, and several circular patches that Stooke believes represent the face of the setting moon. The markings match the relative positions of lunar surface features well enough that Stooke feels justified in calling it a map. Other patterns pecked onto the same stone appear to show the changing orientation of lunar features as the moon rises and sets.

Designs using nested arcs that are stylistically similar to the pecked bands on Orthostat 47 appear all over Knowth. Kerbstone 52, for instance, bears a complex design that some have argued represents a lunar calendar. Investigations into astronomical alignments at Knowth have shown that at certain times moonlight could stream down the entire eastern passage. It's difficult to resist the romantic vision of the pale moon occasionally illuminating a map of itself.

The view of the moon as a perfect crystalline sphere changed forever in 1609, when Galileo Galilei became one of the first to examine the moon through his improved version of a new Dutch invention—the spyglass, later named the telescope. Although only as powerful as a good pair of modern binoculars, Galileo's spyglass revealed features resembling jagged peaks, valleys, and pock-marked plains. Galileo was not the first to sketch the moon as seen through a telescope, but he was the first to publish—in *The Starry Messenger* of 1610—drawings and descriptions of his observations. He studied surface features through the moon's changing phases and recognized their three-dimensional character by the shadows they cast. Galileo noted that the brighter regions of the moon were "uneven, rough and full of cavities and prominences, being not unlike the face of the earth, relieved by chains of mountains and deep valleys" and the dark areas, which he referred to as "large lunar spots," are

> . . . not seen to be broken in the above manner . . . rather they are even and uniform and brighter patches crop up only here or there. Hence if anyone wished to revive the old Pythagorean opinion that the moon is like another earth, its brighter part might very fitly represent the surface of the land and its darker region that of the water.

An existing tradition held that the features on the moon's face reflected an image of the Earth and the dark regions were our seas. Galileo carefully avoided any decisive statement about water on the moon. Nevertheless, each of his lunar spots came to be called a *mare* (Latin for "sea," pronounced MAH-ray, plural *maria*) and, naturally enough, the rest of the moon's surface became known as *terrae* (lands). Today the terrae are more commonly known as the lunar highlands, but the term *mare* still appears in the names of the dusky regions.

Galileo's observations were an important step in proving the Copernican view that the Earth was an ordinary member of the solar system. Isaac Newton, similarly inspired by the moon, extended this line of reasoning to conclude that the force that brought apples to the ground was the same force that kept the moon circling the Earth and the planets revolving around the sun. As astronomers discovered satellites orbiting other planets, they began to appreciate the uniqueness of our own satellite. It is the largest moon in the solar system relative to the planet it orbits, with the exception of distant Pluto and its oversized moon, Charon. Our moon is just over one-fourth the diameter of Earth, with a total surface area slightly larger than Africa and less than one-eightieth of Earth's mass. The force of gravity on the lunar surface is only one-sixth that of Earth's gravity. This is too weak for the moon to hold onto gases escaping from its interior; as a result, the moon has no atmosphere to speak of. Table 2-1 lists some basic facts about the Earth and moon.

After Galileo announced his telescopic discoveries, cartographers set to work mapping the lunar features. The first real map of the entire visible hemisphere was published in 1645 by Michiel Van Langren (1600–1675), an astronomer in the court of Philip IV of Spain. He identified several hundred features, most of them craters, and showed a certain political savvy by naming them for assorted kings and noblemen; for example, Louis XIV and Philip IV. He also honored

Table 2-1. Facts about Earth and Moon

EARTH	
Diameter:	7,927 miles (12,756 km)
Average surface temperature:	59°F (15°C)
Atmospheric surface pressure:	1 bar
Atmospheric composition:	77% nitrogen 21% oxygen 1% water vapor 0.9% argon
Rotation period:	23.93 hours
Obliquity:	23.45° (tilt of rotational axis with respect to orbit)
Sidereal year:	365.26 days (true period of revolution)
Tropical year:	365.24 days (time between successive vernal equinoxes; the seasonal year)
Mean distance from sun:	92.96 million miles (149.60 million km)
MOON	
Diameter:	2,160 miles (3,476 km) 27% that of Earth
Average surface temperature:	Day: 224°F (107°C) Night: –243°F (–153°C)
Sidereal period:	27.32 days (true period of rotation and revolution)
Synodic period:	29.53 days (time between repeating phases, e.g., new moon to new moon)
Mean distance from Earth:	238,870 miles (384,400 km)
Orbit inclined to Earth's:	5.14°

philosophers, explorers, saints, and scientists—including himself, on both a prominent crater and the mare near it. Today only the crater bears his name.

The modern lunar nomenclature originated with Giovanni Riccioli (1598–1671); he used it on the lunar map in his two-volume *New Almagest,* published in 1651. He gave the maria Latin names reflecting qualities or characteristics (Sea of Tranquility, Sea of Serenity, Sea of Cold, Sea of Nectar) and early ideas that connected the moon with weather changes (Sea of Rains, Sea of Vapors, Sea of Clouds, Ocean of Storms). Craters were named for scholars and scientists (Copernicus, Tycho, Kepler) and mountain ranges were named after famous terrestrial ranges, such as the Alps or Apennines. For the next 300 years, as ever larger telescopes revealed finer details on the battered lunar surface and mapmakers strained to keep up with new features and names, the nomenclature Riccioli introduced proved enduring and became formalized.

The known lunar territory began to double in 1959 with the success of the Soviet *Luna 3* mission, which returned 29 grainy images revealing 70 percent of the lunar farside. The Space Age had begun and the moon was center stage. The Soviet Luna and Zond programs provided the first close-up views and the first robotic landing, but the numerous American Ranger, Surveyor, and Lunar Orbiter probes supplied unprecedented detail that paved the way for the highly successful piloted lunar missions of the Apollo program. In 1990, eighteen years after the last Apollo landing and fourteen years after the last Luna mission, Japan became the third nation to successfully fly by, orbit, and impact the moon—with a modest probe named *Hiten.* The United States returned to the moon in 1994 with *Clementine,* a mission designed to map lunar topography and image the surface at several different wavelengths as well as test new technologies. *Clementine* provided the first hint that the moon could still, after centuries of study, serve up surprises.

The idea that ice could exist on an airless, waterless world that is subjected to enormous temperature extremes was first suggested in 1961. Deep craters located near the moon's north and south poles can provide permanent protection for ice because the sun never shines into them. The same objects that made lunar craters—asteroids and comets—no doubt brought water to the moon. Water vapor that drifted into a permanently shadowed crater would find a "cold trap": a place where it could condense as ice and remain stable for billions of years, especially if soil covers or is mixed with the ice.

Radar studies of Mercury in 1991 revealed unusually bright and strongly polarized reflections in craters near both poles. The reflections were similar to those seen by bouncing radio waves from the Greenland ice sheet, the large frozen moons of Jupiter, and the polar caps of Mars; those on Mercury are interpreted as probably being due to ice. In an improvised experiment, *Clementine* detected a similar radar reflection at a location near the moon's south pole and provided the first indication of lunar ice in craters there. Its cameras and laser altimeter determined that the South Pole–Aitken basin, which holds the apparent ice deposits, is the widest and deepest impact structure yet found in the solar system: 1,550 miles (2,500 kilometers) across and nearly 8 miles (13 kilometers) deep.

Another spacecraft, *Lunar Prospector,* provided even greater detail about the mineral composition of the lunar surface. Shortly after its arrival at the moon in 1998, scientists examining data from an instrument designed to detect subsurface hydrogen announced they had found some—presumably in the form of frozen water—at both lunar poles. The signature was stronger at the north pole, where *Clementine* images actually show a smaller permanently shaded area and thus fewer potential cold traps.

"Would I bet my house? The answer is 'yes.' We are certain that water is there. The uncertainty we have is how much," said Alan Binder, lead scientist for the project, at the press conference announcing the findings. Current estimates envision billions of tons of ice, buried under a few inches of lunar soil at both poles.

At the end of the mission, and in an effort to clinch the discovery with something approximating true prospecting, controllers crashed *Lunar Prospector* into a shadowed crater at the south pole. Mission planners had hoped the crash would create a plume of material that could be detectable from Earth, providing ground-based instruments a brief opportunity to find the source of the hydrogen signatures. However, no debris or dust plume was detected.

We've come to understand much about the moon's complex history and the violent origins of the solar system. From 1969 to 1972, six American Apollo missions brought a dozen men to the moon's surface and 843 pounds (382 kilograms) of lunar soil and rocks back to Earth; between 1970 and 1977, Luna probes provided another 11 ounces (300 grams) of surface material from three additional locations on the lunar nearside (the hemisphere that faces Earth). Since then, geologists have identified twenty-six lunar rocks that, incredibly, came to us from the moon all by themselves. To date, geologists have found at least 17 pounds (8 kilograms) of lunar meteorites and, by comparing them with known moon rocks, confirmed them as having originated on the moon. These rocks were blasted off the lunar surface as part of the debris thrown out by an impact, cruised through space for millions of years, and finally fell to Earth where they could be collected by scientists. There is evidence to suggest that the lunar meteorites now in hand come from the moon's farside, a valuable complement to the samples we retrieved, as it were, the hard way.

Seen through a telescope or from orbiting spacecraft, the lunar highlands break up into an endless series of overlapping meteorite craters. These regions took the brunt of a bombardment

Figure 2-5. The full moon. Dark regions are the lunar "seas." (Photo by Bill Sterne)

that formed the solar system's moons and planets through powerful collisions. The top few kilometers of the moon's surface have been repeatedly mixed and pulverized. The lunar highlands—the moon's most ancient terrain—contain samples that solidified within a global ocean of molten rock some 4.4 billion years ago—about 500 million years older than the oldest rocks found on Earth. A crustal shell probably solidified within 200 million years, but molten rock seethed below the surface. The solar system was filled with debris at this time, leftovers from building the planets. Numerous impacts blasted the crust, eroding and mixing the uppermost layers, destroying the oldest lava flows and at the same time throwing out blocks of debris from the deep crust onto the surface.

The maria represent more recent terrain. They cover about 16 percent of the moon's surface, mostly on the nearside. As the moon's surface cooled and its crust solidified, several massive impacts formed huge multi-ringed basins between 3.9 and 3.8 billion years ago. This occurred even as the amount of debris striking the moon began to decrease. Dense basalt magma from the interior oozed its way through the fractured crust and flooded onto the basin floors. The maria represent the frozen remains of ancient dark lava flows that erased the older craters beneath them, which explains why they have far fewer craters than the neighboring highlands. The rate of impacts leveled off around three billion years ago; by then, only small amounts of magma found their way to the surface.

The impacts of the last billion years, such as Tycho (54 miles or 87 kilometers across) and Copernicus (57 miles or 91 kilometers), have gouged the lunar crust and excavated subsurface layers, throwing out blankets of brighter ejecta that highlight the moon's most recent wounds. Blocks of debris thrown hundreds of miles struck as a multitude of smaller impacts, revealing brighter soil and creating the linear rays that radiate away from many craters. Apart from these last few large impacts and many smaller ones, the moon's face has changed little in the past billion years.

The portrait assembled from more than three decades of lunar visits is thus one of a dead world, a geological fossil that preserves evidence of the solar system's distant past. But tales of the dead have a certain fascination all their own. For centuries, lunar observers have reported what we might consider geological ghost stories—puzzling glows, hazes, flashes, color changes, and brief obscurations of lunar features. "Lunar transient phenomena," says Peter Schultz, a geologist at Brown University, "have a long, rich, and controversial history." Lunar observers reported signs of what could be geological activity throughout the 1950s and 1960s, but as it became clear that impacts played the most important recent role in creating lunar features, the "dead moon" paradigm became more widely accepted.

Figure 2-6. Close-up view of an astronaut's footprint pressed into the powdery lunar soil. This photograph was taken during the *Apollo 11* mission. (NASA photo)

A recent group of transients recorded on videotape serves to highlight the problem. At the height of the annual Leonid meteor shower in 1999, independent observers videotaped six brief flashes on the moon's night side; two more confirmed events were seen in 2001. The flashes were from relatively large meteoroids striking the moon. "The recording of Leonid impact flashes at least demonstrates visible events that would very likely not be confirmed by several observers with just optical means," Schultz notes.

Lunar transient phenomena are not distributed randomly around the moon—hundreds of reliable observations have been reported near the bright crater Aristarchus alone. A team of amateur astronomers was mobilized to provide nearly continuous visual coverage of the moon during *Clementine*'s 1994 mission. In several cases, the spacecraft acquired before-and-after images of sites where events had been reported, but the images showed no obvious changes. More recently, Audouin Dollfus of the Paris Observatory reported bright features near the central peak of the crater Langrenus and obtained images and polarization measurements. He suggested that the features could be caused by grains of bright soil lofted above the surface by gases venting from the interior.

Lunar transients seem to be concentrated along the deeply fractured edges of the maria, where we might expect crustal weakness. Fissures connecting to pockets of underground gas deep within the moon may provide a pathway to the surface, where the venting gas could create a visible effect. *Lunar Prospector* scientists announced in 2001 that the craft had detected emissions of radon gas in the vicinity of the craters Kepler and Aristarchus.

Schultz's group at Brown University is studying a feature called Ina, a small but distinctive D-shaped depression on a large dome near Mare Vaporum. Structures like Ina, which were recognized as unusual in Lunar Orbiter images, also tend to be located near the outskirts of the maria. Ina's features appear sharp and distinct, not rounded by erosion from the long barrage of meteorites. Orbiting Apollo astronauts noticed that in a world of lunar grays, Ina appears distinctly bluish.

"Our work on the Ina structure shows that something has happened from inside," says Schultz. "Our best guess at this point is outgassing." Although for much of the past two decades the planetary science community has shown little interest in lunar transient phenomena, he notes, "I think time now allows a discussion of the evidence, especially in the light of data from *Prospector.*" What we may be seeing are the moon's last geological gasps.

Improbable Moon

Accounting for the origin of the moon was a problem for planetary scientists. It was hoped that analysis of actual lunar rocks would eventually favor some theories and disprove others, but in fact no pre-Apollo theory of the moon's birth adequately fits our knowledge of its orbital characteristics and chemical and geological makeup. As chemist Harold Urey once summed up the situation, "All explanations for the origin of the moon are improbable."

Any proposal for the origin of the moon must address several facts: the strange inclination of the lunar orbit, the moon's low density compared to Earth's, geochemical information gleaned from lunar samples, and the high angular momentum contained in the Earth's spin and the moon's orbit. Angular momentum is a property of rotating systems that includes both the speed of rotation and revolution and the masses of the bodies involved. Earth and moon together possess the greatest amount of angular momentum per unit mass of any of the Earth-like planets.

One early model pictured the moon as Earth's "sister," a body that had formed alongside our planet and orbited it ever since. This view requires a moon that is a miniature version of Earth, made of the same ratio of rock and metal. We now know that lunar rocks contain unexpectedly small amounts of elements such as cobalt and nickel that normally accompany iron-containing minerals. They also lack materials such as water that vaporize at low temperatures. This model fails to account for the different densities of Earth and moon or the high angular momentum of the Earth-moon system. Strike one.

We know that the moon is moving away from us as it slows down the Earth's spin. Extrapolating backward in time means that in the distant past the moon must have been closer—and the Earth spinning faster. If we could somehow reel the moon into the Earth today, our planet would "spin up" until a day became just five hours long. George Darwin, a son of English biologist Charles Darwin, suggested in 1879 that when the Earth was molten it spun so rapidly that it threw a piece into space that became the moon; that is, the moon was Earth's "daughter." Although the geochemical aspects are on the right track, the details don't match what we know of the moon. And even an Earth with a five-hour day is not spinning fast enough to do what Darwin proposed. Strike two.

Perhaps the moon formed elsewhere in the solar system and was captured into orbit as it wandered by—becoming Earth's "spouse." We know that lunar rocks formed without the presence of water and volatile elements; we also know that the moon is otherwise similar to rocks in the Earth's mantle. The large satellites of other planets, on the other hand, are composed of mixtures of ice and rock. The likelihood of a capture event is very low to begin with, but for the Earth to have snared a unique body like the moon seems very improbable indeed. It also fails to explain why the Earth and moon—two bodies that, according to this scenario, were created in different parts of the solar system—share the compositional similarities that they do. Strike three.

In the mid-1970s, two groups of scientists independently offered a new scenario. They argued that the moon was made from material blasted from the Earth by a giant off-center impact shortly after it formed—that it was, in essence, a "chip off the old block." A decade later, computer simulations provided an experimental laboratory where scientists could watch the event unfold and see the effects of slight differences in important parameters, such as the mass and speed of the impactor. Although heavily criticized when first proposed—in part because there was a prevailing view that planetary formation was less violent than it now appears to have been—the model successfully accounts for diverse aspects of the moon's chemistry and dynamics. It has since become the generally accepted model.

In its current form, the scenario begins 4.45 billion years ago, about 50 million years after the start of the Earth's formation and very near its last stages. Another body, one with about 10 percent the mass of the Earth and about the size of Mars, had formed in the same part of the solar system and was on a collision course. The two worlds struck one another with a blinding flash; in moments, a jet of vaporized rock shot into space. The collision completely melted the impactor, remelted the surface of the Earth, and blasted away its atmosphere. Earth shuddered as the two bodies merged and it absorbed the momentum of the impactor. Its original modest rotation was accelerated into a five-hour day. Some of the ejected material, most of which came from the mantle of the impactor, fell back to the glowing, wounded Earth. Some escaped into the solar system. But some of it—less than 2 percent of the Earth's mass—went into orbit and formed a disk of debris in the plane of the Earth's equator. From about half of this mass, within a few decades, the moon coalesced at the disk's outer edge, some 20,000 miles (32,000 kilometers) away.

Because it was so close, the moon that first rose over the ancient Earth looked nearly twelve times larger than it does today. Lunar gravity raised waves in what was left of the disk and, over the few hundred years it existed, this interaction increased the tilt of the moon's orbit. Eventually the residual disk material fell back to Earth, leaving the moon alone as impacts and volcanism molded its surface into the pale battered disk we see today.

One of those who proposed the giant impact scenario, William Ward of Harvard University, showed in 1974 that the moon exerts a stabilizing influence on the Earth. The angle that the Earth's axis makes with respect to the ecliptic is called its obliquity and, as previously discussed, this tilt is the reason for seasons. The angle is not fixed; it varies slightly over a period of 41,000 years, and this variation has the potential to directly affect seasonal extremes, since it alters incident sunlight. The obliquity cycle, together with cyclic variations in the shape of the Earth's orbit and a slow wobble known as precession, plays a role in major shifts in Earth's climate. The gravitational tugs of the sun, moon, and planets—especially Jupiter—create these periodic changes, but the strong steady pull of the moon helps the Earth resist dramatic shifts in obliquity. A study by Jacques Laskar and colleagues at the Bureau des Longitudes in Paris found that without the moon the Earth's obliquity changes were, over tens of millions of years, nonlinear, unpredictable, and dramatic. They drew this conclusion:

> It can thus be claimed that the moon is a climate regulator for the Earth. If it were not present, or if it were much smaller . . . the obliquity values of the Earth would be chaotic with very large variations, reaching more than fifty degrees in a few million years and even, in the long term, more than eighty-five degrees. This would probably have drastically changed the climate on the Earth.

Long an inspiration to poets and lovers, the moon remains a symbol of mystery and an eerie beacon of otherworldliness. It is the only astronomical body on which we can explore landforms with binoculars—and the story told by that landscape is one of violence we can hardly imagine.

The moon rules the seas, providing the power for the tides and, perhaps, for important ocean circulation patterns. It anchors Earth's axis and prevents climate excursions far worse than any our planet has experienced. Above all else, though, the moon is an invitation to explore the sky, one that beckons the year round. Remember to enjoy the rhythms of Earth's "next-door neighbor."

3 Morning Stars, Evening Stars: Venus and Mercury

Mighty, majestic and radiant,
You shine brilliantly in the evening,
You brighten the day at dawn,
You stand in the heavens like the sun and moon.

—Sumerian hymn to Inanna, c. 2000 B.C.

Follow the moon's movements faithfully and, sooner or later, they will lead to other discoveries. Some morning just before new moon, or some evening just after it, the slim crescent will share the twilight with a star that outshines all others. If the timing is just right, a second speck of light—fainter, a bit redder—will waver in the unsteady air close to the horizon. With that observation, your grasp of the universe swells over two-hundred-fold, reaching far beyond the orbit of the moon to encompass the planets Venus and Mercury.

These two "stars" never appear more than a few hours ahead of or behind the sun. They emerge into the morning or evening twilight only to reverse course and slip back into the sun's glow. The familiar terms "morning star" and "evening star" have come to mean a planet bright enough to stand out in the glow of dusk or dawn. That definition hardly carries with it the weight of scientific precision—all of the classical planets will sooner or later satisfy it. But only two spend most of their time in the morning and evening twilight, so the titles "evening star" and "morning star" are really best conferred upon Mercury and Venus, the planets whose progress through the sky is most closely tied to the sun.

Actually, Venus so outshines every other planet that it deserves a title all its own. It's the third brightest object in the sky and can be seen even during the day under ideal observing conditions. At its best, Venus swings far enough from the sun to leave the twilight behind and for weeks on end at each appearance skywatchers will see it as a gleaming jewel set high in a darkened sky. The orbit of Venus also brings it within about 25 million miles (40 million kilometers) of Earth, or only about 100 times the distance to the moon. No other planet ever passes as close to Earth. All this adds up to one simple fact: anyone can find Venus, armed with only the most basic information about when and where to look for it.

The same cannot be said of Mercury. Although it mimics the apparent sky motions of Venus, Mercury lacks both its sweep and its brilliance. Even at its best, Mercury hugs the horizon, shining weakly through the haze and twilight, and even its best appearances don't last very long. It bobs up above the predawn horizon for a week or so, retreats back toward the sun, and then shows itself

Figure 3-1. Venus and the crescent moon met in May 2002, a cosmic accent to the clock tower of the Newberry Opera House in Newberry, South Carolina. (Photo by Francis Reddy)

briefly in the west after sunset. To make matters even worse, the time of year also critically affects the planet's visibility. Of course, we prefer to view the situation this way: Mercury presents an observational challenge unmatched by any of the other planets visible to the unaided eye.

When the two planets shine together in the morning and evening twilight, Venus acts as a celestial landmark, pointing the way to the more elusive Mercury. The crescent moon and other planets may join them too, creating arrangements that make interesting astronomical "photo opportunities." The charts and tables in this chapter serve as guides to both Mercury and Venus.

Queen of Heaven

Venus is the brightest, closest, and most visible of all the planets; it has fascinated stargazers and scientists alike for centuries. Venus was probably the first planet noticed by ancient cultures. It was known to the astronomers of imperial China as Taipo, the Great White One, around 300 B.C. and later as Jinxing (Star of Metal). Our name for the planet comes from the Romans, who identified it with their goddess of love and beauty, but it's the Norse fertility goddess Freya who lends her name to the day ruled by Venus: "Freya's day" is Friday.

Venus was an obscure deity in ancient Rome until she became associated with the powerful Greek goddess Aphrodite. Julius Caesar himself enshrined her as Venus Genetrix, the ancestor of his own family. Because the planet Venus alternates between evening and morning appearances without remaining visible all night long, some cultures knew the planet by one name when it appeared in the west and another when it shone in the east. Among the Greeks, both Pythagoras and Parmenides of Elea are credited with realizing that the bright evening star Hesperus and the morning star Phosphoros—the equivalent Roman names were Vesper and Lucifer—were in fact one and the same object.

The practice of associating the "wanderers" with the most important gods originated in Mesopotamia. There Venus was considered a manifestation of Ishtar, a powerful goddess responsible for the fertility of land and beast. It was known earlier by the Sumerian name Ninsianna and was associated with the goddess Inanna (literally "Queen of Heaven"), the forerunner of Ishtar. Hymns to Inanna indicate that by 2000 B.C. she was associated with both the morning and evening apparitions of Venus. The tale of Inanna's descent into the underworld and her death and rebirth was inspired by the movements of Venus. Records dating back nearly four thousand years show that Babylonian observers were thoroughly familiar with the details of the planet's visibility cycle. The evidence comes from a list of dates for the beginning and end of each of the planet's morning and evening appearances during the twenty-one-year reign of King Ammisaduga (1702–1682 B.C.). Appended to the observations are astrological predictions—for example, "a king will send messages of peace to another king" and "the heart of the land will be happy." These were messages from Inanna concerning the way earthly affairs were being run—messages intended only for the king.

Over two millennia later, the Mayan civilization in what is now Belize, Guatemala, and southeastern Mexico independently discerned the pattern of Venus's motions. They knew Venus by several names—Great Star, Wasp Star, Bright Star—and associated it with Kukulcan, Feathered Serpent, god of the wind and inventor of the calendar. Its movements were of such astrological importance that the Maya oriented at least three major buildings with Venus in mind—the Caracol at Chichén Itzá and the Governor's Palace at Uxmal, both on the plains of Mexico's Yucatán Peninsula, and the Temple of Venus at Copan in Guatemala. They devoted six pages to Venus in the Dresden Codex, one of a handful of surviving documents, and included detailed astronomical and religious information. They greatly feared the planet in the days just after its switch to the morning sky. Illustrations in the codex show Venus deities flinging spears at various earthly victims, with singularly unpleasant prognostications nearby—"Woe to the turtle; woe to the warrior and pregnant woman"; "evil excessive sun; the misery of maize seed." Mayan knowledge of the movements of Venus was eminently practical but was driven by religious and military necessity.

For centuries, warfare between Mayan cities consisted mainly of raiding parties in which nobles sought personal glory and captives for religious sacrifice. That changed around A.D. 400, when war imagery began to reflect an influence from the central Mexican civilization of Teotihuacán. There Tlaloc, a rain and fertility god, had been associated with Venus for centuries. The Maya at Tikal in Guatemala embraced this new influence and war took on a new character, as seen in the conquest of the neighboring city Uaxactún in A.D. 378. The Tlaloc-Venus concept became formalized as the standard image of the Mayan conqueror king, and within a couple of generations the Maya began timing their battles to coincide with the actual appearance of Venus and other planets.

Elements of the Mayan pantheon worked their way back to central Mexico and were adopted by the Aztecs, who rose to prominence after the Mayan culture had declined. The Aztec god of wind and fertility was Quetzalcoatl, who represented the predawn appearance of Venus and whose name also means feathered serpent. His twin, Xolotl, the deity of magicians, shone as the evening star. For the Inca in Peru, Venus was identified with Chasca, a fertility goddess, and was worshipped as a consort of the sun god Inti, from whom the Inca believed they were descended.

African peoples generally did not recognize that the evening and morning stars were the same object, although the Karanga and Xhosa tribes in the south did connect the two. Among some of the more imaginative names for Venus in Africa were "evening fugitive," "the watching one," and, with the planet high in the twilight at dinnertime, "peeper into pots." Unlike Mesopotamians and the Maya, the early Egyptians were not inclined to systematic observation. Still, they referred to Venus as "the crosser" or "the star that crosses" and symbolized it as bennu, a legendary heron-like bird in which the reincarnated soul of Osiris resided. Like another legendary bird, the phoenix, bennu would die in flames and be reborn from its own ashes—a suggestion that the Egyptians too knew the true identity of the morning and evening stars. After all, the evening star descends into the flame of the sun only to emerge reborn into the morning sky.

On the astronomical magnitude scale, where smaller numbers indicate greater brightness, Venus hits –4.7 at its best; only the sun and moon are brighter. The planet figures prominently among reports of "unidentified flying objects," and there's even a story about a chagrined air traffic controller who, mistaking the morning star for an arriving flight expected from the east, radioed Venus its landing instructions. The brilliance of Venus still takes us by surprise, as seen in the following examples of misidentification and popular delusion from each of the last three centuries.

On December 10, 1797, while on his way to a victory banquet at Luxembourg Palace in celebration of his successful Italian campaign, Napoleon noticed that the throng lining the streets was looking at the sky instead of paying attention to his procession. He asked what was going on and was told that a star (Venus) could be seen shining above Luxembourg Palace, something that might be looked upon as a timely indication of celestial endorsement. As Venus reached greatest eastern elongation and gained brightness, the public perception changed strangely. The evening star came to be regarded as a comet, noted the astronomer J. J. Lalande—and one on a collision course with Earth:

> On January 16th, people were on the Pont-neuf claiming the existence of a new comet and many were frightened. However it was just Venus, which was seen in daylight in Luxembourg, the very day when 20,000 people, waiting for General Bonaparte, were looking in that direction. We could see it in the same way every nineteen months if we paid attention to it, but we rarely take the opportunity. This time people were overcome with a peculiar terror; all of the shows and clubs talked about comets. *The Comet* and *The End of the World* were performed in the Vaudeville.

A century later, an evening apparition of Venus stirred popular imagination throughout the United States. In the Midwest it was thought to be the signal light of some mystery airship, but New Englanders attributed it to a scientific celebrity. An editorial in the *Boston Evening Transcript* of April 15, 1897, begins:

> A local astronomer was heard to remark the other day in a joking way that he had not been able to work lately, so busy was he kept answering questions about the new Edison experimental star in the western sky. . . . It is two or three months since the story was spread that Edison was experimenting with electric lights, and that it was his desire to learn how far he could signal from a balloon with an electric light. Sober people of Massachusetts have watched the decline in the western sky of this marvellous and brilliant light, and known it for the planet Venus, glowing with unwonted brilliancy, its thin crescent being discerned easily by any possessor of a small telescope.

The American physicist J. Robert Oppenheimer related in a 1950 letter to Eleanor Roosevelt a similar case of mistaken identity that occurred in Los Alamos, New Mexico, in the tense days before the test of the first nuclear bomb.

> I remember one morning when almost the whole project was out of doors staring at a bright object in the sky through glasses, binoculars and whatever else they could find; and nearby Kirtland Field reported to us that they had no interceptors which had enabled them to come within range of the object. Our director of personnel was an astronomer and a man of some human wisdom; and he finally came to my office and asked whether we would stop trying to shoot down Venus. I tell this story only to indicate that even a group of scientists is not proof against the errors of suggestion and hysteria.

While ancient cultures followed and catalogued the movements of Venus, scientists have come to understand its physical nature only with agonizing slowness. Even though Venus is the brightest and nearest of the planets and has been observed over four millennia, little was definitively known about the actual conditions there until the middle of the twentieth century. There is a very good reason for the slow progress: Venus is totally enshrouded in a reflective mantle of bright, pale, nearly featureless yellow clouds (fig. 3-2). Those clouds at once reveal the planet to the stargazer and veil it from the inspection of planetary scientists.

Near the part of its orbit that brings it closest to Earth, Venus appears as a brilliant, featureless crescent when viewed through a telescope. Galileo Galilei recognized in 1610 that Venus mimics the moon by going through a cycle of phases. This was hard evidence that the planet revolved around the sun—evidence that supported the heliocentric ideas proposed by the

Figure 3-2. Venus conceals its true character beneath a yellow veil of thick, sulfurous clouds. The clouds, featureless in visible light, show substantial detail only in images taken through violet and ultraviolet filters. The Jupiter-bound *Galileo* spacecraft, using Venus for a gravity-assist to speed it on its way, returned this image on February 14, 1990, from a distance of nearly 1.7 million miles (2.7 million kilometers). (NASA/Ames photo)

Polish monk Nicolaus Copernicus in 1543. Phases were to be expected under the older geocentric system, but geometry demanded that Venus must always be less than half illuminated—a sequence similar to the moon's was impossible. The Russian astronomer Mikhail Lomonosov saw a faint ring of light around Venus during the transit of 1761, correctly interpreting it as a sign that the planet had an atmosphere. Yet even by 1960 such basic information as the planet's rotation period remained a subject for lively speculation.

What little was known to scientists suggested that Venus was a slightly smaller version of our own planet. Although its proximity to the sun gives it twice the sunlight we receive, its planet-wide cloud layer reflects nearly all of that light back into space. The clouds give the planet its brilliance, but they also ensure that Venus absorbs less solar energy than Earth (and about the same as Mars), despite its nearness to the sun. Some observers believed the thick, featureless cloud deck was formed by water droplets in an atmosphere much like our own. Many thought the length of the Venusian day was about the same as Earth's. In short, Venus appeared to be Earth's twin.

A very different picture emerges from table 3-2, which summarizes the important physical and orbital data for Venus. In size and composition Venus does resemble Earth, but there the similarity ends. The temperature on the planet's surface averages 855°F (457°C)—hot enough to melt tin, lead, and zinc—and shows little variation from equator to pole or between day and night. The bulk of the atmosphere consists of carbon dioxide, which explains the high surface temperature as "global warming" gone wild. The bright clouds reflect away all but 25 percent of the sun's energy and only a small fraction of this actually reaches the surface. But the dense atmosphere makes this small fraction count. Short-wavelength energy (light) reaching the surface is absorbed and then reradiated as heat at longer (infrared) wavelengths. Atmospheric carbon dioxide repeatedly absorbs and reradiates this energy, preventing the heat from quickly escaping into space. By the time the outgoing heat radiation balances the incoming solar energy, there's already enough thermal energy bouncing between the surface and the atmosphere to keep them both plenty hot. This process, nicknamed the "greenhouse effect," also operates in our atmosphere, where water vapor plays the major greenhouse role.

It's reasonable to assume that Venus and Earth were born with similar amounts of water, but there is no water on Venus now and very little in the atmosphere. Planetary scientists speculate that a combination of the greenhouse effects of water vapor, extra solar energy—currently about twice what Earth receives—and a slow increase in the sun's energy output worked to keep Venus much hotter than Earth throughout most of its early history. This would have kept large amounts of water vapor in the atmosphere. In the upper reaches of the atmosphere, ultraviolet solar

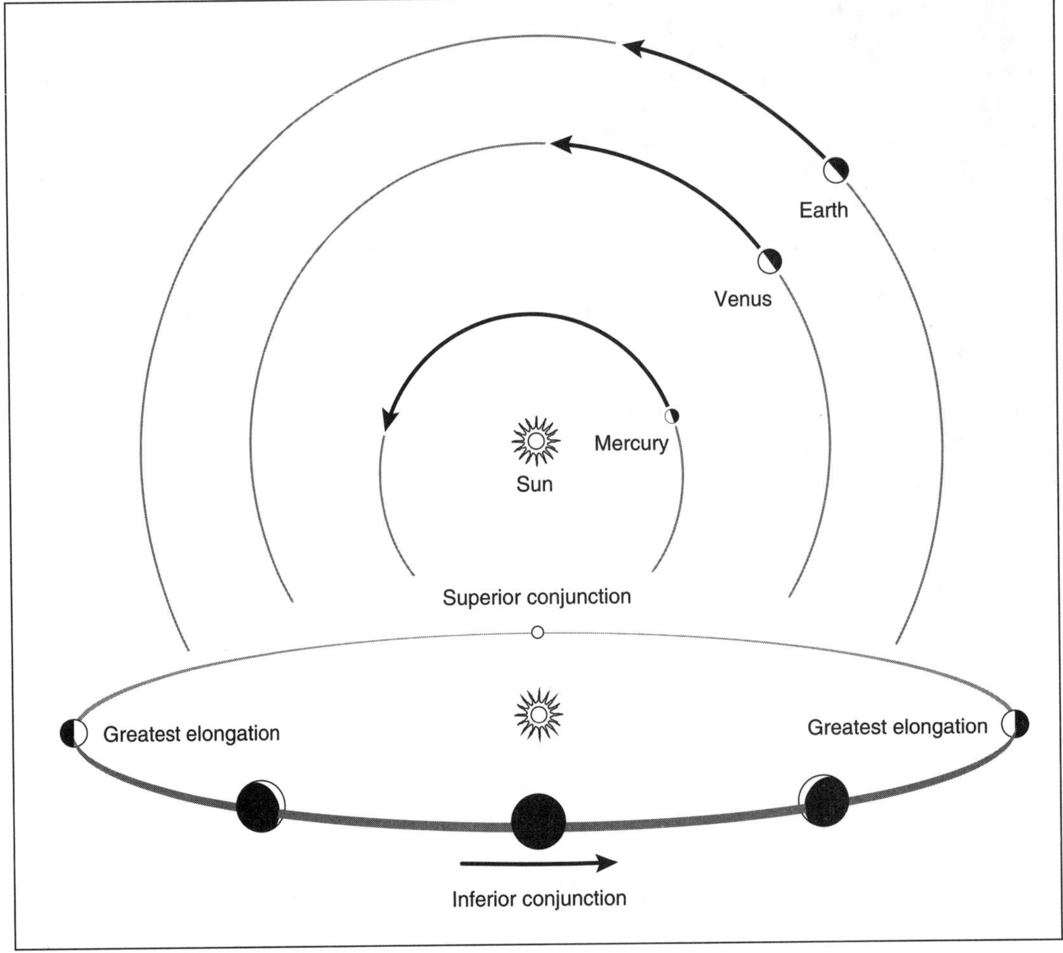

Figure 3-3. Top: A view from high above the "racetrack" of the inner solar system. Arrows indicate the average distance each planet travels in a month. Both Venus and Mercury move faster than Earth. Bottom: How we see Venus or Mercury depends on their positions relative to Earth. The diagram shows the changes in apparent size and phase both planets undergo during their visibility cycle. They pass between Earth and the sun at inferior conjunction.

radiation would have broken the water into its component hydrogen and oxygen and, over eons, the hydrogen would have escaped the planet.

The atmosphere of Venus held still more surprises. In the late 1960s, the Soviet Union attempted to land instrumented capsules on the planet's surface as part of their ongoing Venera series of space missions. The first three attempts that successfully entered the atmosphere ceased operating before they reached the surface. When the next probe, *Venera 7,* survived its descent and sent back surface pressure measurements, it became clear why the earlier Venus landers had failed: they had been crushed as they descended. The dense atmosphere of Venus presses onto the surface with a force more than ninety times greater than Earth's, equivalent to the pressure experienced by a submarine at a depth of over half a mile beneath our oceans.

This catalog of atmospheric horrors would not be complete without mentioning the contents of those perpetual yellow clouds. They aren't made of water droplets; water in any form is scarce on Venus (about 0.01 percent in the atmosphere). Instead, the clouds form from droplets of concentrated sulfuric acid, with traces of hydrochloric and possibly hydrofluoric acids thrown in as well. So in addition to its stifling heat and crushing pressure, the atmosphere of Venus holds the record as being the most corrosive in the solar system.

As of this writing, Venus has seen more terrestrial hardware than any other planet, with twenty Soviet and American space missions returning data since the first attempts in 1961. The Soviet Venera and VEGA missions included flybys, orbiters, atmospheric probes, and landers. Successful U.S. missions included the *Mariner 2* and *5* flyby spacecrafts, the *Pioneer Venus Orbiter* and *Multiprobe*, and *Magellan*. In addition, several missions to other planets—*Mariner 10* as it headed for Mercury, *Galileo* on its way to Jupiter, and Saturn-bound *Cassini*—observed Venus as a target of opportunity; they were in the neighborhood to increase their speed through "gravity assist" maneuvers with the planet. In total, eleven spacecraft have returned data from the surface of Venus, but most survived less than two hours in the hostile environment. Four Soviet landers have even transmitted images from their landing sites, revealing a sterile, rocky, arid landscape bathed in a diffuse orange light. Only about 2 percent of the incident sunlight reaches the surface of Venus, about the same as on a heavily overcast day here on Earth. Images of the surface and chemical analyses of the rocks indicated that all of the areas explored by the landers were volcanic plains.

Since the perpetual clouds block all visible light from the surface, any global analysis of Venus had to be done by radar. The first crude maps were made in the 1960s with large ground-based radiotelescopes, which "pinged" the planet with radar pulses whenever it was nearest Earth. The returned signal contained information about the way radio waves interacted with the surface and allowed the first identification of surface features. It was through these studies in 1961 that scientists were at last able to pinpoint the planet's rotation rate. Venus spins east to west, opposite to the direction of most other planets, and takes 243 Earth days to make one complete rotation. Since it completes one orbit around the sun in just 225 Earth days, the "Venus day" is actually longer than the "Venus year." No one knows why it spins so slowly. The entire atmosphere rotates as well, in the same direction, but takes just four days to do so at the altitude of the cloud deck.

Mapping of the planet from orbit began with *Pioneer Venus Orbiter*, which determined its topography with a radar altimeter, and continued with *Venera 15* and *16*, which carried radar imagers to produce photograph-like pictures of about 25 percent of the surface. The culmination of Venus mapping came with *Magellan*, which between 1990 and 1994 used a radar imager to map 98 percent of the planet in the greatest detail yet. *Magellan* revealed that landforms on Venus consisted of two main types—smooth volcanic plains (80 percent) and intensely deformed elevated plateaus called tesserae (8 percent)—and revealed extensive meandering rift valleys, over 1,700 volcanic landforms or deposits, and over 1,000 impact craters. Like other bodies in the solar system, Venus must have undergone intensive bombardment from comets, asteroids, and smaller debris over the past four billion years, but the density and number of craters, plus the fact that only a few of them are modified by lava flows or geologic faults, indicates that none of the planet's rock units are older than between 300 million and 750 million years. The oldest are the highland tesserae, which formed by intensive folding and faulting of the surface. Various stages of volcanism followed, but the last major episode flooded nearly 90 percent of the planet with basalt lavas, erasing its most ancient landforms and covering all but the highest tesserae. The craters that *Magellan* mapped are scars from impacts received only after this activity had subsided.

Even in its basic geological framework, Venus bears little kinship with Earth. It shows no evidence of plate tectonics—the horizontal motion of large crustal plates that drives earthquakes and volcanoes, builds mountains, and moves continents on Earth. The surface of Venus instead appears to have been repeatedly extended and compressed, warped by the successive rise and fall of plumes of magma from deep within the planet. The apparent detection of lightning by some spacecraft and changes in the amount of atmospheric sulfur dioxide, both phenomena associated with terrestrial volcanoes, suggest that some local volcanic episodes still occur on the face of Venus today.

The View from Earth

Observers had long known that the motions of Venus and Mercury were intimately tied to the sun, but explaining just why this was so proved difficult. To fully appreciate why we see Venus and Mercury more easily at some times than at others, it's necessary to understand just how they move.

If we could view the solar system from a far-flung point high above the sun's north pole, we would see all the planets moving around the sun in their elliptical orbits, much like cars on a racetrack (fig. 3-3). Those in the innermost lanes circle fastest, those on the outermost the slowest. Turn the solar system on its "side"—that is, view it along the plane of the Earth's orbit, the "ground level" of the racetrack—and the planets seem to slide from one side of the sun to the other. From behind the sun, each planet moves to the left (east) until it appears farthest from the sun, at which point it doubles back. Proceeding now to the right (westward), the planet's apparent distance from the sun shrinks. It eventually crosses our line of sight to the sun and continues west until it again reaches a maximum angle, reverses course, and heads east to return to the far side of its orbit.

From our perspective on Earth, we view the solar system not only along the plane of the racetrack, but from one of the innermost lanes. The planets on the outer orbits arc away from the sun and pass behind us, where we can watch them throughout the night. In truth, only two planets exhibit the back-and-forth motion described above. That's because only two planets—Mercury and Venus—move on an inside track as seen from Earth's position. For skygazers, both planets put on their best shows near the time of greatest elongation—the point at which they reach their widest angle east or west of the sun. For Venus, this is between forty-five and forty-seven degrees; for the more variable Mercury, it's between eighteen and twenty-eight degrees.

With that image in mind, we can track the relative positions of Earth and Venus through one complete cycle of visibility. We'll begin as before, with Venus located on the far side of the sun as seen from Earth, at the point termed superior conjunction. Venus, now at its greatest distance from us, is lost in the glare of the sun. If the planet could be seen, a telescope would reveal a very small, fully illuminated disk.

Venus moves farther east each day, setting progressively later than the sun. After a few weeks we can see it low in the west, glimmering in the twilight of dusk before following the sun below the horizon. It continues sliding eastward and pulling away from the sun, each day appearing higher above the horizon after sunset and becoming more noticeable in the evening sky. When Venus reaches greatest eastern elongation (about seven months after superior conjunction), it dominates the early evening and sets a couple of hours after the sun. To telescopic observers, the planet's disk has grown larger, but now only half of its sunlit side faces Earth.

Venus now runs on the near side of its orbit, approaching us as it reverses course and rushes westward. Its disk continues to grow, but a telescope reveals an ever brighter—though ever slimmer—crescent. The planet grows brighter until about five weeks after greatest elongation, when the fading light from its ever-shrinking crescent finally offsets its increasing angular size. Venus falls quickly from its summit in the evening sky, taking just ten weeks to plunge back into the sun's glare. It passes between Earth and the sun (inferior conjunction) and gains a lap on us. So ends the evening visibility period, or apparition, of Venus.

The planet isn't lost in the sun's radiance for long, though; it quickly pulls west of the sun and begins its morning apparition. Venus climbs higher into the predawn sky as rapidly as it fell from the evening sky, glowing brightest about five weeks after inferior conjunction and reaching greatest western elongation five weeks after that. The planet then reverses course and, now on the far side of its orbit, begins a lazy, seven-month-long descent toward the horizon. Venus completes the cycle when its slow eastward slide to the sun brings it back to superior conjunction.

Figure 3-4 tracks Venus throughout typical evening (2008–2009) and morning (2004) apparitions and illustrates its changes in position and speed. Table 3-1 lists the date range during which Venus can be seen as a conspicuous evening and morning star for observers at mid-northern latitudes. Although Venus is bright enough to be seen even in daylight, we limited the dates in the table to times when the planet appears at least ten degrees above the horizon about forty-five minutes after sunset or before sunrise. Looking for Venus closer to dusk or dawn will extend these dates somewhat; see appendix A for additional information.

We mentioned earlier that Venus completes one orbit around the sun in 225 days (its sidereal period), but the planet's visibility cycle takes 584 days, or 1.6 years (its synodic period). The fact that the Earth also moves—that our viewpoint within the solar system's racetrack isn't sta-

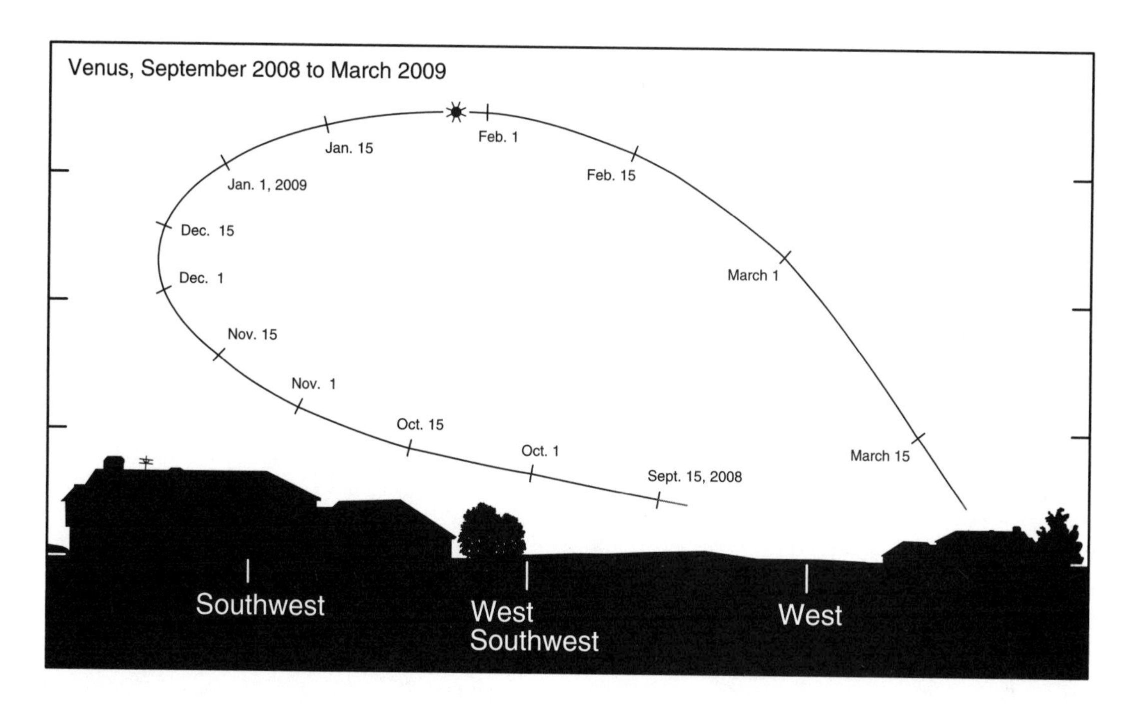

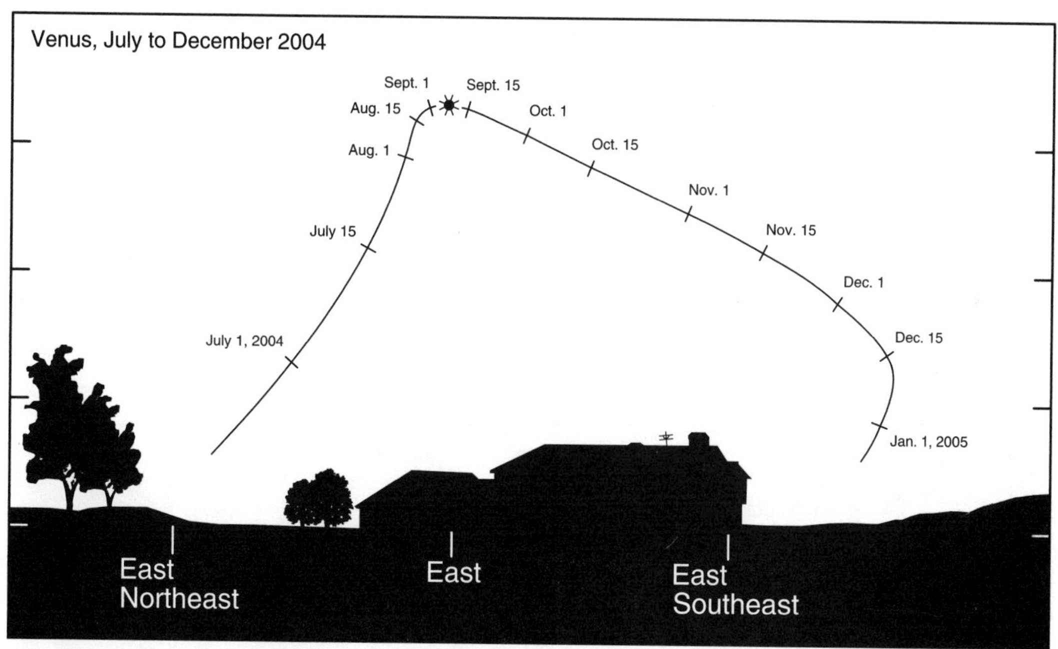

Figure 3-4. Top: Venus arcs through the evening sky from mid-September 2008 to mid-March 2009, as seen forty-five minutes after sunset. The planet reaches its greatest elongation east of the sun on January 14, but keeps climbing above the horizon for another week. Bottom: Venus as it tracks through the morning sky from July 2004 to January 2005, forty-five minutes before sunrise. The planet attains its greatest angle west of the sun on August 17, but continues its climb into the first week of September.

tionary—explains the difference. (We came across a similar discrepancy in chapter 2's discussion of the moon.) For the same geometry to recur between Earth, Venus, and the sun, Venus must make up the extra distance traveled by the Earth before reappearing in the same part of our sky.

Table 3-1. Visibility of Venus, 2003–2010

Each entry gives the range of dates for which an observer at midnorthern latitudes will find Venus at least ten degrees above the horizon forty-five minutes before sunrise or after sunset.

Year	As Evening Star (in the west after sunset)	As Morning Star (in the east before sunrise)
2003	—	Mid-November 2002 to late March. Best in early January, rising about 3¾ hours before dawn.
2004	Late November 2003 to late May. Best in early April, setting nearly 4 hours after sundown.	Early July to late December. Best in mid-August, rising about 4 hours before dawn.
2005	Late July to late December. Best in early December, when Venus sets 3 hours after the sun.	—
2006	—	Late January to early May. Best in late February, when Venus rises little more than 2¾ hours before dawn and remains low in the southeast.
2007	Mid-January to mid-July. Best in mid-May, setting about 3½ hours after the sun.	Early September to early February 2008. Best in early November, rising nearly 3¾ hours ahead of the sun.
2009	Mid-October 2008 to mid-March. Best in late January, when it sets nearly 4 hours after the sun.	Late April to late October. Best in early August, rising 3 hours before the sun.
2010	Early April to early September. Best in early June, but it remains low in the west and sets about 2½ hours after sundown.	Mid-November to mid-March 2011. Best in late December, rising about 3¾ hours before dawn.

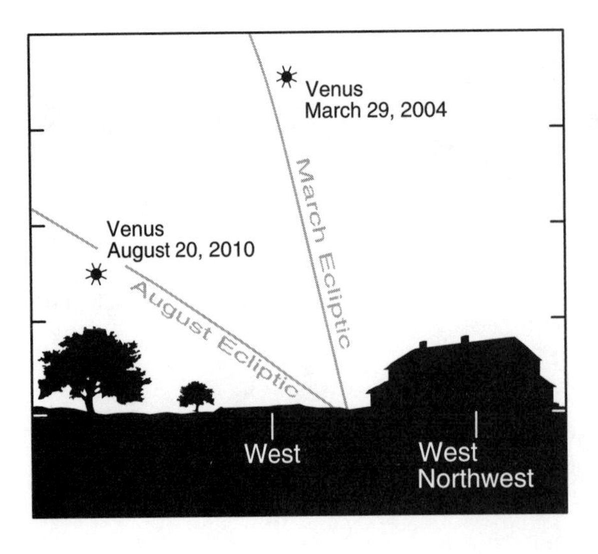

Figure 3-5. Venus gives its best evening shows when its greatest angle east of the sun occurs near the start of spring, which happens in 2004. Its worst evening apparitions occur when it reaches greatest eastern elongation near the start of fall, as in 2010. The planet is forty-six degrees east of the sun on both occasions; the steepness of the ecliptic accounts for the difference in altitude.

Table 3-2. Facts About Venus and Mercury

VENUS	
Diameter:	7,521 miles (12,104 km) 95% that of Earth
Surface temperature:	855°F (457°C)
Surface atmospheric pressure:	93 bars, or 93 times that of Earth's atmosphere. Equivalent to the pressure at a depth of 2,980 feet (907 meters) under the Earth's ocean.
Atmospheric composition:	96.5% carbon dioxide 3.5% nitrogen
Moons:	None
Rotation period:	243.01 days, opposite to the rotational direction of Earth
Obliquity:	177.4°
Sidereal orbital period:	224.70 days
Synodic orbital period:	583.92 days (1.60 years)
Mean distance from sun:	67.2 million miles (108.2 million km) 72.3% that of Earth
Orbit inclined to Earth's:	3.39°

MERCURY	
Diameter:	3,031 miles (4,878 km) 38% that of Earth
Surface temperature:	At perihelion on the equator: 845°F (452°C) Night: –298°F (–183°C) Greatest day/night temperature range of any planet
Surface atmospheric pressure:	Essentially zero
Atmospheric composition:	~60% oxygen ~30% sodium 9% helium < 1% hydrogen
Moons:	None
Rotation period:	58.65 days
Obliquity:	0.1°
Sidereal orbital period:	87.97 days
Synodic orbital period:	115.88 days
Mean distance from sun:	36.0 million miles (57.9 million km) 38.7% that of Earth
Orbit inclined to Earth's:	7.00°

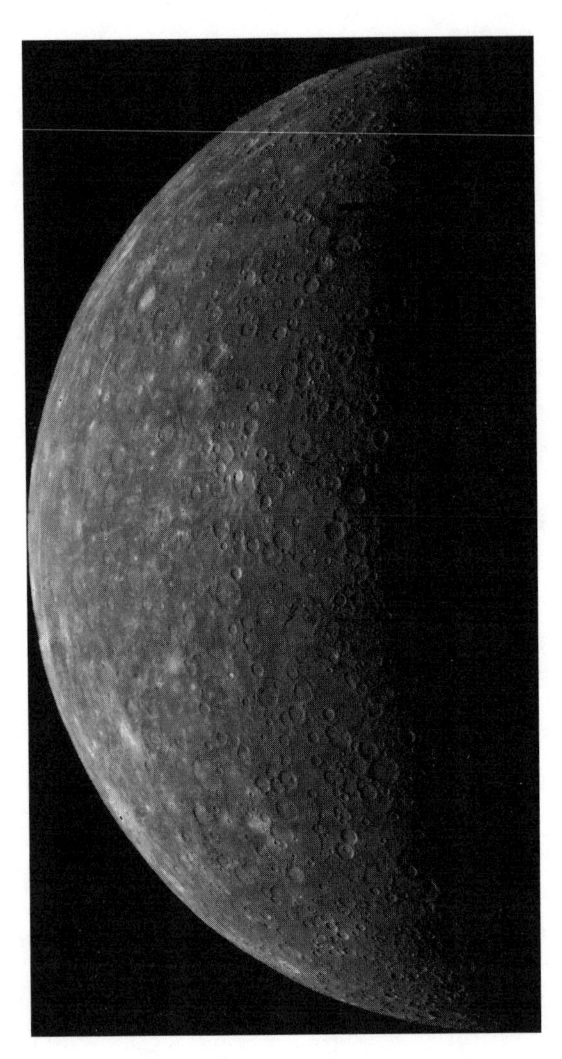

Figure 3-6. *Mariner 10* encountered Mercury three times between 1974 and 1975, photographing almost half of the planet's rugged surface. This photomosaic combines over fifty images acquired during the spacecraft's first encounter and shows about two-thirds of the planet's northern hemisphere. In many respects Mercury resembles an enlarged version of our own moon. (NASA/Mark Robinson, Northwestern University)

Although Venus is always rather easy to find, it only commands attention when its greatest elongation occurs in the right season. At its best, Venus rises nearly four hours before dawn or lingers as long after sunset. All of the planets stay close to the ecliptic, which intersects the horizon most steeply near the start of spring and fall. In the northern hemisphere, Venus gives its best evening displays when greatest eastern elongation occurs near the start of spring, and the worst when it occurs near the end of summer (fig. 3-5). In the span covered by this book, the best evening apparition occurs in 2004, with Venus over thirty-six degrees above the horizon forty-five minutes after sunset; the worst occurs in 2010, with the planet not quite half that distance above the horizon at the same time after dusk.

Earth and Venus share a curious relationship, one that contributed to Mayan and Mesopotamian fascination with the planet. Venus completes five synodic cycles (2,919.6 days) in almost exactly eight years (2,922 days); that is, after every set of five evening and morning apparitions Venus returns to the same relationship with the Earth and sun and replays its performance. For example, the planet's fine morning show in the end of 2004 repeats almost exactly in 2012. The difference between eight Earth years and five synodic Venus cycles is less than sixty hours, so to update the 2004 diagram in figure 3-4 for the

Table 3-3. Mercury's Best Apparitions, 2003–2010

Each entry gives the range of dates for which an observer at midnorthern latitudes will find Mercury at least ten degrees above the horizon thirty minutes before sunrise or after sunset.

Year	As Evening Star (in the west after sunset)	As Morning Star (in the east before sunrise)
2003	April 6 to 24	January 23 to February 7 September 23 to October 1
2004	March 21 to April 4	January 4 to 23 September 5 to 12 December 19 to January 7, 2005
2005	March 5 to 18 June 20 to July 12	August 20 to 29 December 4 to 23
2006	February 18 to 28 June 3 to June 28	August 3 to 11 November 17 to December 5
2007	January 31 to February 12 May 18 to June 12	July 18 to 28 November 2 to 17
2008	January 16 to 27 April 30 to May 23 December 31 to January 10, 2009	October 17 to 29
2009	April 16 to May 4	October 2 to 11
2010	March 30 to April 15	January 15 to 30 December 29 to January 17, 2011

2012 apparition, just subtract two days from the dates beside the planet's track.

Mercury: Messenger of the Gods

The meaning of Mercury's earliest Egyptian name, Sebeg, is unknown but the name is clearly related to Set, and a later text from the tomb of Seti I refers to the planet as "Set in the evening twilight, a god in the morning twilight." Mercury apparently took on the malevolent disposition of Set, brother of Osiris, when it appeared in the evening, but changed identities when it switched to the morning sky.

The Greek name Stilbon (Twinkling Star) seems inspired by the planet's appearance, shimmering in the unsteady air near the horizon. The Greeks associated the planet Mercury with the swift-footed messenger of the gods, Hermes, who watched over travelers and brought good fortune in commerce; our name for the planet comes from his Roman counterpart. The Babylonians associated Mercury with their god of wisdom and patron of scribes, Nabu, and appropriately enough called it Shihtu (Jumping). To the late Chinese it was Shuixing, the Water Star. The Anglo-Saxons named the day ruled by Mercury after their chief deity, Woden, from which we derive our name for Wednesday.

Table 3-2 lists Mercury's vital statistics. Running on the solar system's innermost lane, Mercury completes an orbit around the sun in just 88 days. Its path is more inclined and elliptical than that of every other planet but Pluto. This ellipticity causes Mercury's distance to the sun to vary by 66 percent between its closest point to the sun, called perihelion, and its farthest extreme. Radar studies in 1964 determined that Mercury spins once on its axis every fifty-nine days—exactly two-thirds of its orbital period—so the planet makes three complete rotations for every two orbits around the sun. The coupling of its rotation and orbital periods, together with the elliptical orbit, means that the same side of Mercury faces the sun at alternate perihelion passages. As a result, two locations on opposite sides of Mercury are more sun-baked than any others. These locations are often referred to as Mercury's "hot poles." At perihelion, where the sun appears three times the size it does from Earth, the hot poles can reach 845°F (452°C)—not quite as hot as Venus, despite the proximity to the sun, but still more than adequate for melting zinc. Just as Earth's tidal effects on the moon have locked its rotation period to its orbit, so the sun's tides have locked Mercury into a 3:2 coupling of its spin and orbit.

The telescope reveals little about the planet except its cycle of phases; it took a U.S. spacecraft named *Mariner 10* to give us the first detailed look at Mercury. Its cameras photographed about 45 percent of the planet's surface during three flybys in 1974 and 1975, returning some 3,500 images (fig. 3-6). From a distance, Mercury could be mistaken for our own moon—a similarity that was expected—but a closer look revealed that even Mercury's most heavily cratered areas show fewer craters than the lunar highlands. Mercury's highlands consist of regions rich in craters intermixed with large expanses of gently rolling plains. Because these plains surround and partially cover the cratered areas, they must be younger. Scientists believe they were created by outpourings of lava some four billion years ago. Another landform, the smooth plains, resembles the maria of our moon. Occurring near large impact basins and filling some of the largest craters, the smooth plains probably represent material that flooded onto Mercury's surface some 3.8 billion years ago.

Caloris Basin, named for its location near one of the hot poles, is the largest undegraded impact structure photographed on the planet. About 830 miles (1,340 kilometers) across, the basin floor is marked by a complex pattern of closely spaced crisscrossing ridges and fractures—based on current knowledge, its detailed geology appears to be unique in the solar system. Caloris is thought to have formed around 3.85 billion years ago when an object some 95 miles (150 kilometers) wide smashed into Mercury. The powerful blow transmitted seismic waves around and through the planet; within moments these waves converged on the surface at a location exactly opposite the impact site. The aftermath of the tremendous earthquakes that shook this spot can be seen in the jumbled and heavily fractured terrain opposite the Caloris Basin.

Ground-based radar studies of Mercury in 1991 brought the unexpected revelation that about twenty-seven craters near both poles may contain frozen water. Similar radar studies did not find icelike radar returns near the moon's polar areas—despite the fact that *Clementine* and *Lunar Prospector* both produced evidence that seems to point to the presence of frozen water—but earth-based radar sees farther into polar

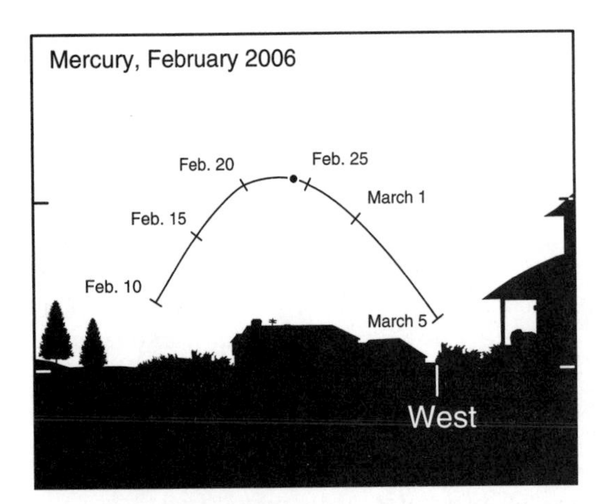

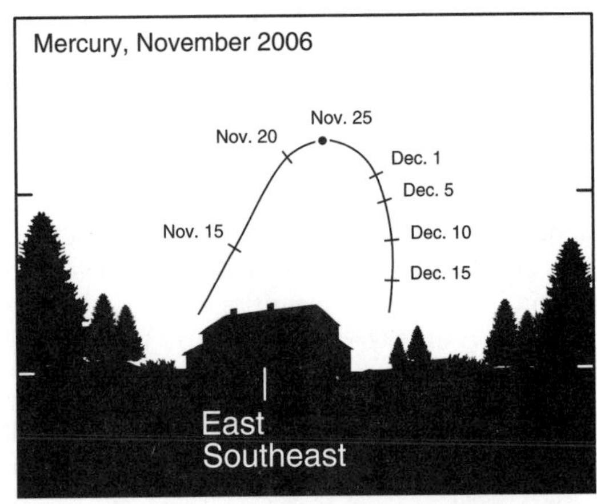

Figure 3-7. Typical evening and morning apparitions of Mercury, as seen about thirty minutes after sunset and before sunrise, respectively. Left: The planet is best placed for evening viewing from February 18 to 28, 2006; greatest eastern elongation (18.1°) occurs February 24. Right: Mercury's track through the morning sky, best from November 17 to December 5, 2006; greatest western elongation (19.9°) occurs November 25.

craters on Mercury than on the moon. With Mercury's near-zero obliquity, there can be no seasons and the sun never shines into craters on the poles. Comparisons of maps made from radar studies and images of the surface returned by *Mariner 10* show a close correspondence between radar-reflective areas and craters. In fact, radar-bright deposits fill most of the polar craters imaged by *Mariner 10* that have intact rims—whatever the nature of the deposits, it appears that Mercury's available cold traps are full. Scientists consider frozen water to be the most likely candidate, but another possibility is sulfur that had been cooked out of the hottest parts of the surface and gradually migrated to the poles.

Radar studies on the side of Mercury not yet imaged provide tantalizing hints of what we may yet learn about the planet's volcanic past.

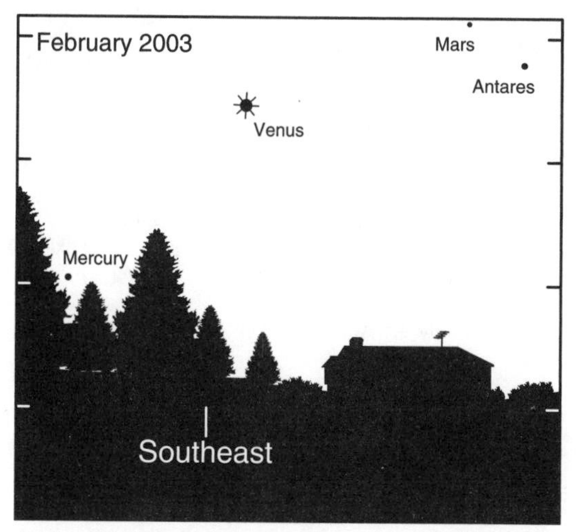

On the morning of February 4, Venus (–4.3) gleams in the predawn light between Mercury (–0.1) and Mars (+1.2), now above and fainter than its stellar rival Antares (+0.9).

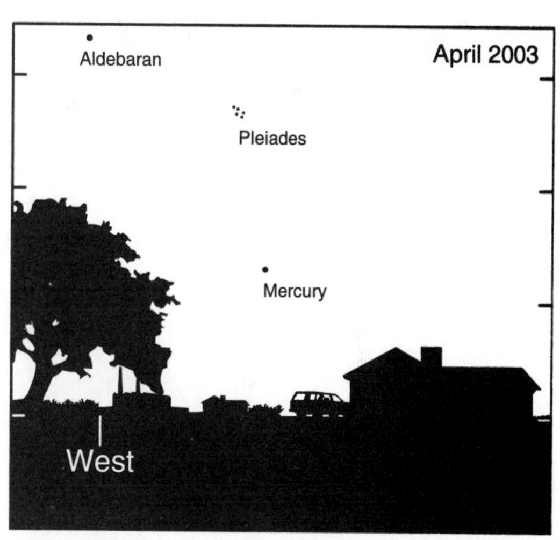

Mercury (+0.1) shines beneath Aldebaran (+0.8) and the Pleiades cluster on the evening of April 16.

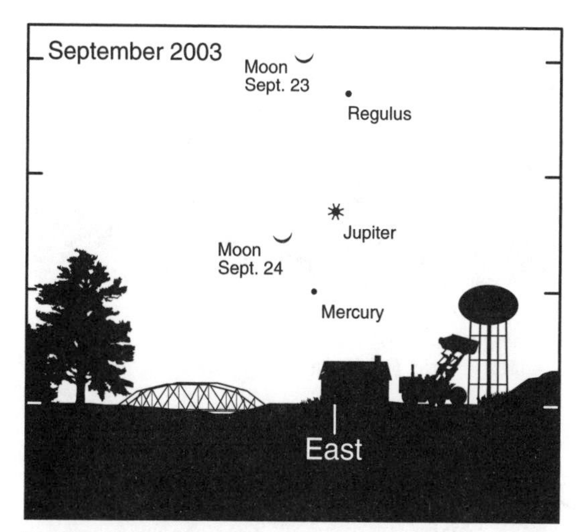

The waning moon passes first Jupiter (–0.9) and then Mercury (–0.1) as it slips into the morning twilight September 23 through 24.

Figure 3-8. Mercury in 2003, looking thirty minutes before sunrise or after sunset. Tick marks along the sides of the horizon diagrams represent altitude intervals of ten degrees—about the distance covered by a fist at arm's length.

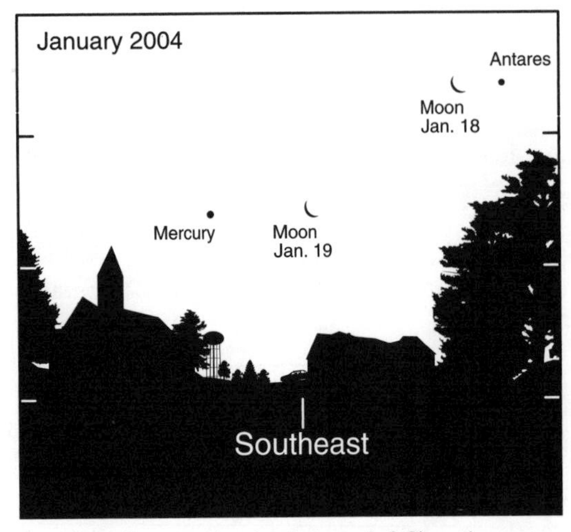

The moon lies near the star Antares (+0.9) on the morning of January 18, then cruises past Mercury (–0.2) January 19.

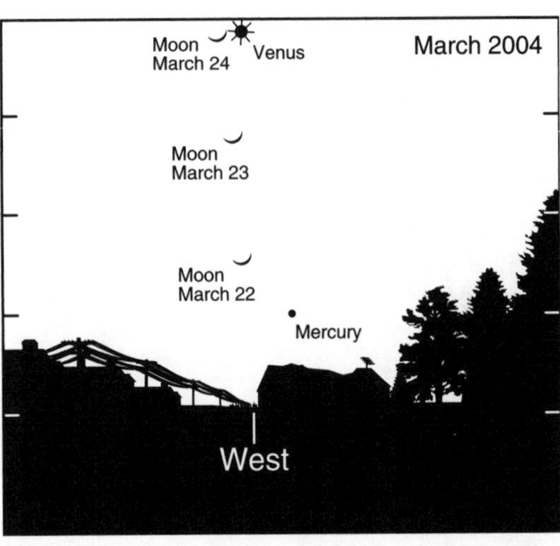

The moon is your guide for a grand tour of the solar system on late March evenings. Starting on March 22, the crescent lies above Mercury (–0.9). The moon, waxing as it goes, visits Venus (–4.3) on March 24, Mars (+1.3) on March 25, Saturn (+1.0) high overhead on March 28, and finally on April 2 meets Jupiter (–1.0) in the eastern sky as it nears full.

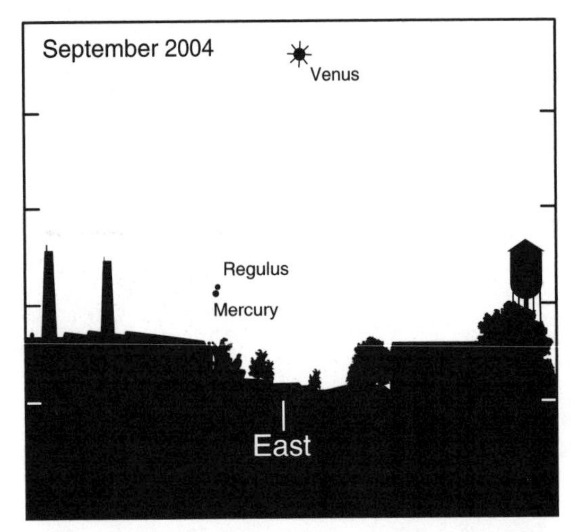

On the morning of September 10, 2004, Mercury (–0.3) shines just below the star Regulus (+1.3), a temporary double star in the predawn sky. The waning moon lies above, between gleaming Venus (–4.1) and Saturn (+0.2).

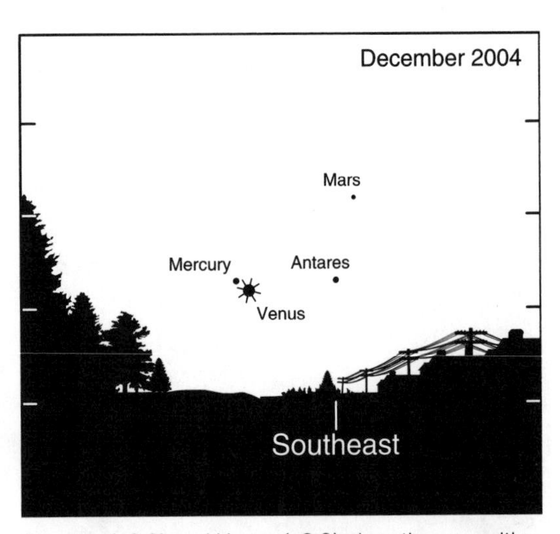

Mercury (–0.3) and Venus (–3.9) close the year with a morning meeting on December 29. Mars (+1.2), above the star Antares (+0.9), chaperones.

Figure 3-9. Mercury in 2004, looking thirty minutes before sunrise or after sunset. Remember to give yourself enough time to get your bearings before the sun rises too high or Mercury descends too low.

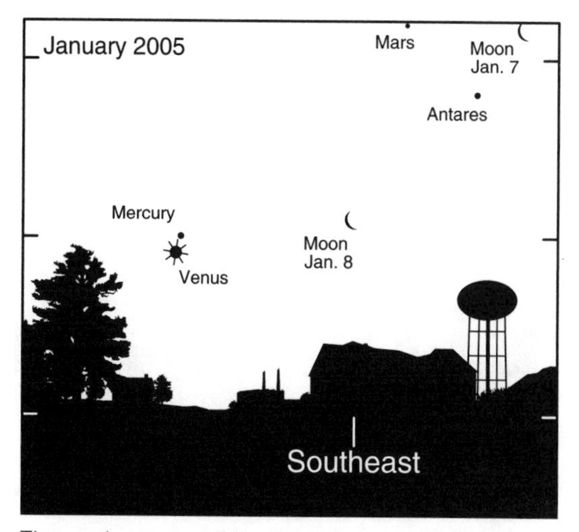

The waning moon slides through a crowded predawn sky, passing first Mars (+1.5) on January 7 and then Mercury (–0.3) and Venus (–3.9) on January 8.

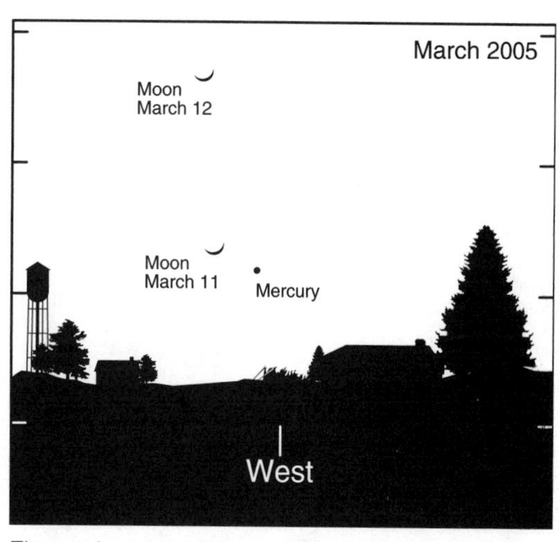

The waxing moon is your guide to Mercury (–0.4) on March 11 and 12. On March 19 it lies close to Saturn (–0.0).

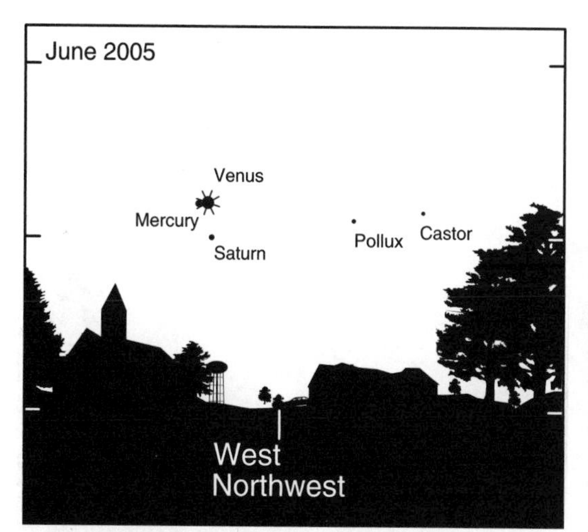

The evening twilight of late June displays a line of planets near two bright stars. Mercury (–0.6), Venus (–3.9) and Saturn (+0.2) form up near Gemini's Castor (+1.9) and Pollux (+1.1) on June 21. Saturn descends, Venus climbs, and Mercury leaps toward them. Venus is closest to Saturn on June 25 (see fig. 6-7). Mercury gleams just below Venus on June 26 and 27.

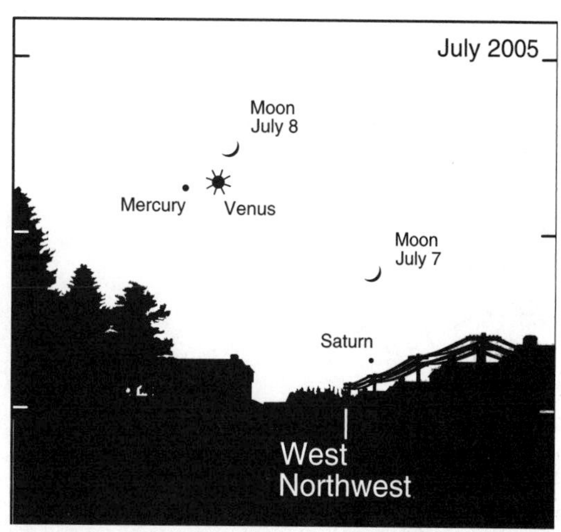

By July 8, Saturn (+0.2) is all but gone from the evening sky as the moon joins Venus (–3.9) and Mercury (+0.5).

Figure 3-10. Mercury in 2005, looking thirty minutes before sunrise or after sunset.

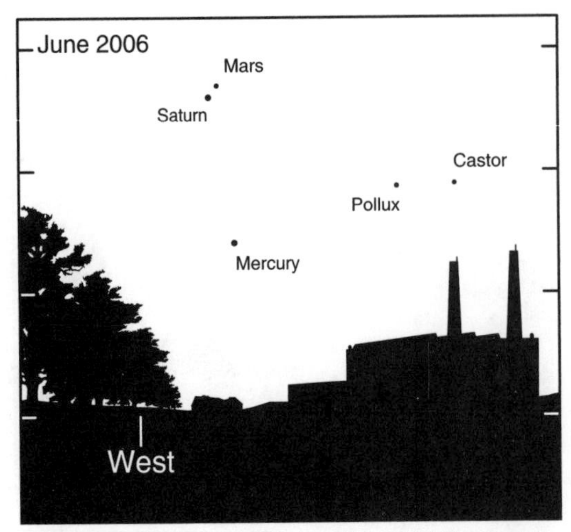

On June 17, 2006, Saturn (+0.3) and fainter, redder Mars (+1.8) meet as Mercury (+0.3) shines near Castor (+1.9) and Pollux (+1.1) in the evening twilight. A glimpse of Saturn and Mars with binoculars will show them near the stars of Cancer's Beehive cluster.

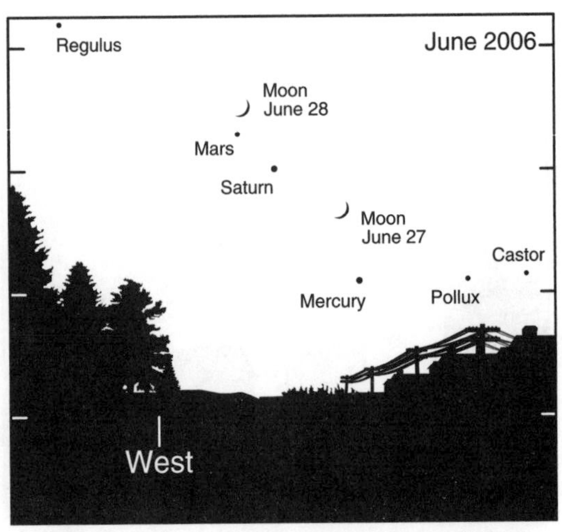

The waxing moon lies below and to the right of Mercury (+1.0) on June 26, between Mercury and Saturn (+0.3) on June 27, and above Mars (+1.8) on June 28.

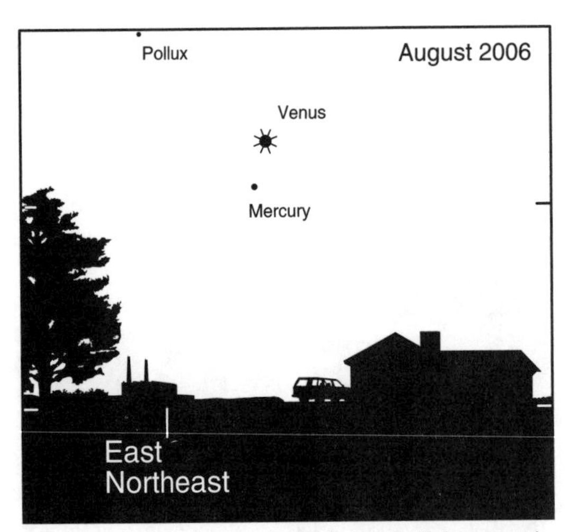

As Venus (–3.9) descends slowly into twilight on early August mornings, Mercury (–0.4) jumps up to meet it.

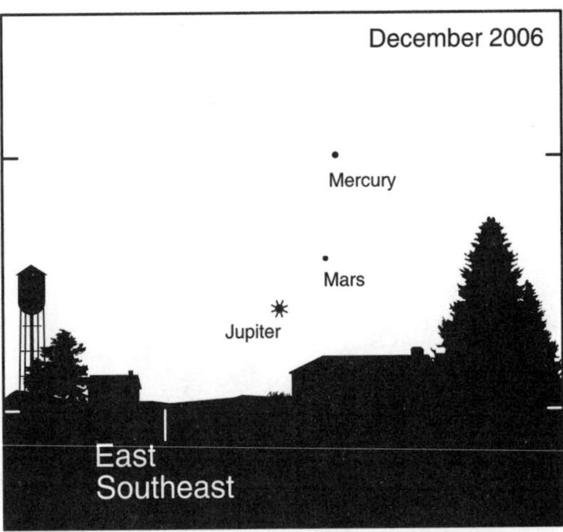

Mercury (–0.6) stands out amid the faint stars of Libra on the morning of December 5. Try locating dim, ruddy Mars (+1.6) and bright Jupiter (–1.7) below it. Binoculars help.

Figure 3-11. Mercury in 2006, looking thirty minutes before sunrise or after sunset.

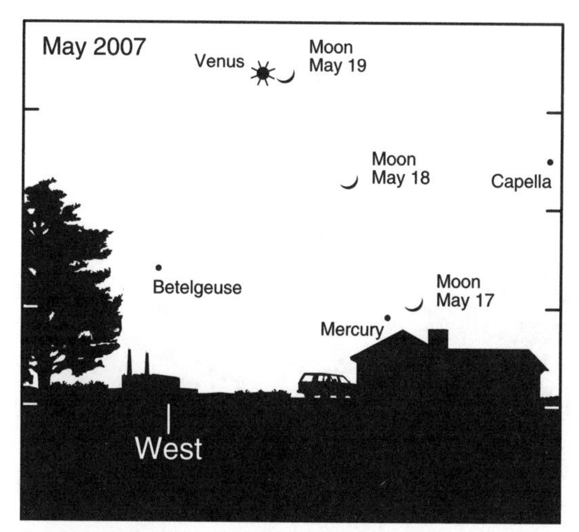

The waxing moon ascends along a chain of planets beginning the evening of May 17. Its thin crescent lies near Mercury (–0.9) on May 17, dazzling Venus (–4.0) on May 19, and Saturn (+0.5) on May 22. When full on May 31 (June 1 UT), the moon rises into the eastern twilight near brilliant Jupiter (–2.3).

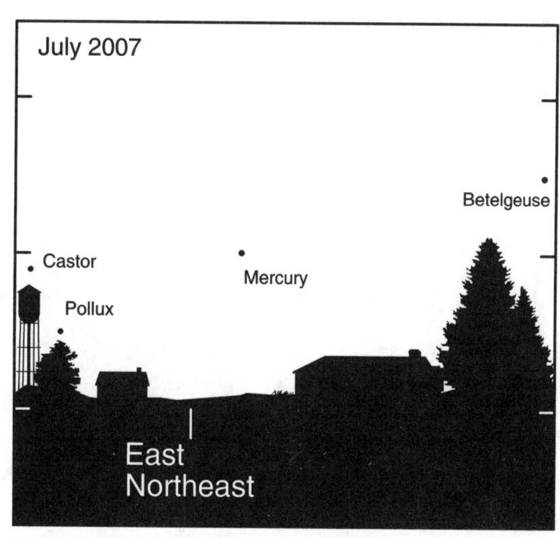

On July 25, Mercury (–0.2) briefly pops into the predawn sky. Look for Mars (+0.6) high in the east as well.

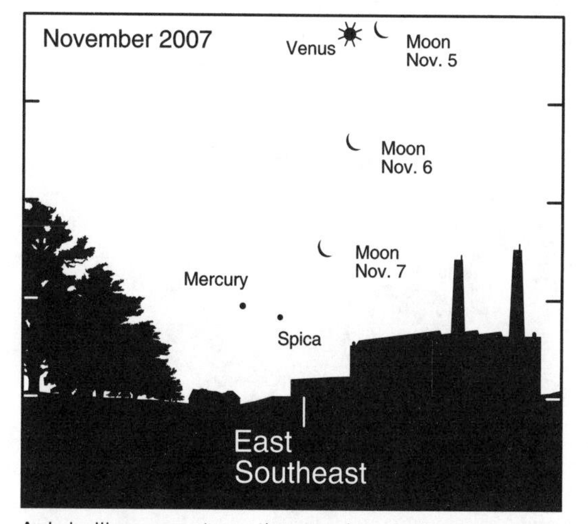

A dwindling moon tours the morning planets at the end of October and early November. A gibbous moon lies near Mars (–0.6) on October 30, and a crescent visits Saturn (+0.8) on November 3, brilliant Venus (–4.3) on November 5, and Mercury (–0.3) on November 7. Also look for the star Spica (+0.9) in Virgo near Mercury.

Figure 3-12. Mercury in 2007, looking thirty minutes before sunrise or after sunset. Tick marks along the sides of the horizon diagrams represent altitude intervals of ten degrees—about the distance covered by your fist at arm's length.

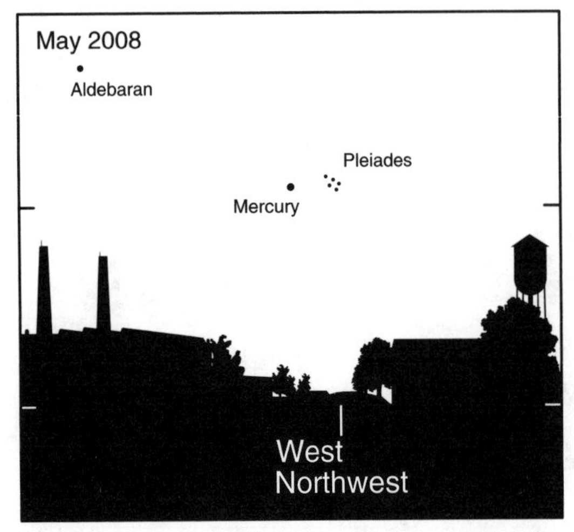

Can you glimpse the Pleiades cluster near Mercury (–0.8) after sunset on May 2?

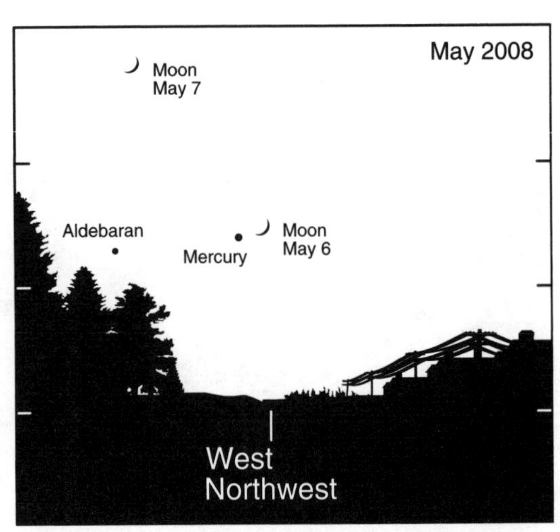

On May 6, the crescent moon joins Mercury (–0.4) and Aldebaran (+0.8) in the evening sky. The moon passes Mars (+1.3) high in the southwest on May 10 and lies near Saturn (+1.0) and Regulus (+1.3) on May 12.

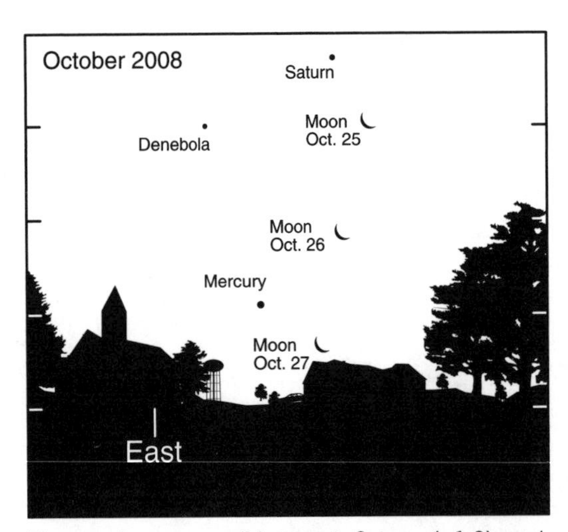

The waning moon slides past Saturn (+1.0) and Mercury (–0.7) in the morning sky between October 25 and 27.

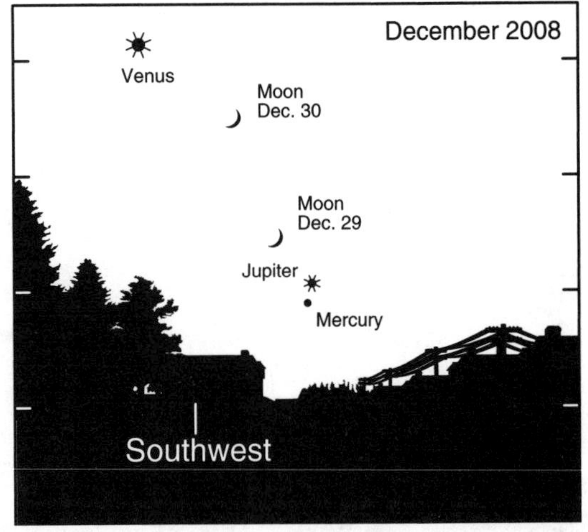

Mercury (–0.7) closes out the year with an evening apparition that includes a close pass to Jupiter (–1.9) while dazzling Venus (–4.1) looks on. The crescent moon lies above the pair on December 29 and appears near Venus on December 31. Mercury is well placed for observing until January 10, 2009.

Figure 3-13. Mercury in 2008, looking thirty minutes before sunrise or after sunset. Remember to give yourself enough time to get your bearings before the sun rises too high or Mercury descends too low.

A radar-bright halo some 310 miles (500 kilometers) across with a radar-dark center about 43 miles (70 kilometers) wide bears some resemblance to the large shield volcanoes found on Earth, Venus, and Mars. With only half the planet mapped at modest resolution, Mercury remains the least known of all the earthlike worlds.

The Hubble Space Telescope cannot point close enough to the sun to view Mercury without risking damage, but two planned space missions will end the long hiatus in exploring this sun-baked world. A NASA spacecraft called *MESSENGER*—short for Mercury Surface, Space Environment, Geochemistry and Ranging—will perform two reconnaissance flybys of the planet in 2008 and will be placed into orbit in 2009. Its instruments will study Mercury's surface composition, geologic history, internal structure, magnetic field, and tenuous atmosphere—and, of course, search for evidence of ice at the poles. An even more ambitious probe will reach the planet in 2012. Following a two-and-a-half-year cruise that includes flybys of the moon, Venus, and Mercury, the European Space Agency's probe *BepiColombo* will settle into orbit around the planet. The name of the mission honors Giuseppe (Bepi) Colombo (1920–1984), an imaginative mathematician and engineer from the University of Padua, whose calculations aided NASA in placing *Mariner 10* in an orbit around the sun that would allow repeated flybys. Plans call for *BepiColombo* to launch a small secondary orbiter designed to study the particles and magnetic field around Mercury and also to drop some type of penetrometer, a device that drives into the surface to provide physical, chemical, and mineralogical readings. With continued funding and a little luck, scientists will have a wealth of new data about Mercury—including the first global maps—before the decade is out.

Mercury's overall motion through our sky resembles that of Venus, with periods of visibility centered on the dates of its greatest elongations. Mercury averages six greatest elongations each year, but they carry the planet no more than twenty-eight degrees from the sun. So although Mercury can rival even the brightest stars, it never climbs high enough into the sky to emerge from the twilight glow of dusk or dawn (fig. 3-7). Earlier we discussed how the steepness of the ecliptic affects the visibility of the young moon and Venus; it proves even more important for Mercury. Table 3-3 summarizes Mercury's best morning and evening apparitions between 2003 and 2010. A glance at the table shows that Mercury puts on its finest shows as an evening star in the spring and as a morning star in the fall.

Locating Mercury is difficult enough that even Nicolaus Copernicus, a founding father of modern astronomy, lamented that it had always given him trouble. But there's no better way to find this speedy planet than by letting the moon and planets point the way. The apparitions illustrated in

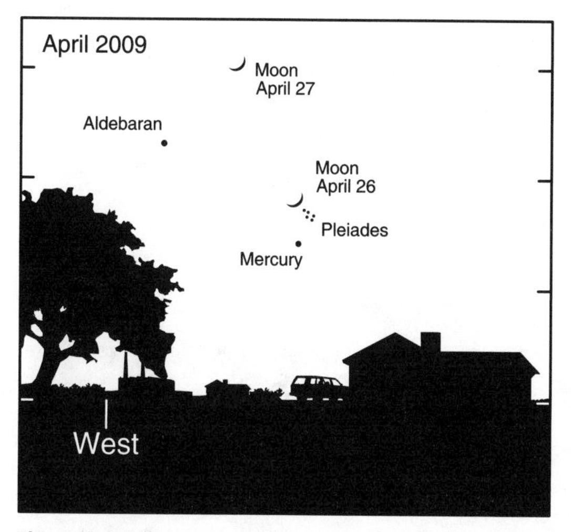

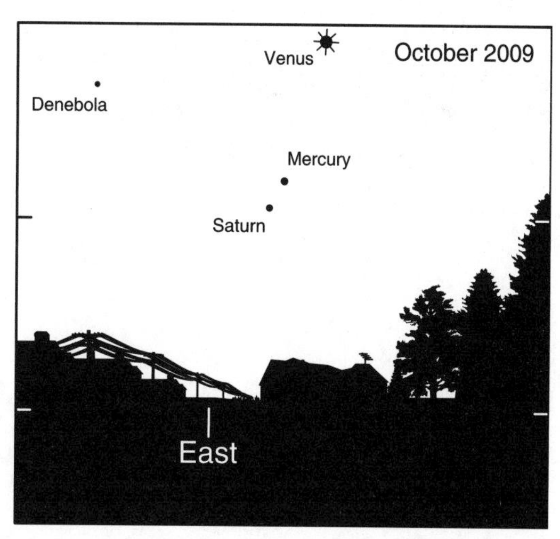

Figure 3-14. Mercury in 2009, looking thirty minutes before sunrise or after sunset. Left: On the evening of April 26 the crescent moon lies near Mercury (+0.2) and the Pleiades. Right: Mercury (–0.5) joins Saturn (+1.2) and Venus (–3.9) in the predawn sky on October 6.

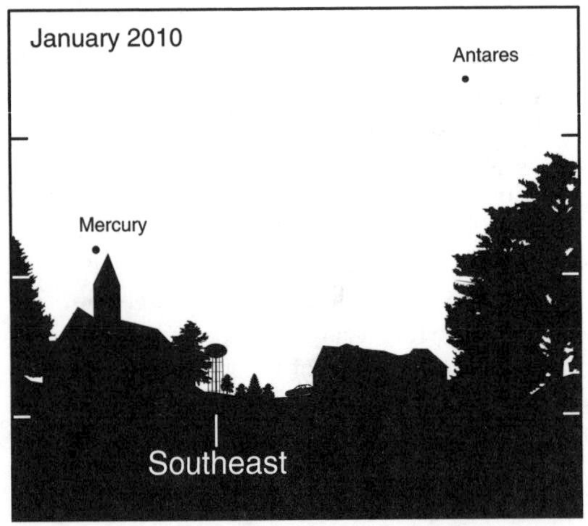

Mercury (–0.3) gleams alone in the southeast on the morning of January 23, but Saturn (+0.7) shines high in the southwest and fiery Mars (–1.2), now just a few days from opposition and its brightest for the year, glows low in the west.

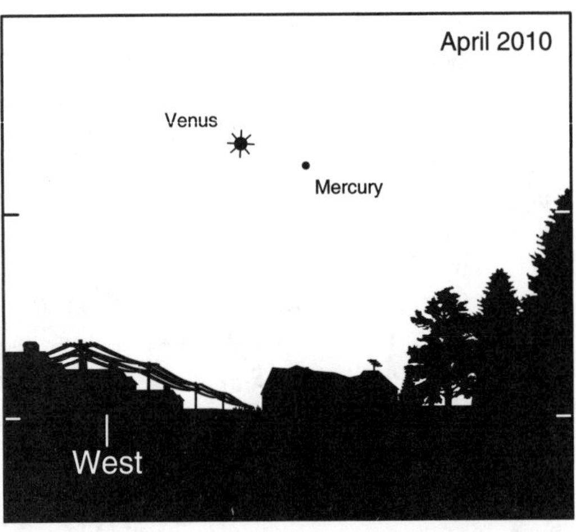

Mercury (–0.5) meets brilliant Venus (–3.9) on the evening of April 4.

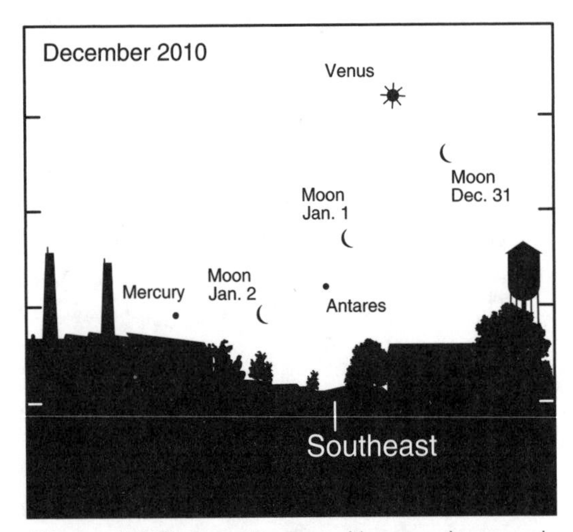

Mercury (+0.3) closes the year with a morning apparition near Antares (+0.9) as dazzling Venus (–4.5) and Saturn (+0.9) look on. The moon is near Saturn on December 28, the star Spica (+0.9) on December 29, Venus on December 31, and Mercury on January 2, 2011.

Figure 3-15. Mercury in 2010, looking thirty minutes before sunrise or after sunset. Tick marks along the sides of the horizon diagrams represent altitude intervals of ten degrees—about the distance covered by your fist at arm's length.

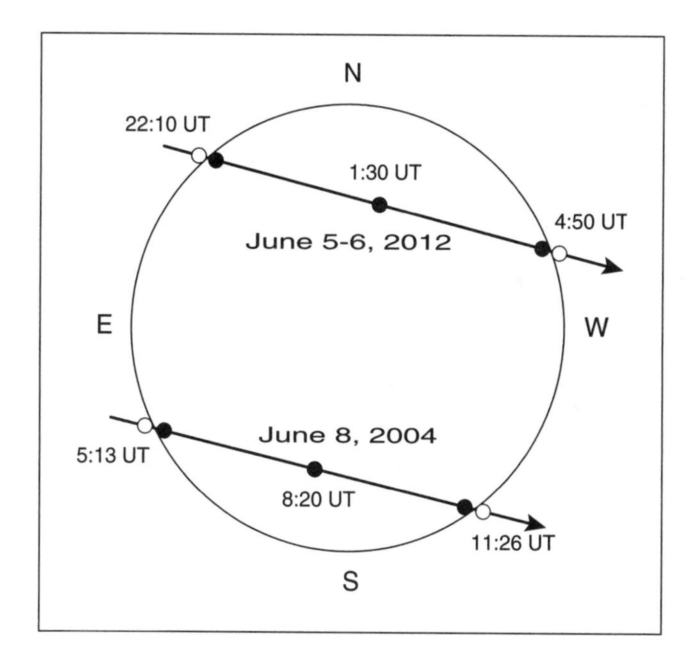

Figure 3-16. Venus transits the sun for the first time in almost 122 years on June 8, 2004—and then does it again in 2012. This figure shows the planet's path across the sun during each of these transits, as seen by an imaginary observer at the center of the Earth. The contact times and actual paths will differ slightly among observation points around the globe.

figures 3-8 through 3-15 show such celestial guideposts, along with each planet's magnitude on the astronomical brightness scale. Like Venus, Mercury also replays its apparitions, but it does so with less precision and over a longer period. The planet completes 41 synodic cycles (4,751.1 days) in a period only three days longer than thirteen years (4,748 days). A forty-six-year cycle works even better, repeating within thirty hours; this was employed by Babylonian astronomer-priests.

Silhouetted Worlds

Since inferior conjunctions bring Mercury and Venus roughly in line between Earth and the sun, it stands to reason that, sooner or later, they will pass close enough to appear in silhouette against the sun's disk. Such events, called transits, occur about thirteen times per century for speedy Mercury and so cannot be considered rare, but no one now living could have seen the last passage of Venus across the sun's face. Only five Venus transits have been observed since the invention of the telescope. In the eighteenth and nineteenth centuries, transits of Venus generated considerable excitement among astronomers and prompted the first international scientific expeditions, because these events seemed to hold the key for determining a poorly known yet essential astronomical measurement: the distance between the Earth and the sun.

Both Claudius Ptolemy and Copernicus had considered the possibility of Mercury and Venus transits, but Johannes Kepler (1571–1630) was the first to make specific predictions. Kepler noticed that Mercury would pass in front of the sun on November 7, 1631, and that, astonishingly, Venus would do the same thing a month later. On the appointed morning, French astronomer Pierre Gassendi (1592–1655) watched for the event from his Paris apartment. He used a telescope to project a magnified image of the sun's disk onto a screen in a darkened room. A few hours before the time Kepler had predicted, Gassendi saw something between clouds that looked like a very small sunspot. Could this tiny black dot—just a two-hundredth of the apparent diameter of the sun—be the planet Mercury? Its progress across the sun's disk removed all doubt.

"I found him out, and saw him where no one else had hitherto seen him," Gassendi triumphantly wrote. The following month Gassendi looked for the Venus transit but failed to see it. We now know that it occurred a few hours later than predicted and was not visible from Europe.

According to Kepler's computations, based on his *Rudolphine Tables*, the next Venus transit would not occur until 1761. But Jeremiah Horrocks, an English clergyman with a passion for mathematics and astronomy, had begun making his own calculations. He was surprised to discover late in October 1639 that Venus would not

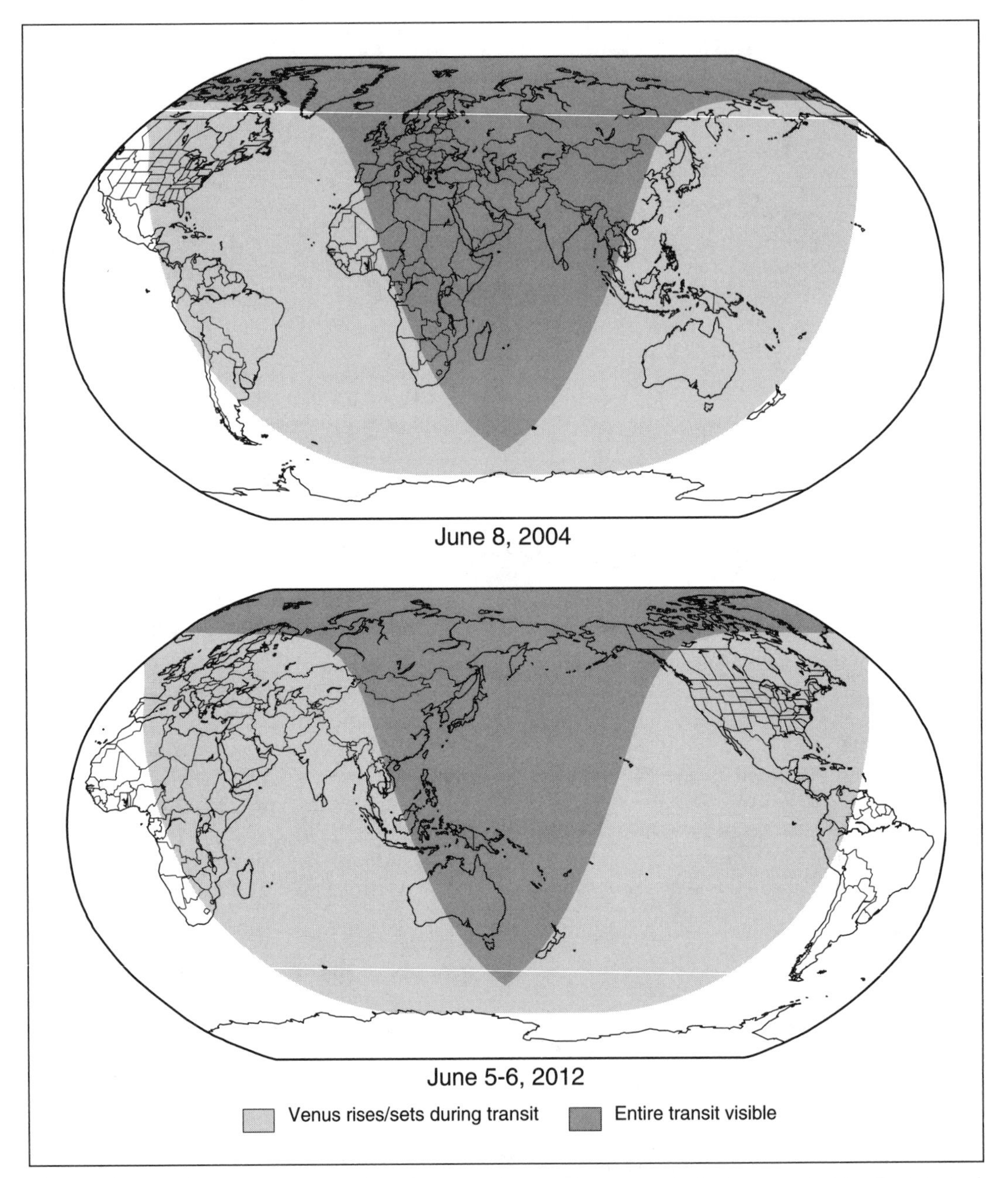

Figure 3-17. Visibility of Venus transits. The shaded portions of these maps indicate the part of the Earth turned toward the sun and Venus while each transit lasts. The darker shading shows areas that will see the entire transit; light gray indicates areas where Venus rises (left) or sets (right) during each transit.

Top: June 8, 2004. Australia, Indonesia, southern Alaska, and the Pacific coast of Asia will see the first part of the transit before the sun sets. Central and eastern Africa, India, the Middle East, and most of China and Europe will see the transit from start to finish. Western Africa, most of eastern South America, and the eastern half of North America will catch Venus on the sun after dawn.

Bottom: June 5–6, 2012. Most of Canada and all of the United States, Central America, and New Zealand will see the beginning part of the transit before the sun sets. Alaska, Japan, most of Indonesia and Australia, and the eastern half of China will see the event from beginning to end. For India, the Middle East, all of Europe, and central and eastern Africa, the end of the transit will occur after sunrise.

pass to the south of the sun as Kepler had determined, but instead would cross the sun's disk—barely a month in the future! He and a friend, William Crabtree, prepared to observe the event from their homes using a telescope to project the sun's image, just as Gassendi had done. Despite cloudy skies, Horrocks monitored the sun from sunrise on December 4 until the early afternoon, when he was required to perform the Sunday services. When he returned the transit was already in progress:

> I then beheld a most agreeable spectacle, the object of my sanguine wishes, a spot of unusual magnitude and of perfectly circular shape, which had already fully entered upon the sun's disc on the left, so that the limbs of the sun and Venus precisely coincided, forming an angle of contact.

Horrocks got back to his telescope less than half an hour before sunset, so he made what measurements he could as quickly as possible. Venus, just a thirtieth of the sun's diameter, was about one-tenth the size some astronomers expected. William Crabtree caught the transit just before sunset and was so overwhelmed by the sight that he almost forgot to make measurements. Horrocks knew that the two of them were probably the only ones to have witnessed the event and, following Gassendi, wrote up a detailed account of their observations. He planned to finish his manuscript for *Venus Visible on the Sun* and meet with Crabtree in early January, but he died suddenly on January 3, 1641. Twenty years later, copies of this manuscript found their way into the hands of professional astronomers, who saw to its publication in 1662.

The following year, Scottish mathematician James Gregory proposed a general method of using transits to measure the distance between Earth and the sun. This number was effectively an astronomical yardstick—with it, only Kepler's laws were needed to determine the scale of the entire solar system. Efforts to measure this distance—by, for instance, observations of Mars at opposition or Mercury transits—failed to produce consistent results; values ranged over a factor of two or more. Enter Edmond Halley (1656–1742), the man who financed the publication of Newton's *Principia*—and coaxed him to write it in the first place—and who became the first to predict the return of a comet, the one that today bears his name. Halley showed in 1716 that Mercury was too close to the sun for observations of its transits to provide effective results, but that Venus was ideal. Looking ahead, he proposed a detailed plan for observations of the 1761 Venus transit and suggested that astronomers be dispatched across the globe to observe and time the planet's passage across the sun. Observers separated by great distances would see Venus track across the sun in slightly different locations. Halley realized that by timing the planet's entrance onto and exit from the sun's disk, the paths seen by each observer could be reconstructed. When combined with the latitude and longitude of the observing sites, the angle between the paths—the parallax of Venus—could be determined, and from this, with a little trigonometry, astronomers could find the distance between the Earth and the sun. Halley believed that his technique could establish the length of the astronomical yardstick to one part in five hundred.

More than one hundred astronomers at over sixty locations throughout Europe observed the 1761 transit and, as Halley had hoped, Britain and France mounted expeditions overseas. Astronomers were sent to Newfoundland, Sumatra, St. Helena, Siberia, Austria, and the Indian Ocean. Unfortunately, the Seven Years War then raging between Britain and France proved a complication. British astronomer Charles Mason and surveyor Jeremiah Dixon were on H.M.S. *Sea Horse* headed for Sumatra when they were intercepted and fired upon by a French frigate; eleven sailors were killed and the badly damaged ship limped back to port. After that, the pair understandably had second thoughts. When they learned that their destination in Sumatra had been taken by the French, they decided to observe from the Cape of Good Hope at the southern tip of Africa. (They would later achieve fame in the United States by surveying the disputed border of Pennsylvania and Maryland, which became known as the Mason-Dixon Line.)

For French astronomer Guillaume Le Gentil, the transit expedition proved to be nothing less than an odyssey. His ship had just arrived in India when news reached the captain that the town of Pondicherry, near the appointed observing site, had been taken by British forces. The ship immediately headed back to Mauritius, but when transit day arrived they were still at sea. Le Gentil watched the event but was unable to make useful observations because his pendulum clocks, crucial for the timings, were useless at sea.

With so little to show for so long a voyage, he decided to remain in the area until the next transit. For much of the next eight years he roamed the Indian Ocean and explored and mapped islands from Madagascar to the Philippines. He set up for the 1769 transit at his original site of Pondicherry, now in French hands again, but on the day of the event clouds—the bane of all skywatchers—rolled in and obscured the sun.

"I was more than two weeks in a singular dejection," he wrote, "and almost did not have the courage to take up my pen to continue my journal." He fell ill and remained so for months, and when he recovered he decided that enough was enough; it was time to go home. After more than eleven years abroad he returned to Paris—only to find that his relatives had declared him dead and his assets had been divided up among his heirs and creditors. He sued to reclaim his property, eventually married happily, and wrote his acclaimed memoirs of his travels.

Even with the multitude of observations—some acquired from remote parts of the globe—astronomers could determine the astronomical yardstick only to within 20 percent. Inadequate knowledge of the position of the actual observing sites—particularly their longitude—contributed to the low precision. More important was an unforeseen problem that foiled efforts to get an exact time for the moment Venus passed completely onto the sun. Instead of seeing a thread of light separating the planet's silhouette from the limb of the sun, observers noted that Venus looked like a droplet with a black tail connecting it to the sun's edge. The black drop could last from seconds to a full minute and seriously compromised the observations. This "black drop effect" is often attributed to the thick atmosphere of Venus, but this explanation cannot be right, because it has been reported at Mercury transits as well. Unsteady air tends to blur telescopic images, and atmospheric turbulence is today considered the most likely cause of the effect—an explanation first put forward by J. J. Lalande in 1770. Other factors, including the diffraction of light within the telescope and the visual perception of individual observers, can magnify the black drop.

Combining the results of the 1761 and 1769 transits further narrowed the margin of error, bringing values of the Earth-sun distance to within 4 percent. But even if the Venus transits could not meet what clearly had been overly optimistic expectations, they had provided astronomers with a much better measure of the scale of the solar system. The transit of 1874 was well observed around the world, but by 1882 most of the scientific enthusiasm for transits had dissipated as other techniques—photographic observations of Mars and asteroids, for instance—promised to whittle down the remaining errors. Now we can measure the distances to Venus, Mars, asteroids, and other solar system objects by pinging them with a pulse of energy from a radio telescope and timing the wait for the returned signal. The distance between the Earth and the sun, formally called the Astronomical Unit and abbreviated AU, is now known with a precision that far exceeds Halley's promise.

The first two of fourteen twenty-first-century Mercury transits occur in 2003 and 2006 (see table 3-4). The orbit of Mercury does not lie in the same plane as Earth's, so usually Mercury passes slightly above or below the sun at each inferior conjunction. For a transit to occur, Mercury must reach inferior conjunction when it lies near one of two points where its orbit intersects the plane of the Earth's orbit—points called the orbit's nodes. For a transit to occur, Mercury must come to inferior conjunction within three

Table 3-4. Transits of Mercury and Venus

Mercury	Venus
—	December 7, 1631
November 13, 1986	December 4, 1639
—	June 6, 1761
November 6, 1993	June 3, 1769
—	December 9, 1874
November 15, 1999	December 6, 1882
May 7, 2003	June 8, 2004
November 8, 2006	June 6, 2012
May 9, 2016	December 11, 2117
November 11, 2019	December 8, 2125

days of May 8 or within five days of November 10. The "transit windows" are not of equal size because Mercury's orbit is very eccentric and perihelion occurs near the November node. Mercury is moving fastest at that time, increasing our chances that we will catch it near the node, so the number of November transits is almost double the number of May transits. Because of the planet's diminutive size, observing a Mercury transit requires a telescope, so these events are beyond the scope of this book and will not be discussed in detail here. Times for the transits are, however, provided in appendix A.

The rarity of Venus transits makes them of special interest to all skywatchers, and the span covered by this book includes the first transit of Venus since 1882. Professional and amateur astronomers will join casual skywatchers in June 2004 to watch Venus glide across the solar disk. The planet is large enough that, with a safe means of viewing the sun such as one of those described on page 83, it will be plainly visible even without a telescope. To transit the sun, Venus must reach inferior conjunction when it lies near one of the nodes of its slightly tilted orbit, which works out to be within two days of June 7 and December 9. Because the orbit of Venus is nearly circular, each window is nearly the same size and about equally likely to experience a transit. Venus transits occur in pairs separated by eight years, so the June 2004 event is followed by another in June 2012. We've included information on both events (figs. 3-16 and 3-17). After a pair of June transits, there is a gap of 105.5 years before a pair of December transits occurs, followed by a span of 121.5 years for the next pair of June transits. The current pattern of paired transits began in 1518, but centuries hence the pairs will dissolve into a single transit at each node.

The next Venus transit occurs on June 8, 2004, and lasts almost six hours. It's convenient to discuss the times of events like this in terms of an imaginary observer located at the center of the Earth, because the exact track of the transit—and so the predicted starting and ending times—depends on each observer's geographic location. These geocentric times are shown on the figures. It's also convenient to express the time as Universal Time (UT); a conversion chart is included in appendix A. Detailed local circumstances for various locations will be available at several of the web resources listed in appendix D, and in any case the times vary by only plus or minus seven minutes across the globe. All that said, the transit begins at 5:13 UT when the disk of Venus touches the eastern edge of the sun, an event called first contact for transits and eclipses. Venus continues to move onto the sun until second contact just before 5:33 UT, the point at which the planet lies completely on the face of the sun. This is one of the moments of contact that earlier transit observers tried to time precisely. Will the black drop effect appear? Australia, Indonesia, Asia, Africa, and parts of Europe can see the beginning of the transit. Before Venus exits the sun, the Earth spins the eastern half of North America and most of South America into view. Another opportunity for seeing the black drop occurs just before 11:06 UT, when the leading edge of Venus touches the sun's western limb. The transit ends around 11:26 UT.

Venus transits the sun again on June 5 and 6, 2012—and it's the last chance to see such an event until 2117. Ingress begins at 22:10 UT on June 5, mid-transit occurs at 1:30 UT on June 6, and Venus exits the sun at 4:50 UT. Western North America, large parts of Asia and the Pacific, and part of Australia can see the event from beginning to end and all of North America can see ingress before sunset.

Once considered an important tool for astronomical progress, transits of Venus have since become novel reminders of the scale, motions, and predictability of the solar system that provide opportunities to reminisce about a heroic age in the history of astronomy. Following the transit of 1882, William Harkness of the U.S. Naval Observatory placed the event in perspective. "When the last transit occurred the intellectual world was awakening from the slumber of ages," he wrote, "and that wondrous scientific activity that has led to our present advanced knowledge was just beginning." As the silhouette of Venus leaves the sun's disk in 2012, it's inevitable that we will momentarily pause to wonder what the world will be like in 2117, the year Venus next crosses the sun.

4 Eclipses of the Sun and Moon

> I shall only say that I have passed a varied and eventful life, that it has been my fortune to see earth, heavens, ocean, and man in most of their aspects; but never have I beheld any spectacle which so plainly manifested the majesty of the Creator, or so forcibly taught the lesson of humility to man as a total eclipse of the sun.
>
> —James Fenimore Cooper, "The Eclipse," c. 1831

The sun travels through the sky along a track astronomers call the ecliptic, which is the plane of Earth's orbit projected onto the sky. The moon and planets loosely travel the same path, deviating from it as a result of each object's particular orbital inclination. Since these objects move at different speeds and follow a similar path around the sky, sooner or later some of them must arrive at the same place in the sky at the same time. When this happens, the nearer of the two objects moves in front of the more distant one, briefly obscuring it from view. Astronomers call these events occultations. The moon frequently occults planets and stars near the ecliptic, as might be expected from its rapid motion through the starry sky, but by far the most sensational occultations occur when the moon passes in front of the sun, blocking its light and creating a brief, eerie darkness in the middle of the day—a total solar eclipse. Something similar, though far less spectacular, occurs at a total lunar eclipse when the full moon darkens and reddens during a passage through the Earth's shadow. The preeminence of solar eclipses explains why the sun's path around the sky—the only location in which they can take place—is known as the ecliptic instead of the "occultic."

The sun's importance to life on Earth was recognized everywhere, which made its sudden, brief disappearance during a total solar eclipse all the more frightening. In mythology, eclipses are most commonly described as attacks on the sun and moon either by heavenly monsters—dragons in China, snakes in Indonesia, the demon Rahu in India, jaguars or wolves in the Americas—or, somewhat more accurately, by one against the other in battle. Some Inuit groups believed that the eclipsed body had simply left its place in the sky to check on earthly affairs. Rio Grande Pueblos feared that when the Sun Father's gleaming shield faded he was displeased and moved away from the Earth. In areas of the South Pacific, eclipses were viewed more romantically as the lovemaking of the sun and moon. In many regions, people were called upon to assist the eclipsed sun or moon by frightening off the being considered responsible for the darkening, usually with loud noises but in some cases—as with the Ojibwa of the upper Midwest—with flaming arrows shot skyward. The midday darkness of a total solar eclipse holds unexpected emotional power even today; some describe it as a religious experience. More than any other event in nature, the moment of totality briefly places us at the crossroads of folklore and science.

Solar Cover-Up

The fact that we see total solar eclipses at all results from two of the most remarkable coincidences in nature. First, as seen from the Earth, the sun and moon both appear to be the same size. The sun is the nearest star, a self-luminous ball of gas 865,000 miles (1,392,000 kilometers) wide that glows as a result of the tremendous energy released by nuclear reactions occurring deep within. While sun and moon differ in size by about 400 times, they also differ in their distance from the Earth by nearly the same factor; thus, both objects appear to us to measure about half a degree across. Both the orbit of the Earth around the sun and the moon's orbit around the Earth are elliptical, and the combination of these out-of-round movements can make either the sun or the moon appear a few percent larger than the other. A total eclipse cannot occur with the angular size of the sun larger than that of the moon. In fact, if the moon were less than 10 percent smaller than it is, all other things being equal, we would miss out on one of nature's grandest spectacles.

The second coincidence involves changes in the moon's orbit over time. Gravitational interactions between the Earth and the moon cause it to recede from us by a small amount each year. Over time, this increasing distance reduces the angular size of the moon's disk. By a happy accident, human civilization arose during a period when total solar eclipses could occur. Astronomers say that one day, some hundreds of millions of years hence, the moon will be too far away to completely cover the sun, forever ending on Earth the phenomenon of a total eclipse of the sun.

Before venturing into a detailed discussion of solar eclipses, we need first to get our bearings. A solar eclipse occurs when the new moon passes in front of the sun so that the sun casts the moon's shadow onto the Earth. Observers on the ground see the moon cover a portion of the sun's disk. The moon's shadow has two components: a broad, diffuse *penumbra,* within which the sun's light is only partially cut off; and a much darker and smaller *umbra,* from which no part of the sun can be seen. The moon's precise path across the sun dictates how the shadow components fall onto the Earth's surface, which in turn determines what type of eclipse we see.

The most common solar eclipses are partial ones, in which the moon covers only a portion of the sun's disk; these are visible over much of the Earth's surface. If the moon passes completely over the sun, but its angular size happens to be too small to cover the disk, the eclipse is called annular—at mid-eclipse a thin ring (annulus) of the solar surface remains visible around the moon. This aspect of the eclipse can be seen only from within a narrow track along the Earth's surface; outside of that path the moon never completely passes onto the sun. The path of totality for total eclipses, in which the moon covers the sun completely, is also narrow. A small portion of solar eclipses are termed annular/total or hybrid eclipses. Along one part of the eclipse's annular path the moon is briefly able to cover the sun; observers within that part of the track witness a total eclipse. Now that we've run though the basics, let's take a look at each type of solar eclipse in a little more detail.

When the moon passes over the sun's disk but the axis of its umbra fails to intersect the Earth's surface, the eclipse is said to be partial. Partial solar eclipses are visible over a large region; for example, one on December 25, 2000, could be seen throughout the contiguous United States. Up to five solar eclipses may occur in any single year—of which four must be partial—but this is quite rare. According to eclipse expert Fred Espenak, of NASA's Goddard Space Flight Center, this happens just fifty-six times in the ten millennia span from 3000 B.C. to A.D. 7000, the last time in 1935 and not again till 2206. The solar-eclipse count for a single year can be as low as two, and both can be partial—as happens in 2007—but combinations of other types are more common. The twenty-first century will see seventy-seven partial eclipses, four of which occur in the span covered by this book. Since a portion of the sun remains visible during partial eclipses—and at times during other types of eclipses when the moon does not completely cover the sun—they cannot be enjoyed directly with the naked eye (see "Viewing the Sun Safely" on page 83).

It's possible for the moon's umbra to point directly toward the Earth and still fail to produce a total eclipse. The ellipticity of the moon's orbit changes its distance to us by over 6 percent from its mean value. Over the course of a year the Earth's distance from the sun—and thus the sun's apparent diameter in the sky—varies by over 3 percent from its mean. Taken together, these differences can inflate the angular size of the sun relative to that of the moon by almost 11 percent. Under such circumstances an annular eclipse occurs. Instead of a blotted-out sun at mid-eclipse, the observer sees a slender ring, or annulus, of uneclipsed sun surrounding the silhouette of the moon. This phenomenon can be seen only from a very restricted geographical range on the Earth—the path of annularity may extend some 10,000 miles (16,090 kilometers) in length but is typically a few hundred miles wide. Observers outside of this track do not see the annulus, but as in a partial eclipse, they still see the moon intrude upon the sun. None of the phenomena associated with totality can be seen during an annular eclipse and, as for partial eclipses, one *must use eye-safe viewing methods at all times.* Annular eclipses outnumber total ones, making up about 33 percent of all eclipses, and seventy-two will occur by 2101. Six are discussed here, including the longest annular eclipse this century (eleven minutes, eight seconds, on January 15, 2010). All of the longest annular eclipses occur close to January 3, the mean date of Earth's perihelion and the time when the sun's disk appears largest. See table 4-1 for a list of other eclipse extremes.

The least common type of solar eclipse is a hybrid, a transition between the conditions favorable for an annular eclipse and those favoring totality. The eclipse is annular everywhere except near the middle of the shadow's track, where the curvature of the Earth brings the surface close enough to contact the moon's umbra; there, observers see a total eclipse. The eclipse is typically quite short in duration, usually less than ninety seconds. The next hybrid eclipse, on April 8, 2005, brings up to forty seconds of totality to the central Pacific; the next one thereafter, in 2013, will produce darkness across the mid-Atlantic and Africa for just one minute longer. Less than 5 percent of all solar eclipses fall into the hybrid category; there will be only seven in this century.

The remaining 27 percent of solar eclipses are total, and of the sixty-eight occurring this century, five are covered in this book. Only one of them brings totality to North America, and only barely so. (In fact, our continent is in something of an eclipse drought. Only portions of Alaska will see the sun partly covered as a result the 2003 annular eclipse, and the partial eclipses of 2004 and 2007. The 2005 hybrid eclipse will cover part

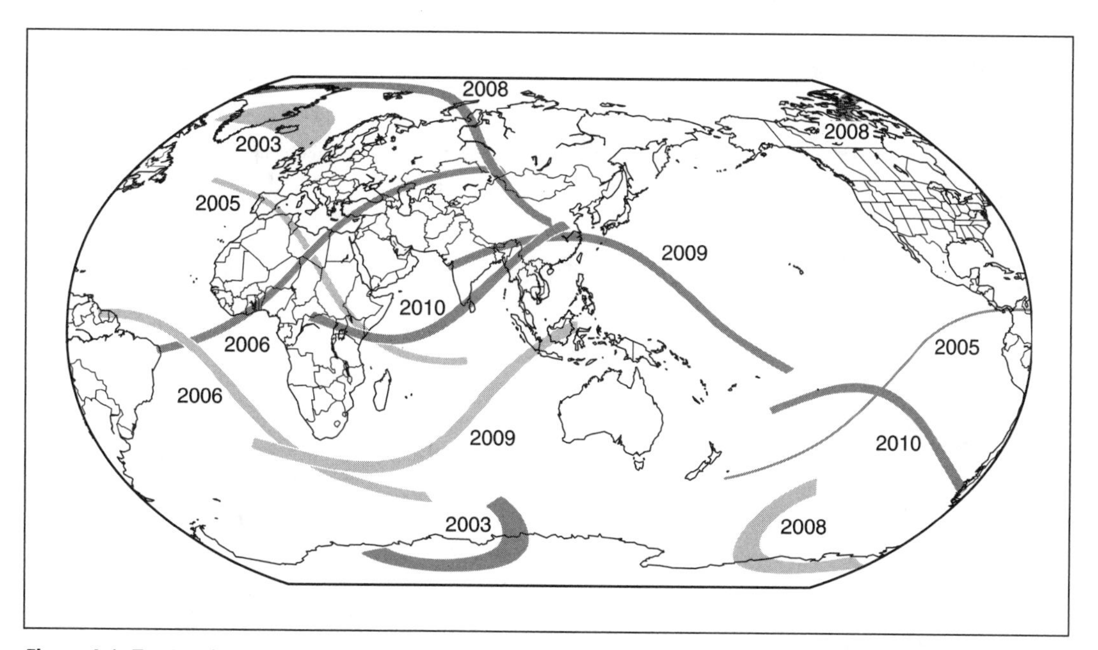

Figure 4-1. Tracks of total and hybrid (dark gray) and annular (light gray) solar eclipses from 2003 through 2010. The eastern hemisphere is clearly more favored this decade.

Table 4-1. Eclipse Facts

Distribution of eclipse types in 2003–2010, long-term frequencies of eclipse types, eclipse extremes, tetrads from 2001–2100, and saros information.

SOLAR ECLIPSES

For the period 2003–2010 there are five total, one hybrid, six annular, and four partial solar eclipses.

Longest total eclipses, 2001–2100:

July 22, 2009	6 min. 39 sec.
Aug. 2, 2027	6 min. 23 sec.
Aug. 12, 2045	6 min. 6 sec.
May 22, 2096	6 min. 6 sec.

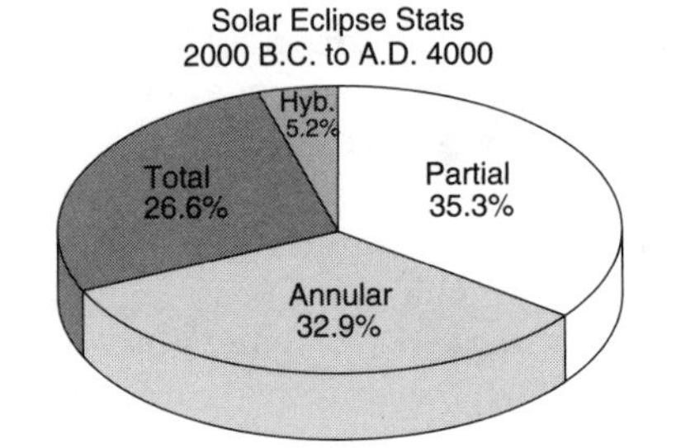

Longest annular eclipses, 2001–2100:

Jan. 15, 2010	11 min. 8 sec.
Jan. 26, 2028	10 min. 27 sec.

INGREDIENTS OF THE SAROS

Synodic month (new moon to new moon):	29.531 days
Node alignment period:	173.310 days
Anomalistic month (perigee to perigee):	27.555 days

Each of these periods equals 18 years 11.3 days (to within 11 hours):
239 anomalistic months, 38 node alignment intervals, and 223 synodic months.

LUNAR ECLIPSES

For the period 2003–2010 there are eight total, five partial, and five penumbral lunar eclipses.

Longest total eclipse, 2001–2100:

July 27, 2018	1 hr. 43 min. 35 sec.

Tetrads—four consecutive total lunar eclipses—from 2001–2100:

2003–2004
2014–2015
2032–2033
2043–2044
2050–2051
2061–2062
2072–2073
2090–2091

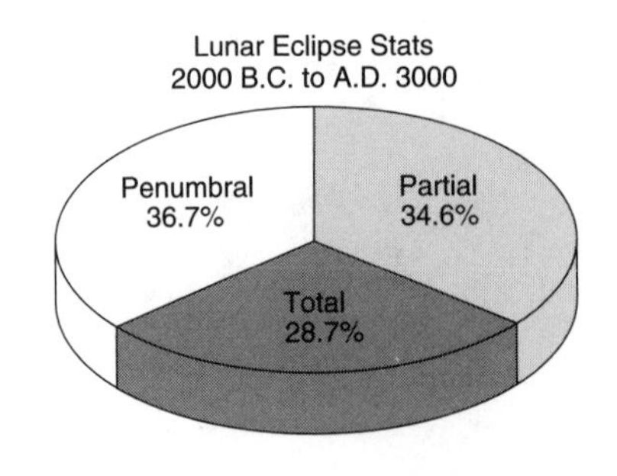

of the sun as seen from the southern United States.) For the 2008 total eclipse, the path of totality crosses the north coast of Greenland and reaches into northernmost Canada; the rising sun will appear partly eclipsed from Hudson Bay to Maine. As something of a consolation prize for a totality-poor decade, the footloose will have the opportunity to experience the century's longest span of totality (six minutes, thirty-nine seconds) in 2009 in the western Pacific. The paths of upcoming annular and total eclipses are plotted in figure 4-1; see also table 4-2 for a list of all eclipses occurring through 2010.

Astronomers estimate that every location on Earth experiences totality within 375 years, but this is a frequency averaged over time. The totality drought for North America ends dramatically in 2017, when the moon's shadow arcs across the United States from Oregon to South Carolina, and just over six years later, in 2024, residents of southern Illinois and eastern Missouri will see totality again (fig. 4-2).

Lacking the good fortune of being in exactly the right place at exactly the right time, the only way to see a total solar eclipse is by planning a trip to intercept the moon's shadow. Over 100,000 people journeyed to Hawaii and Mexico to witness the great total solar eclipse of July 11, 1991; hotels were booked years in advance. In August 1999, nearly a million eclipse watchers reportedly descended on Cornwall, England, to see the moon's shadow first come ashore. Eclipse viewers of the champagne-and-caviar set rode through the umbra aboard the supersonic Concorde, which moved fast enough to extend the duration of totality for several minutes. Millions more watched along a track that brought totality across the most populous region of Europe and the Middle East. Jordan and Syria declared national holidays. Iran issued 600,000 sun-safe eclipse

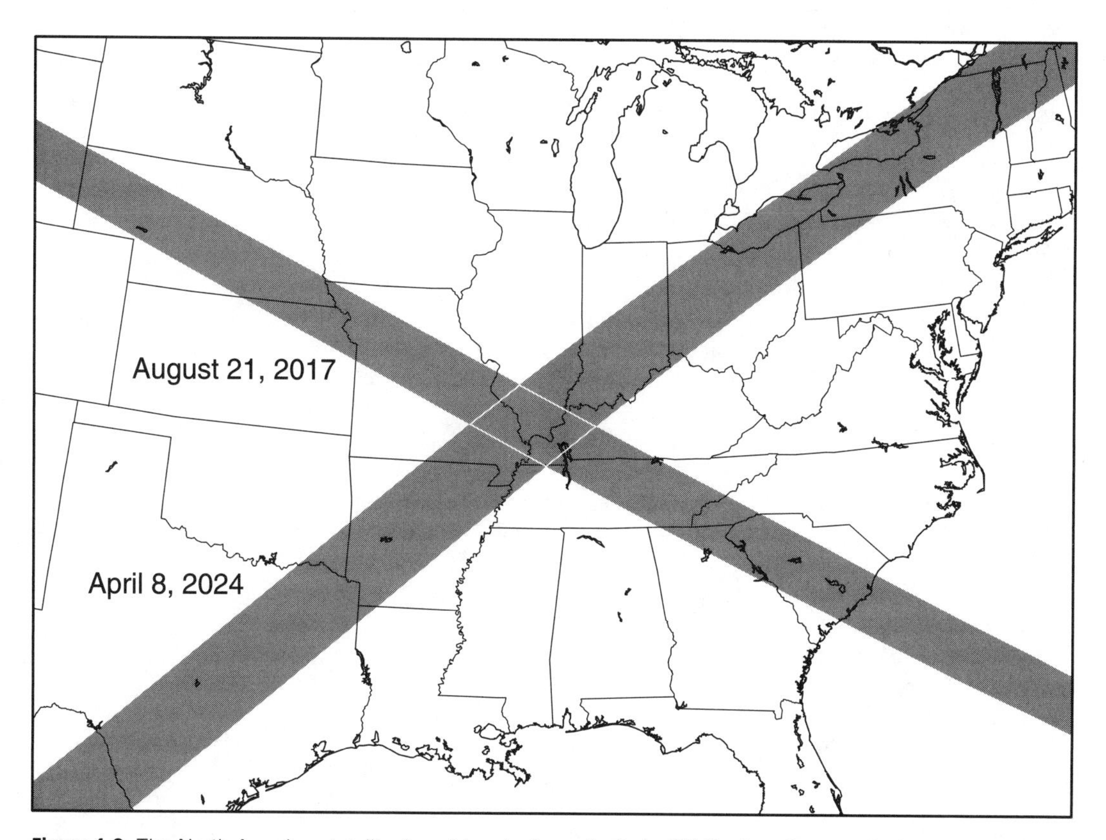

Figure 4-2. The North American totality drought ends dramatically in 2017, when the moon's shadow darkens the United States along a track from Oregon to South Carolina. Just six years later, another totality track runs over some of the same ground. The region of overlap (white box) includes Marion and Anna, Illinois; Cape Girardeau, Missouri; and Paducah, Kentucky.

Table 4-2. Upcoming Eclipses, 2003–2010

Solar and lunar eclipses dates, types, geocentric times of mid-eclipse, geographic range, and the page number of a detailed map, if provided.

Date	Lunar or Solar	Type	Greatest Eclipse (UT)	Geographical Region of Visibility	Page Where Illustrated
2003					
May 16	Lunar	Total	03:40	Central Pacific, Americas, Europe, Africa	97
May 31	Solar	Annular	04:08	Greenland, Iceland, Scotland	84
Nov. 9	Lunar	Total	01:19	Americas, Europe, Africa, central Asia	98
Nov. 23	Solar	Total	22:49	Antarctica	—
2004					
April 19	Solar	Partial	13:34	South Atlantic, southern Africa	—
May 4	Lunar	Total	20:30	South America, Europe, Africa, Asia, Australia	99
Oct. 14	Solar	Partial	02:59	Northeastern Russia, Japan, Alaska, Micronesia	85
Oct. 28	Lunar	Total	03:04	Americas, Europe, Africa, central Asia	100
2005					
April 8	Solar	Hybrid	20:36	New Zealand, southern Pacific, western South America, Central America, Caribbean, southern United States	86
April 24	Lunar	Penumbral	09:55	Eastern Asia, Australia, Pacific, Americas	—
Oct. 3	Solar	Annular	10:32	Africa, Europe, western Asia, India	87
Oct. 17	Lunar	Partial	12:03	Asia, Australia, Pacific, North America	101
2006					
March 14	Lunar	Penumbral	23:47	Eastern South America, Africa, Europe, Asia	—
March 29	Solar	Total	10:11	Northern and central Africa, Europe, Iceland, central Asia, northern India	88
Sept. 7	Lunar	Partial	18:51	Africa, Europe, Asia, Australia, Indonesia	102
Sept. 22	Solar	Annular	11:40	Eastern South America, western Africa	89
2007					
March 3	Lunar	Total	23:21	Eastern Americas, Africa, Europe, central Asia	103
March 19	Solar	Partial	02:32	Eastern Asia and western Alaska	90
Aug. 28	Lunar	Total	10:37	Eastern Asia, Australia, Pacific, western North America	104
Sept. 11	Solar	Partial	12:32	Central and southern South America, Antarctica	—
2008					
Feb. 7	Solar	Annular	03:55	Antarctica, New Zealand, eastern Australia	91
Feb. 21	Lunar	Total	03:26	Americas, Africa, Europe	105
Aug. 1	Solar	Total	10:21	Northeastern North America, Asia, India	92
Aug. 16	Lunar	Partial	21:10	Eastern South America, Africa, Europe, central Asia	106
2009					
Jan. 26	Solar	Annular	07:59	Southern Africa, Antarctica, Indian Ocean, southern India, western Australia and Indonesia	93
Feb. 9	Lunar	Penumbral	14:38	Eastern Asia, Indonesia, Australia, Pacific, western North America	—
July 7	Lunar	Penumbral	09:39	Australia, Pacific, western Americas	—
July 22	Solar	Total	02:35	Eastern India, eastern Asia, central Pacific, Hawaii	94
Aug. 6	Lunar	Penumbral	00:39	Eastern North America, South America, Africa, Europe	—
Dec. 31	Lunar	Partial	19:23	Europe, Africa, Asia, western Australia	107
2010					
Jan. 15	Solar	Annular	07:06	Western Europe, Africa, Indian Ocean, India, Indonesia	95
June 26	Lunar	Partial	11:38	Australia, Indonesia, Pacific, western Americas	108
July 11	Solar	Total	19:33	South Pacific, western South America	96
Dec. 21	Lunar	Total	08:17	Northeast Asia, Eastern Pacific, Americas	109

glasses; Tehran Radio announced that prayer during the eclipse was mandatory for Muslims. In 2001, over 21,000 tourists sought totality in Zambia; hotels in Lusaka were filled to capacity and authorities were prepared to set up tents to handle overflow.

Upcoming solar eclipses offer many travel opportunities—the paths of totality and annularity particularly favor Africa. The rarity of these events, plus the fact that none of the phenomena accompanying totality can be seen during other types of eclipses, explains part of the excitement. These reasons are sufficient for the more astronomically inclined, but they fail to explain why so many people will travel so far. There is another aspect to the moment of totality, something that is difficult to express—a primal reaction more felt than thought, one that is sensed differently by each observer. It elevates totality, at least in the human mind, to something grander than the clockwork of celestial mechanics. To give a taste of that experience, we include here an excerpt from an evocative first-hand account of totality.

A Writer in the Umbra

James Fenimore Cooper is often considered America's first great novelist. While living in Paris, friends asked him to write up his recollections of the June 16, 1806, total solar eclipse. As the moon's shadow swept across the United States from Baja California to Massachusetts, the then-seventeen-year-old Cooper had watched it from his family home in Cooperstown, New York. "The Eclipse," an unpublished essay written around 1831, was printed many years after his death, in anticipation of another total eclipse that tracked through the eastern United States in 1869. The epigram that began this chapter is the last sentence of Cooper's essay.

> Throughout the belt of country to be darkened by the eclipse, the whole population were in a state of almost anxious expectation for weeks before the event. . . . We were all exulting in the feeling that a grand and extraordinary spectacle awaited us—a spectacle which millions then living could never behold. There may have been a tinge of selfishness in the feeling that we were thus favored beyond others, and yet, I think, the emotion was too intellectual in its character to have been altogether unworthy. . . .
>
> When I left the Court House, a sombre, yellowish, unnatural coloring was shed over the country. A great change had taken place. The trees on the distant heights had lost their verdure and their airy character; they were taking the outline of dark pictures graven upon an unfamiliar sky. The lake wore a lurid aspect, very unusual. All living creatures seemed thrown into a state of agitation. The birds were fluttering to and fro, in great excitement; they seemed to mistrust that this was not the gradual approach of evening, and were undecided in their movements. . . .
>
> I once more took my position beside my father and my brothers, before the gates of our own grounds. . . . The birds, which a quarter of an hour earlier had been fluttering about in great agitation, seemed now convinced that night was at hand. Swallows were dimly seen dropping into the chimneys, the martins returned to their little boxes, the pigeons flew home to their dovecots, and through the open door of a small barn we saw the fowls going to roost. . . .
>
> Suddenly one of my brothers shouted aloud, "The moon!" Quicker than thought, my eye turned eastward again, and there floated the moon, distinctly apparent, to a degree that was almost fearful. The spherical form, the character, the dignity, the substance of the planet, were clearly revealed as I have never beheld them before, or since. It looked grand, dark, majestic, and mighty, as it thus proved its power to rob us entirely of the sun's rays. . . . We are accustomed to think of the sun, and also of the moon, as sources of light, as etherial, almost spiritual, in their essence. But the positive material nature of the moon was now revealed to our senses, with a force of conviction, a clearness of perception, that changed all our usual ideas in connection with the planet. This was no interposition of vapor, no deceptive play of shadow; but a vast mass of obvious matter had interposed between the sun above us and the Earth on which we stood. . . . Darkness like that of early night now fell upon the village. . . .

At twelve minutes past eleven, the moon stood revealed in its greatest distinctness—a vast black orb, so nearly obscuring the sun that the face of the great luminary was entirely and absolutely darkened, though a corona of rays of light appeared beyond. The gloom of night was upon us. A breathless intensity of interest was felt by all. There would appear to be something instinctive in the feeling with which man gazes at all phenomena in the heavens. The peaceful rainbow, the heavy clouds of a great storm, the vivid flash of electricity, the falling meteor, the beautiful lights of the aurora borealis, fickle as the play of fancy—these never fail to fix the attention with something of a peculiar feeling, different in character from that with which we observe any spectacle on the Earth. . . . That movement of the moon, that sublime voyage of the worlds, often recurs to my imagination, and even at this distant day, as distinctly, as majestically, and nearly as fearfully, as it was then beheld. . . .

Thus far the sensation created by this majestic spectacle had been one of humiliation and awe. It seemed as if the great Father of the Universe had visibly, and almost palpably, veiled his face in wrath. But, appalling as the withdrawal of light had been, most glorious, most sublime, was its restoration! The corona of light above the moon became suddenly brighter, the heavens beyond were illuminated, the stars retired, and light began to play along the ridges of the distant mountains. . . . I can liken this sudden, joyous return of light, after the eclipse, to nothing of the kind that is familiarly known. It was certainly nearest to the change produced by the swift passage of the shadow of a very dark cloud, but it was the effect of this instantaneous transition, multiplied more than a thousand fold. . . .

The changes of the unwonted light, through whose gradations the full brilliancy of the day was restored, must have been very similar to those by which it had been lost, but they were little noted. . . . Every living creature was soon rejoicing again in the blessed restoration of light after that frightful moment of a night at noon-day.

Men who witness any extraordinary spectacle together, are apt, in after-times, to find a pleasure in conversing on its impressions. But I do not remember to have ever heard a single being freely communicative on the subject of his individual feelings at the most solemn moment of the eclipse. It would seem as if sensations were aroused too closely connected with the constitution of the spirit to be irreverently and familiarly discussed. . . .

Shadow Play

In all types of solar eclipses, the moment when the moon first encroaches on the disk of the sun is known as first contact. (At no point during a partial eclipse is it *ever* safe to look directly at the sun without some sort of eye protection. See page 83 for details.) Over the course of about an hour, the dark silhouette slides over the sun, giving it the appearance of a bright cookie slowly being eaten. The eclipse ends when the limb of the moon detaches from the sun, a moment known as fourth contact. This description holds true for the partial stages of total and annular eclipses as well. Only those inside a narrow path will see more than just a partial obscuration of the sun; annular and total eclipses present additional moments of contact for those fortunate enough to be within that track.

The moon covers the sun to the maximum degree of eclipse and then, just as slowly, slides off the sun's face. For a partial eclipse, this expanding and receding cookie-bite represents the extent of the visible phenomena. The specific circumstances of each eclipse and of the observer's location on the Earth determine whether or not a partial eclipse is visible and, if so, how deeply the moon appears to penetrate. Most people will not notice any change in the level of sunlight around them even with 70 percent of the sun covered.

During an annular eclipse, the moon is too small to cover the sun and instead fits within its disk. The umbra of the moon points toward but fails to reach the Earth's surface; technically, it is the sweep of the antumbra, a negative shadow, that creates the path of annularity. The moment of greatest interest comes at second contact, when the body of the moon has passed completely onto the sun. From this point on, for a period of up to twelve and a half minutes, a bright ring of sunlight surrounds the silhouetted moon. Third contact, when the eastern limbs of both disks come together and break the ring, ends the period of annularity.

For total eclipses, the time between second contact and third contact marks the duration of totality. Since the moon appears wider than the sun, the definitions of these moments are slightly different than for annular eclipses. Second contact is the moment when the moon just touches the eastern edge of the sun; third contact is the moment when the moon begins to reveal the western edge of the sun. The path of totality spans thousands of miles but is typically just a few hundred miles across. The shadow sweeps eastward through space at about 2,100 miles (3,380 kilometers) per hour near the Earth. Our planet rotates at a speed of about half that value at the equator, slower closer to the poles; it spins in the same direction that the shadow travels. All of these factors work to lengthen the duration of totality by slowing down the apparent speed of the umbra as it passes an observer on the ground. All of the longest total eclipses occur close to July 3—the mean date of Earth's aphelion, the point at which it is most distant from the sun, so the sun's disk appears smallest—but the theoretical maximum duration of totality is just seven and a half minutes.

At totality, after the hour-long wait to reach the onset of the main event, skywatchers must suddenly come to terms with a rush of new sensations and varied phenomena. It's helpful to know what to look for in advance. What follows is a typical sequence, in countdown fashion, of things to watch for as the umbra approaches and passes by.

T minus 60 minutes and counting: First contact, when the western edge of the sun meets the limb of the moon. The sun's disk develops a progressively larger bite as the dark moon glides into view. Its slow progress can be viewed directly through protective devices or indirectly by projecting the sun's image onto a screen. Large sunspot groups make the viewing more interesting as they are occulted by the oncoming moon (fig. 4-3).

T minus 20 minutes: By this time, most people are at least vaguely aware of an unusual character in the light of the landscape around them; some may report that everything has a peculiar yellowish cast. The color of the sky has also changed; the rich blue has become duller, flatter. The temperature has fallen noticeably. In a humid climate, the temperature change may be sufficient for clouds to begin forming in what was previously a clear sky—an unexpected source of drama that all eclipse viewers could live without! Multiple overlapping images of the crescent sun form in the shade of foliage—the small gaps between intersecting branches and leaves act as tiny pinhole cameras.

T minus 15 minutes: Now the pace picks up. The crescent sun is dwindling—it's about 80 percent covered—the light is failing noticeably, and the sky and landscape are shaded a steely blue gray. Animals respond to the falling light levels; flowers close up as if dusk were really falling. Insects seem to react most dramatically—bees swarm back to their hives, butterflies nestle in the grass, and nocturnal insects emerge. Viewing an eclipse from Tonga in 1911, William Lockyer described the burst of insect noise at totality as "most impressive, and will remain in my memory as a marked feature of the occasion." Many bird species go to roost, cows come home, bats may appear. From observing locations with an unobstructed view of the western horizon, a dusky shading reminiscent of a gathering storm becomes visible. This is the oncoming shadow of the moon, already bringing totality to sites located a few hundred miles downrange.

T minus 5 minutes: A few minutes before and after totality, when the exposed portion of the sun forms a thinning crescent, narrow bands of light and shadow race across the ground. First described in 1706, these shadow bands occur because wind-blown pockets of warmer and cooler air refract light from the narrow crescent slightly differently. Both the cause and the effect resemble the ripples of light seen traveling across the bottom of a swimming pool.

T minus 1 minute: The crescent sun's remaining light can be blocked with a finger or solar filter to reveal a ghostly halo around the dark circle of the moon. The corona begins to reveal itself and becomes steadily more obvious.

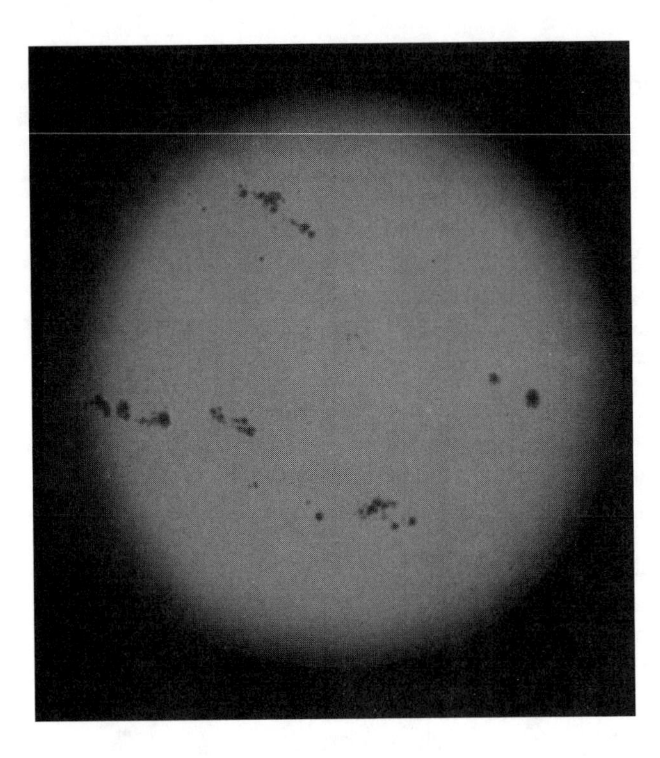

Figure 4-3. The visible surface of the sun, called the photosphere, has a temperature of 10,000°F (5,500°C). Sunspots are slightly cooler areas that routinely pepper its surface. Their numbers, recorded since 1750, rise and fall over an eleven-year cycle. This image shows the sun during the 1957–1958 sunspot maximum, the greatest on record. (Courtesy of The Observatories of the Carnegie Institution of Washington)

T minus 15 seconds: In the coming seconds, the moon will obscure all of the sun, but the limb of the moon is not perfectly circular. Lunar mountains penetrate the sliver of sun sooner than valleys. The narrowing crescent breaks up into several bright beads of sunlight shining through deep valleys on the lunar limb. These are Baily's beads, named for English amateur astronomer Francis Baily (1774–1844), who called attention to them during the annular eclipse of 1836 as "a row of lucid points, like a string of bright beads." They can be seen for a few seconds along the moon's limb at second and third contacts during annular and total eclipses. The last bead to fade seems so dazzling against the dark sky and the black moon that it conjures up the image of a gleaming jewel set in a pearly ring. This is called the "diamond ring effect."

Totality! Second contact begins when the diamond ring winks out—now it's safe to view the sun without eye protection through cameras, binoculars, and telescopes. The temperature cools several degrees more—over the course of the eclipse it may fall by more than twenty degrees Fahrenheit—and the landscape grows about as dark as evening twilight. Not exactly "night at noon-day," but dark enough to reveal the brightest stars and planets. The glow of dusk appears all along the horizon—the moon's shadow covers such a small region that sunlight from the areas outside the umbra tints the sky near the horizon with a twilight reminiscent of sunset.

The big attraction, of course, is the sun. For a few seconds, the eastern rim of the sun shows a bright pink or rosy coloring. This is the chromosphere, the lowest and coolest layer of the sun's atmosphere, Above it, huge arcs of hot gas called prominences lie suspended by intense magnetic fields (fig. 4-4). The prominences extend into space like tongues of reddish flame. As the moon progresses, these too disappear.

With the sun's brilliant light completely obscured, the pearly white corona at last becomes fully visible. The corona is the sun's extremely hot, tenuous outer atmosphere, about a million times fainter and up to two hundred times hotter than the solar surface. Its outermost portion expands into interplanetary space, providing the gusts and gales known as "space weather." About as bright as a full moon, the corona extends visible streamers several times the sun's diameter; the structure within it is readily apparent. The corona also changes its overall shape from eclipse to eclipse—for example, it was circular in 1991 and elliptical in 1998 (fig. 4-5). The shape of the corona is more asymmetric in times of low solar activity, with long streamers extending from the equatorial region and less dramatic streaks near the poles. When solar activity is high, the polar corona expands and its glow looks more circular.

Totality ends with another chance to spot the pink glow of prominences and chromosphere on the sun's western edge, then a second diamond ring at third contact. Now eye protection again becomes necessary. Another appearance of Baily's beads quickly follows; after that comes an uninterrupted sliver of sunlight. For a few seconds after totality, from observing sites with a clear view of the eastern horizon, the retreating shadow of the moon can be seen as it races across the landscape. Maria Mitchell of Vassar College described this moment of the eclipse she observed from Denver in 1878:

> Happily, some one broke through all rules of order, and shouted out, "The shadow! the shadow!" And looking toward the southeast we saw the black band of shadow moving from us, a hundred and sixty miles over the plain, and toward the Indian Territory. It was not the flitting of the closer shadow over the hill and dale: it was a picture which the sun threw at our feet of the dignified march of the moon in its orbit.

Spacecraft now allow us to view that picture from a vantage point Mitchell could only imagine (fig. 4-6). Today many of the unique observing opportunities that eclipses provide are available to astronomers by other means. Satellites carrying instruments above the atmosphere can observe the sun in greater detail and over a broader range of its emitted radiation than is possible from the Earth's surface. Space-based observatories study the faint outer atmosphere of the sun with instruments called coronagraphs. These use an opaque disk to occult the sun, but they also block the innermost corona, which is bright enough to scatter light within the device. For

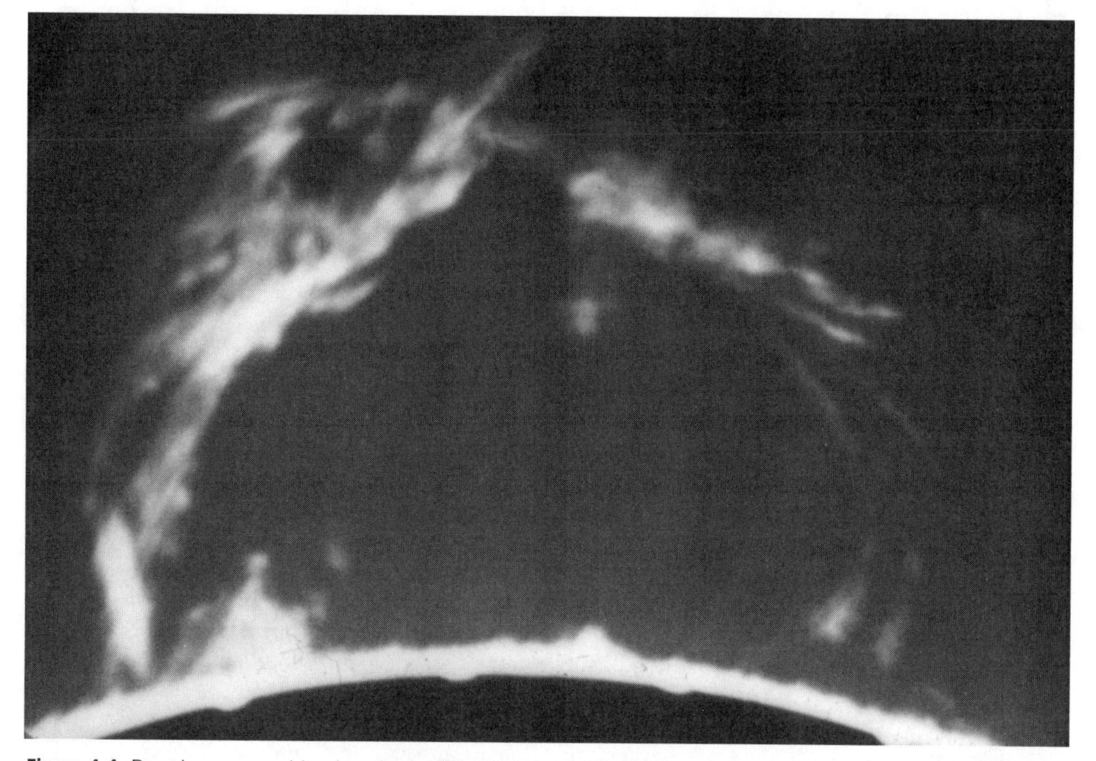

Figure 4.4. Prominences arching hundreds of thousands of miles into space can be seen above the solar surface during an eclipse. Magnetic forces suspend the hot gas and their collapse can release energy and material that impacts the Earth. This prominence was photographed in 1957 with the help of a coronagraph, a device that creates an artificial eclipse. (Courtesy of The Observatories of the Carnegie Institution of Washington)

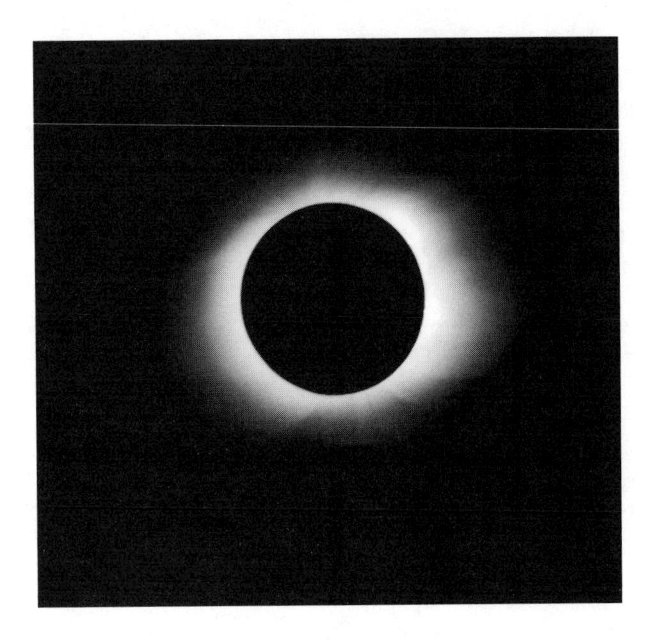

Figure 4-5. With the solar surface blocked by the moon, the tenuous streamers of the sun's corona became visible during the February 1998 total eclipse as seen from Curaçao. (Photo by Bill Sterne)

example, the Large Angle Spectrometric Coronagraph (LASCO) aboard the *Solar and Heliospheric Observatory (SOHO)* places more than twice the sun's diameter in artificial eclipse. Ground-based instruments can see much closer to the sun than their space-borne counterparts, but eclipse observations still offer a better view of the innermost regions of the lower corona and chromosphere. Moreover, eclipse trips cost hundreds of times less than a space-borne experiment and can be planned in months rather than years, enabling researchers to use the latest technology available. Although now a scientific niche, eclipse observations remain a valuable complement to other methods of studying the sun, and professional astronomers will continue to chase the moon's shadow for the foreseeable future.

Tales of the Shadowlands

The visual impact of solar eclipses has occasionally shaped human events. The most dramatic example is recorded by Herodotus, the first Greek historian, who wrote around 430 B.C. Two of the major military powers in Asia Minor, the Lydians and the Medes, had been fighting one another with about equal success for five years. In the sixth year, as they engaged in another battle, day was suddenly changed into night. This was taken as a serious portent—the combatants stopped fighting and their leaders made overtures of peace that led to a treaty sealed by the marriage of the Lydian king's daughter to the son of the Median king.

Working with the regnal dates of the kings in the story and modern eclipse calculations, astronomers generally agree that the eclipse mentioned occurred on May 28, 585 B.C. Herodotus also records that the year of this eclipse was predicted by the Greek philosopher Thales of Miletus. The claim is vague and difficult to reconcile with the state of astronomy in Mesopotamia, where we know a framework for predicting lunar eclipses was becoming established. But even centuries later they could not predict where on Earth a solar eclipse would be total.

Knowledge of an upcoming eclipse could be a useful tool for persuading those who did not know their cause. During his fourth voyage to the West Indies, Christopher Columbus and crew found themselves in caravels so infested with shipworms that they were no longer seaworthy and had to be beached in Jamaica. While awaiting the arrival of a relief ship, his crew traded with the natives for food and other supplies. But after six months and a mutiny of half the crew, Columbus was effectively out of tradeworthy goods and the Jamaicans had lost interest in providing aid. Three days before a lunar eclipse in February 1504, Columbus warned the native chieftains that the Christian god was angry with them for not

Figure 4-6. The moon's shadow swept over the western hemisphere on February 26, 1998. These images show the total solar eclipse from the unusual perspective of the *GOES 10* weather satellite.

Top: At 15:01 UT totality falls on the central Pacific—the shadow zone seems to bulge outward from the Earth's night side.

Middle: The shadow approaches Panama and Colombia at 17:01 UT.

Bottom: Moving over the Earth's surface at over 1,000 miles (1,609 kilometers) per hour, the moon's umbra shades the Lesser Antilles by 18:31 UT.

(Images courtesy of the GOES Project, NASA/Goddard Space Flight Center) supplying food and would give them a sign in the heavens. The eclipsed full moon had the desired effect and the Jamaicans kept Columbus supplied until relief came.

Tecumseh and his brother Tenskwatawa used a similar technique. They were influential members of the Shawnee tribe in the Ohio River valley in the early 1800s. Both recognized that the only way to stop the increasing westward advance of white settlers was for the different tribes of the area to put aside their differences and unite against a common threat. Tenskwatawa, known as The Prophet, was a popular religious leader who preached a rejection of all white customs and a return to traditional cultural values. The governor of the Indiana Territory, William Henry Harrison, challenged Tenskwatawa to provide "some proofs at least of his being the messenger of the Deity." Tecumseh heard about an upcoming solar eclipse from a scientific expedition and shared the news with Tenskwatawa, who then announced that on June 16, 1806, the Great Spirit would hide the sun from the world. Tenskwatawa—on hand at Greenville, Ohio, for the moment of totality—demonstrated his connection with the Great Spirit by restoring the darkened sun. Tenskwatawa's followers grew as word of the miracle spread, but the new confederation collapsed in 1811 with Harrison's raid on its capital, Prophetstown, near the Tippecanoe River.

These historical incidents provided inspiration to novelists. The hero of Mark Twain's *A Connecticut Yankee in King Arthur's Court* uses knowledge of a total solar eclipse to bargain his way out of being burned at the stake. H. Rider Haggard's protagonist in *King Solomon's Mines* similarly interprets a lunar eclipse to his own advantage. In both cases the eclipses are fictional.

Not surprisingly, eclipse observations frequently found their way into the astronomical records of many cultures. We've previously mentioned that the Earth's rotation is slowing down—that is, the length of the day is increasing over time—because of the friction caused by tides raised on the Earth. Eclipse information can be used to check the Earth's slowdown across historical time. They show an increase in the length of the day averaging 1.7 milliseconds per century over the past three millennia. That result is significantly smaller than what would be expected through tidal friction alone (see page 18). Nontidal factors acting over the same period make additional contributions to the length of the day, either speeding or slowing the Earth. They include the ongoing rebound of continents compressed by the weight of Ice Age glaciers and interactions between the Earth's core and mantle. Long-term changes in the length of the day have implications for geologists as well as astronomers.

On the face of it, this may not seem like much of a change—a day in 500 B.C. was just 0.043 second shorter than today's—but it does have consequences. Astronomers use a uniform time scale to compute the positions of the sun and moon at, for example, a total solar eclipse. But the path of totality will be visible only from a limited region and its exact location depends on a slowly changing time scale based on the rotation of the Earth. The further back we go in time, the more Earth's rotation runs ahead of schedule, diverging from the uniform time scale and the day length that forms the basis of its definition. In the year A.D. 1000 that difference is less than an hour, but it rises to over two hours by A.D. 100. The divergence is nearly five hours for 500 B.C., which means that the path of an eclipse in that era computed without accounting for this effect would be misplaced by as much as seventy degrees in longitude.

While solar eclipses have played an important role in our current understanding of the sun, the years between 1840 and 1920 supplied the true scientific bonanza. Two important technologies emerged during this period: photography and spectroscopy. Photography allowed a means of recording the event for later analysis. Spectroscopy allowed astronomers to determine the composition of the sun by looking for lines characteristic of each chemical element in the solar spectrum. In 1863, William Huggins (1824–1910) showed that the sun and stars are primarily composed of hydrogen gas. In 1868, French scientist Jules Janssen (1824–1887) and British astronomer J. Norman Lockyer (1836–1920) called attention to a yellow line in the spectrum of the corona that did not seem to belong to any known element. They daringly proposed that it was an element not yet discovered. Lockyer named it helium, after the Greek sun god Helios. The following year, two more astronomers claimed to have discovered another new element, which they called coronium.

One particular eclipse from the middle of this period offers an interesting glimpse of American science—and celebrity—at the time. On July 29, 1878, the shadow of the moon raced southeast across the United States, passing through the Montana and Wyoming Territories, the new state of Colorado, Oklahoma Territory, Texas, and Louisiana. The path of the umbra passed right across the Rocky Mountains. The prospect of clear, dry high-altitude observing sites attracted some of the world's most distinguished astronomers. The new transcontinental railroad made it much easier to move personnel and equipment; the Pennsylvania Railroad even gave astronomers a special discount on tickets. Simon Newcomb (1835–1909) of the U.S. Naval Observatory hoped to spot a new planet (more on that later). Lockyer joined a party led by Henry Draper (1837–1882) of New York University. Samuel Langley (1834–1906), director of the Allegheny Observatory, led a rugged group to the summit of Pike's Peak in Colorado. Maria Mitchell (1818–1889) of Vassar College traveled to Denver.

But the best-known observer of the great eclipse of 1878 was not an astronomer. He was a thin, graying thirty-one-year-old New Jersey inventor named Thomas Alva Edison (1847–1931). He had already patented over 150 inventions, including important improvements to both the telegraph and the telephone. In late December 1877, Edison tested his most original invention, one that catapulted him to a level of fame he had not yet experienced. It was the phonograph—the first machine capable of recording and reproducing sound. Newspapers and magazines raved about it all winter. The National Academy of Sciences asked for a demonstration during its April meeting in Washington, D.C.—so many people crammed into the hall to hear Edison's presentation that the doors had to be taken off their hinges. During this meeting, he mentioned that he had designed a super-sensitive gadget for measuring heat, an offshoot of his telephone improvements. He called it a tasimeter. George Barker, a professor at the University of Pennsylvania, was heading west with the Draper party and wanted to use a tasimeter to attempt to measure the heat of the corona. To make sure he got one, he asked Edison along.

In 1878, Wyoming still had a dozen years to go before it would become a state. The site chosen for the Draper expedition was the tiny town of Rawlins, a railroad switching point that consisted of a dozen or so unpainted buildings, a hotel, and about eight-hundred people. Thanks to the eclipse, the town could boast among its visitors some of the leading astronomers of the day—and the world's most famous inventor. Newspapers along the Rockies enjoyed the presence of the scientists, or "wise men from the east" as one called them. Edison, though, was a bonus for the press, and headlines such as "Professor Edison attended by a party of scientists" proved a source of mild annoyance to the astronomers; Edison was mostly self-educated, and his oft-quoted disdain for academics had won him few friends among professional scientists.

Edison shared his hotel room with Edwin Fox, a reporter for the *New York Herald.* The night before the eclipse, the two were jolted awake by thunderous knocking on their door. "Upon opening the door," recalled Edison, "a tall, handsome man with flowing hair, dressed in western style, entered the room." In stepped Texas Jack, eyes bloodshot and hands on his gun belt.

"Which one of you is Edison?" he said.

The inventor gulped hard and introduced himself. Just then the hotel manager arrived and asked Jack not to make so much noise. The manager was promptly shoved out of the room.

Texas Jack explained that he was the best pistol shot in the West and wanted to meet the great inventor of the phonograph he had read about in the newspapers. Then he pulled his Colt revolver from its holster and fired it out the window, setting a weathervane atop the freight depot across the street into a wild spin.

"The shot awakened all the people, and they rushed in to see who was killed. It was only after I told him I was tired and would see him in the morning that he left," said Edison. Fame, he was discovering, had its drawbacks.

Tourists flocked to towns all along the eclipse path. Weather had been a problem for some of the sites but, in the words of one Wyoming paper, the sky was "as slick and clean as a Cheyenne free-lunch table." Astronomers busied themselves as the moon slowly covered the sun and darkness gathered. An eerie wind arose, kicking up whorls of dust, and then the twilight of totality arrived.

A dozen miles west of Rawlins, Simon Newcomb's group searched for the hoped-for new planet. At this point of astronomical knowledge, one quirk of Mercury's orbit continued to frustrate astronomers: although Newton's theory of gravity successfully accounted for most of the motions of Mercury, it consistently underestimated the advance of the perihelion point, which crept along the planet's orbit by almost one minute of arc per century. Many astronomers—including Urbain Le Verrier, who had predicted the existence of Neptune in 1846 from discrepancies in the orbit of Uranus—believed that the unexplained portion of Mercury's perihelion advance was due to a gravitational influence not yet accounted for—a new planet circling the sun in a much tighter orbit than Mercury's. It was even given a name: Vulcan, after the Roman god of fire and metalworking. Newcomb planned to telegraph the position of any planet his team spotted to astronomers in Texas, who would try to confirm its presence when totality came their way. James Watson of the University of Michigan thought he saw an object south of the sun, but when the critical moment came, Newcomb was busy with his own observations and neglected to send the information—a failure for which he publicly apologized. Watson announced his discovery to the press.

At Rawlins, Edison set up a borrowed telescope in the yard of the railroad superintendent. "I had my apparatus in a small yard enclosed by a board fence six feet high, at one end there was a house for hens," he recalled years later. "I noticed that they all went to roost just before totality. At the same time a slight wind arose, and at the moment of totality the atmosphere was filled with thistle-down and other light articles." As the sun darkened, he placed his pocket-sized infrared detector at the end of the telescope, connected the battery, and watched the swinging needle of a galvanometer. (In a more colorful version of this story that later arose, Edison sets up in the henhouse doorway and, as darkness falls, is besieged by the arriving hens.)

He announced to reporters that he had detected the heat of the corona, but the scientists weren't convinced and ignored his results. Edison's name appears nowhere in the official eclipse report produced by the U.S. Naval Observatory and even Edison himself quickly dismissed the effort. His tasimeter was far more sensitive than existing infrared detectors, but it was also unstable, poorly calibrated, and largely untested for its astronomical role. Then again, the corona turned out to be far hotter than anyone expected at the time. In the 1970s, John Eddy of the High Altitude Observatory in Boulder, Colorado, took another look at Edison's data and came to the conclusion that the tasimeter was as sensitive as its inventor had claimed—and it had indeed detected coronal heat.

After the climax of the eclipse, the Draper expedition moved on to hunting and fishing. Evening scientific discussions turned to the new discoveries in electric lighting. "Just at that time," recalled Edison, "I was looking for something new." He quickly lost interest in the tasimeter and never even bothered to patent it.

Validation for Lockyer's belief in helium came in 1895, when William Ramsay identified the new element in a uranium-bearing mineral called clevite. In contrast, the green spectral line attributed to that other new element, coronium, was not identified until 1941. It proved to be characteristic of iron atoms that have been stripped of thirteen electrons, a highly ionized state that could only occur in an extremely hot, highly rarefied gas. The low density prevents particles from colliding very frequently; the high temperature guarantees that the collisions are very energetic. The coronium line became classified as a "forbidden line," one never seen in the laboratory because the required conditions could not be achieved there, although elsewhere in the universe forbidden transitions are very common.

And what of Vulcan? Watson's reported discovery of an intramercurial planet spurred a few searches for decades; however, the problem of Mercury's peculiar orbit would be solved in an entirely unexpected way. What was required was nothing less than a new era in physics—and another total eclipse of the sun.

In 1905, an obscure patent clerk rose to prominence in the world of physics with a trio of groundbreaking papers that helped usher in that new era. Albert Einstein (1879–1955) is, of course, best known for the general theory of relativity that he completed a decade later, describing the distortion of space that occurs in the presence of a strong gravitational field. Near the end of 1915, he enthusiastically described his efforts in a letter to another physicist:

> . . . I have lived through the most exciting and the most exacting period of my life; and it would be true to say that it has also been the most fruitful. . . . The wonderful thing that happened was that not only did Newton's theory result from it *as a first approximation,*

but also the perihelion motions of Mercury, *as a second approximation.*

Einstein's theory seemed to explain Mercury's behavior as a natural consequence, but he was aware of additional phenomena that could be used to test it. In particular, he believed that the warping of space near a massive object like the sun would bend the path of any light passing close to it. Light from a star near the edge of the sun, where the effect is strongest, would be deflected by a tiny yet detectable amount so that the star would appear to have moved from its normal position. An early analysis showed that this deflection could exist under a Newtonian framework, but Einstein's completed relativity theory predicted a deflection of twice its value. Thus, an accurate measurement of the bending of starlight near the sun would favor one theory over the other. The only way to accomplish this at the time was, of course, during an eclipse.

In August 1914, a German expedition to Crimea had planned to put this prediction to the test by taking photographs of stars near the eclipsed sun. Instead, August opened with Germany's declaration of war on Russia and the prompt arrest of the astronomers, who were returned in a few weeks as part of a prisoner exchange. As World War I finally drew to a close, British astronomers made plans to test Einstein's theory. The eclipse of May 29, 1919, was considered ideal for the purpose, with the sun among the bright stars of the constellation Taurus. Two teams, one at Sobral in northern Brazil and the other at Príncipe Island off the west coast of Africa, would observe the eclipse and photograph the darkened sun and nearby stars. By comparing the star positions during the eclipse with those on photographic plates exposed when the sun was in a different part of the sky, astronomers hoped to be able to measure the displacement with sufficient accuracy to favor either Newton or Einstein.

Arthur Eddington (1882–1944), long a supporter of Einstein's theories, led the expedition to Príncipe. After a month of preparations, eclipse day began with heavy rain but by the time of totality the sky was only partly cloudy. Eddington wrote in his diary, "I did not see the eclipse, being too busy changing plates, except for one glance to make sure it had begun and another halfway through to see how much cloud there was." Clouds interfered with the star images on many plates, but he was optimistic that some of the last six photographs would be suitable. "One plate that I measured gave a result agreeing with Einstein"—a moment Eddington later referred to as the greatest of his life. The 1919 measurements confirmed that the sun bent light rays by roughly the right amount—less than predicted in Príncipe, more than predicted in Brazil. When the dramatic eclipse results were made public in November and it was clear that the predictions of relativity had surpassed those of Newton, the international press immediately made Einstein a household name.

Observations from a 1922 eclipse showed even better agreement, but the errors associated with all of these measurements remained relatively large and thus not accurate enough to rule out later theories of gravity that challenged Einstein's version. By the 1970s, radio astronomy offered opportunities to test the deflection of radio waves—like light, a form of electromagnetic radiation—without an eclipse. The positions of bright radio sources known as quasars were monitored as the sun approached and occulted them; these studies reduced the measurement errors to about 1 percent and validated relativity over its challengers. More recently, emphatic confirmation came from the European Space Agency's astrometric satellite *Hipparcos,* which between 1989 and 1993 measured over 100,000 star positions with unprecedented accuracy. Whereas previous observations of light deflection had been confined to objects seen within a degree or two of the sun's limb, *Hipparcos* detected the bending of light-rays as far as ninety degrees from the sun. According to *Hipparcos* scientists, Einstein's prediction is correct to within one part in a thousand.

Eclipse Cycles

Since the moon courses through the ecliptic once each month, why don't we enjoy lunar and solar eclipses with the same frequency? Remember, the ecliptic represents the sun's apparent annual path through the sky, the plane of Earth's orbit around the sun. If the moon followed exactly the same path as the sun—that is, if the plane of its orbit around us coincided with the ecliptic—we would see a total solar eclipse with every new moon and a total lunar eclipse with every full moon. However, the moon's orbit carries it a bit more than five degrees above and below the ecliptic, so the new moon usually does not cross in front of the sun and the full moon usually misses the Earth's shadow (fig. 4-7).

An eclipse can occur only when a new or full moon lies near one of the nodes of the moon's orbit—one of the two points at which it intersects the ecliptic—and sun, moon, Earth, and the nodes are almost aligned. For example, the sun can be eclipsed any time it lies within 18.5 degrees of one of the moon's nodes. The sun slides along the ecliptic by about one degree each day, so it remains within the "solar eclipse window" for thirty-seven days. Since a new moon occurs every synodic month (29.53 days), we're guaranteed at least one solar eclipse every time one of the nodes lines up with the sun. Such alignments recur in just under six months because the nodes themselves move, sliding westward along the ecliptic. Alignment of the nodes with the sun occurs every 173.31 days.

These numbers combine to form an important cycle—the *saros*—first recognized in Mesopotamia sometime before 500 B.C. There, astronomer-priests kept detailed records of eclipses and other sky events because of their astrological significance as dispatches from heaven—commentaries by the sky deities on the king and his conduct of earthly affairs. With a sufficiently long record of observations available, anyone looking for a pattern could find one, and what the Mesopotamian priests discovered was an interval of 18 years, 11.3 days separating very similar eclipses. Astronomers believe that the cycle was first established for total lunar eclipses because they can be seen over a greater geographical range than total solar eclipses.

The saros arises because three different lunar cycles are nearly commensurate with one another. We know how long it takes for the geometry required for an eclipse to recur (173.31 days). We also know that solar and lunar eclipses depend on certain lunar phases, which repeat every synodic month. The saros is a length of time that is almost evenly divisible by both the synodic month and the node-alignment interval. As it happens, 223 synodic months nearly equals the time required for thirty-eight node alignments—the difference is just eleven hours.

A third period of importance, called the anomalistic month, also nearly meshes with the synodic month. The anomalistic month, which is 27.55 days long, is the time required for the moon to move from one perigee—its closest point to

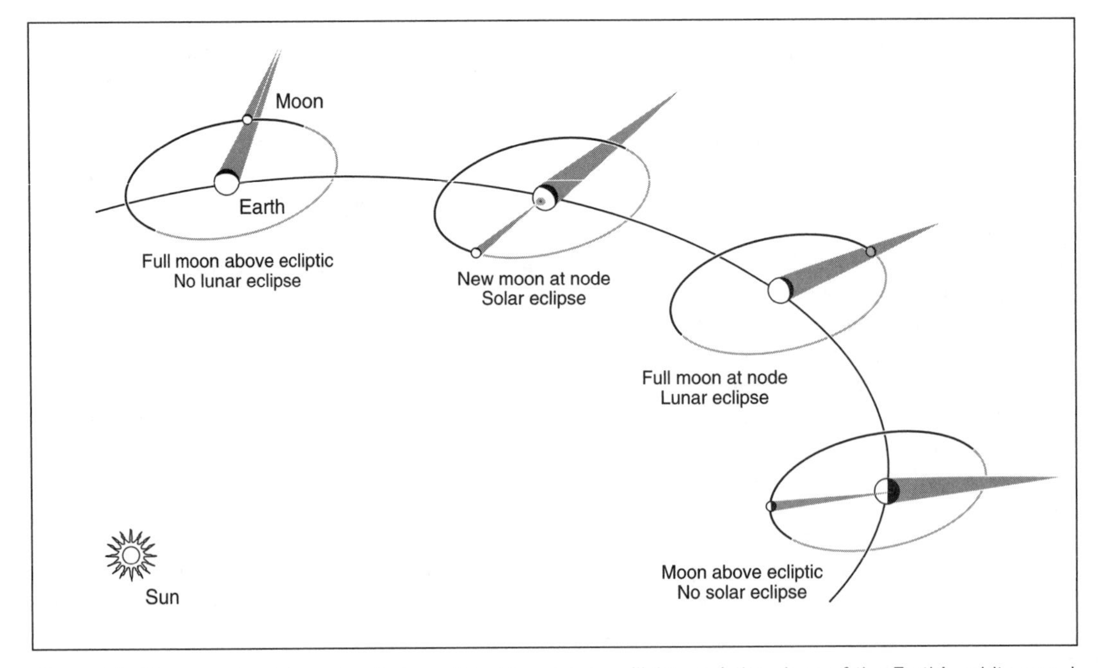

Figure 4-7. The moon's orbit carries it above (black) and below (light gray) the plane of the Earth's orbit around the sun. The moon must lie near that plane, the ecliptic, at new or full moon in order for a solar or lunar eclipse to occur. This happens about once every six months.

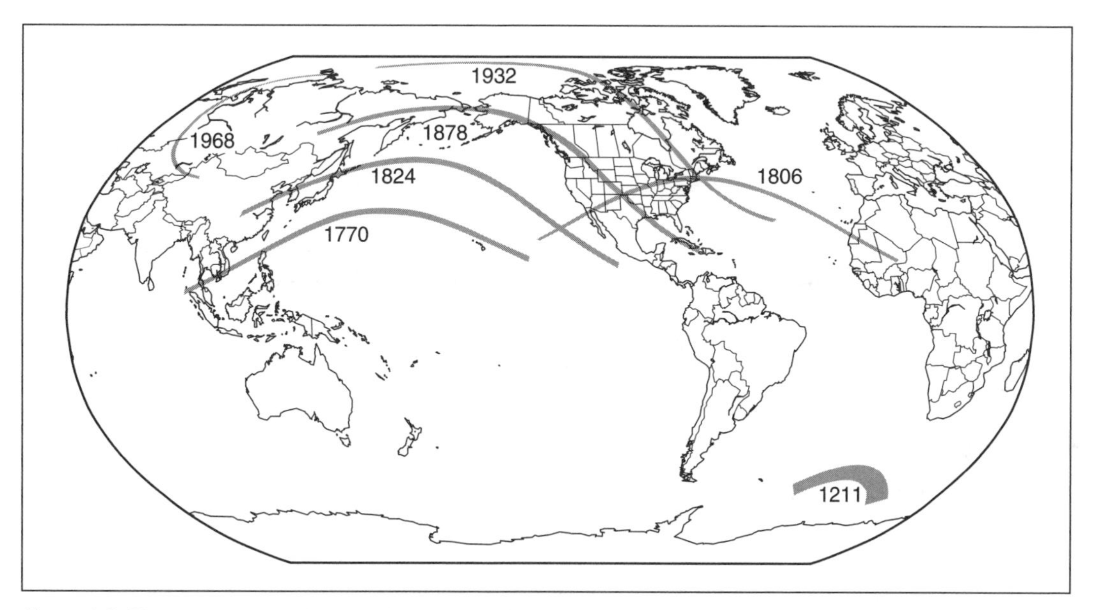

Figure 4-8. The totality paths of Saros 124 shifted in both longitude and latitude. The 1806 eclipse passed through the United States, but one saros interval later, 1824, it tracked westward by about one-third of a day. The paths of the 1770, 1824, 1878, and 1932 eclipses are separated by three saros periods and occur along a similar range of longitude, but shift into more northerly latitudes.

Earth—to another. With an excess of just a few hours, 239 anomalistic months occur in the same period as 223 synodic months. So, 18 years and 11.3 days after an eclipse, the moon returns to the same phase, lies nearly the same distance from us (and thus has about the same apparent size), and is again aligned with the sun, the Earth, and one of its nodes.

Any two eclipses separated by a saros interval share similar characteristics and occur near the same date. For instance, during the eclipse of August 21, 2017, the curve of the moon's shadow across the Earth will be almost identical to the one it made during the total solar eclipse of August 11, 1999. But that fraction of a day in the saros period affects the locations on Earth from which the path of totality can be seen. Each succeeding eclipse in a saros occurs about a third of a day later, so Earth is rotated eastward by an additional eight hours when the eclipse begins. Totality ran through Europe in 1999, but the Earth rotates an extra 120 degrees before the 2017 eclipse begins, swinging Europe out of the way and bringing the United States into the path of the moon's shadow.

Since the region of visibility for each succeeding eclipse in a saros moves westward by about one-third of a day, it stands to reason that the third eclipse will return to more or less the same geographic region. The path of totality for the June 1806 solar eclipse—the one seen by Tenskwatawa and James Fenimore Cooper—ran across the United States from California to New England, crossed the Atlantic, and ended in western Africa. The next eclipse in this series, occurring one saros interval later in 1824, brought totality to China, Korea, Japan, and the northern Pacific. In 1878, three saros periods after the 1806 eclipse, a strip of totality ran from Russia to Cuba and cut straight through the United States. This was the eclipse of 1878 seen by Edison, Lockyer, and Newcomb. The three-saros interval, called the *exeligmos* and equal to 54 years, 33.9 days, is useful for predicting when similar eclipse circumstances will return to roughly the same longitude of the globe (fig. 4-8).

A typical saros lasts thirteen centuries and consists of more than seventy eclipses, but because there is an eleven-hour difference between the lunar phase cycle and the node-alignment cycle, a single series cannot run forever. When one series ends, a new one begins. Since there are several solar eclipses each year, it's obvious that multiple saros cycles run concurrently; typically,

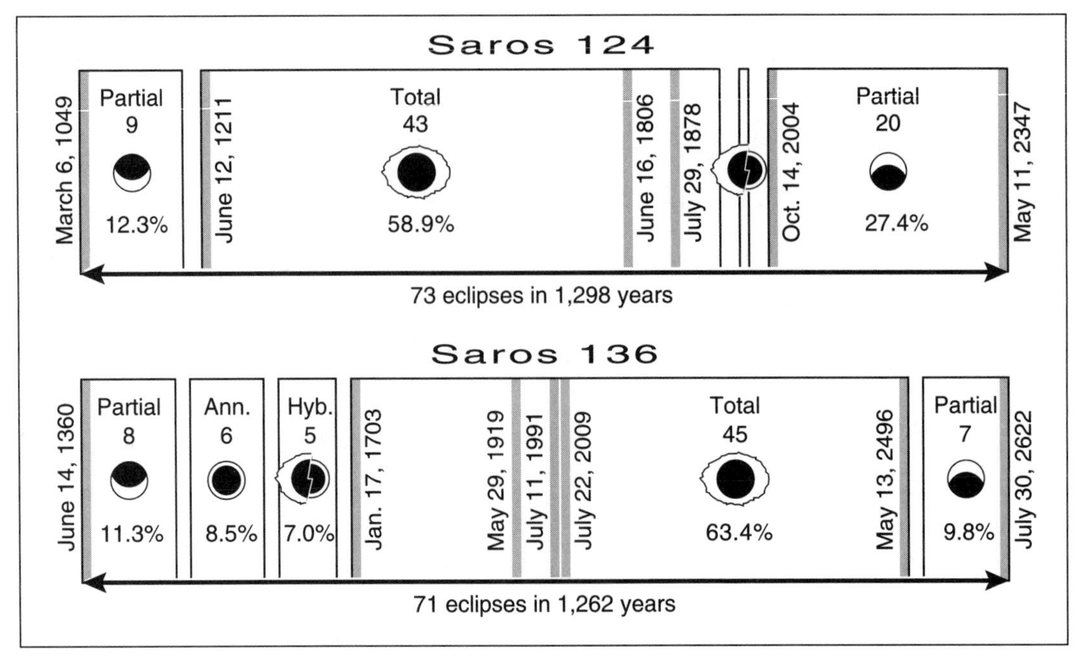

Figure 4-9. This graph breaks down the pattern of eclipses within two active eclipse families. The duration, total number of eclipses, distribution of eclipse types, and location of selected eclipses are shown for Saros 124 and Saros 136.

forty or so are in progress at any given time. The related eclipses separated from each other by one saros cycle make up a saros series, a family of similar eclipses running into the past and the future.

Following a numbering system put forward by astronomers in 1955, the eclipses seen by Cooper and Edison belong to Saros 124. We'll take a brief look at other eclipses of this family to understand the rise and fall of a typical saros. Every saros family starts with a modest partial eclipse visible only from high northern latitudes (for an odd-numbered saros) or deep southern latitudes (even-numbered saros). So begins the story of Saros 124, with an insignificant partial eclipse—with less than 2 percent of the sun covered—visible only from Antarctica on March 6, 1049. As time passed, the slight flaws in the eclipse cycle slowly improved the alignments in this series. The next eight partial eclipses were progressively deeper until, in the summer of 1211, the first of forty-three total eclipses darkened the sun along a track across the southern Atlantic. Improvement continued until, thirty eclipses later, Saros 124 produced its best. The duration of totality on May 3, 1734, was the longest of the series, reaching five minutes forty-six seconds along a path from the east coast of South America to India.

Then began a rapid decline. For the 1806 eclipse, the longest duration along the path of totality did not even reach five minutes. Three eclipses later, when Newcomb and Edison were viewing in Wyoming, the greatest duration of totality barely exceeded three minutes. Another triple-saros interval later, in 1932, an eclipse darkened the sun for less than two minutes on a path that ran through Canada and the northeastern United States. Saros 124's last total eclipse curved through China and Russia in 1968, with totality lasting less than forty seconds. October 1986 brought the only hybrid of the series: the eclipse was annular except for a spot off the coast of Greenland where the sun blinked dark for less then two-tenths of a second. The next Saros 124 eclipse, in October 2004, marks the beginning of the end, ushering in a final phase of dwindling partial eclipses that spans three centuries. Saros 124 expires in May 2347 with a small partial eclipse visible from northern Canada and Alaska, after producing a total of 73 solar eclipses over a period of 1,298 years (fig. 4-9).

There is another eclipse family of particular interest during the period covered by this book. Saros 136, now near the height of its totality-producing power, generated the six longest total eclipses of the twentieth century. These include the 1919 eclipse that put general relativity to the test and the 1991 eclipse over Hawaii and Mexico. The series continues this trend, creating three of the four longest totalities in the twenty-first century. For the next eclipse, in July 2009, the umbra sweeps across India, Bhutan, China, and Japan's Ryukyu and Bonin Islands—totality reaches its peak near Iwo Jima—and then arcs across Micronesia and Kiribati. This series will produce total eclipses until 2496 and then wind down with seven partial eclipses, the last of which occurs in 2622.

Bad Moons Rising

Just as Earth occasionally passes through the moon's shadow, so the moon sometimes passes through the shadow cast by the Earth. Lunar eclipses also require a precise geometry between Earth, sun, and the nodes of the lunar orbit, and their periodicity is similarly ruled by the saros cycle. The apparent size of the Earth's umbra at the moon's distance is over two and a half times the moon's angular width, so the lunar version of totality is measured in hours, not minutes. At any one instant the entire night side of the Earth can view the moon immersed in shadow. Lunar eclipses are not nearly as impressive as their solar counterparts, but they have an eerie beauty all their own that more than rewards the small effort required to see them.

Stonehenge, the famous megalithic monument near Salisbury in southern England, has been associated with lunar eclipses since the 1960s. Stonehenge was built in four stages between 2800 B.C. and 1500 B.C., beginning as little more than a circular embankment and evolving into the imposing stone circle we see today. Increased computer power allowed investigators to test the monument's many possible alignments against objects in the sky at various stages of its construction. Such research led two astronomers, Gerald Hawkins and Fred Hoyle, to propose that Stonehenge incorporated an impressive amount of astronomical knowledge—so much, in fact, that it could have been used to predict when lunar eclipses would occur or, in a weaker form, to predict the "danger times" when eclipses were possible.

Today, few astronomers and even fewer archaeologists agree with these imaginative suggestions. We should first recognize that while it may have been *possible* to use Stonehenge as some sort of eclipse warning system, we have no evidence that it was used in such a fashion. There are solar and possibly lunar alignments built into Stonehenge, but they lack the precision often claimed for them. Sightlines to the sun or moon are too short—much shorter than at other megalithic monuments. A given observation, such as the summer solstice sunrise, would not shift appreciably within a week on either side of the solstice. At other megalithic sites, horizon landmarks could have served as long and accurate sightlines, but the horizon seen at Stonehenge is largely flat and featureless. Stonehenge remains an enigma, built by an ancient people for a purpose we have not yet completely fathomed. What we do know is that it functioned as a ritual center, not as an astronomical observatory.

Without knowing its cause, any eclipse is disturbing because it appears to be a dramatic violation of the natural order. The Bible contains many allusions to events that sound suspiciously like eclipses, usually with a stock description along the lines of "the sun shall be turned into darkness, and the moon into blood," and all of them are mentioned in connection to events leading up to the Day of Judgment. Islamic tradition is more specific about this association, holding that both a solar and a lunar eclipse during the month of Ramadan will occur before Judgment Day. Such a situation does occur periodically. The next set of Ramadan eclipses, both of them total, occurs in November 2003.

This tradition may have played a role in the reaction of Turkish soldiers to the total lunar eclipse of July 4, 1917, which also occurred during Ramadan. Thomas Edward Lawrence, better known as Lawrence of Arabia, served as a British adviser during World War I; he helped organize the tribes of what is now Saudi Arabia into a guerrilla force operating against Turkish troops of the Ottoman Empire. Lawrence planned to take Aqaba, a strategic port on the eastern side of the Sinai Peninsula, by attacking it from the relatively poorly defended desert approach. He crossed the desert with fifty Bedouin fighters, supplemented

Figure 4-10. These photographs, taken at intervals of ten minutes, follow the moon as it leaves Earth's umbra (beginning at right) during the August 1989 total lunar eclipse. (Photos by Bill Sterne)

them with local Arab rebels, and moved on to the first of two well-fortified outposts on the way to the port. "By my diary," wrote Lawrence, "there was an eclipse. . . . and the Arabs forced the post without loss, while the superstitious soldiers were firing rifles and clanging copper pots to rescue the threatened satellite." The second outpost fell a few days later and Aqaba surrendered without a fight.

The moon passes through the Earth's shadow moving from west to east, its exact path varying greatly from one eclipse to another. The shadow has the same structure as the moon's—a broad, faint penumbra surrounding a darker, more compact umbra. Earth's penumbra is so large, in fact, that the entire moon can pass through it without crossing into the umbra. Penumbral eclipses comprise about 37 percent of all lunar eclipses, but any darkening of the moon that results is so subtle that these usually go unnoticed by casual observers. Five penumbral eclipses occur between 2003 and 2010 but they are so inconspicuous that we do not illustrate them here; they are, however, listed in table 4-2 and appendix A.

When only a portion of the moon's disk dips into the umbra, the eclipse is said to be partial. Partial eclipses make up about 35 percent of all lunar eclipses; there are five before this decade is out. As the moon contacts and enters the umbra, an arc of darkness expands across its face. It reaches maximum extent at mid-eclipse and then gradually withdraws as the moon passes out of the shadow. During partial eclipses—and the partial phases of total eclipses—the Earth's shadow looks almost black in contrast with the part of the moon still in sunlight (fig. 4-10).

The eclipse is total only when the moon passes completely into Earth's umbra. The remaining 28 percent of lunar eclipses are total; eight of them occur through 2010. A total lunar eclipse may last nearly six hours from start to finish. The moon spends about an hour traversing the penumbra, the outermost shadow zone within which it still receives some sunlight. Expert observers will notice a dusky shading on the eastern edge of the moon a little more than ten minutes after it contacts the penumbra, but most people will not notice a darkening for another half hour or so. The moon then enters the umbra, and for the next hour a dark circular shadow creeps across its face. At the end of this time the moon's disk lies completely in shadow, shining with a coppery to ruddy glow that imaginative ancient writers compared with blood. The moon can remain in the umbra for as long as 114 minutes. Once the moon's eastern edge exits the umbra, another hour passes before it emerges. This is followed by about an hour of traversing the penumbra, after which the eclipse is over.

The color of the moon at totality comes not from the moon itself but from sunlight scattered through the ring of atmosphere around the limb of our own planet—without it, a moon immersed in the umbra would disappear completely. Longer wavelengths of light (orange, red) penetrate Earth's atmosphere better than shorter wavelengths (blue, indigo)—this is why the sun looks reddish at sunrise and sunset.

A variety of hues may be used to describe the color of the eclipsed moon: bright coppery orange or red, brick-colored, deep red or rusty, brownish (see color plate 5). It may even darken so much that it becomes all but invisible to the unaided eye. Its appearance depends on many factors, such as weather conditions in the regions on the Earth's limb and the amount of dust and other matter in the atmosphere at the time of the eclipse. Exceptional volcanic eruptions, such as those of El Chichon in 1982 or Mt. Pinatubo in

1991, enhance the population of sulfuric acid droplets in the stratosphere for years afterward. This often gives rise to dark, very red eclipses.

Imagine what a lunar observer would see during totality. The silhouetted Earth blots out the sun far better than the moon ever could, for its apparent width is about four times greater. The black disk, rimmed by the ruddy colors of sunset, hangs in space against a ghostly backdrop—the streamers of the sun's pearly outer corona.

One final note on an interesting pattern of total lunar eclipses: up to four consecutive lunar eclipses can be total, each separated by exactly six lunations. Such clusters are called tetrads and they occur infrequently and variably—there are only five this century. Between 1582 and 1908 there were none at all, but there are sixteen between 1909 and 2156—followed by a tetrad drought until 2448. One tetrad occurs during the span of this book, from 2003 into 2004.

Eclipse Maps

The primary question concerning any eclipse is simply "Will I be able to see it?" The following pages provide maps illustrating solar and lunar

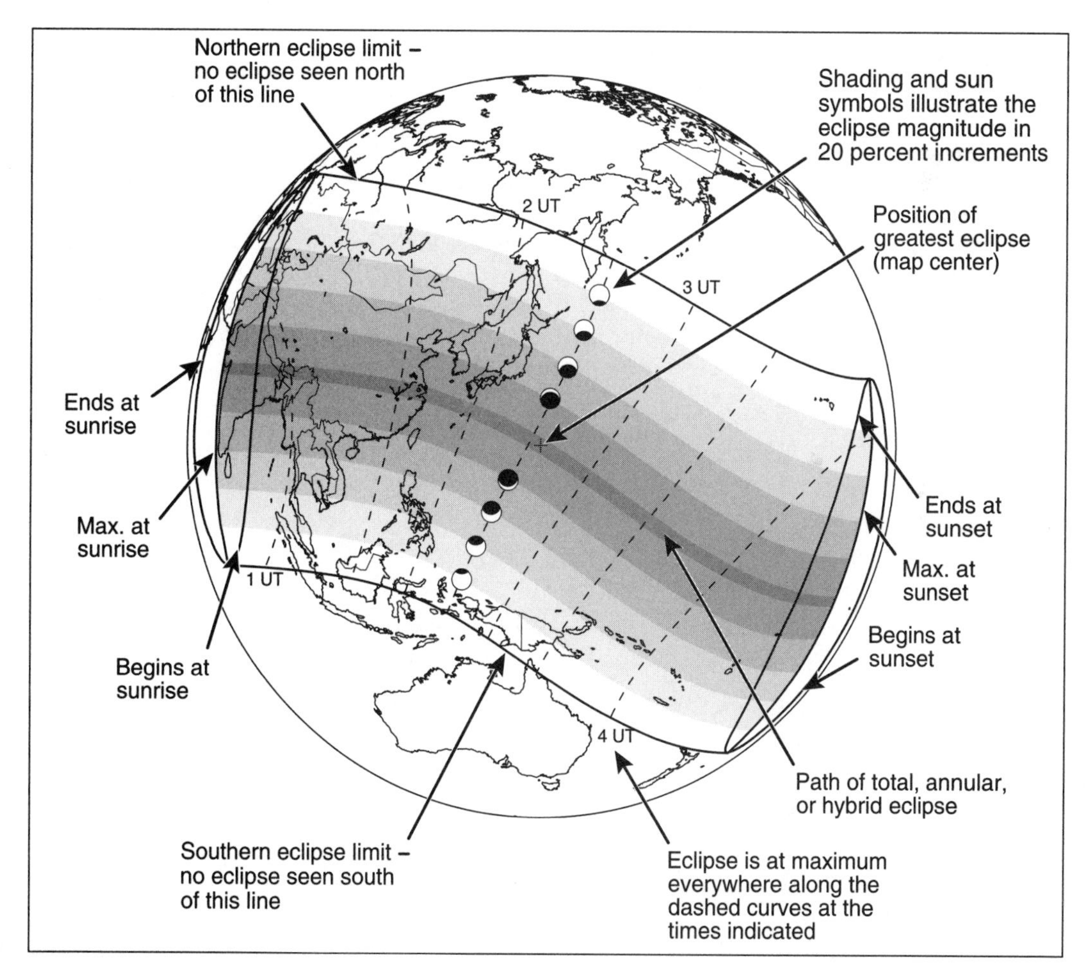

Figure 4-11. Key to the information provided in the solar eclipse maps, using the July 2009 eclipse as an example. Shading and sun symbols indicate the maximum obscuration of the sun in terms of eclipse magnitude, the percentage of the sun's diameter covered by the moon. Dashed curves show the UT times of maximum eclipse every half an hour. At the center of each map is the position of greatest eclipse, the instant when the axis of the moon's umbra passes closest to the center of the Earth. This is approximately the location where the eclipse has its greatest duration and deepest magnitude. In fact, the correspondence is better for total eclipses than for annular ones, but the circumstances at greatest eclipse give us a simple way to compare both types.

eclipses through 2010. The solar eclipse maps, figures 4-12 through 4-24, consist of a view of the Earth from space over the point of greatest eclipse, where the axis of the umbra passes closest to the center of our planet. A saddle-shaped grid on each map encloses the portion of the Earth's surface touched by the moon's penumbra. All locations within this region experience at least a partial eclipse. Just how deep the partial eclipse will be at a given location depends on how close that location is to the path of the umbra. The easiest way to discuss the appearance of a solar eclipse is to think in terms of the percentage of the sun's diameter covered by the moon, so in a 50-percent eclipse, at maximum the moon slides halfway across the sun. Shaded curves on the grid represent the eclipse percentage at 20-percent increments.

Figure 4-11 provides a key to the type of information on the maps, using the total eclipse of July 2009 as an example. Observers in Hawaii, in the least shaded part of the grid, see less than 20 percent of the sun obscured. Those in parts of Japan and Korea see the moon cover over 80 percent of the sun. The darkest shading indicates areas where the eclipse is total.

The grid also contains two great loops, one on the left and one on the right. The outermost line of the left (western) loop passes through all the locations where the eclipse ends at sunrise. Next comes the line of maximum eclipse at sunrise, which is where the shaded curves begin, and then the inside line of the loop, which marks the locations where the eclipse begins at sunrise. Similarly, the lines of the eastern loop represent, from left to right, eclipse ending at sunset, maximum eclipse at sunset, and eclipse beginning at sunset. Lines passing through the path of totality indicate the Universal Time (UT) hour when maximum eclipse occurs. Rather than provide tables of local circumstances, we refer you to Fred Espenak's Eclipse Home Page and the NASA Reference Publications available there (see appendix D).

The lunar eclipse maps are easier to understand. Figures 4-25 through 4-37 illustrate all total and partial lunar eclipses through 2010. There are two diagrams for each eclipse. The top drawing simply shows the path of the moon through the Earth's penumbral and umbral shadows and the UT of its contacts for a geocentric observer. The bottom drawing is a world map that shows the regions on the Earth where the umbral stages of an eclipse will be visible; see the captions for details.

Viewing the Sun Safely

In addition to visible light, the sun emits infrared and ultraviolet radiation that can seriously damage the light-sensitive cells within the human eye. Our normal reaction to the sun's brightness is to squint and turn away, but when a large portion of the sun's surface is covered up during a deep eclipse, we can tolerate the glare and may be tempted to take a longer look. Even in the reduced light, though, the cornea and lens of your eye can focus damaging levels of solar heat and ultraviolet radiation onto your retina. Cases of eye damage are reported after almost every eclipse—some of them result in permanent vision problems. It is *extremely dangerous* to view the sun directly through any material that decreases sunlight to tolerable limits but allows the damaging infrared and ultraviolet wavelengths to pass through. *Never* use sunglasses, smoked glass, CD-ROMs, floppy disks, or exposed color-photographic film to protect your eyes during direct solar viewing. They do not provide enough protection!

Sun-safe filters: Safe filters are easily available and inexpensive. They include #14 welder's glass and various products using materials long shown to be sun-safe, such as aluminized mylar. Some commonly encountered brand names are Eclipse Shades, Solar Viewers, and SolarSkreen. These types of products are available from vendors such as American Paper Optics, Inc. (www.3dglassesonline.com), Rainbow Symphony, Inc. (www.3dglasses.net), and Science Stuff (www.sciencestuff.com); see also advertisements in astronomy magazines. Use these filters only as intended—that is, use a naked-eye filter only for viewing with the eye, not through binoculars or a telescope. Handle the filters carefully and inspect them before each use for any scratches or punctures that would allow unfiltered light into the eye.

Pinhole cameras: This method takes advantage of the basic principle that sunlight passing through a pinhole aperture naturally forms a focused image on a screen—as you can see in the dappled shade under a tree, in which sunlight passing through the pinhole apertures of overlapping leaves and twigs projects many small sun images on the ground. The width of the sun's image is approximately one-hundredth the distance between the aperture and the screen onto which it is projected.

It's easy to construct your own pinhole camera. Cut a hole in a large piece of cardboard. Tape a single piece of aluminum foil over the hole. Carefully pierce the foil with a single hole from a pushpin. A sheet of white paper opposite the pinhole serves as the projection screen. Hold the pinhole between the sun and the screen and angle it so that a bright spot of light appears on the paper. For a larger image, you can build the camera into a box or shipping tube.

Projection from binoculars: Those with binoculars can obtain a larger and more satisfying image by projecting the sun's image onto a sheet of paper. Keep the lens caps on one of the binocular tubes. *Never* look through the binoculars to view the sun. With the sun behind you, adjust the binoculars until they cast their smallest and most circular shadow. The sun's disk will appear within it as a bright, out-of-focus circle of light. Adjust the size of the image by adjusting the distance between the binoculars and the paper, then focus. To provide shade for easier viewing of the projected image, attach a piece of cardboard to the binoculars (without blocking the sunlight entering the open tube). Since heat build-up can soften the cement used to attach some internal parts of the binoculars, expose the open tube to the sun for no more than a minute at a time, then let the binoculars cool by moving them off the sun for a few minutes.

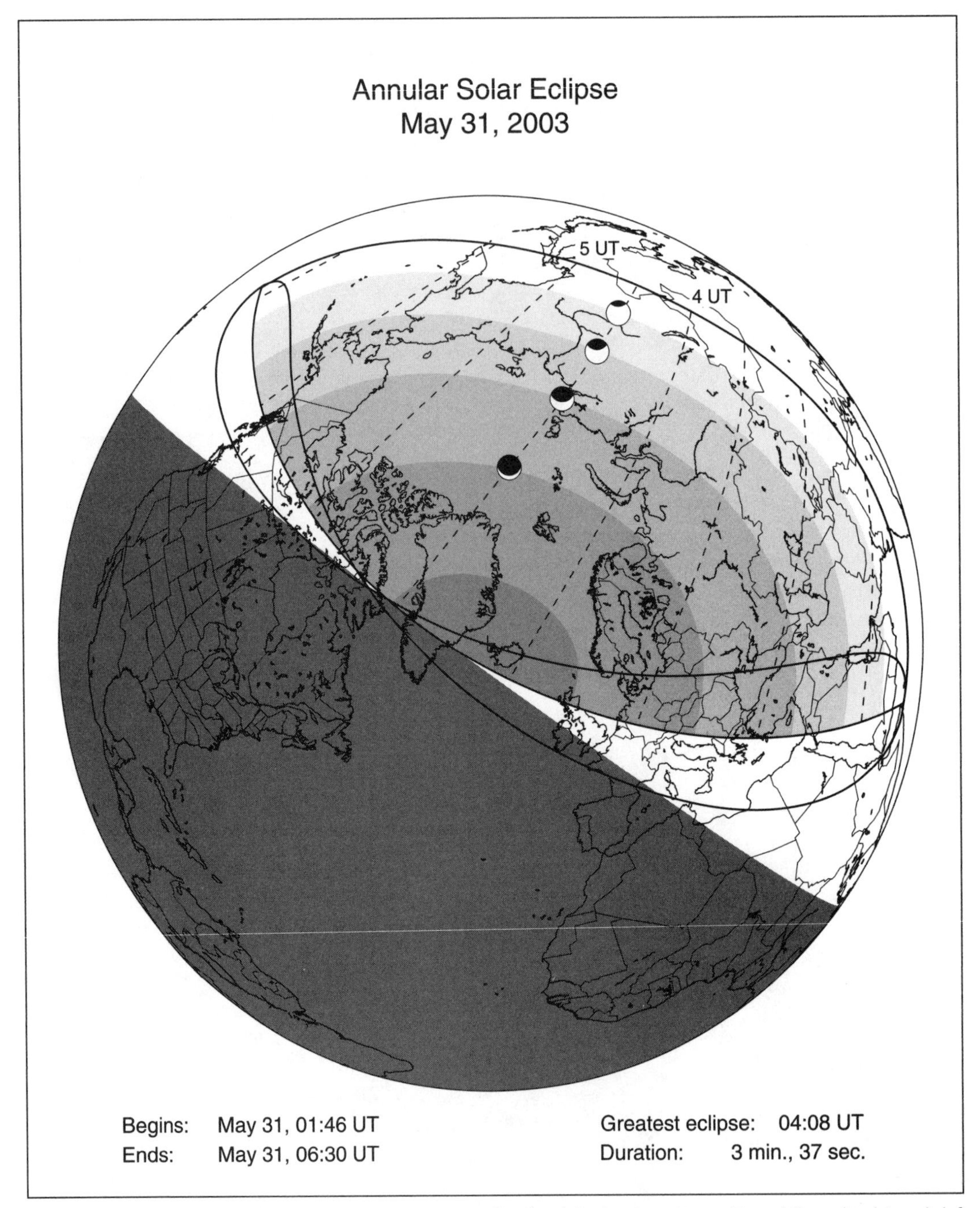

Figure 4-12. The May 31, 2003, annular eclipse treats Scotland, Iceland, and a portion of Greenland to a brief "ring of fire" sunrise. The eclipse is unusual in that the moon's shadow passes over the North Pole before reaching the Earth's surface, a situation that makes the shadow appear to move from east to west in a reversal of the usual state of affairs. The sun will stand just three degrees above the horizon when the eclipse is maximum (4:04 UT) at Reykjavik, Iceland, where observers will see the moon cover all but a thin golden ring of sun for about three and a half minutes. From Fairbanks, Alaska, observers will see 59 percent of the sun's disk covered at maximum eclipse (5:21 UT, which when converted to local time changes the date to May 30). This eclipse is a member of Saros 147.

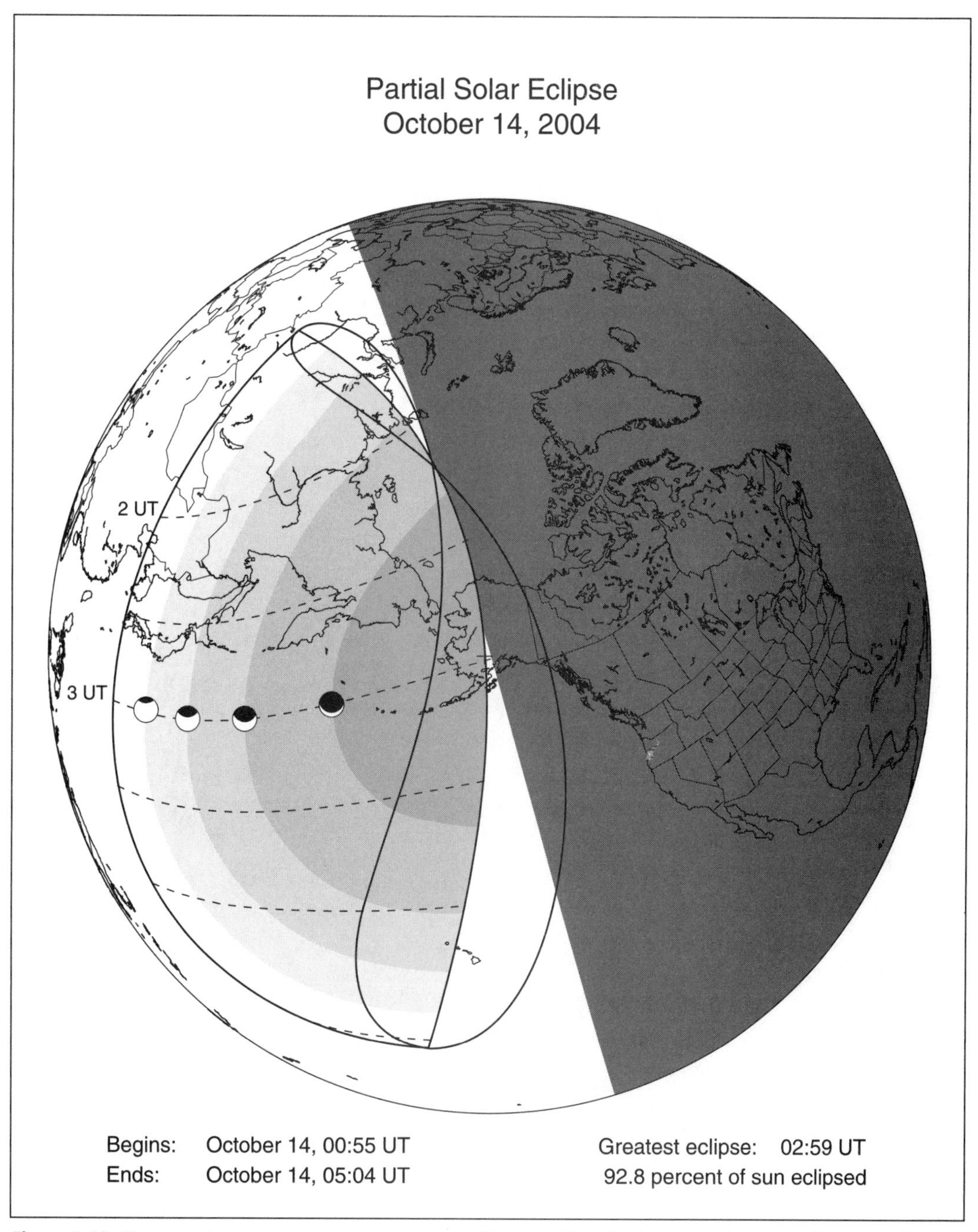

Figure 4-13. The moon's penumbra sweeps across northeastern Russia, Japan, and western Alaska on October 14, 2004. It will be night for most of North America, but observers in the western half of Alaska will see just over 90 percent of the setting sun in eclipse. The date of the eclipse for Alaskans is actually October 13, thanks to the conversion from UT to local time. Observers in Bethel, Alaska, which lies very near the point of greatest eclipse (map center), will see 92 percent of the setting sun covered. This eclipse is a member of Saros 124.

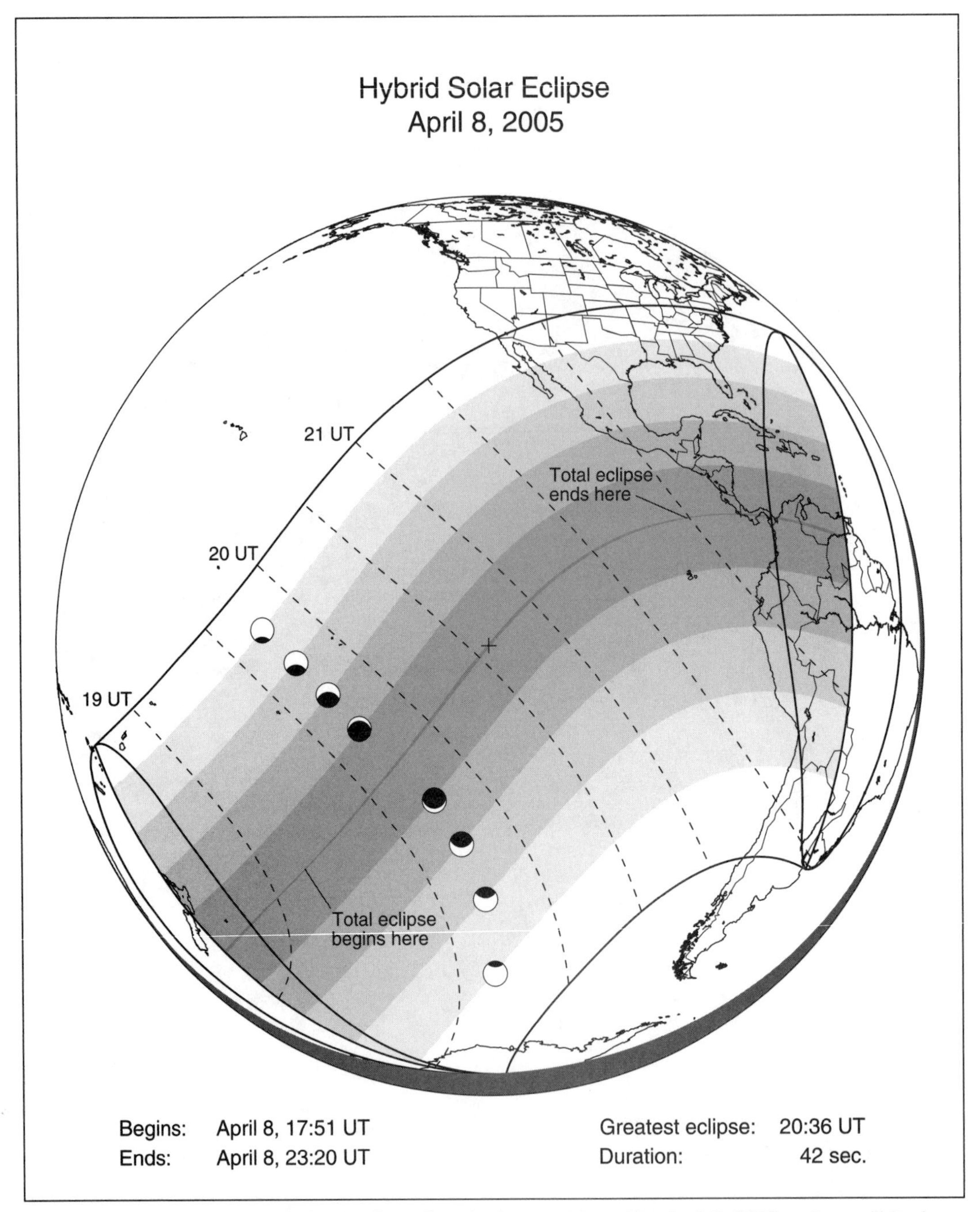

Figure 4-14. A hybrid, or annular/total, solar eclipse is the rarest type. The April 8, 2005, eclipse will begin as annular because the moon appears slightly smaller than the sun's disk. But as the shadow proceeds northeastward along its track, the surface of the Earth will curve toward it and the apparent size of the moon will exceed that of the sun, resulting in a total eclipse. Greatest eclipse will occur in mid-ocean, about 1,100 miles (1,770 kilometers) east of the Marquesas Islands of French Polynesia, and will deliver a forty-two-second glimpse of totality along a path just 17 miles (27 kilometers) wide. The length of totality will then shorten along the ground track as the Earth's surface curves away from the moon; the eclipse will revert to annular about 500 miles (800 kilometers) north of the Galapagos Islands. Observers on the path of annularity in Panama, Colombia, and Venezuela will see a ring of afternoon sun lasting between about ten and twenty seconds. This eclipse is a member of Saros 129.

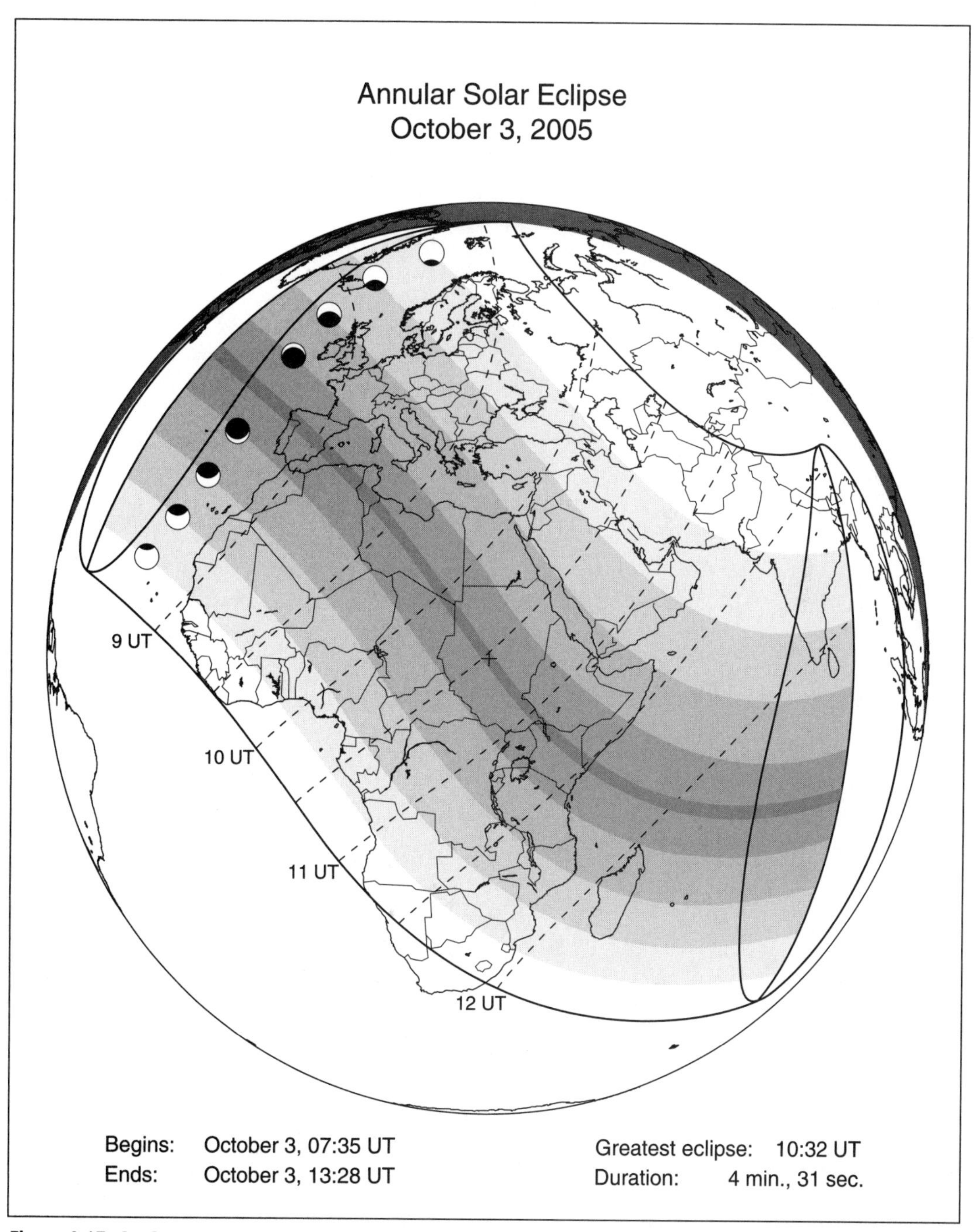

Figure 4-15. On October 3, 2005, the moon's shadow will sweep from the Iberian Peninsula to the Indian Ocean. Madrid, Spain, lies near the center of the path of annularity; observers there will see a ringlike sun for over four minutes beginning at 8:55 UT. The shadow will cross the Mediterranean and make landfall at Algeria, bringing just under four minutes of annularity to Algiers (9:04 UT) and a bit over four minutes of it to Setif (9:08 UT). Greatest eclipse will occur northeast of Salim, Sudan. The shadow will graze Ethiopia, arc across Kenya, and catch the southernmost portion of Somalia (skywatchers at Kismaayo will see nearly three minutes of annularity at 11:29 UT) before rushing into the Indian Ocean. This eclipse belongs to Saros 134.

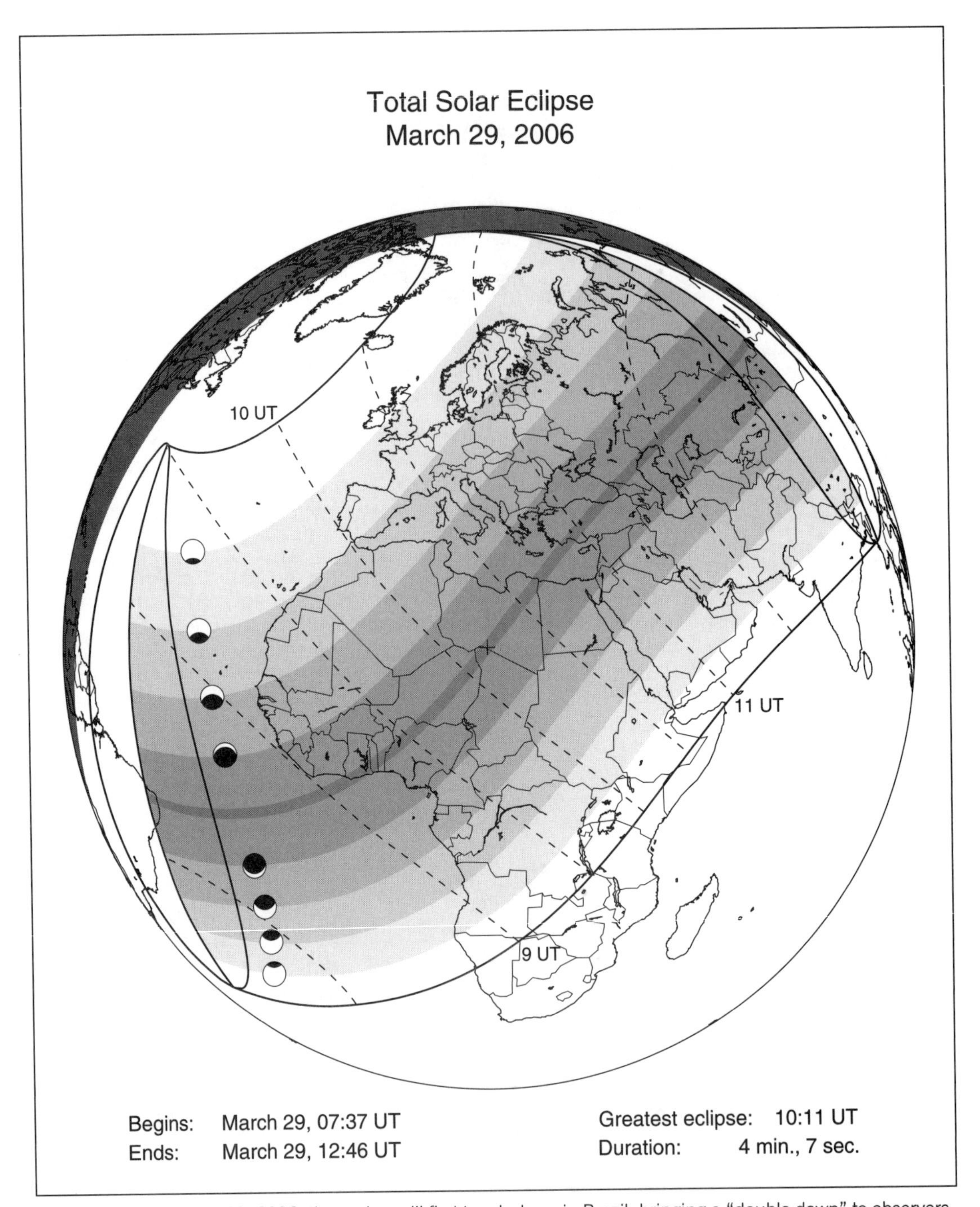

Figure 4-16. On March 29, 2006, the umbra will first touch down in Brazil, bringing a "double dawn" to observers. At Natal, for example, the sun will rise 80 percent eclipsed and will be completely obscured just eight minutes later (8:35 UT, duration ninety seconds). The shadow will cross the Atlantic and come ashore at Ghana, bringing three minutes of totality to the capital of Accra beginning at 9:09 UT. Greatest eclipse will occur on the border shared by Chad and Libya. After leaving the Libyan Desert and crossing the Mediterranean, the umbra will move over Turkey. The city of Tokat lies near the center of the shadow track; observers there will see three and a half minutes of totality starting at 11:06 UT. The moon's umbra will then sweep over the eastern Black Sea, cross over the Volga River delta, and proceed across Kazakhstan. This eclipse is a member of Saros 139.

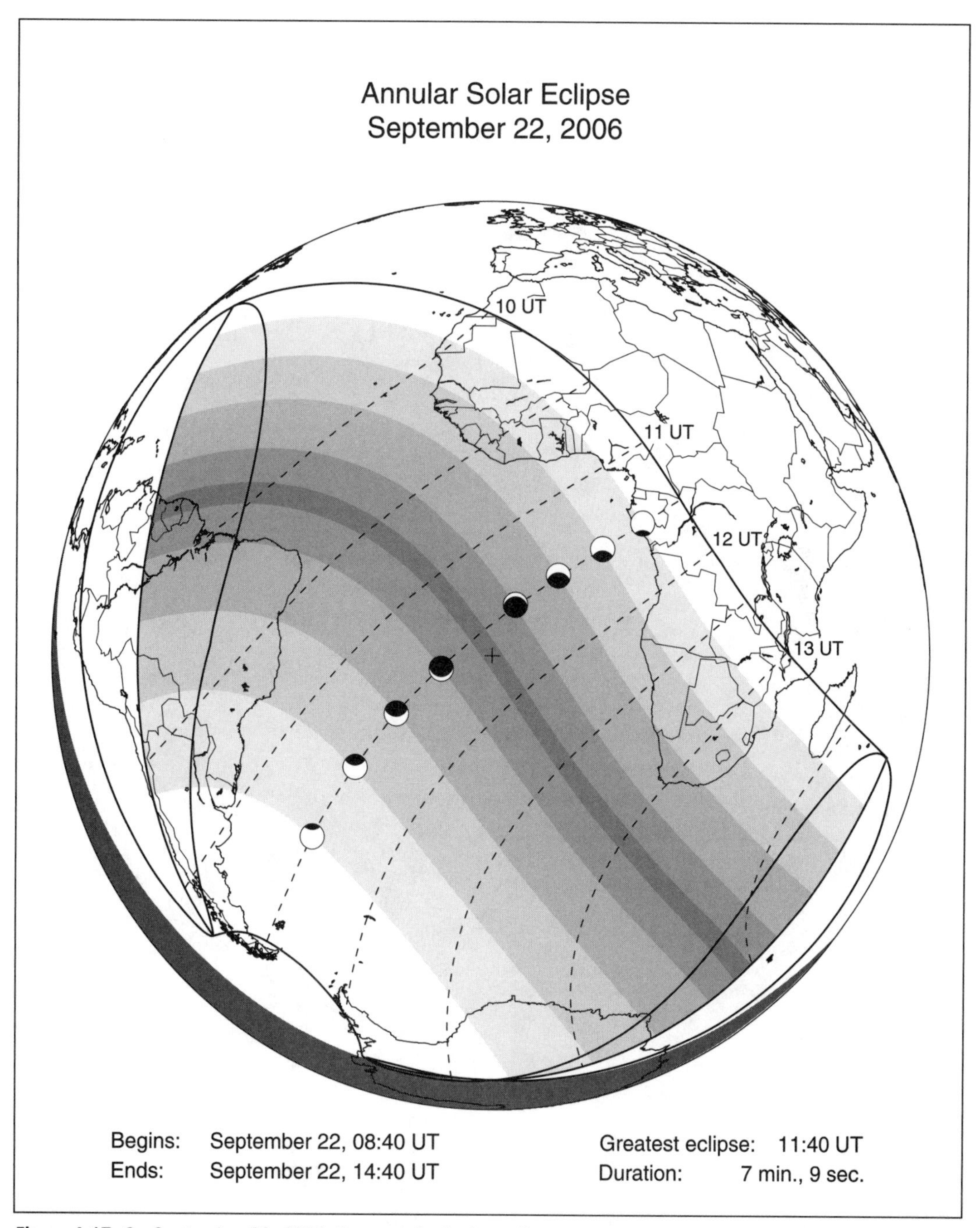

Figure 4-17. On September 22, 2006, the moon's shadow will track almost completely over the open ocean of the South Atlantic. Among the few cities along its path are the capitals of Suriname (Paramaribo) and French Guiana (Cayenne). Observers in the northern half of these countries, together with those in portions of Guyana and Brazil, will see the sun transformed into a golden ring of light within a few minutes of dawn. Paramaribo skywatchers will see five minutes of annularity starting at 9:48 UT, but those in Cayenne, which lies nearer the center of the eclipse path, will see the annular sun for forty seconds longer (starting at 9:49 UT). This eclipse is a member of Saros 144.

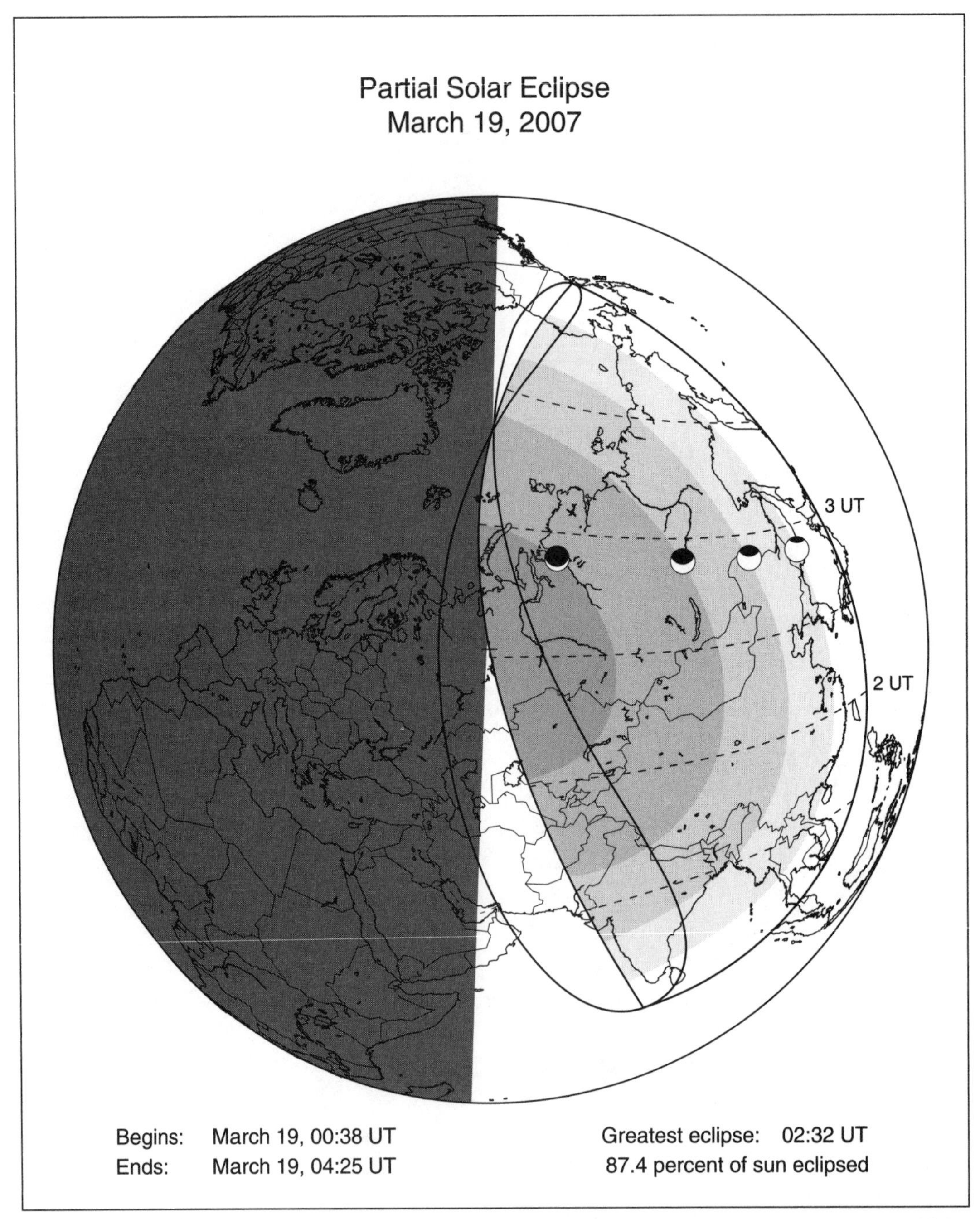

Figure 4-18. The moon's penumbra will touch down on March 19, 2007, bringing a partial eclipse to much of Asia. It will be night for Europe, Africa, and most of North America, but observers in the western half of Alaska will see up to 20 percent of the setting sun in eclipse. The date of the eclipse for Alaskans is actually March 18, thanks to the conversion from UT to local time. Observers in Prudhoe Bay, on the northern coast, will see 23 percent of the setting sun obscured (3:49 UT); those in Fairbanks (3:55 UT) will see a 9 percent "bite" taken out of the sun. The point of greatest eclipse will fall in Russia east of the Ural Mountains. Skywatchers in Beijing, China, will see a maximum eclipse of 39 percent at 2:23 UT. This eclipse is a member of Saros 149.

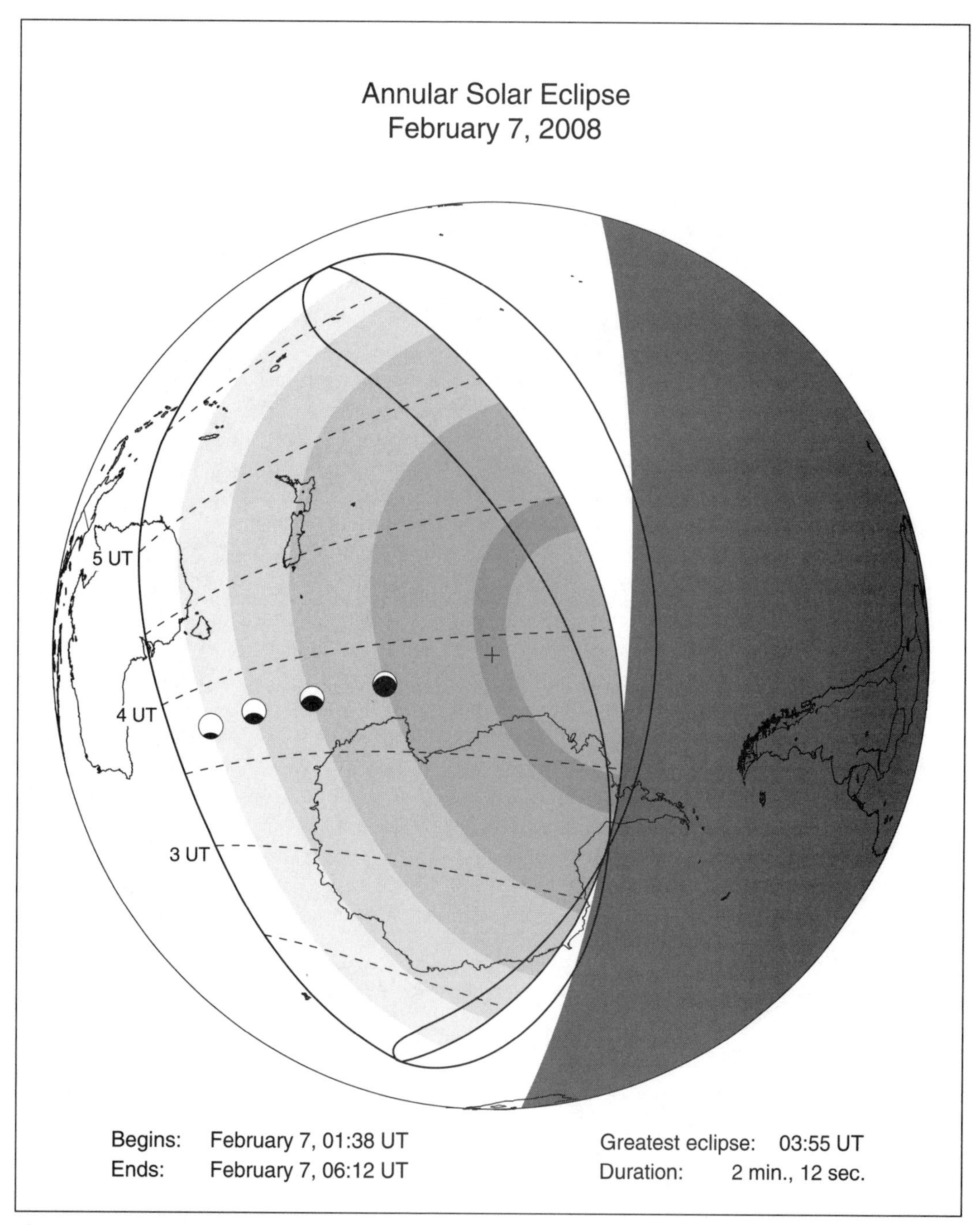

Figure 4-19. The moon's shadow will arc across Antarctica and the southern Pacific on February 7, 2008. Although the annular eclipse itself comes only to very remote regions, New Zealanders will see the sun well obscured at maximum: 74 percent at the Chatham Islands (4:40 UT); 63 percent at Christchurch (4:37 UT) and Wellington (4:42 UT); and 58 percent at Auckland (4:52 UT). Australians at Sydney see a 22-percent eclipse at 4:42 UT. At Apia on Western Samoa, the eclipse will reach its maximum (32 percent at 5:30 UT) with the setting sun just six degrees above the horizon. This eclipse is a member of Saros 121.

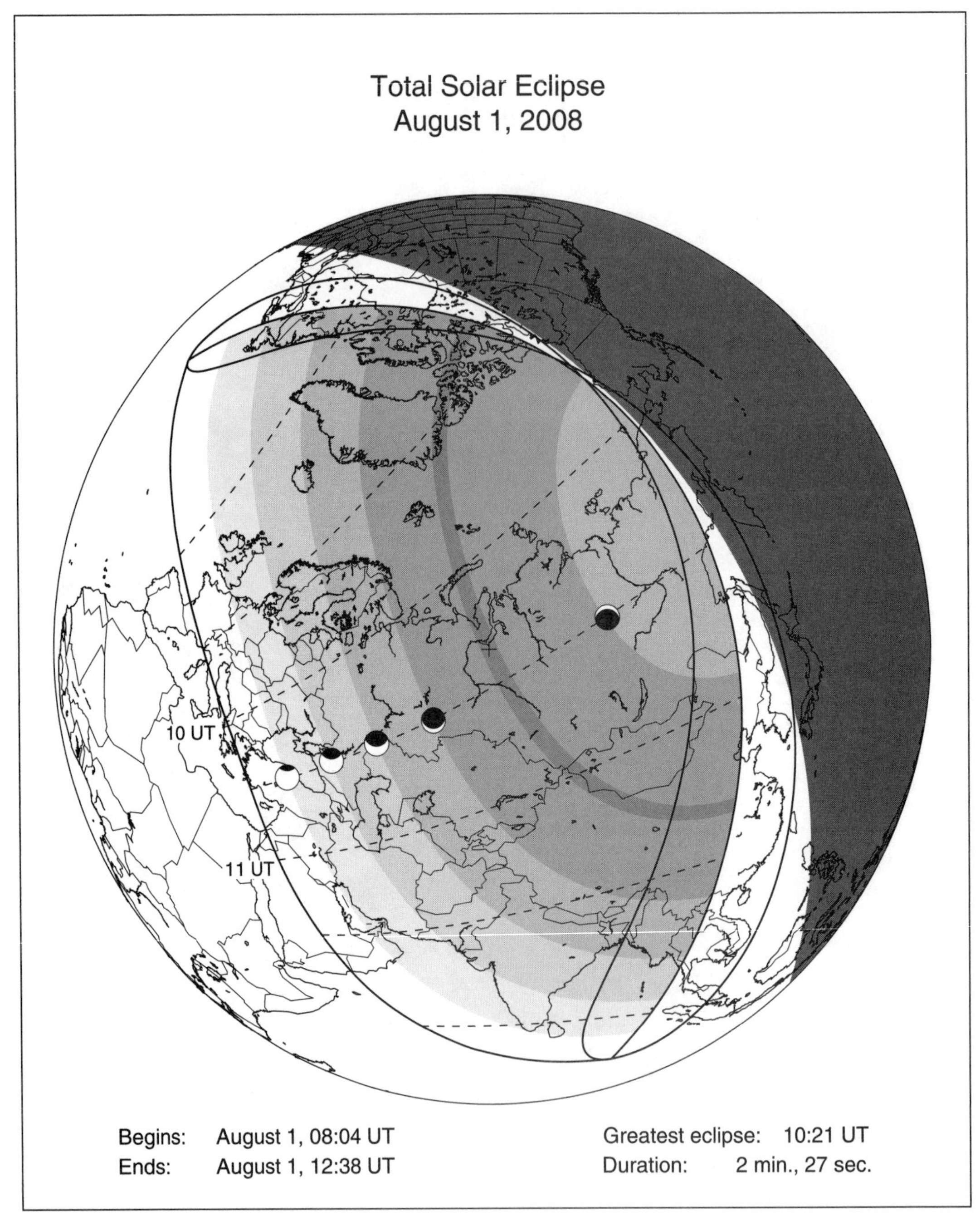

Figure 4-20. The moon's umbra will touch down on the northernmost part of North America on August 1, 2008. The event brings with it the possibility of seeing a partially-eclipsed sunrise for those along the northeastern coast. Observers in Caribou, Maine, and Halifax, Nova Scotia, will see a rising sun about 25-percent eclipsed. At St. John's, Newfoundland, maximum eclipse will occur about fifteen minutes after sunrise (32 percent at 8:43 UT). Skywatchers in Nadym, Russia, near the point of greatest eclipse, will experience almost two and a half minutes of totality (10:20 UT). As the shadow moves southward, darkness lasting more than two minutes will fall on Novosibirsk (10:45 UT) and Barnaul (10:47 UT). The umbra will cross into China before leaving the Earth's surface. Observers at Luoyang and neighboring villages will see one minute of totality with the setting sun less than two degrees above the horizon—a "double dusk" event. The eclipse is a member of Saros 126.

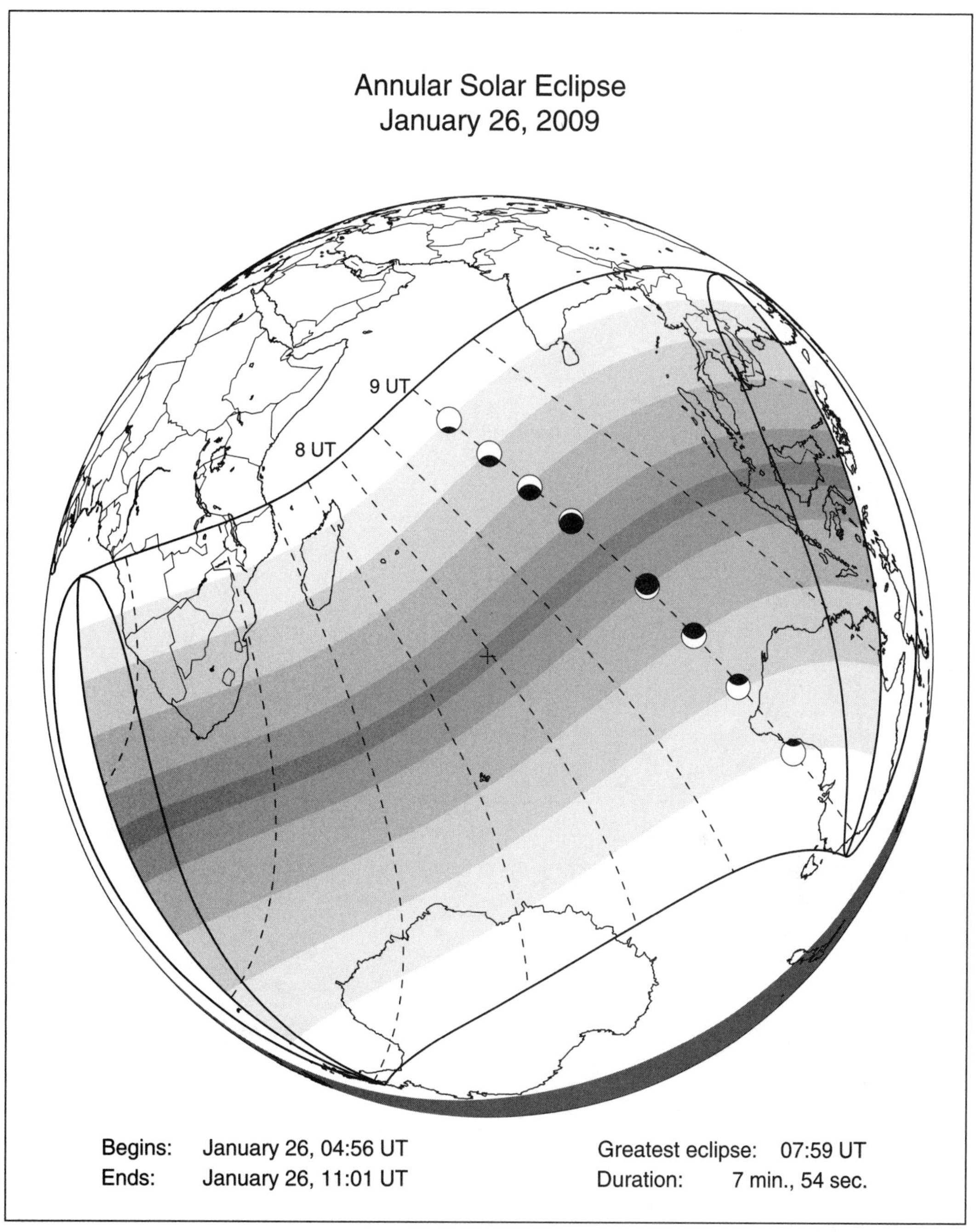

Figure 4-21. The path of the annular eclipse of January 26, 2009, will avoid landfall until the moon's shadow is nearly ready to leave the Earth's surface. Observers on the Indonesian islands of Sumatra and Java will be the first to see the sun transformed into a ring of light. Over six minutes of annularity will come to the Sumatran city of Tanjungkarang-Telukbetung at 9:38 UT, when the sun will be twenty-three degrees above the horizon. The moon's shadow will then cross the Java Sea and sweep over Borneo; observers in Samarinda will see an off-center solar ring for nearly two and a half minutes (9:48 UT). This eclipse is a member of Saros 131's family.

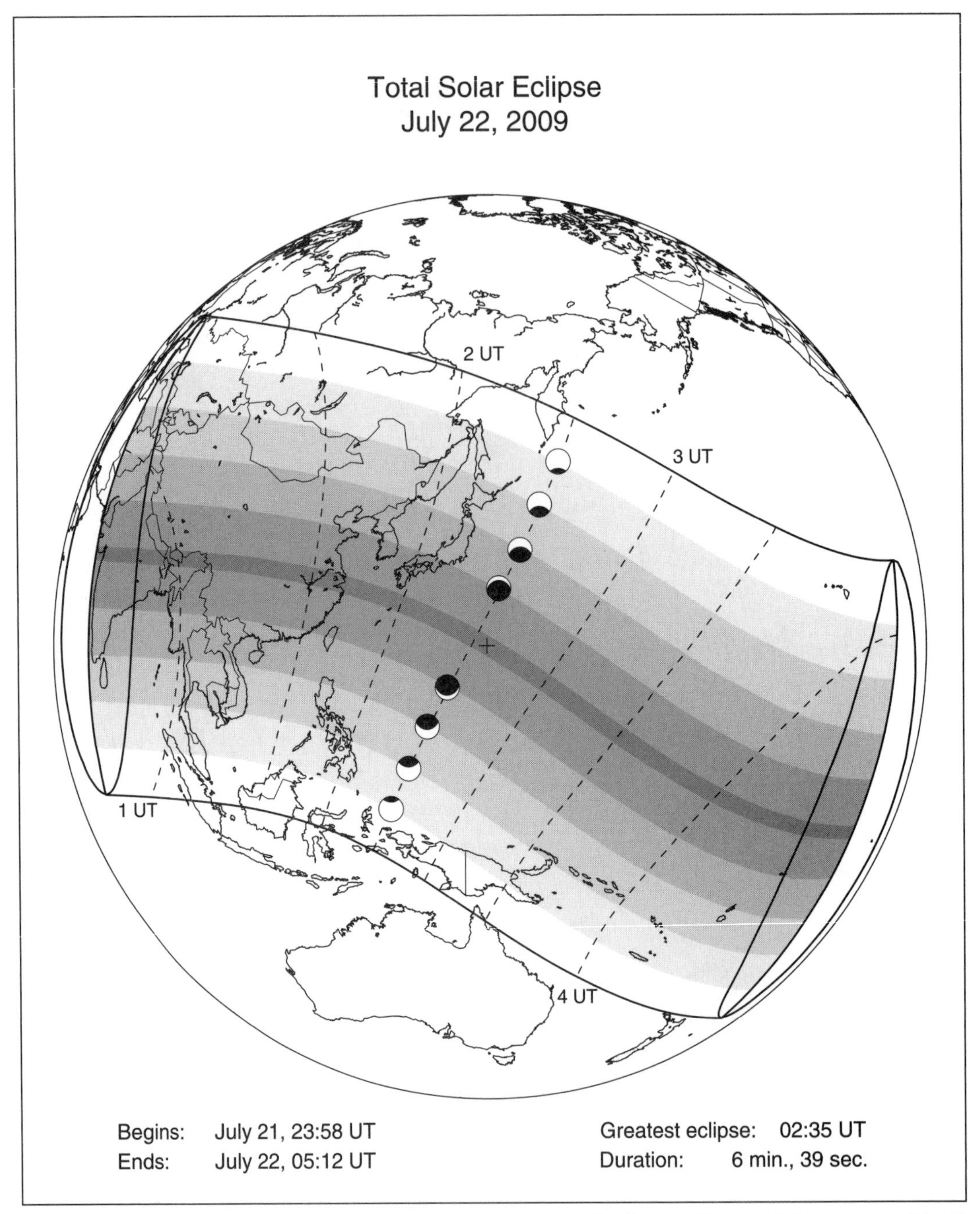

Figure 4-22. Saros 136 produced six of the seven longest-lasting total eclipses of the twentieth century and it will generate three of this century's longest spans of totality. The first and longest of those three will occur on July 22, 2009. The umbra will touch down in the Arabian Sea and move eastward across India. Skywatchers at Sirat (0:51 UT) and Indore (0:52 UT) will see more than three minutes of darkness shortly after sunrise. Moments later the shadow will bring over two minutes of totality to Thimphu, the capital city of Bhutan. Sweeping across China, the shadow will fall first on Wuhan (1:24 UT, five and a half minutes of totality) and then Shanghai (1:37 UT, for five minutes) before it passes into the East China Sea. It will sweep over Japan's Ryukyu Islands (1:53 UT, totality lasts over six minutes) and move into the Pacific. Greatest eclipse will occur a couple of hundred miles northeast of Iwo Jima.

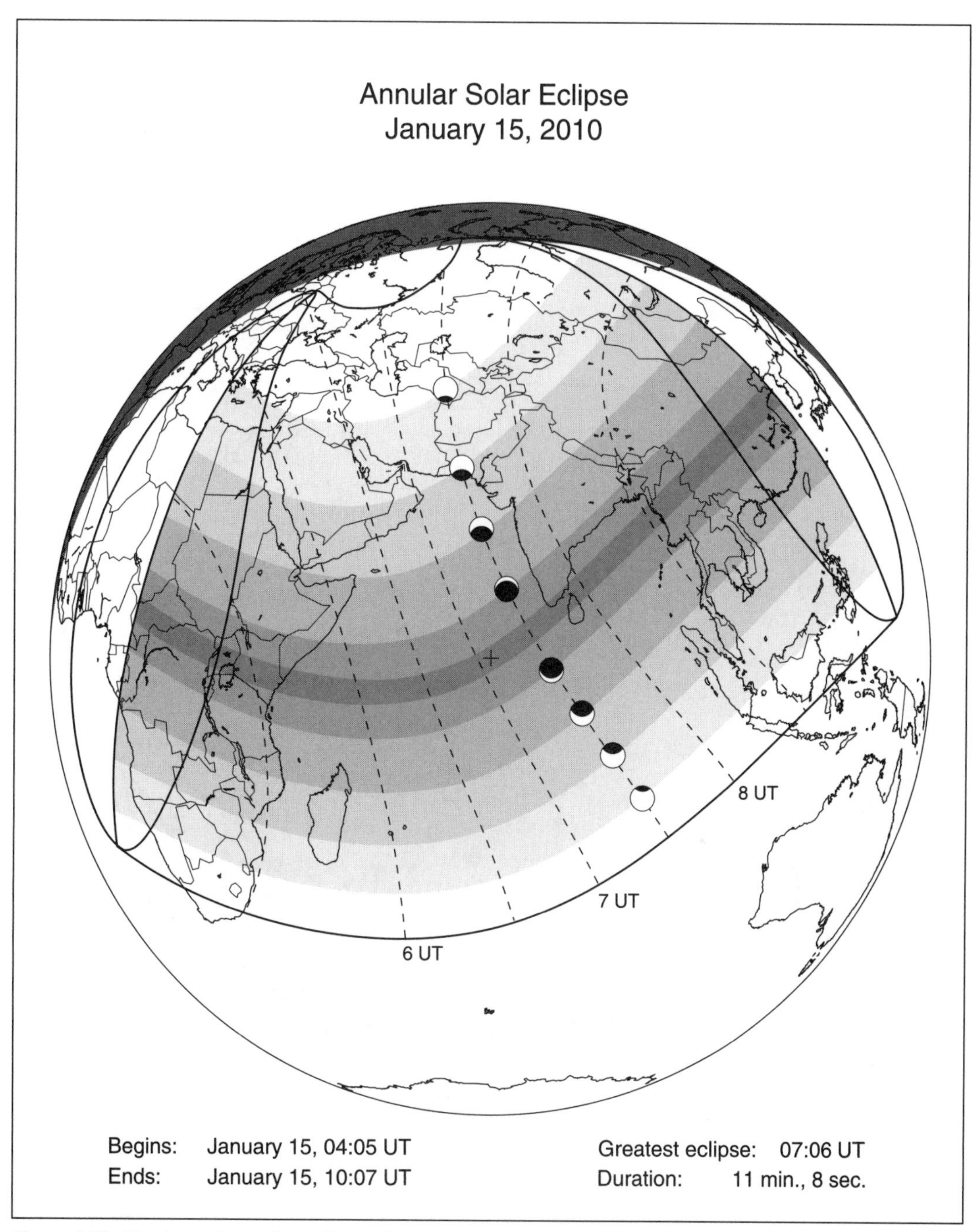

Figure 4-23. The longest annular eclipse of the millennium will occur on January 15, 2010. An early morning annulus will appear to observers in the capital cities of three African nations: Bangui, Central African Republic (5:15 UT, annular duration of four minutes); Kampala, Uganda (5:21 UT, over seven and a half minutes of annularity); and Nairobi, Kenya (5:26 UT, annular duration of almost seven minutes). Greatest eclipse will occur in the Indian Ocean. Shortly thereafter, the shadow will bring over ten and a half minutes of annularity to Male, Maldives (7:20 UT). It will then glide over southernmost India and cross the Bay of Bengal. The shadow will make landfall near the coastal city of Sittwe in Burma (maximum eclipse at 8:32 UT), and will sweep into China before leaving the Earth's surface. This eclipse is a member of Saros 141.

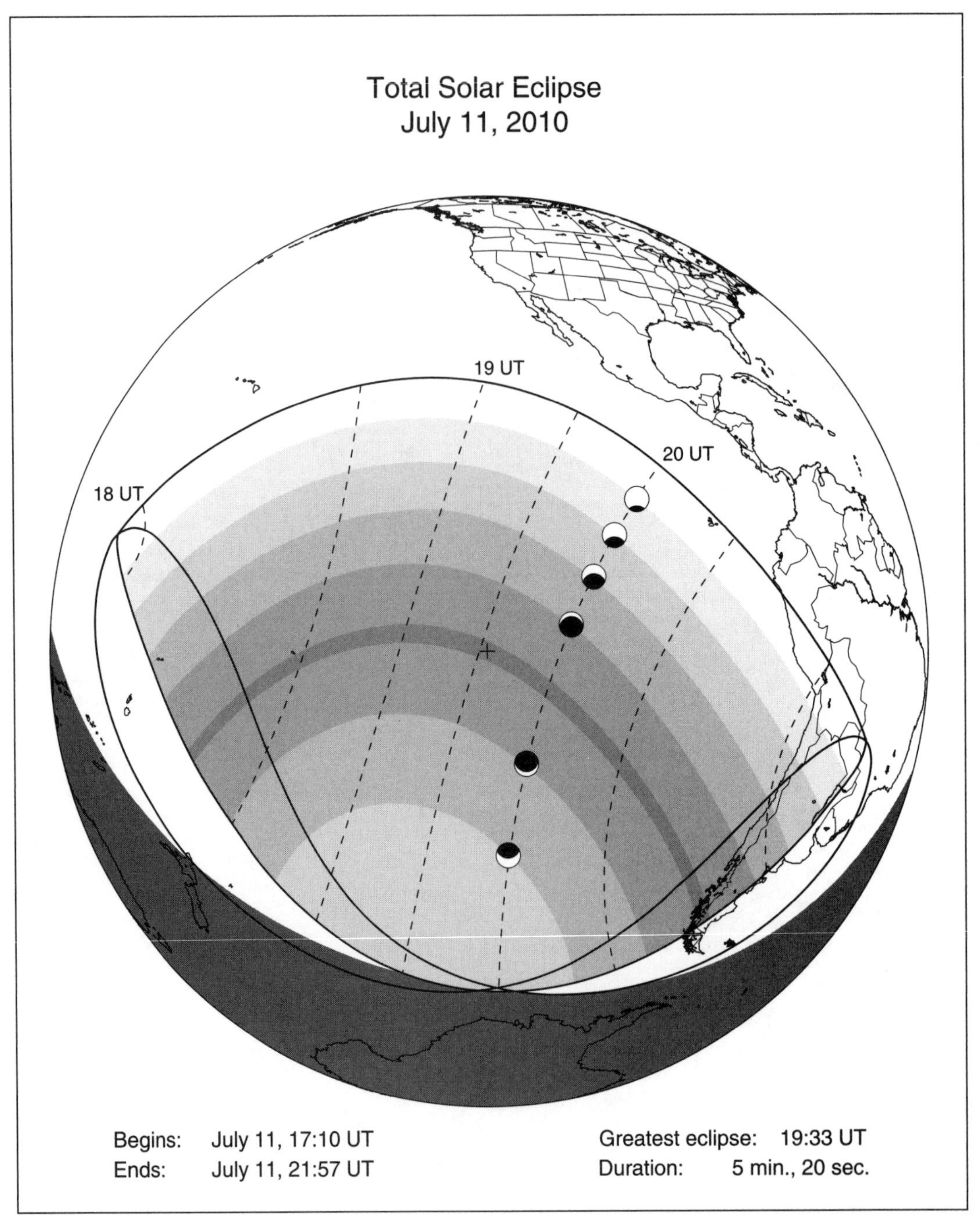

Figure 4-24. The moon's umbra will arc over the southern Pacific Ocean on July 11, 2010. The path of totality passes just south of Tahiti at 18:27 UT, but ten minutes later skywatchers on a few islands of the Tuamotu Archipelago will see up to four minutes of totality. Greatest eclipse will occur in mid-ocean. The moon's shadow will next make landfall on Easter Island (maximum eclipse at 20:11 UT, totality lasting nearly five minutes). From there the umbra sweeps through open ocean until it reaches Wellington Island, Chile, where observers will see the setting sun darken for almost three minutes at 20:48 UT. The shadow will pass into Argentina before leaving the Earth's surface. This eclipse is a member of Saros 146.

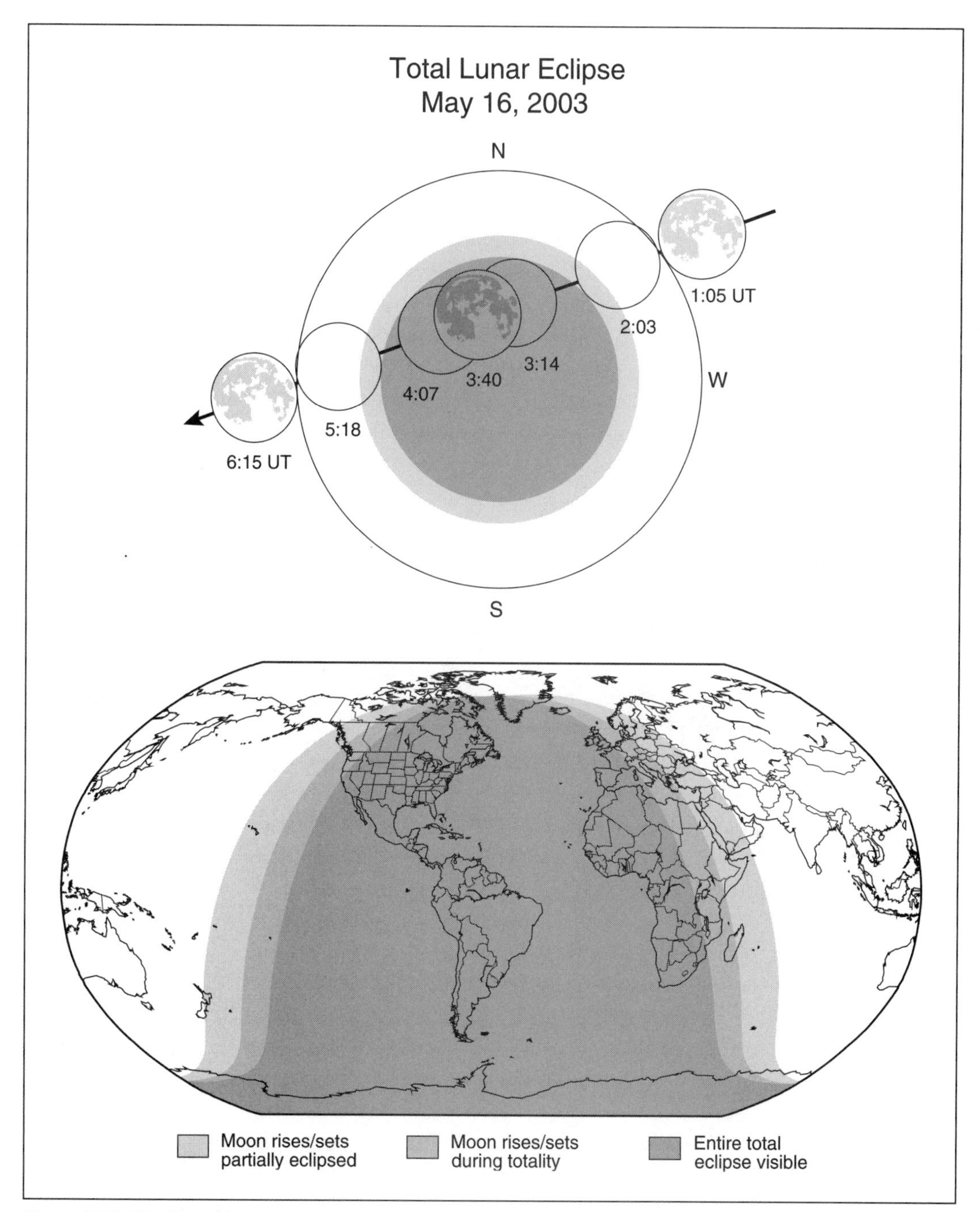

Figure 4-25. The first of four consecutive total lunar eclipses will take place on May 16, 2003. It will begin on the evening of May 15 for North Americans, with mid-eclipse occurring at 3:40 UT. Top: The drawing shows the moon's position and times of contact with the Earth's penumbra (outer circle) and umbra (inner circle) throughout the eclipse; note that east and west are reversed on the sky. Bottom: The shaded areas on the map illustrate where in the world skywatchers will see the moon in the umbra. Observers in western Europe, Africa, South America, and much of North America will see totality in its entirety. From the Pacific Northwest and Tahiti, the moon will rise already totally eclipsed; from Germany, Italy, and a band of western Africa, the moon will set before totality ends. In Hawaii, Samoa, and part of New Zealand the moon will rise after it has begun its exit from the umbra; in eastern Europe and the Middle East the moon sets before it has completely entered the umbra. This is a member of lunar eclipse Saros 121.

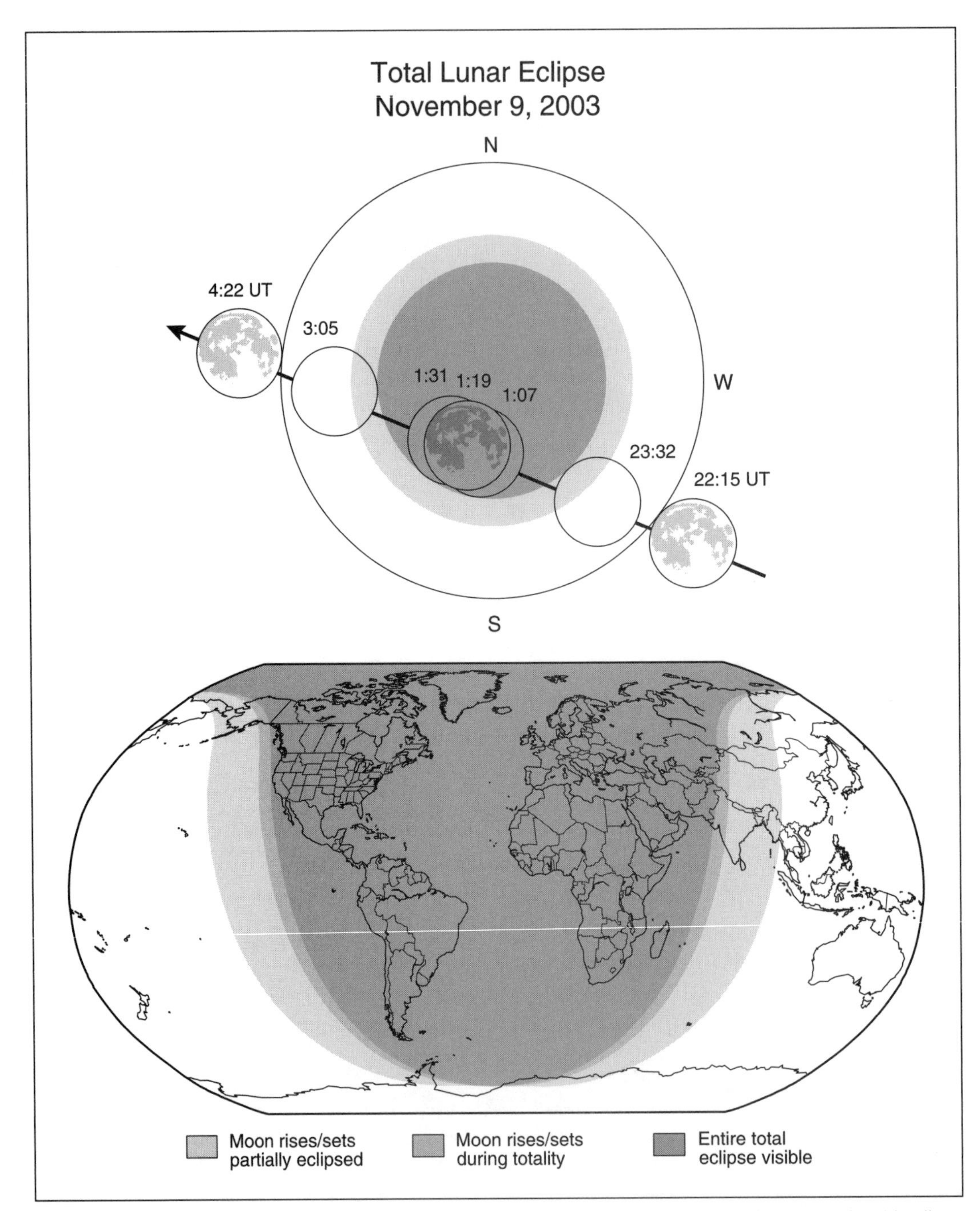

Figure 4-26. The moon will enter Earth's umbra on the evening of November 8 for North Americans. At mid-eclipse (1:19 UT), observers will find the Pleiades to the east of the darkened moon; Mars will shine brightly in the south. Top: The drawing shows the moon's position and times of contact with the Earth's penumbra (outer circle) and umbra (inner circle) throughout the eclipse. Bottom: The shaded areas on the map illustrate where in the world skywatchers will see the moon in the umbra. Observers in South America, most of North America, Africa, Europe, and eastern and central Asia will see the moon's complete passage through the umbra. From India, eastern China, and much of Alaska, only the moon's entrance into or exit from the umbra will be visible. This event is part of the Saros 126 family of lunar eclipses.

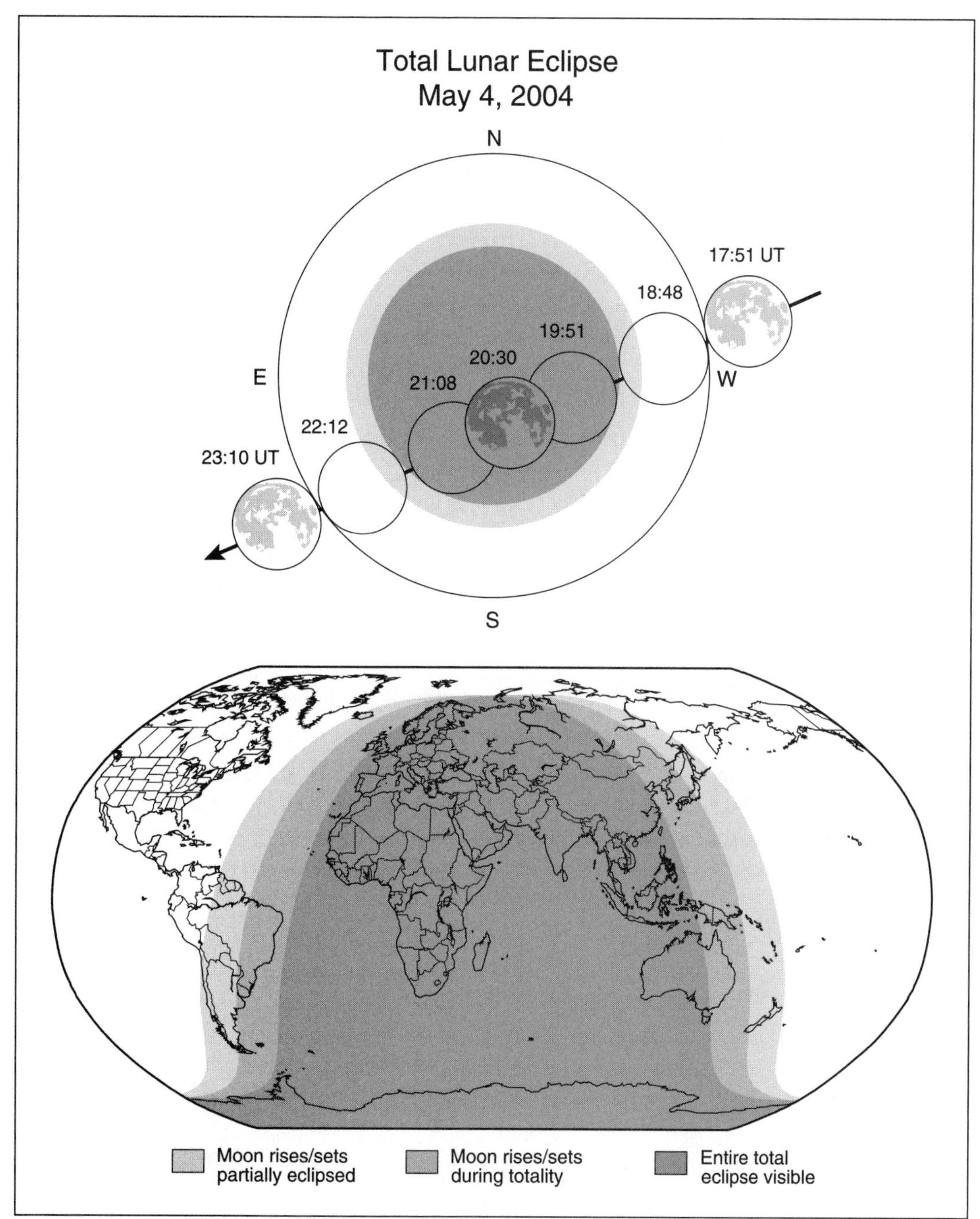

Figure 4-27. The moon will pass through the Earth's umbra on May 4, 2004. Top: The drawing shows the moon's position and times of contact with the Earth's penumbra (outer circle) and umbra (inner circle) throughout the eclipse. Bottom: The shaded areas on the map illustrate where in the world skywatchers will see the moon in the umbra. The moon's entire umbral passage will be visible from western Australia, most of Indonesia, most of Asia and Europe, and all of Africa. The moon will rise in total eclipse as seen from Ireland, Scotland, the Azores, eastern Brazil, and the Falkland Islands. It will set during totality as seen from eastern China, Korea, southern Japan, Papua New Guinea, and eastern Australia. Skywatchers in central South America will see the moon rise after it has begun its exit from the umbra. Observers in Vanuatu, New Caledonia, and most of Japan and New Zealand will see the moon set before it completely enters the umbra. This eclipse is a member of Saros 131.

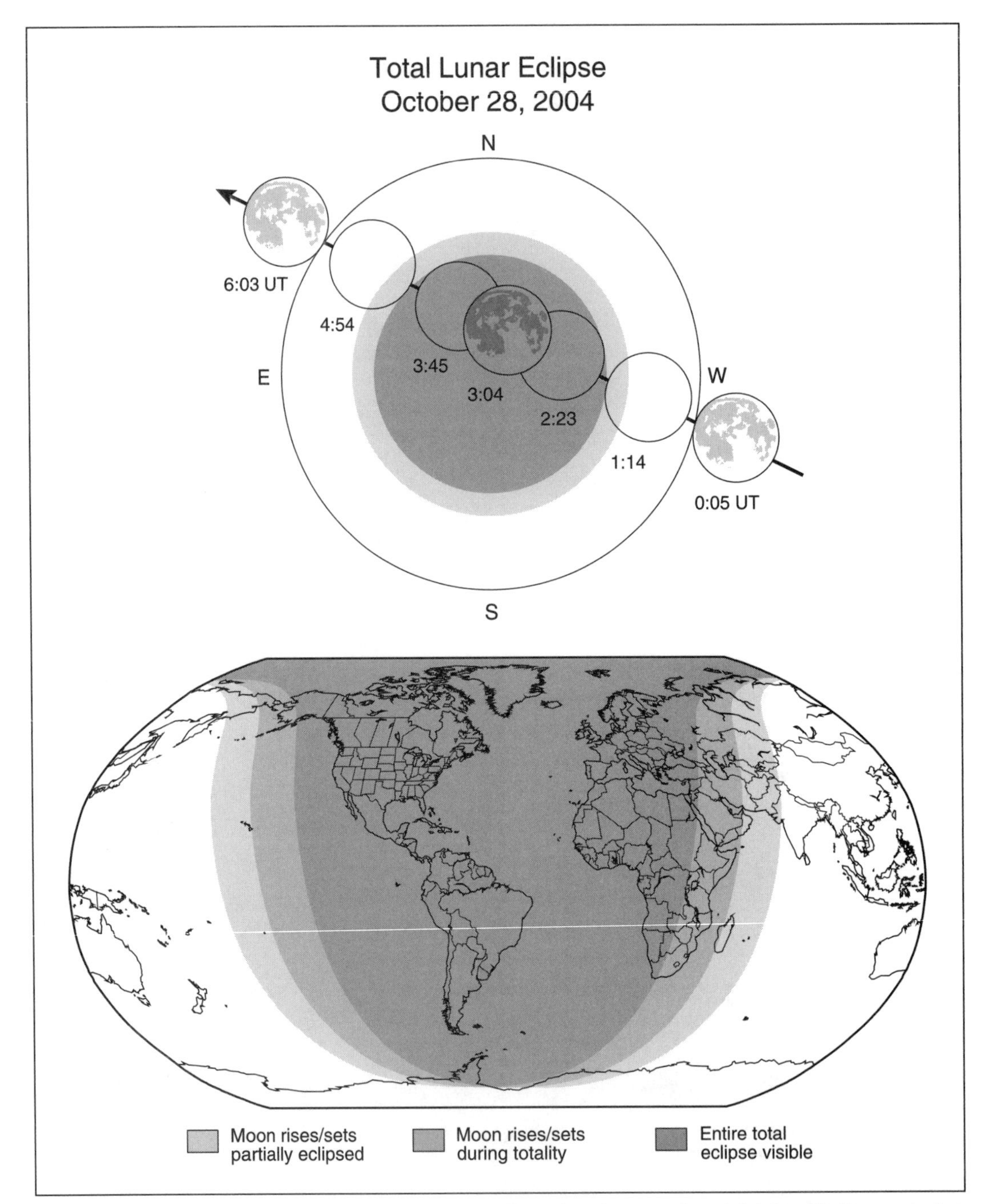

Figure 4-28. The moon enters the Earth's umbra on the North American evening of October 27, the concluding event of the total lunar eclipse tetrad of 2003 and 2004. Mid-eclipse will occur at 3:04 UT. Top: The drawing shows the moon's position within the Earth's penumbra (outer circle) and dark umbra (inner circle) throughout the eclipse. Bottom: The shaded areas on the map illustrate where in the world skywatchers will see the moon in the umbra. The moon's entire umbral passage will be visible from Iceland, Europe, the western two-thirds of Africa, and nearly all of North and South America. The moon will rise in total eclipse as seen from westernmost Alaska; it sets during totality as seen from eastern Africa and the Middle East. As seen from Hawaii and Tahiti, moonrise will occur after the moon has already begun its exit from the umbra; from Madagascar, Oman, Afghanistan, and Pakistan, the moon will set before its complete immersion into Earth's umbra. This event is part of the Saros 136 family of lunar eclipses.

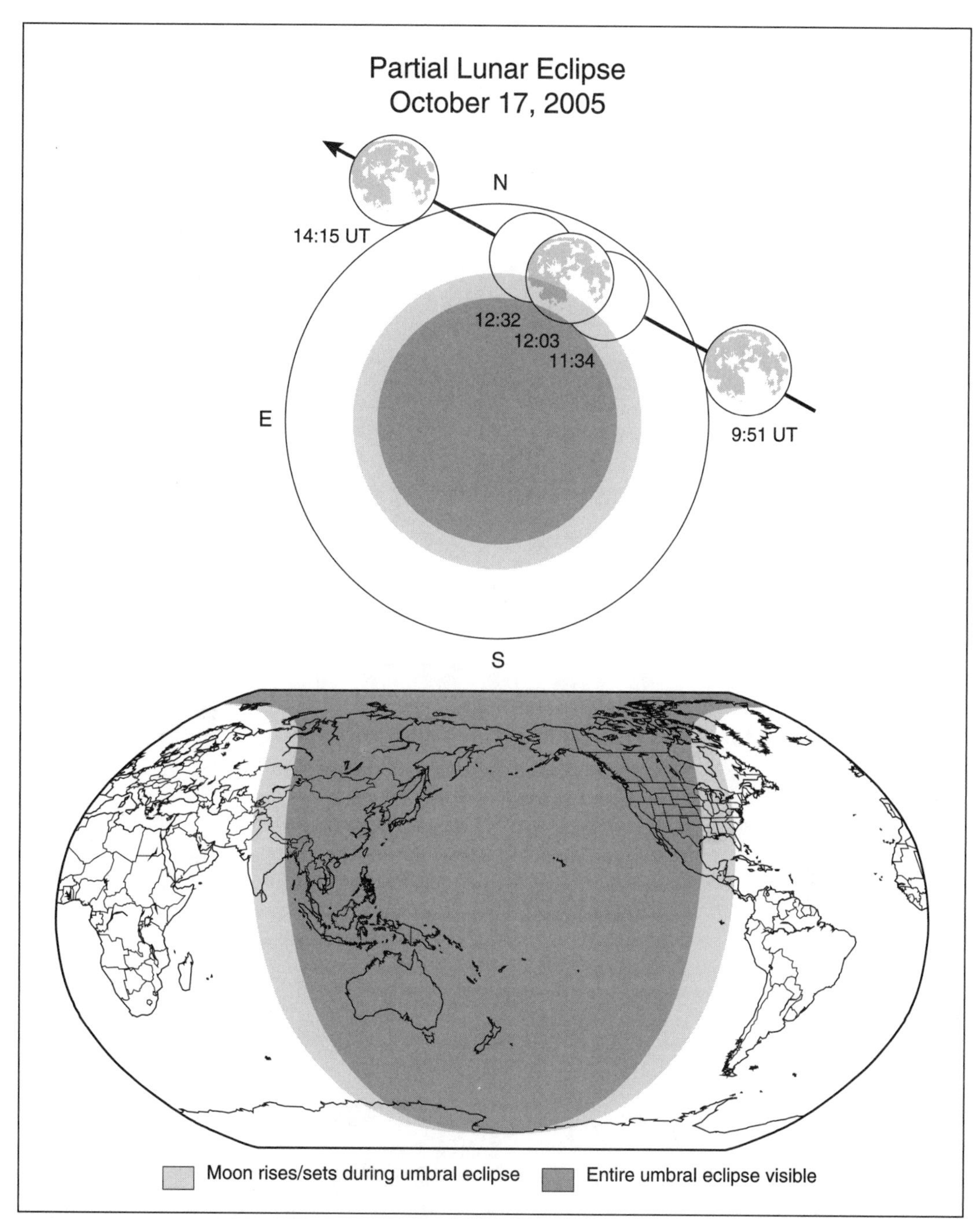

Figure 4-29. The moon will graze the darkest portion of the Earth's shadow on October 17, 2005; mid-eclipse will occur at 12:03 UT. Top: The drawing shows the moon's position within the Earth's penumbra (outer circle) and dark umbra (inner circle) throughout the eclipse. Bottom: The shaded areas on the map illustrate where in the world skywatchers will see the moon in the umbra. Observers in Hawaii, New Zealand, Australia, Indonesia, the eastern half of Asia, and the western half of North America see the moon's complete umbral passage. This eclipse is a member of Saros 146.

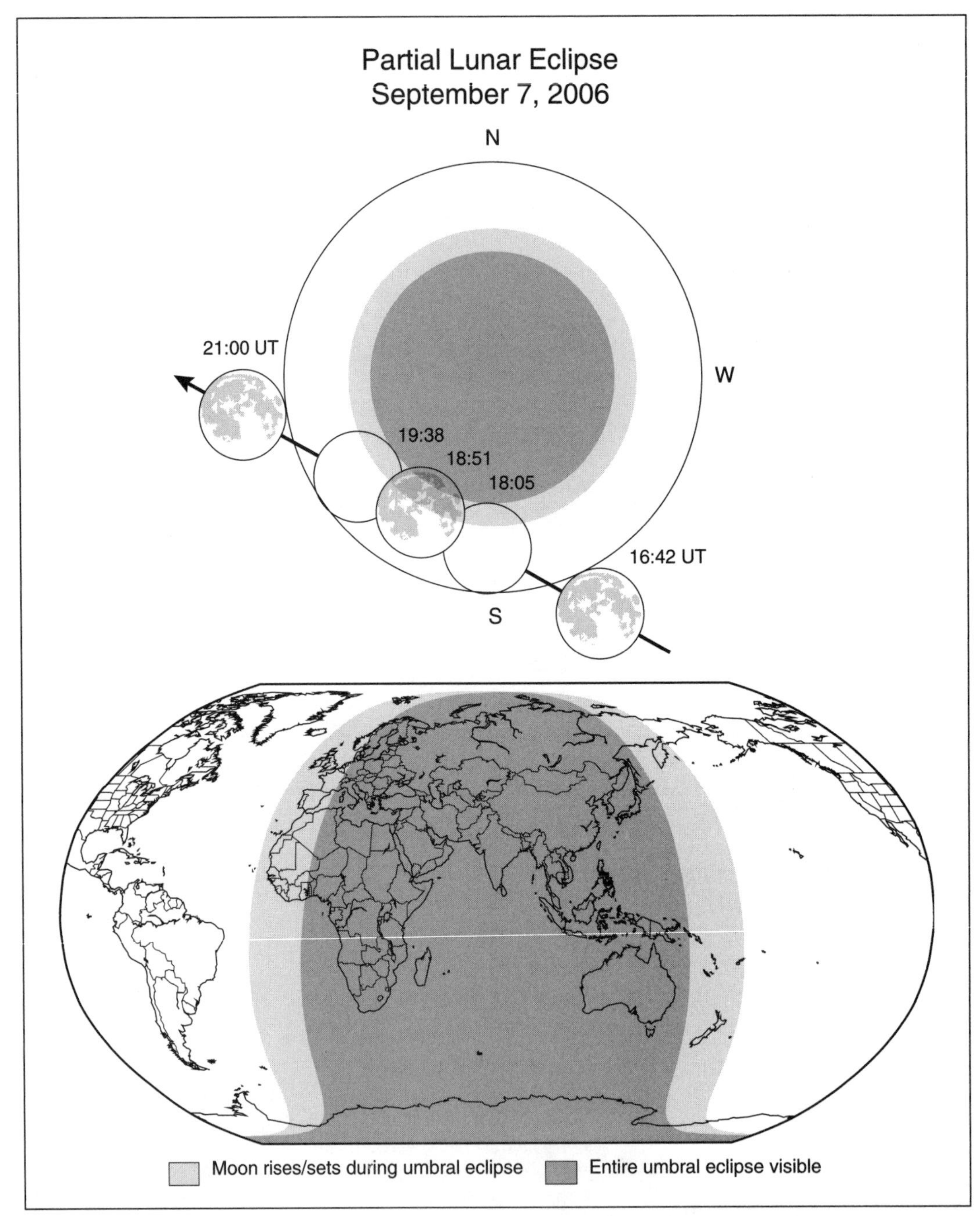

Figure 4-30. A partial lunar eclipse will occur on September 7, 2006. Top: The drawing shows the moon's position within the Earth's penumbra (outer circle) and dark umbra (inner circle) throughout the eclipse. Bottom: The shaded areas on the map illustrate where in the world skywatchers will see the moon in the umbra. The moon's complete passage through the umbra will be visible from central Europe, the eastern two-thirds of Africa, Indonesia, Australia, and most of Asia. New Zealand observers will see entry into the umbra before the moon sets; the western third of Africa will see the rising moon already immersed. Saros 118 produces this eclipse.

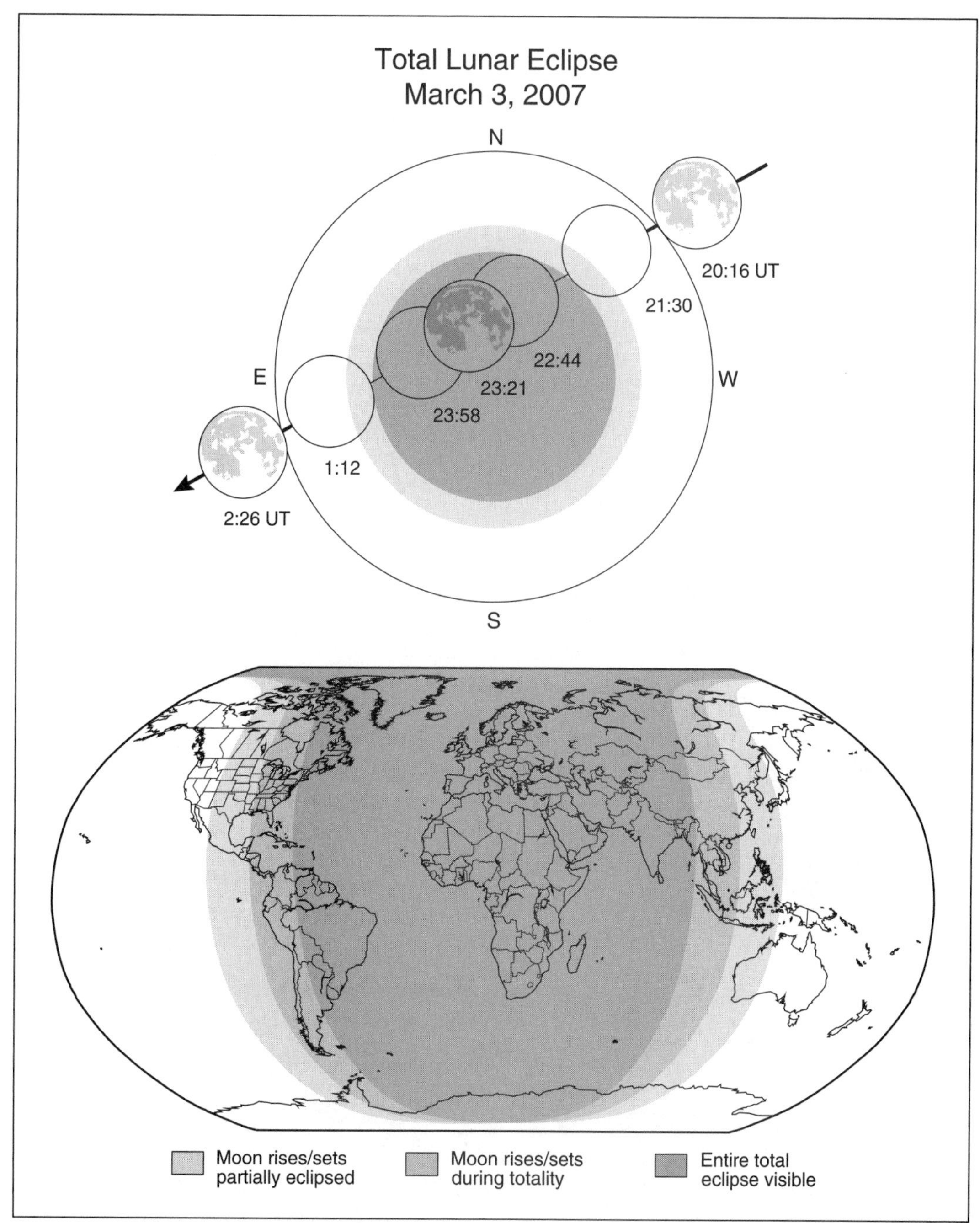

Figure 4-31. March 3, 2007, brings us the first total lunar eclipse in two and a half years. Mid-eclipse occurs at 23:21 UT, which translates to early evening for North American observers. Top: The drawing shows the moon's position within the Earth's penumbra (outer circle) and dark umbra (inner circle) throughout the eclipse. Bottom: The shaded areas on the map illustrate where in the world skywatchers will see the moon in the umbra. Observers throughout Europe, Africa, and western Asia will see the moon's entire passage through the umbra, as will those in the eastern half of South America and the easternmost parts of the United States and Canada. The moon will rise during totality as seen from Cuba, the western half of South America, and part of the U.S. Midwest. The moon sets before totality will end as seen from Indonesia, southeastern Asia, and central China. The eclipse is a member of Saros 123.

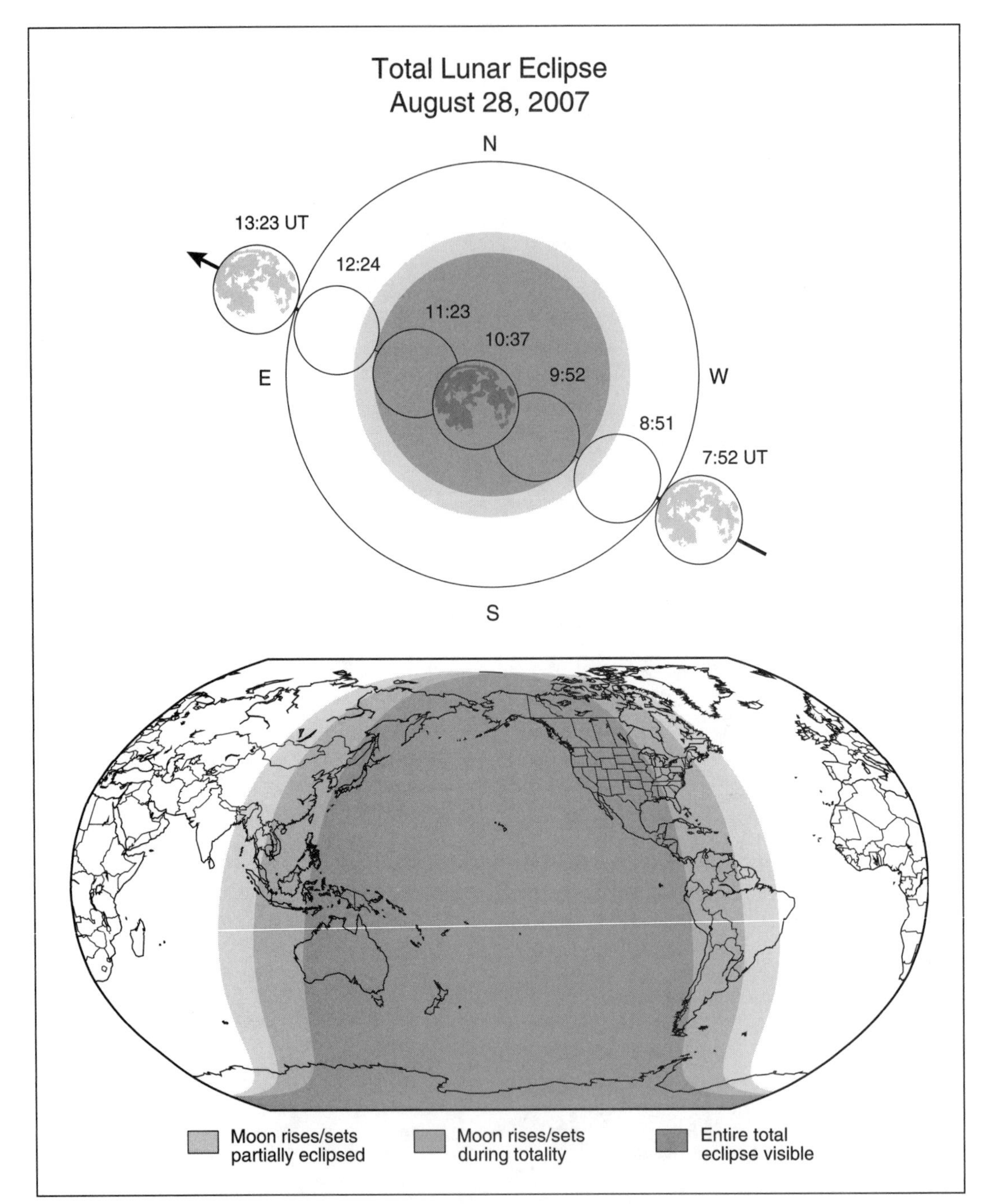

Figure 4-32. A total lunar cover-up will occur on August 28, 2007, with the moon in mid-eclipse at 10:37 UT. Top: The drawing shows the moon's position within the Earth's penumbra (outer circle) and dark umbra (inner circle) throughout the eclipse. Bottom: The shaded areas on the map illustrate where in the world skywatchers will see the moon in the umbra. All of the total phase of the eclipse will be visible throughout the Pacific Rim, including Japan, New Zealand, most of Australia, and western North America. Observers in Indonesia and eastern China will see the moon rise in totality; those in Cuba, the eastern third of the United States, and much of western South America will see moon set while still immersed completely in the umbra. Saros 128 produces this eclipse.

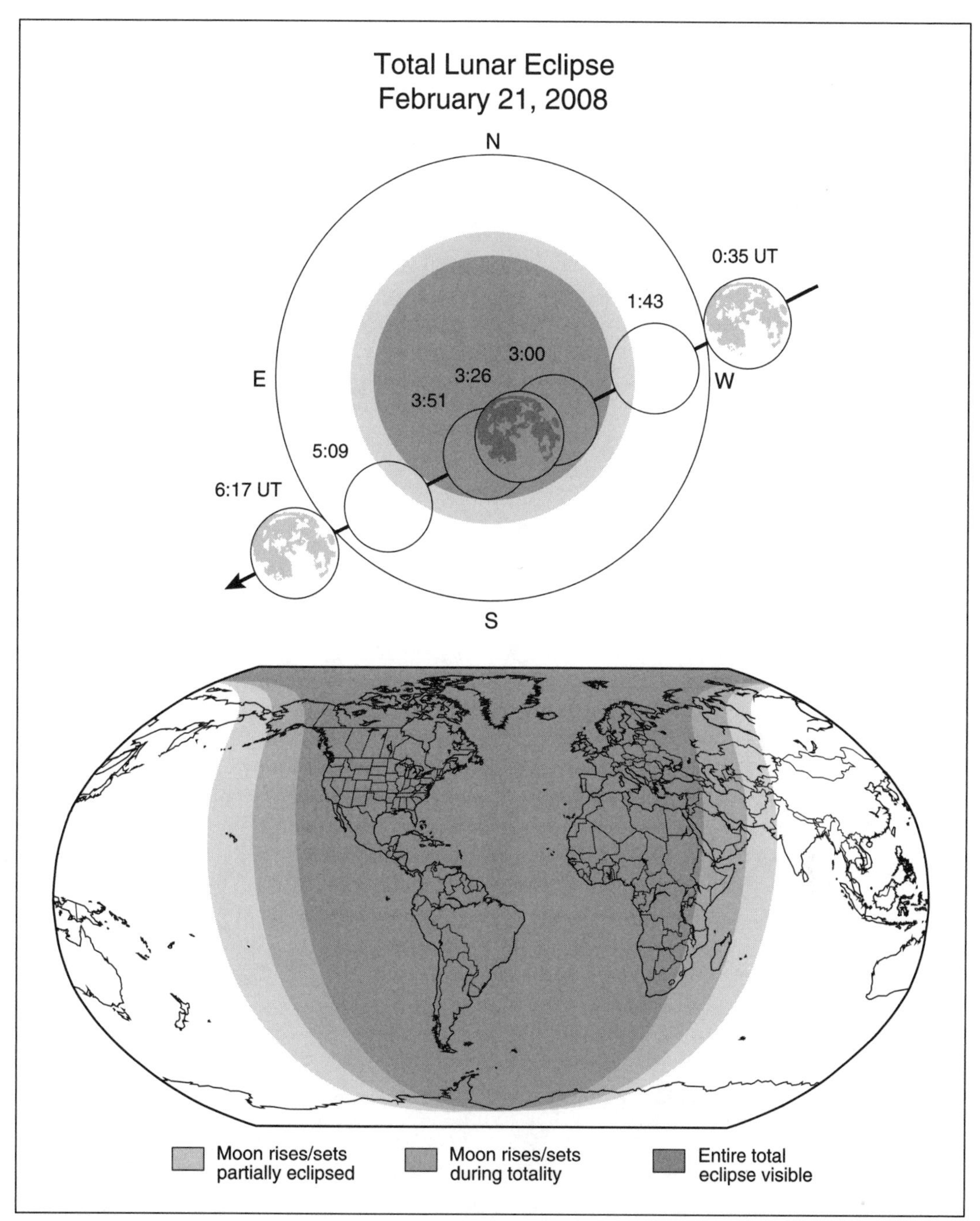

Figure 4-33. This eclipse will occur on the evening of February 20 for North Americans, all of whom will be able to see at least a portion of the moon's encounter with Earth's umbra. The darkness of mid-eclipse (3:26 UT) will reveal Saturn and the star Regulus flanking the ruddy moon. Top: The drawing shows the moon's position within the Earth's penumbra (outer circle) and dark umbra (inner circle) throughout the eclipse. Bottom: The shaded areas on the map illustrate where in the world observers will see the moon within the umbra. From all of North America (except western Alaska), South America, Europe, and the western two-thirds of Africa, the moon will be visible throughout its entire umbral passage. Western Alaska, Madagascar, and most of the Arabian Peninsula will see some portion of totality. Hawaii and Tahiti will see the moon rise after totality but still partially in shadow. Mauritius, Pakistan, and a band of central Asia will see the moon set before totality begins. The eclipse is a member of Saros 133.

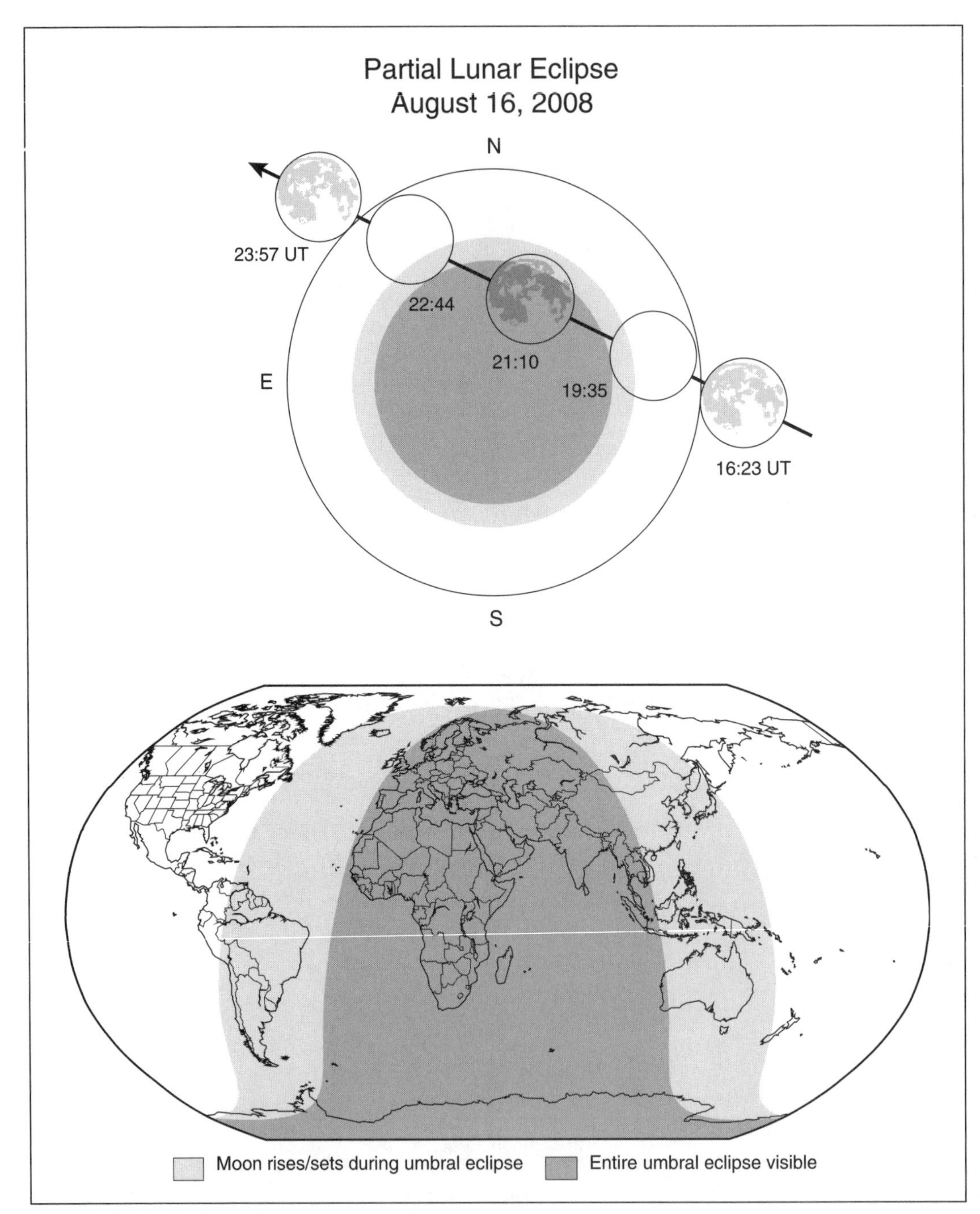

Figure 4-34. Saros 138 delivers a deep partial lunar eclipse to much of the eastern hemisphere on August 16, 2008 (mid-eclipse, 21:10 UT). Top: The drawing shows the moon's position within the Earth's penumbra (outer circle) and dark umbra (inner circle) throughout the eclipse. Bottom: The shaded areas on the map illustrate where in the world observers will see the moon within the umbra. Skywatchers in all of Africa, India, central Asia, westernmost Australia, and most of Europe will be able to watch the moon's motion through the umbra from start to finish. Observers located in Indonesia and eastern China, as well as those in most of Japan, Australia, and South America, will see the moon rise or set in partial eclipse.

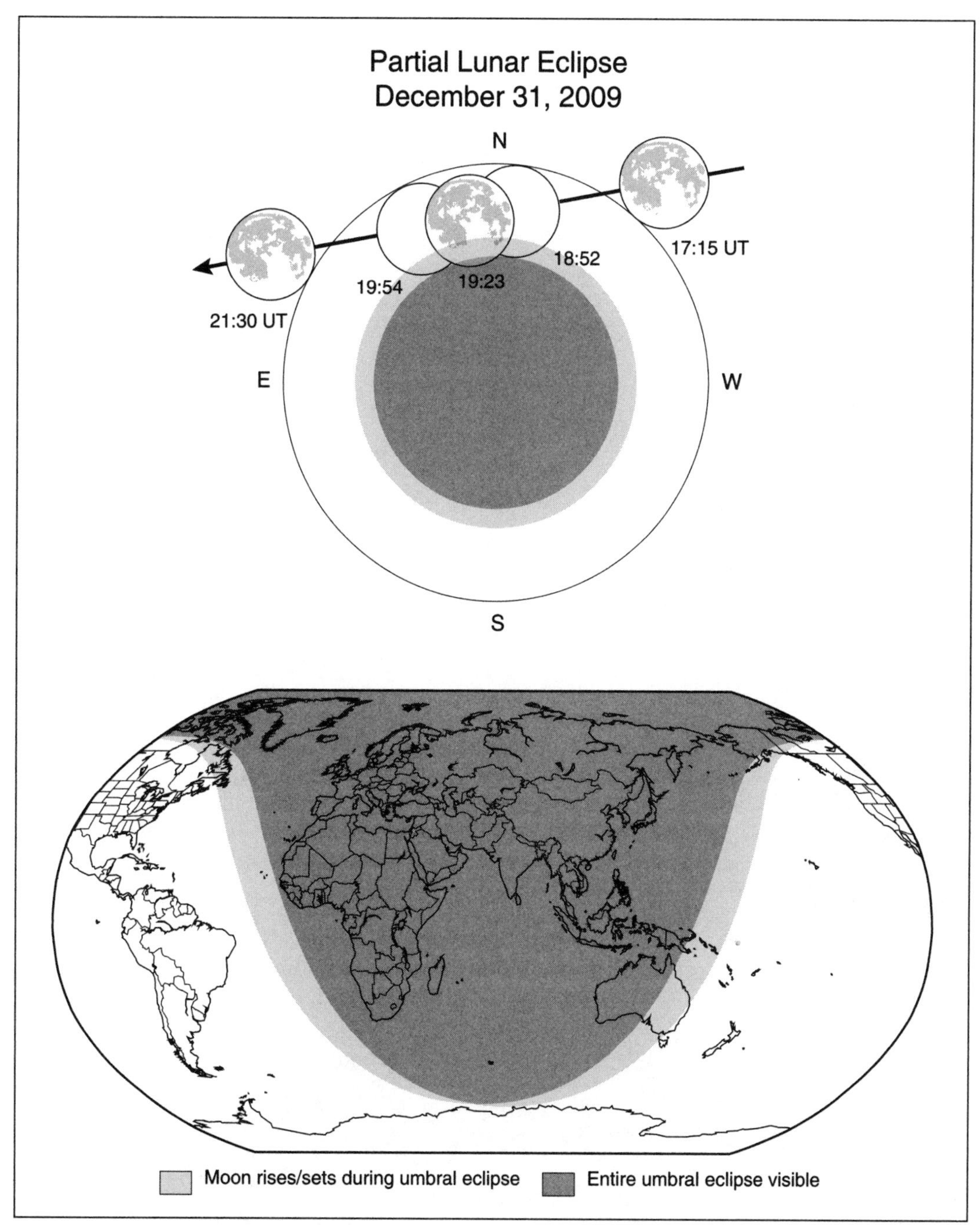

Figure 4-35. Following a trio of eclipses where the moon traversed only the Earth's penumbra, the moon will graze the umbra for a partial eclipse on December 31, 2009 (mid-eclipse at 19:23 UT, Saros 115). Top: The drawing shows the moon's position within the Earth's penumbra (outer circle) and dark umbra (inner circle) throughout the eclipse. Bottom: The shaded areas on the map illustrate where in the world observers will see the moon within the umbra. The moon's entire voyage through the umbra will be visible from all of Africa, Europe, Asia, Indonesia, the western half of Australia, and most of Alaska. Skywatchers on the Cape Verde Islands, the northeastern reaches of Canada, and the eastern half of Australia will see the moon rise or set while still in the umbra.

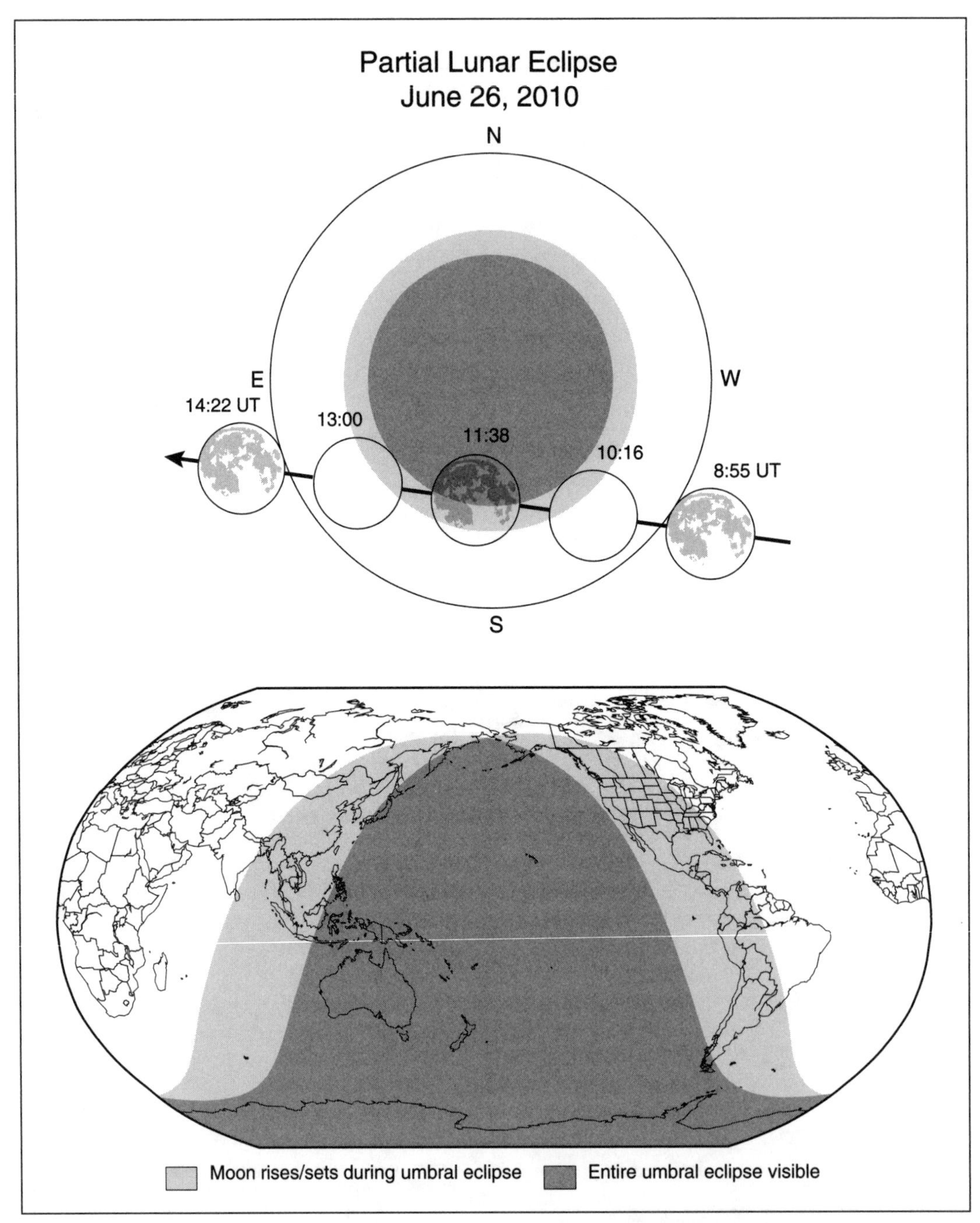

Figure 4-36. The moon will pass into Earth's umbra for a modest partial eclipse on June 26, 2010 (mid-eclipse at 11:38 UT, Saros 120). Top: The drawing shows the moon's position within the Earth's penumbra (outer circle) and dark umbra (inner circle) throughout the eclipse. Bottom: The shaded areas on the map illustrate where in the world skywatchers will see the moon within the umbra. Observers in Australia and the islands of the Pacific—Hawaii, Tahiti, Fiji, Samoa, New Zealand, Papua New Guinea, Vanuatu, and most of Japan and the Philippines—will see the entire umbral eclipse. Those in eastern Asia and the western halves of North and South America will see the moon rise or set while still in the umbra.

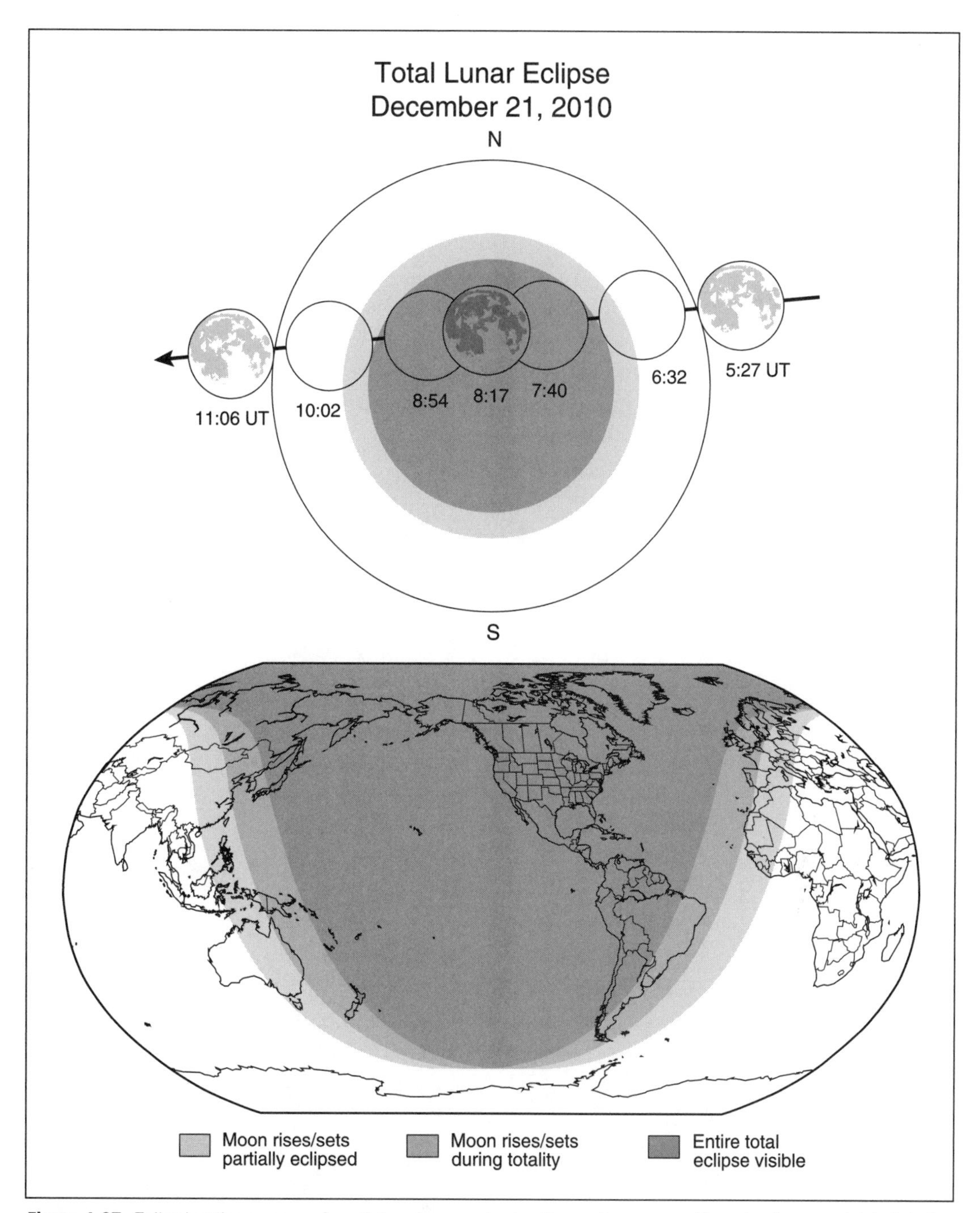

Figure 4-37. Following three years of partial and penumbral eclipses, the moon will again slip completely into the Earth's umbra on December 21, 2010 (a member of Saros 125, mid-eclipse at 8:17 UT). It's a pre-dawn event for North Americans. Top: The drawing shows the moon's position within the Earth's penumbra (outer circle) and dark umbra (inner circle) throughout the eclipse. Bottom: The shaded areas on the map illustrate where in the world observers will see the moon within the umbra. Skywatchers throughout North America, the Caribbean, Hawaii, Tahiti, Samoa, Fiji, Vanuatu, and in most of Japan and South America will witness totality from beginning to end. The moon will rise in total eclipse as seen from Korea and northeastern China, Papua New Guinea, and most of New Zealand; it will set before totality ends as seen from western Europe, the Canary and Cape Verde Islands, and the easternmost portion of South America. The moon's entrance into or exit from the umbra will be visible to observers in central China, the Philippines, Tasmania, eastern Australia, western Africa, and central Europe.

5 Mars: The Red Wanderer

To account for these phenomena, the explanation that at once suggests itself is, that a direct transference of water takes place over the face of the planet, and that the canals are so many waterways.

—Percival Lowell, *Mars,* 1895

At the close of the nineteenth century, Mars was imagined to be the most likely abode of extraterrestrial life. The available science hinted that conditions on its surface were similar to those on Earth. Observations of unusual linear surface features by some of the leading astronomers of the day ultimately led one to promote fanciful notions of a dying martian race trying to irrigate its desert world. Even among scientists, the belief that Mars should have *some* form of life proved hard to shake—as late as the 1950s, some astronomers felt that color changes detected on the martian surface were best explained by the seasonal growth of vegetation. By the mid-1970s, microscopic life was the most advanced organism anyone seriously expected to find there, but biological experiments sent to the surface detected nothing. More recently, in 1996, investigators claimed to have found microscopic fossils in a meteorite thought to have come from Mars. Over the course of the century, in the face of growing knowledge of actual conditions on the planet, proponents have had to scale back the complexity of any imagined martian life.

While the early speculation about martian civilization was quickly discredited, the idea rippled through popular culture and inspired writers from H. G. Wells to Ray Bradbury. Their stories fueled the public imagination about the possibilities of alien contact. In contrast to the declining prospects for martian biology seen over the past century, a 1999 Gallup poll found that more than a third of Americans believe some form of life exists there today.

Long before it was considered a home to extraterrestrials, Mars had established itself in the human imagination. Its reddish coloring, which contrasts beautifully with the deep blue of a twilight sky, is unique among the planets. Mars also undergoes exceptional changes in brightness within a single apparition—and its peak brightness varies from one appearance to the next. Near the time when Mars shines best, a point called opposition, it takes a seemingly chaotic whirl through the starry sky. Every planet makes one of these retrograde loops, but that of Mars is by far the most obvious and dramatic. Its distinctive color, remarkable brightness variations, and bizarre sky motion combine to make Mars the most outstanding of the "wanderers." So, in both a cultural and an astronomical sense, Mars is the archetypal planet.

Mars seems anything but a wanderer when it first appears in the morning sky, just a faint orange "star" lingering for weeks above the eastern horizon. But a closer look shows that the background stars are progressing noticeably westward each week and Mars is holding its position against the trend—indeed, it is traveling eastward through the constellations. By the time Mars rises in the east around 9:00 P.M., it's moving very slowly, or not at all, through the background stars. When the Red Planet shines brightly in the south at midnight, it has managed to reverse course and is moving backward (westward) through the stars. And when it appears in the west after sunset, Mars again lingers in the sky as the background stars slip toward the sun. From its first visibility in the east before sunrise to its fade-out in western twilight, Mars cruises across two-thirds of the ecliptic.

The Ancient View

In Mesopotamia and the classical world, Mars was associated with gods of war: Nergal of the Babylonians, Ares of the Greeks, and, of course, the Roman Mars. Rome was believed to have a special relationship with Mars, for he fathered the mythical twins Romulus and Remus who founded the city. His name was given to the first month of the Roman calendar, March, but the Anglo-Saxon war god Tiw is the one who gives his name to the day of Mars: Tuesday. It's often said that the planet's association with war stems from its reddish appearance, suggestive of bloodshed, but Mars is really rather more orange than crimson. If color is an imperfect explanation, perhaps its idiosyncratic departure from the order of the heavens justifies its identification with war, which is itself a radical deviation from the ordinary rhythm of life.

Chinese astronomers called the planet Ying-huo (Dazzling or Sparkling Deluder) and Huoxing (Fire Star), a name that nicely evokes its ember-like hue. To them, Mars was a portent of a variety of troubles—including war—and astrological texts were quick to point to its color, as in this omen from the T'ang Dynasty (A.D. 618–907): "When Sparkling Deluder enters the Southern Dipper [eastern Sagittarius] and its color is like blood, there will be a drought." The Chinese thought Venus to be a better indicator of coming war, while Mars was more of a force of nature with judicial functions: "Sparkling Deluder is the Master of the Proprieties; when the proprieties are misdone, then the punishment issues from it." Other names that T'ang astronomers used for Mars—Star of Punishment, Holder to the Law—suggest just the opposite of the chaos of war.

Among the Skidi Pawnee of southeastern Nebraska, Mars was associated with Morning Star, a powerful god who created the sun to provide heat and light. Evening Star, or White Star Woman—probably associated with Venus—enticed Morning Star, but as soon as he moved toward her she placed many hurdles in his path. Only Morning Star was powerful enough to overcome these hardships and through their union they brought about the peopling of Earth. Every few years, when the need to appease Morning Star was great and the celestial signs were right, the Skidi Pawnee captured a maiden from a neighboring tribe. Her captor dedicated her to Morning Star by speaking his name—Opirikuts—and, after months of ceremonies, she was sacrificed to him to ensure the fertility of the land. Although earthly needs were probably most important in the timing of the sacrifice, the celestial wanderings of Mars and Venus together appear to have played a role as well.

The Maya of Mesoamerica also maintained an interest in the Red Planet. The principle aim of Mayan astronomical observation appears to have been the discovery of commensurate relationships between the seasons, their 260-day sacred calendar, and various other celestial cycles. In the case of Venus, such a cycle was relatively straightforward, but the erratic wanderings of Mars would seem to be another matter altogether. The Dresden Codex, one of four surviving Mayan texts, contains a table that was first identified as having something to do with Mars a century ago. It lists ten intervals of seventy-eight days each, a number close to the average time (seventy-five days) it takes Mars to execute a retrograde loop. The ten intervals together equal 780 days, very close to the planet's mean synodic period (see table 5-1), and that number happens to equal three cycles of the sacred calendar—just the sort of the thing that would catch the eye of Mayan

Table 5-1. Facts about Mars

Diameter:	4,217 miles (6,786 km) 53% that of Earth
Surface temperature:	Average: –64°F (–53°C) Range: –199°F (–128°C) during polar night to 80°F (27°C) on the equator at noon at perihelion
Surface atmospheric pressure:	~6 millibars, less than 1/150 that of Earth
Atmospheric composition:	95.3% carbon dioxide, 2.7% nitrogen, 1.3% argon, 0.13% oxygen, 0.08% carbon monoxide, 0.19% water and other trace gases
Moons:	Phobos Deimos
Rotation period:	24.62 hours
Obliquity:	25.19°
Sidereal orbital period:	686.98 days (1.88 years)
Synodic orbital period:	779.94 days (2.14 years) Longest of any planet
Mean distance from sun:	141.6 million miles (227.9 million km) 1.52 times that of Earth
Orbit inclined to Earth's:	1.85°

astronomers. They appear to have used the cycle as an aid in predicting when the planet would first be visible in the morning sky and when it would begin its unusual motion. But the time between these two events could vary widely between apparitions and no single cyclic relationship could take these changes into account.

Harvey and Victoria Bricker of Tulane University, together with Colgate University's Anthony Aveni, have called attention to another table in the Dresden Codex, one that reveals a particularly ingenious solution to the problem of tracking Mars. In a paper published in 2001, they argue that Mayan astronomers discovered two directly observable time cycles that together "not only accurately described the planet's motion, but also related it to other cosmic and terrestrial concerns." The longer cycle included the time Mars spent in its retrograde loop (702 days); the shorter cycle (about 543 days) did not. They then linked multiples of these periods together to arrive at a simple and practical formula: 7 long + 1 short + 7 long + 1 short + 8 long + 1 short; thereafter, the pattern repeats. The twenty-five time spans represented in this sequence contain nearly the same number of days it takes for Mars to revolve around the sun twenty-five times, so the formula tracks Mars relative to the stars and the seasonal year. The values chosen for the long and short intervals are less precise than they could be, probably so that they would be commensurate with the 780-day synodic period. Both the synodic period and the long interval are even multiples of seventy-eight, and the short interval very nearly is, too. A Mayan astronomer could think of all of these cycles as built from different numbers of seventy-eight-day units. Finally, the last four terms of the Mars formula match the number of days in twenty synodic Venus cycles to within about one day. Remarkably, the Maya found an empirical way to integrate the Red Planet's errant synodic motions with the seasonal year, their own sacred calendar, and even the appearances of Venus.

As Western philosophers took up the challenge of explaining the causes of planetary motion, Mars proved to be a dazzling deluder indeed. The problem has three parts. First, the planets do not move at constant rates; second, they vary in brightness; finally, they actually change direction

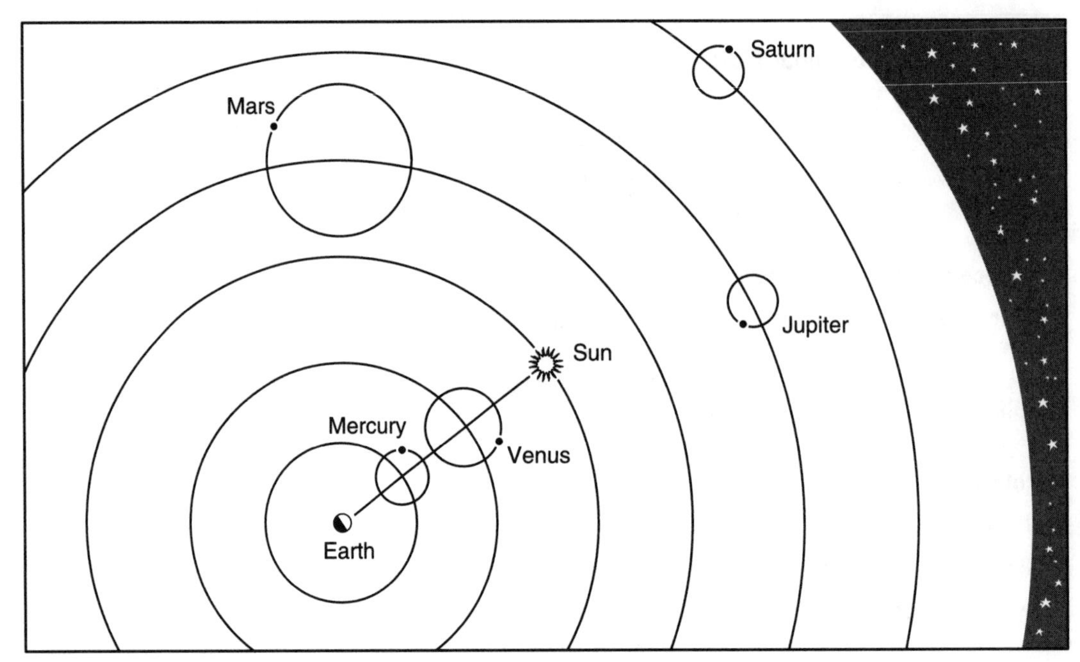

Figure 5-1. The Ptolemaic system of deferents and epicycles could explain the motions of Mars. Carried around the Earth on its deferent, the planet also revolves on a separate circle called an epicycle. Mars appears to move backward when it passes through the half of the epicycle nearest Earth.

occasionally, temporarily plying that retrograde or westward path before resuming their normal eastward motion. As we have seen, these variations are especially dramatic for Mars.

The Greeks were the first to attempt a theoretical framework that explained the motions of the planets. Constrained by the purely philosophical considerations of Plato (c. 427–327 B.C.), Greek cosmologists allowed the planets to move around the Earth only in perfect circles and only at a constant velocity. The earliest such system was devised by one of Plato's students, Eudoxus of Cnidus, in the fourth century B.C. He placed the planets on concentric spheres centered on the Earth. The sun and moon each required three moving spheres, the planets required four apiece, and a single sphere held the stars. Callippus (c. 370–300 B.C.), a student of Eudoxus, later refined the system by adding another seven spheres; another of Plato's students, Aristotle (384–322 B.C.), made further refinements that brought the total to fifty-five.

"It was an extremely ingenious system," wrote historian Arthur Koestler, "and completely mad, even by contemporary standards; as shown by the fact that in spite of Aristotle's enormous prestige, it was quickly forgotten and buried." Although imprecise, the nested-spheres models offered at least qualitative agreement with the peculiarities of planetary motion—but they failed to account for changes in appearance that today we know are caused by changing distances from the Earth. The dramatic brightness variations of Mars and Venus, and changes in the size of the moon made apparent by annular and total solar eclipses, were simply ignored. On the other hand, the fact that these models were even qualitatively successful could be seen as validating the dogma of uniform circular motion.

To be sure, there were other voices. Most notable was Aristarchus of Samos (c. 310 to c. 230 B.C.), the first to hold the radical view that the sun, not the Earth, lay at the center of the universe. A heliocentric system was intellectually repugnant because it went against the teachings of Plato and Aristotle, who argued that the Earth was immovable. Early sun-centered models retained circular orbits and uniform motion, but refining them would have proved much easier than refining Earth-centered theories. Instead, the heliocentric alternative lay fallow in antiquity—never completely forgotten, but also never percolating toward the mainstream of astronomical thought.

A geocentric system that enjoyed phenomenal success was the purely practical system of epicycles, sketched in simplified form in figure 5-1. Its two main proponents, Hipparchus of Nicea (fl. c. 125 B.C.) and Claudius Ptolemy (c. A.D. 90–168), focused more on merely computing planetary positions than on explaining the physical nature of the cosmos. To get around the limitation of uniform circular motion, Ptolemy arranged multiple circles of different sizes and allowed them to move at different speeds. The perfected system contained forty circles—the sun, moon, and planets rode on circular epicycles, which were set on larger circular *deferents* that spun around the central Earth. As clumsy as this may now seem, there was no arguing with the results tabulated using Ptolemy's system. Nothing better would come along until the seventeenth century.

In 1543, a Polish cleric named Mikolaj Kopernigk published *On the Revolution of the Heavenly Spheres,* a book that resurrected the idea of a sun-centered universe. We know him today as Nicolaus Copernicus (1473–1543), a physician, lawyer, church administrator and, in his spare time, an astronomer. He was neither an avid skywatcher—he disliked making observations—nor a revolutionary, choosing to publish his ideas only near the end of his life for fear of ridicule. His original motivation was to refine the Ptolemaic system. Instead, he came up with something new, crystallizing and formalizing the heliocentric ideas that had been casually discussed from the time of Aristarchus. Copernicus freed himself from the Aristotelian mandate of an unmoving Earth, but he retained uniform circular motion—so his system still needed epicycles, although fewer of them. Predictions derived from the Copernican model were at best only marginally better than those made within a Ptolemaic framework, and the motions of Mars remained equally flawed in both systems. Thus the initial response to the heliocentric hypothesis was one of surprising indifference—but as the century wore on and new discoveries called other elements of Aristotelian astronomy into question, the Copernican system took on greater importance.

One adherent of the new system was Johannes Kepler (1571–1630), an eccentric assistant to the most famous astronomer of the age, Tycho Brahe (1546–1601). Tycho rejected Copernicus's ideas but made his own observations in support of a model he was developing, which freed him from the slavish acceptance of classical astronomy that bedeviled many of his day. Among Tycho's best traits was a passion for accurate observation; his treatise on the new star of 1572 and the comet of 1577 spread his fame throughout Europe. Denmark's King Frederick II made nearly 1 percent of the Danish government's annual income available to Tycho for his research, a level of government support that astronomers since could only dream of. With this extraordinary funding he built on the island of Ven an extraordinary pair of observatories and a residence for himself and eight assistants, as well as a windmill, a paper mill, and fishing ponds. Here he recorded thousands of planetary and stellar positions, using high-quality instruments of his own design—the pinnacle of naked-eye observation.

Even before their meeting in 1600, Kepler realized the importance of Tycho's observations to any theory of planetary motion. He also understood that erratic Mars would be the planet to make or break any model of the solar system. "For Mars alone enables us to penetrate the secrets of astronomy which otherwise would remain forever hidden from us," he wrote. Kepler details his years of torturous work on the Red Planet—he calls it his "war against Mars"—in his book *The New Astronomy,* published in 1609. Tycho's observations ultimately led Kepler to two great discoveries: the planets move in ellipses, not circles, and their orbital speeds change predictably as their distances from the sun vary. (He would publish a third law of planetary motion nine years later.) "The sun will melt all the Ptolemaic apparatus like butter," wrote Kepler, "and the followers of Ptolemy will disperse partly into the camp of Copernicus, partly into the camp of Brahe." As with Copernicus, Kepler's book was not immediately appreciated for the groundbreaking work it contained. But near the end of his life he published tables for the calculation of planetary positions, all computed with his techniques and within a heliocentric framework, that set new standards for precision and placed the hypothesis of Copernicus on a firm observational and theoretical footing.

A Matter of Life

On the heels of Kepler's success a new tool, the telescope, became available to astronomers. Although the first telescopes were too crude to permit interesting discoveries on Mars, it wasn't long before improved instruments revealed a planet much more interesting than the bland Venus. By 1677 astronomers had discovered polar icecaps, along with bright and dark markings that were regarded as deserts and seas. These features allowed astronomers to measure the length of the martian day, which, at twenty-four hours, thirty-seven minutes, is remarkably similar to Earth's. The icecaps were seen to grow and shrink with the martian seasons, and the bright and dark patches also varied from year to year. These characteristics suggested a striking resemblance to Earth.

That resemblance was briefly enhanced by the "discovery" of another type of feature—the canals of Mars. They first appeared in the work of an Italian astronomer, Pietro Secchi, during the 1860s. He plotted several vague linear features on the planet and called them *canali* (channels). The term was picked up by Giovanni Schiaparelli (1835–1910), who during the close opposition of 1877 found them to be sharper, more distinct, and greater in number. "They traverse the planet for long distances in regular lines, that do not at all resemble the winding courses of our streams," he later wrote. At the next two oppositions Schiaparelli also reported that some of the canali appeared to double. Meanwhile other astronomers strained to see the canali at all. They were visible only under the best observing conditions, and successive Mars oppositions had brought the planet to more distant parts of its orbit, making detection more difficult.

Only as Mars returned to more favorable approaches, after 1886, did reports of canali—now translated into English as canals—begin again. Not all observers saw them and, perhaps more important, those who did were not always seeing the same ones. The scientific question of whether the lines were real features on the planet's surface or simply optical illusions had not yet been decided. But the possibility that the canals were indeed some sort of artificial geometric network propelled an intense burst of popular interest in astronomy as the favorable 1892 opposition drew closer. Even a few scientists found themselves caught up in the excitement. Camille Flammarion, a French astronomer and writer of popular science, announced in 1892 that "the present inhabitation of Mars by a race superior to ours is very probable."

One astronomer who heard of the canals, and subsequently believed he saw them, was Percival Lowell (1855–1916). Lowell soon became convinced that the canals were created by an advanced race of beings to irrigate the planet's vast deserts. The wealthy Bostonian built an observatory in Flagstaff, Arizona, specifically to acquire high-quality observations of the planet. Lowell catalogued over 180 canals, more than four times the number Schiaparelli had observed, and believed that he was seeing not the irrigation channels themselves but the strips of fertilized land that bordered them. He wrote three popular books expounding his theory of a martian civilization. (Another of Lowell's theories fared much better. He predicted the existence of a planet beyond Neptune, based on discrepancies in the orbits of Neptune and Uranus. In 1930, fourteen years after his death, astronomer Clyde Tombaugh discovered Pluto from the observatory Lowell founded. Interestingly, Pluto is not massive enough to have caused the discrepancies that led to its discovery and it's generally believed that the calculations showing them were flawed.)

The opinions of the scientific community were diverse. The canals were close to the resolution limit of telescopes at the time and many astronomers remained skeptical that the canals even existed, let alone that they served as proof of a martian civilization. Others accepted the canals but interpreted them as great cracks in the planet's crust. Still others argued that the canals were small geographical features blurred together by the turbulence of Earth's atmosphere. Today we know that the canal network was a product of the limited resolution of the telescopes at the time, the smearing effect of the atmosphere, and wishful thinking on the part of observers. The canals do not, in fact, correspond to any natural features on the planet.

Although by the 1920s astronomers had rejected any interpretation of the canals as artificial, they had no difficulty in believing the planet capable of plant or even animal life. Hope for animal life faded in the 1930s as it became clear that oxygen did not exist in any appreciable amount in the martian atmosphere. Plant life was still considered possible, if unlikely, by the end of World War II, and shortly thereafter a new discovery reinvigorated the search. In 1947 Gerard Kuiper (1905–1973) detected emissions from carbon dioxide, a key ingredient for photosynthesis by plants, in the martian atmosphere. Comparison of the dark grayish areas on Mars with different types of plants on Earth eliminated most possibilities, but Kuiper pointed out that lichens were consistent with the observations. "The hypothesis of life," he wrote in 1955, ". . . appears still the most satisfying explanation of the various shades of dark markings and their complex seasonal and secular changes." As the Space Age dawned, the proponents of martian life again had cause for optimism.

Mariner 4 sped past Mars in July 1965, returning twenty-one images that covered about 1 percent of the planet's surface. Only about half of the images contained any appreciable detail, but those that did revealed a pockmarked landscape of overlapping impact craters reminiscent of the moon. Instruments measured frigid temperatures and an extremely low atmospheric pressure of about ten millibars, less than half the value expected from telescopic studies and equivalent to the pressure at an altitude of 17 miles (27 kilometers) in the Earth's atmosphere. It was a glimpse of the planet that surprised and disappointed astrobiologists. Nothing changed with the results from *Mariner 6* and *7*, which together imaged about 20 percent of the surface. Carbon dioxide turned out to be the main ingredient of the atmosphere. The polar caps appeared to be frozen carbon dioxide—dry ice—and not water. There was no getting around the fact that Mars was an environment hostile to any form of life that we knew.

In November 1971, *Mariner 9* settled into orbit around Mars. A great planet-wide dust storm raged below, obscuring everything but four large spots and the south polar ice cap. There was little to look at until the storm abated in January 1972. As the dust cleared, it became apparent that these spots were enormous mountains—all ancient volcanoes—that reach up to 15 miles (24 kilometers) above the surface. *Mariner 9* also found an enormous rift valley, dubbed Valles Marineris, that spans over one-fifth of the planet's circumference and in places plunges to a depth of 6 miles (10 kilometers). If transported to Earth, it would run the length of the continental United States.

Planetary scientists were surprised and delighted by the unexpected diversity of landforms among the more than 7,300 images the spacecraft returned. The earlier Mariners had all passed over heavily cratered areas that were not representative of the rest of Mars. Figure 5-2 shows the planet's appearance from space; see also color plate 6. The apparent seasonal changes that Earth-based observers had seen in dark areas were caused by the windblown redistribution of surface materials. *Mariner 9* detected water vapor in the atmosphere over the south polar ice cap. Scientists interpreted this as indicating that the polar caps were primarily made of frozen water, acquiring only a veneer of dry ice as carbon dioxide snows fell during the winter. This meant that each cap held about half the volume of frozen water as the Greenland ice sheet on Earth. By far the most important discovery was a wide variety of features that could only be formed by a flowing liquid: flood plains, canyons, and what looked like dried-up river beds. The atmospheric pressure on Mars is too low for water to run freely on its surface today, but could the situation have been different in the geologically recent past?

There are good reasons to expect dramatic changes in the martian climate. Like the Earth, Mars has seasons because its rotational axis tilts toward its orbital plane. The angle of that tilt is known as obliquity. The Earth experiences only minor changes in obliquity due to the stabilizing influence of the moon. Mars, even closer to the disrupting gravitational tugs of Jupiter that drive some of these changes, has only two small moons—probably captured asteroids—that cannot perform the same function. So the obliquity of Mars changes chaotically, usually cycling between fifteen and thirty-five degrees but ranging from eleven to as high as sixty degrees over the past few million years. The planet's tilt is also sensitive to geological processes that change its mass distribution, such as the volcanic outpourings that occurred near the geographic rise of the Tharsis region. As one astronomer told us, "You could almost change Mars's obliquity just by looking at it wrong." The effect on climate is that summer temperatures at the poles are much warmer at high values of obliquity than at low ones. Another factor affecting the martian climate is the planet's eccentric orbit (fig. 5-3). The pole tilted toward the sun at perihelion has warmer summers than the other. Right now that's the south pole, but because of a slow change in the direction of the spin axis—a wobble called precession—the hot and cold poles swap hemispheres over a 51,000-year cycle. Finally, variations in the shape of Mars' orbit, which also occur cyclically and can change

Figure 5-2. Planetary scientists processed about one thousand *Viking Orbiter 1* and *2* images to create global mosaics of the Red Planet. Contrast and shading of the darker regions have been slightly exaggerated in this view. The white area at the top is the north polar ice cap. Composed largely of frozen water, with a veneer of dry ice added every martian winter, the north polar cap covers an area half as large as Texas and holds about half the volume of water as Earth's Greenland ice sheet. Canyons and troughs up to half a mile deep arc across the ice cap, creating a glacial terrain apparently unique to Mars. Near the planet's left limb sits the solar system's largest volcano, Olympus Mons. The trio of spots below it are also huge volcanoes. Below center is the great equatorial canyon system of Valles Marineris, long enough to span the United States. (NASA/USGS photo)

chaotically, provide still another vehicle for martian climate change.

Taken together, these effects may have warmed Mars enough to unfreeze some of the carbon dioxide and water locked under the planet's surface and in the ice caps. Increasing amounts of both of these atmospheric gases would give rise to increased "greenhouse effect" warming, creating a positive feedback that would liberate more gases and increase the pressure still further. If Mars was once warmer and wetter than it is today, then perhaps microbial life did indeed develop—and some of it may have managed to evolve in step with the deteriorating climate.

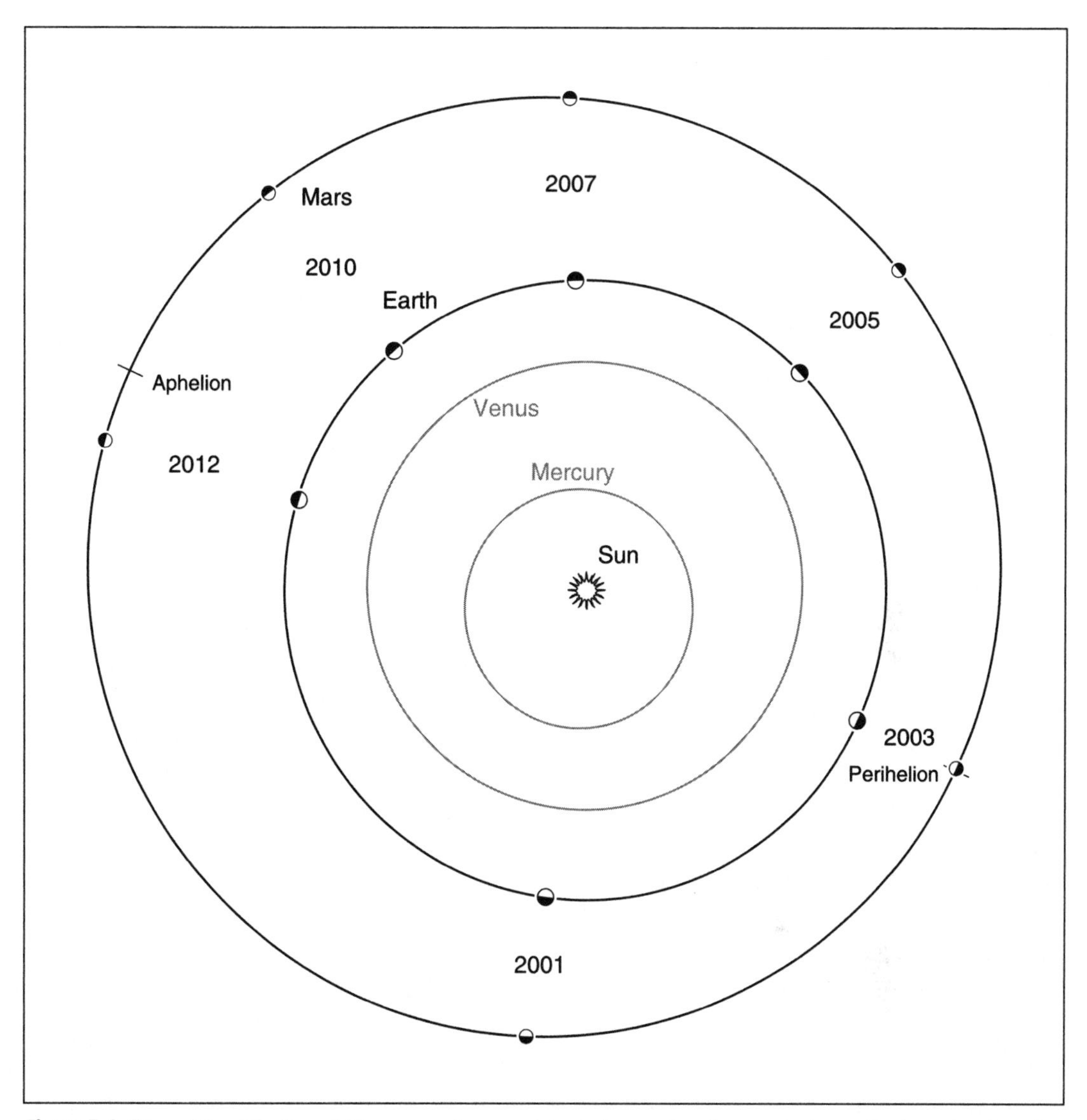

Figure 5-3. The orbits of Earth and Mars are not concentric circles, so the distance between the two planets varies from opposition to opposition. As shown here, the opposition distance between Earth and Mars steadily increases after 2003.

The U.S. Viking program represents one of the most ambitious planetary missions ever undertaken. Twin spacecraft, each consisting of an orbiter and a sophisticated lander, arrived at Mars in 1976. The two orbiters provided high-resolution imaging of the planet, while the landers served as weather stations, biological laboratories, and even geological probes. Soil experiments showed that iron-rich clays cover much of the planet's surface, giving Mars its rusty hue. Of greatest interest, of course, were the results of the three biology experiments. Although officially labeled inconclusive, most scientists agree that the experiments failed to find any sign of martian life. Another test looked for organic molecules, such as methane, hydrocarbons, and amino acids. Organic compounds are always associated with life on Earth and they were expected on Mars, even if life did not exist, because meteor dust, meteorites, and impacting comets would deliver them. The sun's ultraviolet light eventually destroys organic material at the surface, so the experiment was designed

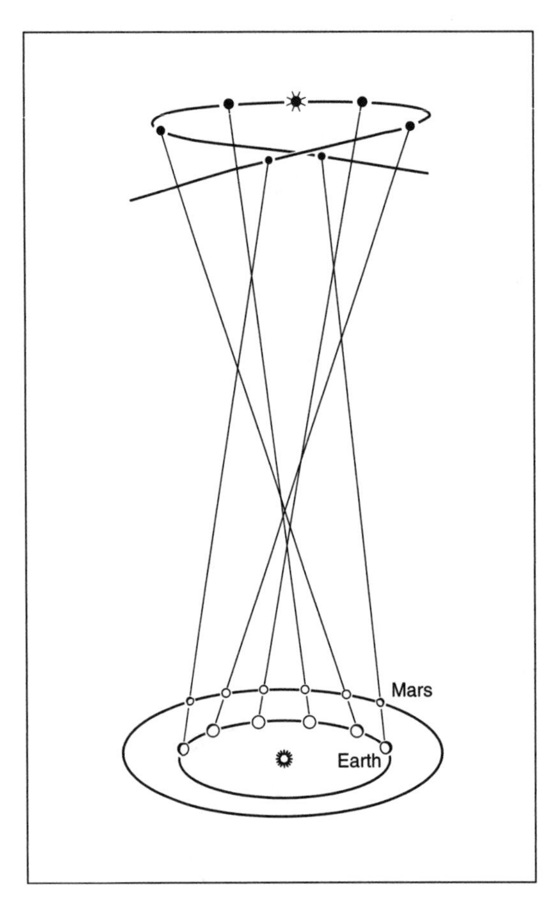

Figure 5-4. The remarkable loop of Mars is less mystifying when seen from space. The loop at the top shows both the path Mars takes through the stars and the planet's changes in brightness. As Earth catches up to Mars, it appears to halt its motion among the stars and as we overtake it the Red Planet reverses its motion through the stars. As our angle between the sun and the Red Planet increases, its orbital motion once again directs its apparent motion.

to be extremely sensitive. Yet it found no organic molecules to a level of a few parts per billion, a finding that has been called the most surprising single discovery of the mission. Because the molecules should be there even without life, some scientists have suggested that the martian surface contains a powerful oxidizing agent—a substance that transforms organic compounds into chemicals the Viking experiment could not detect. The presence of a "superoxide" might explain some of the biology results as well. Nevertheless, the early optimism about finding martian microbes had been dealt a hard blow. Two decades would pass before the question of martian life would again create widespread excitement.

Viking's detailed study of atmospheric composition allowed planetary scientists to identify a small group of meteorites as rare visitors from Mars. The Shergotty, Nakhla, and Chassigny (SNC) class of meteorites are named for the locations in India, Egypt, and France, respectively, where the first three members of the type were found; twenty-five specimens are now known. To be launched from the surface, these rocks had to be accelerated to martian escape velocity, about 3 miles (5 kilometers) per second. The only natural process capable of doing this is a large impact event, which would excavate a crater and eject surface materials. It's the same process responsible for bringing us meteorites from the moon, but it's more problematic for Mars. The higher escape velocity requires an event of much greater violence, one closely approaching the point where any ejected rocks might be completely destroyed. On the other hand, all of the rocks are volcanic and most of them solidified less than 1.5 billion years ago. Only the solar system's largest bodies could have retained enough internal heat to be producing molten rock so recently, a factor that makes Mars a top candidate. What clinches the martian origin of the rocks, though, is the close match between the composition of gases trapped inside the meteorites and the distribution of elements and isotopes the Viking landers found in the martian atmosphere.

One SNC meteorite cruised through space for some sixteen million years before crashing onto the ice fields of Antarctica about thirteen thousand years ago. There it lay buried in the ice until scientists recovered it from the Alan Hills region in 1984, the first specimen to be found in that year's Antarctic meteorite search and thus designated ALH 84001. Its martian origin was recognized a decade later. ALH 84001 is a softball-sized igneous rock that crystallized about 4.5 billion years ago, making it the oldest member of this select group of meteorites. In August 1996, a team led by David McKay of NASA's Johnson Space Center in Houston made the surprising announcement that ALH 84001 contained organic molecules, microfossils, and minerals possibly created by biological processes. "None of these observations is in itself conclusive for the existence of past life," the team reported. "Although there are alternative explanations for each of these phenomena taken individually, when they are considered collectively . . . we conclude that they are evidence for primitive life on early Mars."

In the years since, a few research teams have offered support for this view, but many more have put forward other plausible chemical and terrestrial interpretations. However, the most lasting legacy of this work is likely to be the very debate it rekindled, one that had been effectively dead since the days of Viking. News of the "Mars rock" ignited popular interest—the possibility that life had developed on Mars no longer seemed quite so theoretical. There is a scientific legacy as well, because the techniques employed in the study of ALH 84001 will be refined and extended with an eye toward the day when fresh martian samples can be examined up close and personal.

We are now in the midst of a new assault on Mars. In July 1997 *Mars Pathfinder,* protected within an envelope of air bags, literally bounced onto the Red Planet as a demonstration of low-cost methods for exploring the surface. The mission captured the public's imagination. Related NASA websites scored record numbers of hits in the week of the landing, and CNN doubled its viewership on landing day by providing especially heavy coverage. By the time contact was lost in late September, *Pathfinder* had returned over 16,000 images. The results from investigations carried out by both the lander and the small rover, *Sojourner*, seemed to validate the idea that Mars was once warmer and wetter than it now is.

Mars Global Surveyor entered orbit around the planet in late 1997. By the end of 2001 it had

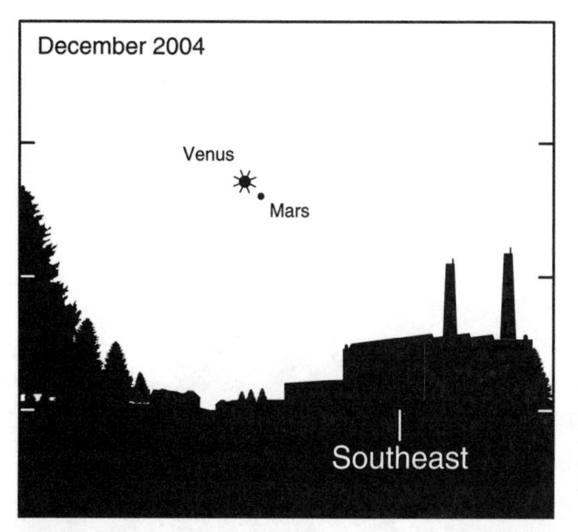

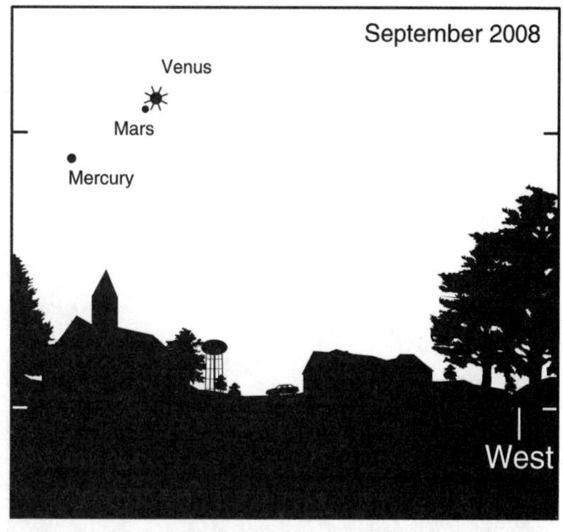

Figure 5-5. Left: Venus (–4.0) and Mars (+1.7) gleam together in the morning sky on December 5, 2004. Look east-southeast forty-five minutes before sunrise; binoculars help in finding Mars. Jupiter (–1.8) shines high above the pair. Right: Mars (+1.7) in conjunction with and very close to Venus (–3.9), low in the western sky after sunset on September 11, 2008. Binoculars help. Mercury (+0.2), also difficult to spot despite reaching greatest eastern elongation on this date, lies below and to the left of the pair. Jupiter (–2.4) gleams high in the south; the waxing moon, approaching full, rises in the southeast.

returned over 100,000 images at resolutions of a few meters and hundreds of millions of topographic measurements using a laser altimeter. Scientists found city-block-sized systems of small, apparently uneroded gullies that resemble terrain cut by flash floods on Earth. Elsewhere, large floods appear to have originated from the same vents that produced extensive lava flows, providing evidence that volcanism and the release of water have occurred on Mars in the geologically recent past—possibly even the present. Portions of the walls of Valles Marineris contain hundreds of alternating light and dark layers suggestive of sedimentary deposits. As dramatic as these features are, it's not yet clear if they are consistent with the notion of a balmy, water-rich, Earth-like Mars. They may have been created by something more typical of the Mars we see today, such as subsurface ice melted by impacts or nearby volcanic activity.

The case for water beneath the surface, though, has become impressive. In early 2002 *Mars Odyssey* arrived and began mapping the planet's surface composition. After its first week of data collection, mission scientists announced that several instruments had detected large amounts of hydrogen just below the surface, likely in the form of frozen water, over a broad area centered on the south pole and extending into the middle latitudes. Similar readings were found over a much smaller area in the north. In May project scientists announced that the amount of ice so far detected provided a source of water twice the volume of Lake Michigan. "This is really amazing," said William Boynton of the University of Arizona, Tucson, principal investigator for the suite of instruments that made the discovery. "We were hopeful that we could find evidence of ice, but what we have found is much more ice than we ever expected," he said. *Mars Odyssey* project scientist R. Stephen Saunders summed the discovery up more simply: "Mars has surprised us again."

Most planetary scientists now consider the probability of finding living organisms on Mars to be vanishingly small. Many think it somewhat more likely that life once had a toehold on the planet, but there are simply too many unanswered questions about the history of the martian climate and even of the origins of life itself. As the debate over ALH 84001 illustrates, it's entirely possible that we may not immediately recognize fossilized martians even if we happen to collect the right rock. In any case, Mars will be examined in unprecedented detail throughout the coming decade. Space agencies in the United States, Europe, and Japan have planned a veritable invasion of the Red Planet with a variety of orbiters, landers, and rovers. And planetary scientists are

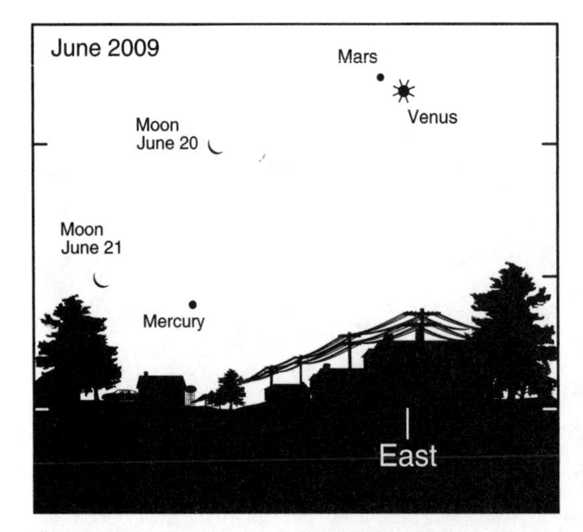

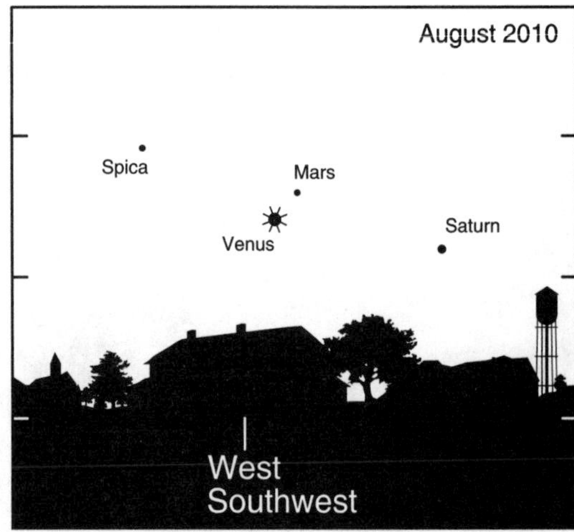

Figure 5-6. Left: Venus (–4.2) and Mars (+1.1) shine together in mid-June 2009. They are well placed in the east forty-five minutes before dawn. A waning crescent moon lies above the pair; can you glimpse Mercury (+0.1) below them? Jupiter (–2.5) gleams high in the south. Right: Venus (–4.4) is closest to Mars (+1.5) on August 19, 2010, in the western sky in the hour after sunset. Saturn (+1.0) shines below and to the right of the pair. To their left is the bright star Spica (+0.9) in Virgo.

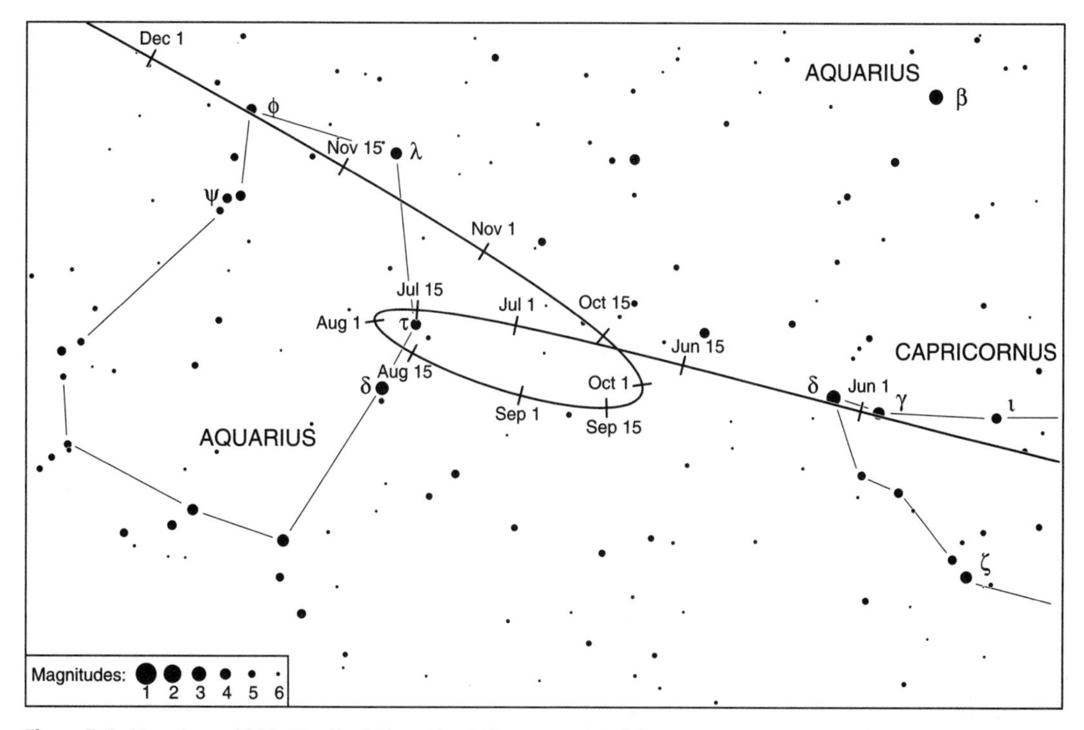

Figure 5-7. Mars loop, 2003. The Red Planet is stationary on July 29, at opposition August 28, and stationary again on September 27. This opposition brings Mars closer to Earth than at any time in the past several thousand years. (Drawing by Robert Miller)

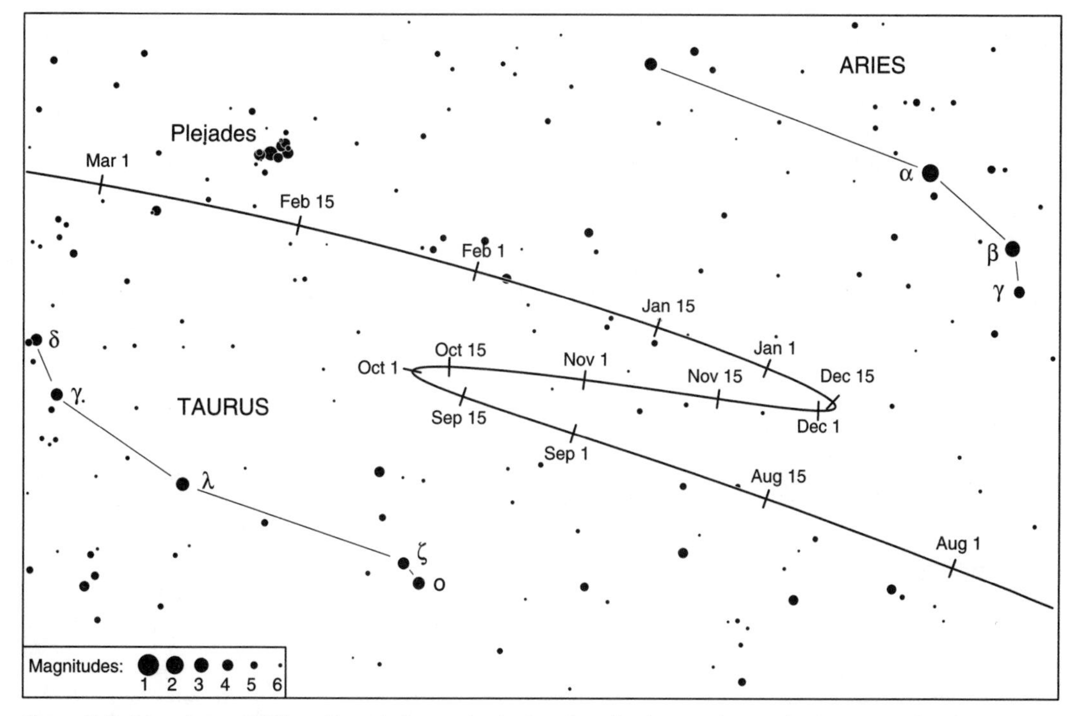

Figure 5-8. Mars loop, 2005—although it may be better described as a zigzag. Stationary on October 5, Mars reaches opposition on November 7 and completes its loop with the stationary point on December 10. (Drawing by Robert Miller)

already looking beyond 2010 with missions to collect samples from the surface of Mars and return them to the Earth.

The Martian Sky Show

Mars runs on an outer lane of the solar system racetrack. To put its motions in the context of a single apparition, let's take a look at how they play out for the 2010 opposition. We'll begin in early February 2009, when Mars is in the constellation Capricornus and emerging from the sun's glare, just five degrees above the eastern horizon thirty minutes before sunrise. Earth's orbital motion nudges the stars noticeably farther west each week. This westward motion tends to carry the planets along, too—but not in the case of Mars, whose eastward motion counteracts the effect of Earth's travels. Looking at Mars half an hour before sunrise a month later, we find that it remains five degrees above the eastern horizon, even though Capricornus is rising two hours earlier. By May, the Red Planet has passed through Aquarius and lies among the stars of Pisces, gaining only another five degrees in altitude. Now, though, the pace begins to pick up. In early June, as Mars is joined by Venus in the constellation Aries, it has gained almost another ten degrees of altitude when observed thirty minutes before dawn. Mars is not particularly bright, because of its distance from us, but these long sojourns in morning or evening twilight give it ample opportunity to meet up with other planets. We've illustrated the most interesting of these arrangements in figures 5-5 and 5-6.

The Red Planet progresses through Aries in June, Taurus in July and August, Gemini in September, and Cancer in October, entering Leo in November. By December 20, 2009, Mars is rising at around 9:00 P.M. Its eastward motion finally grinds to a halt as Mars reaches its stationary point, where its motion reverses and the retrograde loop begins. This also marks the start of prime Mars viewing, with the planet at a magnitude of –0.6 and growing brighter until opposition.

Now moving westward, Mars charges back into the stars of Cancer and reaches opposition on January 29, 2010. The Red Planet is now opposite the sun, visible all night long and gleaming at its brightest for this apparition (–1.3). In 2010 Mars gives its least impressive performance, shining with less than one-fourth of its peak brilliance in 2003. That's because the 2003 opposition occurs with Mars near perihelion, but the planet's orbit swings it farther away at each successive opposition.

On March 10, 2010, Mars halts its motion and accelerates eastward, once again defying the

Table 5-2. Oppositions of Mars, 2003–2010

Dates, constellation, brightness, date of closest approach, and minimum distance for Mars at upcoming oppositions.

Opposition Date	Constellation	Mag.	Nearest to Earth	Distance from Earth When Closest
Aug. 28, 2003	Aquarius	–2.9	Aug. 27	0.37274 AU 34.6 million miles (55.8 million km)
Nov. 7, 2005	Aries	–2.3	Oct. 30	0.46405 AU 43.1 million miles (69.4 million km)
Dec. 24, 2007	Gemini	–1.6	Dec. 19	0.58933 AU 54.7 million miles (88.1 million km)
Jan. 29, 2010	Cancer	–1.3	Jan. 27	0.66403 AU 61.7 million miles (99.3 million km)

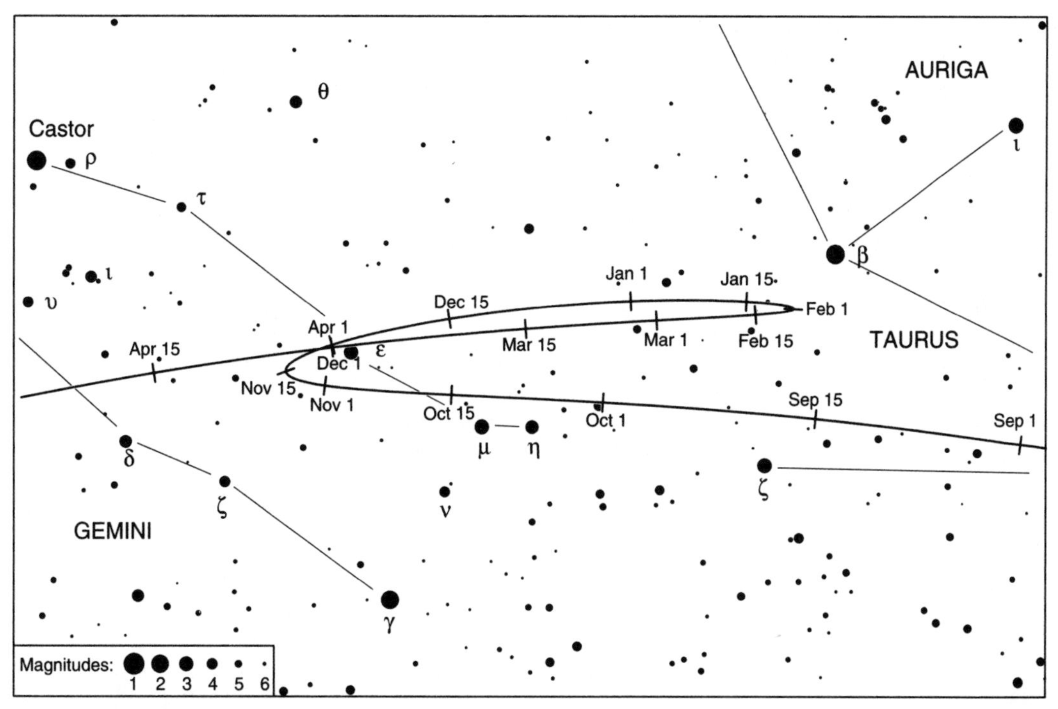

Figure 5-9. Mars loop, 2007–2008. Mars is stationary November 15, at opposition December 24, and stationary again January 20, 2008. (Drawing by Robert Miller)

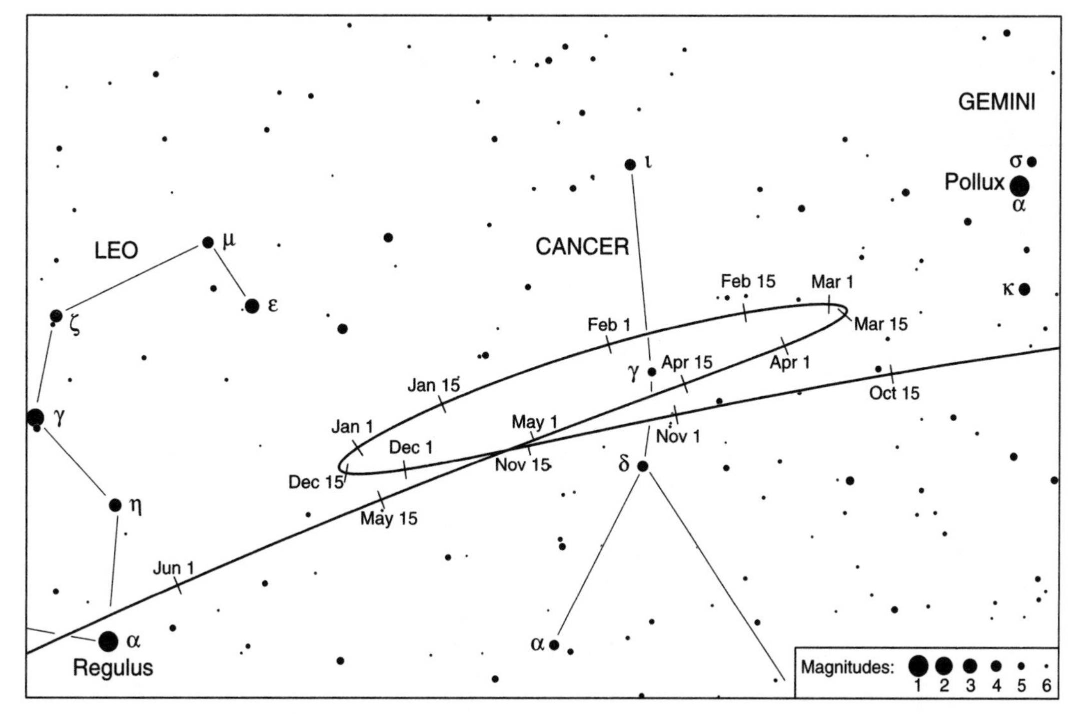

Figure 5-10. Mars loop, 2009–2010. Although this is the Red Planet's least impressive apparition this decade, Mars has no competition among the faint stars of Cancer. It's stationary December 20, 2009, at opposition January 29, 2010, and stationary again on March 10. (Drawing by Robert Miller)

general westward drift of the stars. The Red Planet lingers in the western sky, coursing through Leo and Virgo in the process and meeting Venus and Saturn in August. Finally, Mars rides into the glow of sunset in October.

Its motions in the sky, which mystified all astronomers prior to Kepler, continue to give us a delightful exhibition of celestial geometry. Table 5-2 lists the Red Planet's upcoming oppositions through 2010; figures 5-7 through 5-10 chart the Red Planet's changing location among the stars during each of its coming retrograde loops. The angular size of the loops shows an interesting pattern—they become progressively wider with each apparition, from ten degrees in 2003 to just over nineteen degrees in 2010. Mars becomes ever more distant from us throughout the decade, an effect that in principle would decrease the size of the retrograde loops. But the speed of Mars relative to the Earth is more important here than distance. When Mars is farther out, it is moving more slowly and the difference in speed between the two planets is more pronounced.

As we follow Mars around the sky, we can reflect on the accomplishments of the Maya, the insight of Copernicus, the mathematical labors of Kepler, the fantasy of Lowell, the ups and downs of scientific understanding—and the armada of spacecraft that may once again alter our views of the Red Planet.

6 Distant Giants: Jupiter and Saturn

And it may sound unprofessional, but a lot of the people up in the Imaging Team area are just standing around with their mouths hanging open watching the pictures come in, and you don't like to tear yourself away to go and start looking at numbers on a printout.

—Bradford A. Smith, imaging team leader, March 4, 1979, as *Voyager 1* approached Jupiter

After following the breathless wanderings of Mars, we turn now to planets that proceed through the sky at a much more leisurely pace. Jupiter and Saturn, the largest planets of the solar system, lie much farther from the sun—and us—than Mars. Jupiter's lane of the solar system racetrack is about five times the size of Earth's orbit and Saturn's track is twice the diameter of Jupiter's. As a result of both their longer circuits and slower speeds, the wanderings of Jupiter and Saturn through the constellations are much less dramatic than the splendid whirl of Mars, although as outer planets they exhibit most of the same motions. They go through retrograde loops each year as Earth slips past them and they are brightest near opposition. Tables 6-1 and 6-2 list the dates on which the two planets are at opposition, directly opposite the sun and visible to the south at midnight. Unlike Mars, which courses through much of the zodiac during each apparition, these planetary giants make seasonal appearances that approximate those of the background stars. Jupiter will travel through roughly one constellation each year and Saturn about half that, so skywatchers can count on seeing Jupiter and Saturn only slightly later each successive year. The two giants shine close together every two decades when Jupiter catches up to and laps Saturn. Since this last happened in May 2000, they move farther apart for the rest of this decade. They appear opposite one another in the sky by 2010 and then, over the following decade, close this distance to gleam together in the twilight of December evenings in 2020.

In addition to their stately motions, Jupiter and Saturn represent a distinctly different class of planet than those we've discussed up to this point. They are the largest and nearest of the four gas giants of the outer solar system, huge planets largely composed of hydrogen and helium—the two lightest elements in the cosmos. The small rocky worlds of the inner solar system have more in common with the largest moons of the gas giants than with the giants themselves. These planets are simply enormous—as a group, they contain 99.5 percent of the solar system's planetary mass. Jupiter alone holds 318 times the mass of our planet in a volume large enough to contain

Table 6-1. Oppositions of Jupiter, 2003–2010

Opposition Date	Constellation	Mag.	Nearest to Earth	Distance from Earth When Closest
Feb. 2, 2003	Cancer	–2.6	Feb. 2	4.32714 AU 402 million miles (647 million km)
March 4, 2004	Leo	–2.5	March 4	4.42567 AU 411 million miles (662 million km)
April 3, 2005	Virgo	–2.5	April 4	4.45665 AU 414 million miles (667 million km)
May 4, 2006	Libra	–2.4	May 6	4.41271 AU 410 million miles (660 million km)
June 5, 2007	Ophiuchus	–2.6	June 7	4.30442 AU 400 million miles (644 million km)
July 9, 2008	Sagittarius	–2.7	July 10	4.16106 AU 387 million miles (622 million km)
Aug. 14, 2009	Capricornus	–2.9	Aug. 15	4.02783 AU 374 million miles (602 million km)
Sept. 21, 2010	Pisces	–2.9	Sept. 20	3.95393 AU 368 million miles (591 million km)

1,300 Earths. It contains more than twice the combined mass of all the other planets in the solar system; in fact, one could argue that the planetary system consists of Jupiter plus debris. Saturn is a distant second to Jupiter, but still weighs in at an impressive 95 Earth masses in a volume large enough to hold 750 Earths.

Celestial Kingpins

The regal pace at which Jupiter and Saturn drift through the constellations of the zodiac led to their association with the most powerful members of ancient pantheons. In Babylon, Marduk was regarded as the creator of the world and the god who established cyclic order in the cosmos by vanquishing Tiamat, one of two primordial creative elements whose blind chaotic energy dominated the early universe. As a reward for this deed, Marduk was made lord and ruler of the gods. He adopted as his personal star the planet that most closely follows the sun's path through the stars, Jupiter (Niburu). Over a twelve-year period Jupiter completes the same circuit through the zodiac that the sun makes every twelve months—significant to the Babylonians because of the importance of the number twelve in their culture. Jupiter could be seen as a night watchman, keeping order with its steady pace through the sky and guiding the stars and other planets.

The Greek name Zeus is derived from the Sanskrit Dyaus (Shining One) and our name for the planet stems from the Sanskrit Dyauspitar (Shining Father), through Zeuspater (Father

Color plate 1. Our moon gives us a night light, rules the tides, provides a stepping stone for human exploration of the deeper solar system, and stabilizes the Earth's axis against the gravitational tugs of other planets. This multiple-exposure image, in which the camera's shutter was opened every five minutes, shows the full moon rising over Tulsa, Oklahoma. (Photo by Bill Sterne)

Color plate 2. The crescent moon and the bright planet Venus set over Tulsa, Oklahoma, in April 1988. Note how the separation between moon and planet changes in the three hours needed to make this multiple-exposure sequence (start at the top). The moon moves so swiftly that its eastward orbital motion carries it noticeably farther from Venus by the time the pair sets. (Photo by Bill Sterne)

Color plate 3. The partial phases of solar eclipses are particularly photogenic at sunrise or sunset. The silhouetted moon seen here, clearly too small to cover the sun, was photographed during the partial phases of the January 4, 1992, annular eclipse from Dana Point, California. This eclipse is a member of Saros 141. The next eclipse in this family, also annular, occurs January 15, 2010, and is visible from central Africa to eastern Asia. (Photo by Bill Sterne)

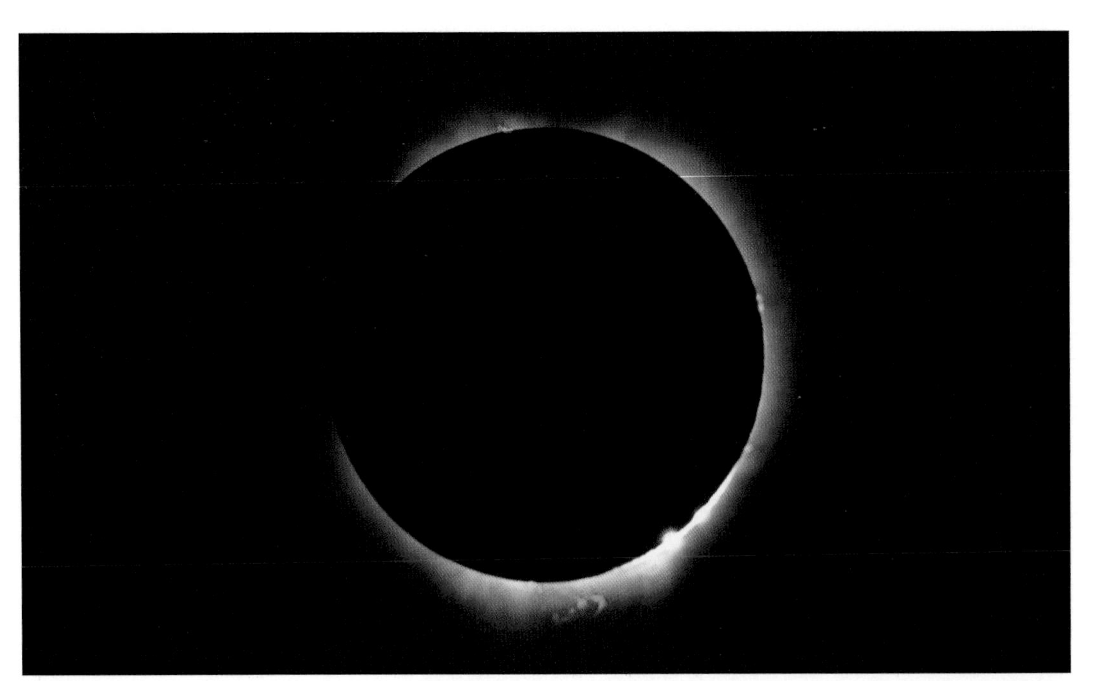

Color plate 4. Set within the pearly light of the solar corona, the black disk of the moon is rimmed by the pink glow of the chromosphere and bright prominences. This image of totality was captured during the July 11, 1991, eclipse from Cabo San Lucas, Mexico. From Mexico the sun remained darkened for nearly seven minutes—the longest span of totality until 2132. This eclipse is a member of Saros 136; the next related eclipse is also total and takes place July 22, 2009, when the moon's shadow courses across India, China, southern Japan, and the central Pacific. (Photo by Bill Sterne)

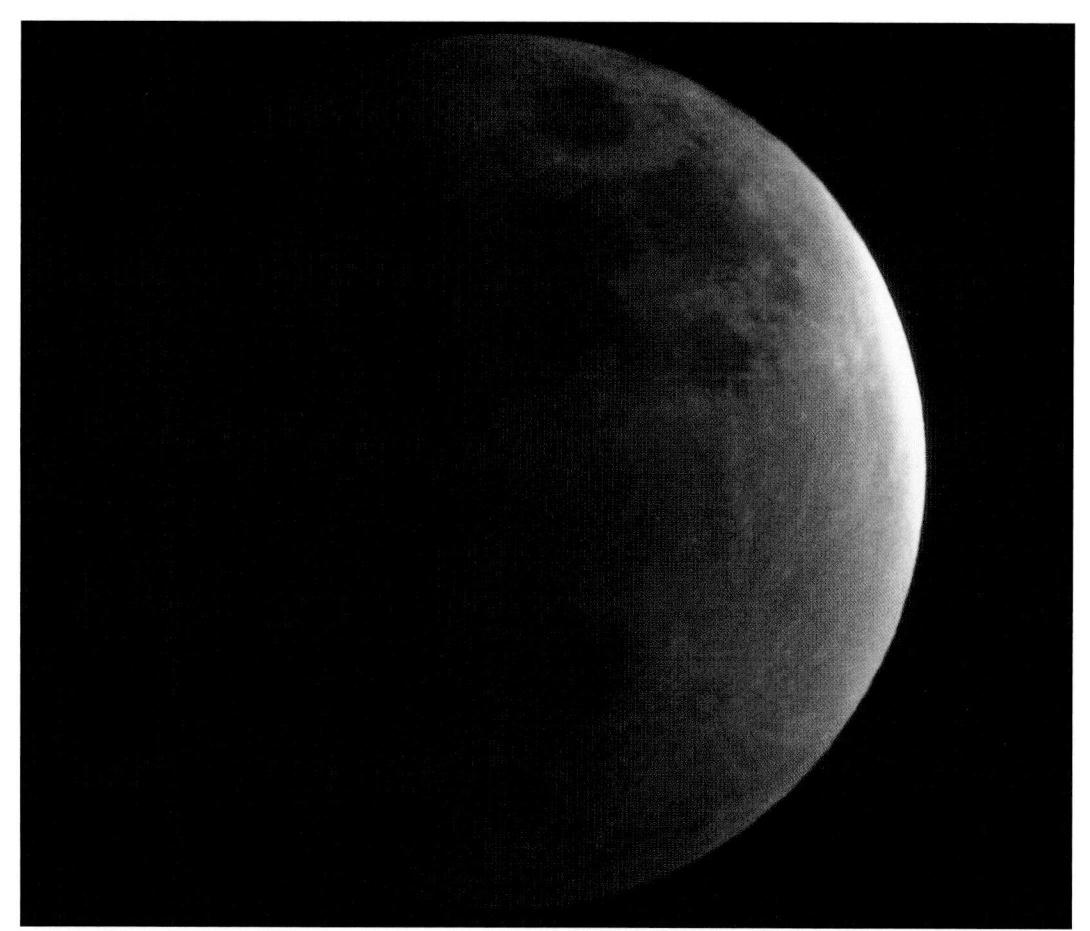

Color plate 5. The moon enters the deepest part of the Earth's shadow during the total lunar eclipse of January 20, 2000. (Photo by Robert Miller)

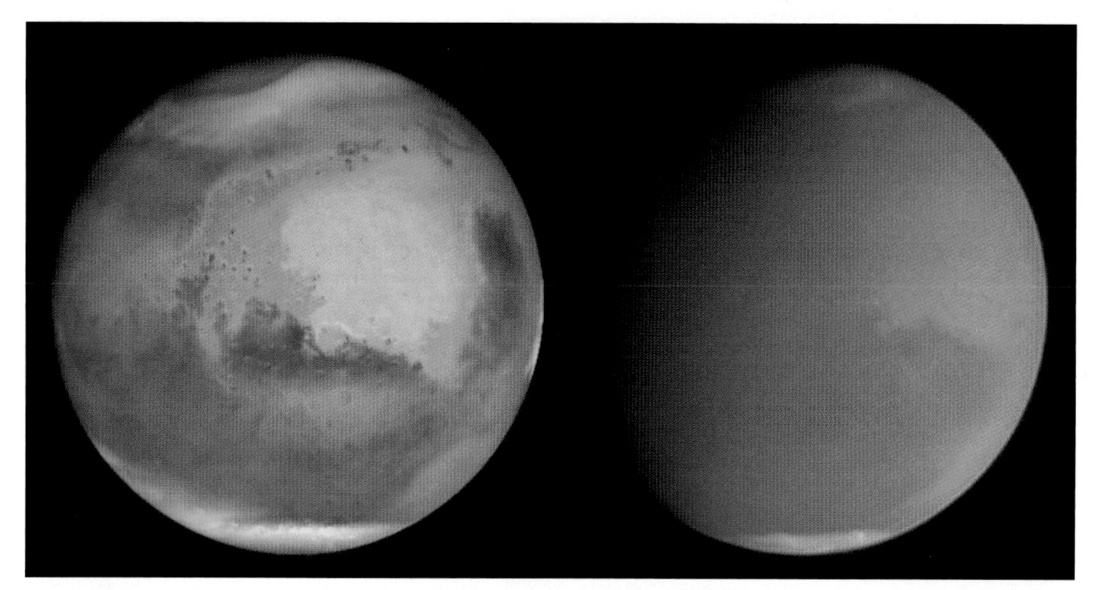

Color plate 6. In 2001 the Hubble Space Telescope watched the development of the strongest dust storm seen on Mars in decades. In June, when Mars was near opposition, storms could be seen brewing in the giant Hellas Basin (oval at lower right in left image) and near the northern polar cap (left). When photographed in early September, the storm had been raging across the planet for nearly two months, obscuring all surface features (right). Seasonal global Mars dust storms have been observed from telescopes for over a century. Mars looks gibbous in the right image because our viewing angle has changed. (NASA/STScI/AURA photo)

Color plate 7. Jupiter as seen in a combination of four images taken by the *Cassini* spacecraft on December 7, 2000. Jupiter's moon Europa is casting the shadow on the planet at left. (NASA/JPL photo)

Color plate 8. This composite of the jovian system includes the edge of Jupiter, showing an oblique view of its Great Red Spot, along with the planet's four largest moons, known as the Galilean satellites. From top to bottom, the moons shown are Io, Europa, Ganymede, and Callisto. Europa is about the size of our moon; Ganymede is the largest moon in the solar system. All images except that of Callisto were taken by NASA's *Galileo* spacecraft in 1996. The Callisto portrait is from the 1979 Voyager flybys. (NASA/JPL photo)

Color plate 9. The Hubble Space Telescope captured this image of Saturn in late 1998. The image was processed to render the planet's cloud bands in their natural subtle shadings. The small black dot near the planet's center is the shadow of its moon Enceladus. Saturn's most distinguishing feature is its fabulous ring system, which consists mostly of chunks of frozen water. Although it appears as if the disk is composed of only a few rings, it actually consists of tens of thousands of thin "ringlets." This image also shows two classic gaps long known from Earth-based observation—the narrow Encke gap and the broad Cassini division. (NASA/STScI/AURA photo)

Color plate 10. Orion the Hunter is a key constellation for finding your way around the winter sky. The contrasting colors of orange Betelgeuse and bluish Rigel are particularly striking. The middle star of the vertical trio below Orion's belt is the stellar nursery known as the Orion Nebula. (Photo by Robert Miller)

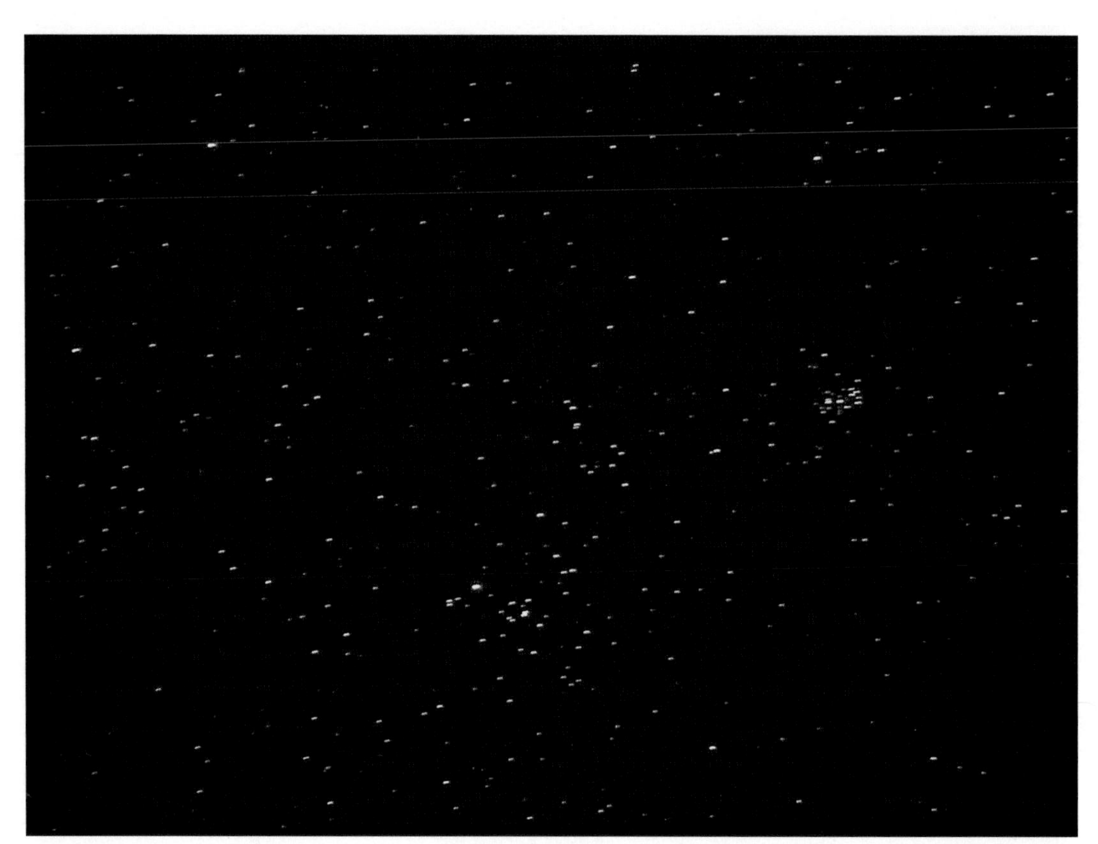

Color plate 11. The constellation Taurus contains two well-known star clusters: the Hyades and the Pleiades. The *V*-shaped face of the bull is formed by the Hyades cluster, although the brightest star of Taurus, Aldebaran, is not itself a member. The distinctive Pleaides cluster, one of the most familiar elements of the winter sky, can be found in folklore worldwide—and may even be present in Paleolithic cave art. (Photo by Robert Miller)

Color plate 12. The Big Dipper is a helpful guide to the spring sky. It's really an asterism, an easily recognized pattern of stars that is part of a larger, formally recognized constellation. The stars forming the Dipper are the brightest of Ursa Major, the Greater Bear. (Photo by Robert Miller)

Color plate 13. The brightest stars of the constellation Cygnus, the Swan, form an asterism known as the Northern Cross. From a dark sky Cygnus seems to be flying south down the faint glow of the Milky Way. Its brightest star, Deneb, marks the tail of the swan and is one of the trio of stars of the Summer Triangle. (Photo by Robert Miller)

Color plate 14. Clouds of stars characterize the southern portion of the summer Milky Way in the vicinity of Sagittarius and Scorpius. The center of our galaxy lies in the direction of Sagittarius but is hidden from us by intervening dust. (Photo by Robert Miller)

Color plate 15. Cassiopeia is an easily recognized constellation most of the year, but in autumn skies it serves as a guide to Pegasus, Perseus, and Andromeda. (Photo by Robert Miller)

Table 6-2. Oppositions of Saturn, 2003–2010

Opposition Date	Constellation	Mag.	Nearest to Earth	Distance from Earth When Closest
Dec. 31, 2003	Gemini	–0.5	Jan. 1	8.05013 AU 748 million miles (1,204 million km)
Jan. 13, 2005	Gemini	–0.4	Jan. 14	8.07562 AU 751 million miles (1,208 million km)
Jan. 27, 2006	Cancer	–0.3	Jan. 28	8.12683 AU 755 million miles (1,215 million km)
Feb. 10, 2007	Leo	–0.1	Feb. 10	8.20037 AU 762 million miles (1,227 million km)
Feb. 24, 2008	Leo	+0.2	Feb. 24	8.29141 AU 771 million miles (1,240 million km)
March 8, 2009	Leo	+0.5	March 9	8.39445 AU 780 million miles (1,256 million km)
March 22, 2010	Virgo	+0.5	March 21	8.50382 AU 791 million miles (1,272 million km)

Zeus). Zeus was actually a third-generation god in Greek mythology. In one Greek creation myth, Gaea, Mother Earth, arose from chaos and gave birth to Uranus. Together Gaea and Uranus engendered such strange creatures as the one-eyed Cyclopes before giving birth to the Titans. But eventually Uranus exiled the Cyclopes and an angry Gaea persuaded the Titans to attack him. Kronos, the youngest Titan, led the rebellion and became its leader. As Uranus lay dying, he prophesied that Kronos, equivalent to the Roman Saturn, would be similarly overcome by his own offspring. Kronos hoped to avoid the prophecy by swallowing his children, but his wife Rhea decided to substitute a stone for their youngest son, Zeus; she then hid him on the island of Crete. When Zeus grew up, he returned to confront his father and gave him a potion that made him vomit up the other children. They then pleaded with Zeus to lead them in a rebellion to overthrow the Titans. And so he did, defeating Kronos and the Titans and assuming rule over the universe. Zeus was thought to make his presence known to mortals with his lightning bolts—and it is the Norse god of thunder, Thor, who gives his name to the fifth day of the week, Thursday.

The Egyptians of the New Kingdom (c. 1540 to 1070 B.C.) saw Jupiter and Saturn, together with Mars, as manifestations of the sky-god Horus. Jupiter was Horus Who Bounds the Two Lands, Horus Mystery of the Two Lands, or Horus Who Illuminates the Two Lands; Saturn was Horus the Bull of the Sky. The "Two Lands" were Upper and Lower Egypt, which were united around 3000 B.C.

To the ancient Chinese, Jupiter was Suixing, the Year Star. As the name suggests, Jupiter served a calendrical function for the Chinese from about the seventh century B.C., based on its twelve-year cycle of residence in certain zones of the sky. These regions followed the celestial equator, an imaginary line midway between the north and south celestial poles, as opposed to the ecliptic.

Jupiter comes to opposition twelve times in just over twelve years, and the twelfth opposition returns the planet to nearly the same stars as the first. The Chinese came to associate each of the twelve sky intervals with an animal, and as Jupiter moved from one zone to another the year took on the characteristics of each successive animal realm it was in. So the traditional Oriental cycle of names for the year—Year of the Rat, Year of the Ox, and so on—derives in part from Jupiter's twelve-year journey through the stars.

To the Chinese, Saturn was Zhenxing, Quelling Star—or, following a later system of elemental correspondences, Tuxing (Soil Star). Among the Babylonians it was associated with Ninurta, originally a war god and hunter but also a fertility deity and the personification of the south wind. The god Saturn seems to have retained his association with agriculture when transported to the Italian peninsula. The Roman Saturnalia festival, a sort of harvest celebration held just prior to the winter solstice, was celebrated with unusual abandon—even slaves were given a day of freedom. Today many of us may have similar feelings of release on the last day of the week, which gets its name from the god of the Saturnalia.

The Maya were particularly interested in the motion of Venus, but they also timed some events to coincide with the two stationary points in the retrograde loops of Jupiter and Saturn. Some Mayan rulers even appear to have adopted patron planets. Inscriptions that herald events in the life of Chan Bahlum, king of Palenque, suggest that the dates were chosen with Jupiter's retrograde motion in mind. He may have made this choice after using a celestial spectacle to legitimize his rule and seal his bond of kinship with the gods of creation. On the evening of July 20, A.D. 690, a gibbous moon, Jupiter, Saturn, and Mars came together in Scorpius, an event that the Maya interpreted as the First Mother rejoined by her three planetary children. This initiated three days of rituals that culminated with a small offering of Chan Bahlum's own blood, a sacrifice that symbolized the actions of the First Mother at the most recent cycle of cosmic creation. The rituals and offering forged a link that joined the new king to the entire royal line at Palenque—and ultimately to the gods themselves. Royal blood was similarly offered at a Jupiter-Saturn conjunction in October 709, which came a few months after the birth of a son to the king of Yaxchilán. The sacrifice helped cement the child's future claim to the throne of that city.

Star of Wonder?

Mayan kings weren't alone in their appreciation of the power of planetary conjunctions, especially those involving Jupiter. As noted previously, astrologers in Mesopotamia, ancient China, and medieval Europe looked to planetary gatherings as a sort of barometer of coming events. The advent of the new millennium rekindled astronomical interest in the Star of Bethlehem, the celestial event believed to have revealed the birth of Jesus as recorded in the New Testament account of Matthew 2:1–16. Over the centuries, many astronomers have proposed that this too was a conjunction of planets. Recently, though, one astronomer has argued that the astrological meaning of one planet's motions is sufficient to explain the story. That planet is Jupiter.

First, let's take a look at what astronomers see in the story and the various other explanations that have been put forward. Biblical scholars believe that Matthew was writing fifty to sixty years after the crucifixion, around A.D. 80–90. Astronomers have struggled with the behavior he attributes to this star: ". . . and, lo, the star which they had seen in the east, went before them, till it came and stood over where the young child was," as found in the familiar King James translation. One obvious way around any astronomical problem is to conclude that the star is a miracle and therefore scientifically inexplicable. However, Matthew himself never calls it a miracle and the Magi who follow it seem to consider it an astrological portent rather than a supernatural apparition. It's also possible to dismiss the story entirely, writing it off as an invention by Matthew to legitimate Jesus as the one and only Messiah by connecting him to a unique sky event. This conclusion obviates the need for an astronomical identity of the star, but it isn't very satisfying. So throughout history a few astronomers have searched for a natural celestial event that might fit the biblical requirements given by Matthew.

A bright comet would be sure to get the attention of the Magi and, with a long tail, could be seen as pointing them to Judea—or at least to the astrological sign representing Judea. A bright comet would also be just as obvious to Herod and the people of Jerusalem as it was to the Magi. Yet Matthew's account indicates that they were unaware of the portent until the Magi began asking for the location of the newborn King of the Jews.

Comets are a bad choice for another reason. Claudius Ptolemy, in his influential astrological treatise *Tetrabiblos* written around A.D. 150, noted that comets "show, through the parts of the zodiac in which their heads appear and through the directions in which the shapes of their tails point, the regions upon which the misfortunes impend." They were overwhelmingly viewed as bad news in the Greek and Roman world, often seen as heralding a military loss or the death of a king.

Johannes Kepler observed two sky events that some have put forward as explanations for the Star of Bethlehem. The first was a triple conjunction of Mars, Jupiter, and Saturn in the constellation Ophiuchus in 1604. The second event fell in the midst of the first—the sudden appearance of a brilliant new star between Jupiter and Saturn. We know today that what Kepler saw was a relatively nearby supernova. The brightest members of a class of exploding stars, supernovas brighten tremendously in a short time and can blaze forth for months. Kepler wondered whether the triple planetary conjunction had caused the appearance of the new star. He calculated that such conjunctions recur about every 805 years and noted that the three planets had come together in the constellation Pisces in 6 B.C., close to the time of Jesus' birth. Despite this computation and his notion that a triple conjunction might produce a new star, Kepler considered the Star of Bethlehem itself to be "a special miracle moved in the lower layer of the atmosphere."

Following Kepler's lead, if not his reservation, others have suggested that the star was either a supernova or its more common but less spectacular relative, a nova. Chinese records do show that a nova appeared in the constellation Aquila in 5 B.C. Some have argued that a sequence of events—a conjunction of Jupiter and Saturn in 7 B.C., followed by the triple conjunction in 6 B.C., with a nova the following year—is what sent Chaldean astrologers on their way to Judea. But no surviving Middle Eastern or Western document records the nova and, more importantly, there is no record of any astrological significance accorded to the appearance of any new star. The planetary conjunctions, however, do have some potential and many have offered one or the other—or both together—as the identity of the Star of Bethlehem.

At this point we should note that the Christian era was established in A.D. 533 by a monk named Dionysius Exiguus, who proposed that years should be numbered from the birth of Jesus. He then proceeded to determine how much time had elapsed by adding up the lengths of the reigns of the Roman emperors. He selected December 25, 1 B.C., as the birth date of Jesus and began the Christian era the following week, on January 1, A.D. 1. Somewhere along the way, though, he dropped a few years in his calculations. Many biblical scholars contend that Jesus was born no later than 4 B.C., so the conjunctions mentioned above do occur at about the right time.

Planetary gatherings are appealing to the astronomically minded because they are visually striking, at least approximating our Christmas-card impression of what the Star of Bethlehem might have looked like. But to astrologers, planetary conjunctions could indicate many things, good or bad, depending on the constellation in which they occurred and the location of the sun and moon at the time. The Magi in Matthew's account had the very specific notion that the omen they followed meant the birth of a king in Judea. So, is there a celestial event that could be viewed as indicating a regal birth, that occurred before 4 B.C., and that took place in a constellation that astrologers of Roman times associated with Judea? The answer, says Rutgers University astronomer Michael Molnar, is a resounding yes—but it lies in subtler sky events.

Molnar's hobby is collecting ancient Roman and Greek coins that have celestial symbols. In 1990 he purchased a bronze coin from ancient Antioch, Syria, that portrayed the zodiacal sign of Aries the Ram looking back at an overhead star. The coin dates from around A.D. 6 and probably commemorates the annexation of Judea by the Romans of Anitoch. "I will never forget my astonishment," he writes, "when I first consulted Ptolemy's *Tetrabiblos* for the meaning of Aries on one of my Antiochene coins." Molnar had thought it well established that Pisces was the zodiacal constellation of importance to Judea, but Ptolemy said it was Aries. "After some thought," he writes, "I realized that the clue to the biblical star was sitting in my coin box: the theories about the Magi's star having appeared in Pisces were wrong." He went on to examine historical and astrological records, recounting his exploration of the subject in the book *The Star of Bethlehem: The Legacy of the Magi.*

Molnar found that astrologers viewed Jupiter as the regal planet, the one that conferred kingships; they believed that its power was amplified when it was close to the moon. Jupiter's effects were further enhanced when it lay within the same constellation as the sun—but was rising well ahead of it. Between 10 B.C. and A.D. 5, Molnar found, Jupiter rose in Aries as a morning star only once: on April 17, 6 B.C. Matthew quotes the astrologers as saying that they have seen the star "in the east." Molnar thinks this refers to Jupiter's heliacal rising—its emergence from the dampening astrological influence of the sun. Jupiter was still too close to the sun's glare to be visible, but this did not affect its astrological import. Furthermore, Jupiter underwent another significant astrological event the very same day: the moon passed in front of and briefly obscured, or occulted, the planet. This was actually the year's second Jupiter occultation; the first, in March, happened with Jupiter too close to the sun's astrological dampening zone, which counteracted its influence.

Like their Mayan counterparts, Chaldean astrologers accorded special significance to the stationary points in a planet's retrograde loop. Jupiter left Aries and moved into Taurus, appearing to halt as it reached its first stationary point in late August. Then it reversed its course and headed westward, reentering Aries in late October. Astrologers of the time described this as "going before" (in Greek, *proegeseis*); that is, westward motion or movement in the same direction in which the stars move. Molnar believes that Matthew's use of "went before" *(proegen)* is garbled astrological jargon for Jupiter's westward motion. The planet continued on through Aries until it halted there in late December. This was a secondary royal portent for Judea and, Molnar argues, the point at which Jupiter "stood over." This, he says, is another poorly communicated astrological term. The Greek word usually translated as "above" *(epano)* in the works of Ptolemy can also mean "over" and is translated that way in biblical works. With these revised meanings Molnar would have us paraphrase Matthew: ". . . and, lo, the star which they had seen at its heliacal rising, went westward before them, till it became stationary above and showed where the young child was."

"The Star of Bethlehem turned out to be something very different than I expected," Molnar writes. "Like other people I had anticipated something visually dramatic rather than arcane and cerebral. Nevertheless," he concludes, "we can be assured that the extraordinary conditions of April 17, 6 B.C., were as real and dramatic as any blazing comet or exploding supernova."

Critics argue that astrological interpretation was not quite so standardized as Molnar believes it to have been, and some historians favor other birth years for Jesus. We may never know if his explanation is correct, but as we watch Jupiter course through the sky we think it's fun to contemplate its potential role as the Star of Wonder.

King of the Planets

Efforts to explain the motions of the planets ultimately gave humanity a new perspective on its place in the universe. As we have seen, though, Mars played the pivotal role in the Copernican revolution. Jupiter and Saturn came into their own only after the invention of the telescope. In the spring of 1609, word of a new invention reached Galileo Galilei, the professor of mathematics at the University of Padua in Italy. He fashioned his first crude telescope from glass lenses and lead pipe, then quickly improved on this first model. It took him little time to turn his new telescope toward the heavens.

> On the seventh day of January in the present year 1610 . . . Jupiter presented itself to me; and, as I had prepared a very excellent instrument for myself, I perceived (as I had not done before on account of the weakness of my previous instrument) that beside the planet there were three starlets, small indeed, but very bright. Though I believed them to be among the host of fixed stars, they aroused my curiosity somewhat by appearing to lie in an exact straight line parallel to the ecliptic. . . . But returning to the same investigation on January eighth—led by what, I do not know—I found a very different arrangement. The three starlets were now all to the west of Jupiter, closer together, and at equal intervals to one another. . . .

Galileo was quick to realize that he was seeing orbital motion edge-on and recognized that Jupiter and its four satellites—a term introduced by Kepler—were an unequivocal demonstration of celestial motion that did not have Earth at its center.

Galileo called the four bright moons the "Medicean stars" after his patrons, the Medici. Today these satellites—Jupiter's largest—are called the Galilean moons in honor of their discoverer. The German astronomer Simon Marius (1573–1624) later claimed to have observed the jovian moons weeks before Galileo, but as he never published his early observations, the claim is impossible to verify. Galileo referred to the individual moons by number based on their distance from Jupiter, a practice that continued for centuries. On a suggestion from Kepler, Marius proposed a more palatable nomenclature for the jovian satellites, based on the mythological lovers of Zeus. The scheme was finally adopted in the mid-1800s, but only after the need to number new satellite discoveries made it necessary. In order of their distance from Jupiter, the moons are named Io, Europa, Ganymede, and Callisto. As befits a giant planet, Jupiter's moons are supersized. Ganymede is slightly larger than the planet Mercury and is the largest satellite in the solar system. Callisto is slightly smaller, and Io and Europa are about the size of Earth's moon.

In March, 1610, Galileo published his telescopic findings in a booklet called *The Starry Messenger.* Elsewhere we have noted that works of Copernicus and Kepler—two of the most significant books in the development of Western astronomical thought—caused little sensation, even in academic circles, when they first appeared. Not so Galileo's little book. *The Starry Messenger* caused a tremendous stir, in part because the observations reported in it were so specific and remarkable—mountains on the moon, faint stars in the Milky Way too numerous to count, stars circling Jupiter—but also because Galileo presented them clearly, simply, and succinctly.

Improved telescopes soon revealed fascinating details on the planet itself. First astronomers noted cloud bands; later, the bands were resolved into swirls and festoons. The most remarkable feature of the planet, the Great Red Spot, was first noticed by Robert Hooke (1635–1703) in 1664. This amazing feature, almost three times the diameter of the Earth, is akin to an enormous high-pressure system that has remained on the planet for over three hundred years. It rotates once every six days and interacts with other storms at the same latitude. Features such as the Great Red Spot allowed astronomers to time the rotation of Jupiter to an amazing 9.8 hours, a spin so rapid that it causes the planet to bulge noticeably at the equator (see figure 6-1 and color plate 7). Telescopic observations, along with the laws of physics derived by Kepler and Newton, enabled Earth-bound astronomers to discern the bulk properties of both giant planets, which are summarized in table 6-3.

The mythical Zeus threw lightning; his planetary namesake hurls asteroids and comets. Asteroids that orbit the sun in even multiples of Jupiter's twelve-year circuit are said to be in an orbital resonance with it. For example, an asteroid that circles the sun three times for every revolution Jupiter makes is in a 3:1 resonance. The asteroid makes a close approach to Jupiter every twelve years, regularly feeling an extra-strong tug in nearly the same place in its orbit. These periodic nudges force a steady change in the asteroid's orbit, moving its perihelion closer to the sun and its aphelion farther away. Over time, the orbit plunges deep into the inner solar system, crossing lanes occupied by the inner planets. We don't, in fact, see many asteroids in the 3:1 resonance because Jupiter has perturbed most of them into planet-crossing orbits. We also don't see many asteroids at the 2:1, 5:2, 7:3, or 9:4 resonances for the same reason. Close encounters with the inner planets or with Jupiter can further alter an asteroid orbit, sometimes quite drastically, and greatly enhance the possibility of a collision. What we know about the composition of asteroids that cross the orbits of Mars (the Amor class) and Earth (the Apollo and Aten classes) indicates that they come from every part of the asteroid belt. It's likely that collisions among larger asteroids knock some fragments into the resonance zones, where Jupiter can subsequently toss them sunward.

Not all gravitational resonances result in such a snowplow effect. In fact, just the opposite happens at the 1:1 resonance, where over 1,200 asteroids cluster in two dynamically stable zones. Collectively known as the Trojans, half of this entourage orbits sixty degrees ahead of Jupiter and the other half follows by the same angle. In principle, any planet could retain similar swarms of bodies, but none has yet been found accompanying Saturn, Uranus, or Neptune.

Figure 6-1. Giant Jupiter, the solar system's largest planet, consists mostly of the lightest element—hydrogen. This *Voyager 1* image, returned in 1979, shows zones of light-colored, rising clouds that alternate with bands of dark, descending clouds. They circle the planet in alternating eastward and westward belts. The Great Red Spot (oval shape toward the lower left) is an enormous anticyclonic storm that has persisted for centuries. (NASA/USGS photo)

Current thinking suggests that Jupiter's Trojans have been in the planet's neighborhood since its formation; the other giants were unable to retain their retinues. On the other hand, tiny Mars happens to be accompanied by six Trojan attendants, so perhaps the discovery of Trojans around the other giants is only a matter of time.

What Jupiter does to asteroids, it also does to comets. The short-period comets show a decidedly jovian influence—twice as many reach perihelion in a semicircle centered on Jupiter's own perihelion than in a semicircle centered on its farthest point from the sun. Sometime in the late 1920s or early 1930s, Jupiter captured a small object into a polar orbit. On occasion this orbit brought it quite close to the planet, but on July 8, 1992, it passed within 13,000 miles (21,000 kilometers) of the jovian cloud tops. This was

Table 6-3. Facts About Jupiter and Saturn

JUPITER

Diameter:	88,850 miles (142,984 km) 11.21 times that of Earth	
Atmospheric composition:	90% hydrogen 10% helium	
Number of moons:	39 (total includes S/1999 J1, S/2000 J1 - J11, and S/2001 J1 - J11)	
Largest moons:	Ganymede	3,270 miles (5,262 km) 7.8% larger than Mercury and largest moon in solar system
	Callisto	2,996 miles (4,821 km) 1.2% smaller than Mercury
	Io	2,264 miles (3,643 km) 4.6% larger than our moon
	Europa	1,940 miles (3,122 km) 10% smaller than our moon
Rotation period:	9.84 hours	
Obliquity:	3.12°	
Sidereal orbital period:	4,332.71 days (11.86 years)	
Synodic orbital period:	398.88 days (1.09 years)	
Mean distance from sun:	483.63 million miles (778.33 million km) 5.20 times that of Earth	
Orbit inclined to Earth's:	1.30°	

SATURN

Diameter:	74,901 miles (120,536 km) 9.45 times that of Earth	
Atmospheric composition:	97% hydrogen 3% helium	
Number of moons:	30 (total includes S/2000 S1 - S12)	
Largest moon:	Titan	3,200 miles (5,150 km) 5.4% larger than Mercury and the second largest in the solar system
Rotation period:	10.23 hours	
Obliquity:	26.73°	
Sidereal orbital period:	10,759.50 days (29.46 years)	
Synodic orbital period:	378.09 days (1.04 years)	
Mean distance from sun:	886.72 million miles (1,426.98 million km) 9.54 times that of Earth	
Orbit inclined to Earth's:	2.49°	

Figure 6-2. Saturn puts on a show as the planet and its magnificent ring system nod majestically over the course of its twenty-nine-year journey around the sun. These Hubble Space Telescope images, captured from 1996 to 2000, show Saturn's rings opening up from just past edge-on to nearly fully open as it moves from autumn toward winter in its northern hemisphere. Throughout the next decade the rings will slowly close, becoming edge-on once more in 2009. (NASA/STScI/AURA photo)

too close—the object was shattered into a score of fragments by Jupiter's powerful tides and the pieces continued on in the original orbit, forming a "string of pearls" train of debris and dust. On March 23, 1993, astronomers discovered the unusual object and it became known as comet Shoemaker-Levy 9 (now designated D/1993 F2; the D indicates that it is "defunct"). Astronomers had seen Jupiter capture or disrupt comets before, but they soon realized that the pieces of Shoemaker-Levy 9 would meet a singularly dramatic end by plunging one by one into the planet's atmosphere at a speed of 37 miles (60 kilometers) per second.

Heidi Hammel led a team of astronomers using the Hubble Space Telescope to observe the impacts. "Prior to the event," she wrote, "no one knew for sure whether the collisions would produce phenomena detectable from Earth." The unprecedented nature of the collision guaranteed that the *Galileo* space probe (then en route to Jupiter), various Earth-orbiting satellites, and observatories around the world would be watching on July 16, 1994, when the first fragment was expected to strike.

"We gathered in the basement control room at the Space Telescope Science Institute to watch with breathless anticipation as our first image appeared on the screen. Down on the lower left side of Jupiter was a small bright spot," she wrote. Was this a satellite emerging from behind Jupiter? As astronomers scrambled to account for the locations of the jovian moons, the next image appeared, and it was clear that the odd spot was a plume of material ejected high above the cloudtops of Jupiter. Over the next few days the other twenty-one fragments exploded in the atmosphere. Infrared telescopes detected the heat of the fireballs as they entered; *Galileo* detected visible flashes from some of them; satellite and ground-based telescopes saw plumes of hot gas rise above the limb of Jupiter; and infrared observations revealed glowing spots as the ejected material fell back and heated the upper atmosphere. The larger impacts, estimated to have detonated with the energy equivalent of 25,000 megatons of TNT, created Earth-sized brownish clouds that remained visible for months. The physical and chemical effects of the impacts were far more complex than anticipated.

With the advent of the Space Age, planetary scientists no longer had to be content to observe Jupiter from afar. Four U.S. flyby missions and one orbiter have investigated the weather, moons, and radiation environment of Jupiter. The first such probes were the *Pioneer 10* and *11* spacecraft. Launched in 1972 and 1973 respectively, these robotic investigators carried eleven instruments, from particle detectors to a relatively crude imaging device. The solar energy at Jupiter is only 4 percent the amount available on Earth, so powering the craft with solar panels was impossible. Instead, the probes relied on a form of nuclear power. *Pioneer 10* reached Jupiter after a twenty-one-month trip that included a proof-of-concept passage through the asteroid belt. One major discovery was the intensity of the radiation belts created by Jupiter's powerful magnetic field; a significant amount of scientific data was lost when the radiation disrupted spacecraft operations. *Pioneer 10* was followed a year later by *Pioneer 11,* which continued on to Saturn. The Pioneer missions garnered major scientific findings in their own rights, but their most important role was that of blazing a trail for the spectacularly successful Voyager missions that followed.

Launched in 1977, the two Voyager spacecraft continue to collect data about the solar environment. With luck, they will serve as humanity's first interstellar probes in the next couple of decades. For a modest per-capita annual investment—roughly half the cost of a candy bar—the United States sent two probes past Jupiter and Saturn, discovered dozens of moons, acquired awe-inspiring pictures, and collected a wealth of data from which scientists still tease new discoveries. *Voyager 1*'s planetary odyssey ended at Saturn, but a fortuitous planetary arrangement—together with some talented engineering and a bit of luck—enabled *Voyager 2* to swing past Uranus and Neptune as well.

The jovian cloud bands are the visible manifestation of east-west jet streams that alternate direction closer to the poles. They carry oval weather systems of all sizes, up to the size of the Great Red Spot. The major constituent of the visible clouds is frozen ammonia, but the cloud colors come from some as-yet-unknown substances, probably created through chemical reactions driven by ultraviolet radiation or charged particles entering the atmosphere. Descending through the cloud layers, we would find first ammonia ice crystals, then particles of ammonium hydrosulfide. We cannot see past these clouds, but atmospheric scientists expect that the next layer is made from frozen water, like cirrus clouds on Earth. Deeper still, at a pressure of about eight Earth atmospheres (or eight bars), the clouds are thought to contain droplets of a water/ammonia mixture. The *Galileo* spacecraft, which was placed into orbit around Jupiter in late 1995, dropped a probe that descended far below this level before it ceased to function; it detected an unexpectedly small amount of water. The *Galileo* orbiter has detected lightning from what appear to be thunderstorm-like clouds at the level where water is expected, and it's thought that the probe—which failed to detect lightning—fell into a dry atmospheric "sinkhole" that was not representative of the rest of the atmosphere. The probe fell to depths with temperatures hot enough to melt metal and is now a part of the very atmosphere it measured; the orbiter will join it at the end of its mission.

Voyager scientists used minute frequency changes in the spacecraft's radio signals to map the structure of Jupiter's gravitational field. This in turn enabled them to describe in some detail the planet's internal structure forever hidden by its clouds. Pressures and temperatures increase steadily below the cloud layers, but the hydrogen atmosphere simply grows denser and hotter with depth. There is no distinct layer at which the gaseous molecular hydrogen turns into liquid hydrogen. At pressures of a few hundred thousand bars the atmosphere becomes very similar to a hot liquid. The fundamental property of all of the gas giant planets is that, in the words of Mark Marley of New Mexico State University, they have "essentially bottomless atmospheres." About 20 percent of the way toward Jupiter's center, where pressures reach an unimaginable two million bars and temperatures soar to 12,000°F (6,700°C), molecular hydrogen becomes a more exotic substance. Liquid metallic hydrogen, an electrically conductive soup of protons and electrons, makes up most of the mass of Jupiter. Some 31,000 miles (50,000 kilometers) below this region, at a depth just 10 percent of the way from the center of Jupiter, the pressure rises to around forty million bars and the temperature is about 41,000°F (23,000°C). Only here does the composition gradually begin to change into something we're more familiar with—a dense rocky core slightly larger than the Earth.

The description of Jupiter's interior applies to Saturn as well, although Saturn's lower mass and therefore lower pressures allow for a smaller metallic hydrogen region. Uranus and Neptune, less massive still, lack one altogether.

Chief among the Voyager achievements at Jupiter was a close-up look at the Galilean moons. Bruce Murray, director of the Jet Propulsion Laboratory during the Voyager encounters, summarized the reaction of planetary scientists to the first Jupiter flyby:

> *Voyager 1* discovered a miniature solar system surrounding Jupiter. Those four orbiting moons are as unusual and different from one another as four bits of rocky debris orbiting close to the sun—Mercury, Venus, Earth, and Mars. *Voyager 1* had zoomed in on the four dark smudges near the gaudy telescopic image of Jupiter, revealing worlds and circumstances beyond our imaginations.

Galileo arrived at Jupiter in 1995 and circled the planet for seven years, making repeated close passes of all four moons. It examined in detail what the Voyagers had only glimpsed. Callisto is the least complicated world, a battered sphere of ice and rock that has undergone few changes driven by internal geologic activity. Large bodies tend to have organized interiors, with denser materials like rock settling toward the center and less dense matter, like ice, moving toward the surface. This process started at Callisto but was never completed. Its interior is a half-baked hash of ice and rock enveloped by an ice-rich crust. Some *Galileo* observations point to the surprising possibility of a thin layer of briny ocean under the crust.

Ganymede, the next world in, is three-quarters the size of Mars and larger than both Pluto and Mercury. It is very different from Callisto, with a complex surface history that better suits a moon of such planetary dimensions. Dark, heavily cratered—and therefore presumably older—areas cover about 40 percent of the surface, with the rest occupied by a brighter, smoother terrain corrugated with intricate grooved patterns. These bright swaths cut across the older dark terrain; scientists believe that they represent regions where subsurface water flooded onto the surface. The grooves appear to be formed by stretching and faulting of this fresh veneer of ice. Internally, Ganymede evidently completed the differentiation that Callisto could not. *Galileo* discovered an internally generated magnetic field around Ganymede about 1 percent as strong as Earth's, which implies the existence of a partially molten metallic core. Ganymede's interior must have reached temperatures hot enough to melt rock and stayed hot long enough for metals in the rock to drift to its center.

Europa's icy surface is among the brightest in the solar system. An extensive network of darker fractures crisscrosses the frozen plains. Europa is also very smooth, its most prominent topography a few ridges that rise no higher than the length of several football fields. Voyager and *Galileo* images reveal only a handful of impact craters. These observations all point to the conclusion that geologic forces have been at work on the surface recently. The paucity of craters alone indicates that the surface is very young, perhaps just tens of millions of years old. Galileo's most detailed views of Europa's "chaos terrain" reveal large plates of ice that have been broken apart, displaced, and rotated into new positions—strikingly similar to the rafting of pack ice in Earth's polar oceans. Between the plates, new crust has formed, probably from slushy ice welling up from below. *Galileo* did not detect active "icy volcanoes" during its Europa flybys. Scientists had speculated since the Voyager encounters that Europa could harbor a global ocean beneath its icy crust, and *Galileo* results strongly suggest, but cannot prove, that liquid water exists there. Europa is clearly a world that planetary scientists want to visit again, and plans for a dedicated mission to this moon are now under study.

The most surprising of the jovian moons was Io. *Voyager 1*'s first color views of its vivid red and orange sulfur-stained disk invited immediate comparison to a pizza (color plate 8). At any given moment, half a dozen or more geyserlike eruptions can be seen. Some of their umbrella-shaped plumes extend up to 250 miles (400 kilometers) above the surface. Io's largest volcanic complex, Loki Patera, contains a lava lake larger than the Big Island of Hawaii. The outpouring of material from Io's geysers and lava flows is so great that it has erased any impact craters. Io is differentiated: it has an iron-rich core that occupies about half its diameter and above it a thoroughly molten mantle capped by a thin rocky crust.

The progression of increasing geologic activity from Callisto to Io is no accident. Io, Europa, and Ganymede orbit Jupiter in a 1:2:4 resonance—every time Europa and Ganymede come closest together, Io is on the opposite side of Jupiter. The gravitational interaction forces the orbits of Io and Europa to maintain a slight eccentricity, which results in tides that create friction and heat the interiors. This resonance does not seem capable of fully explaining Ganymede's internal heat, but other resonances may have existed in the past that could have done the job.

Lord of the Rings

Saturn has been an icon of space itself for a long time. Its bright, broad ring system is the most dramatic reminder that matter behaves differently in space from the way it does here on Earth. Despite the familiar close-up images from *Voyager 1* and *2*, Saturn remains the object that makes the deepest immediate impression through a small telescope. No one ever forgets that first clear telescopic view of Saturn, in large part because it looks so unexpectedly unnatural. Brad Smith, imaging team leader for the Voyager Saturn encounters, told journalist Henry S. F. Cooper, Jr.: "There is something about Saturn that makes it hard to believe it's real. . . . You have to see it through a telescope. You never forget it—ever after, it remains a sort of focal point in the sky." Although we now know that all of the giant planets have rings, Saturn's stand alone in terms of brightness, breadth, and complexity.

The first telescopic observations of Saturn were made by Galileo. Because of the relatively poor quality of his telescope, he didn't have a clear view of the now-famous rings. He did detect two points of light on either side of the planet and took them to be moons—but was mystified when, two years later, those satellites had completely disappeared from his view. He recovered sight of them in 1616, but was puzzled why they didn't drift back and forth like the moons of Jupiter. Saturn was thought of as a "triplet" planet for some time.

In 1656, the Dutch scientist Christiaan Huygens (1629–1695) viewed Saturn and noticed a thin dark shadow across the planet's disk. Huygens realized that he was seeing a ring of material edge-on. As the planet continued in its orbit, the terrestrial viewing angle gradually changed and the ring reappeared (fig. 6-2). Huygens published his findings in 1659, but for a while there was resistance to the idea of a giant ring floating in space unconnected to the planet. Huygens had solved the geometrical problem, but the argument over the nature of the rings went on for centuries.

In 1676, Giovanni Domenico Cassini (1625–1712) observed that the ring was divided into two separate rings; the gap is known today as the Cassini Division. This gap and others are caused by gravitational resonances with saturnian satellites; in this specific case the culprit is Mimas. The main rings cover an area of just over 15 billion square miles (40 billion square kilometers), or eighty times the total surface area of the Earth, and span 174,000 miles (280,000 kilometers)—about 73 percent of the distance separating Earth and the moon. It's little wonder that they vanish when edge-on to Earth—the rings are probably less than 100 feet (30 meters) thick.

In 1858, physicist James Clerk Maxwell (1831–1879) published his analysis of the ring structure, proving that it had to be made up of billions of individual particles, most no larger than a few inches, orbiting independently. The particles in the rings range in size from smoke particles to sugar grains to blocks as large as houses, with smaller sizes outnumbering the larger ones, and they are believed to resemble loose lumpy snowballs. The total amount of material in the rings is surprisingly small—about the same mass as Saturn's moon Mimas (120 miles or 195 kilometers across). Cameras on the Voyager spacecraft resolved each of the larger rings into thousands of tiny ringlets—some kinked or clumpy or braided, others distorted by the presence of moonlets within the rings. The images revealed that density waves and corrugations ripple throughout the system, and electrically charged dust particles float above the rings, creating the appearance of spokes. The dazzling closeups forced physicists to push their dynamical theories to new limits to accommodate what the Voyager cameras showed them. After *Voyager 2*'s flyby, the journal *Science* summed up the missions this way: "For sheer intellectual fun there has never been anything like the Voyager missions. Volcanoes on Io, ringlets around Saturn, *braided* rings—the observations are outrageous."

Over time, and with many mutual collisions, the ring particles must lose energy and eventually fall into the atmosphere. Without replenishment, Saturn's glorious ring system is ultimately an evanescent phenomenon, albeit one with a lifespan measured in tens of millions of years. Perhaps

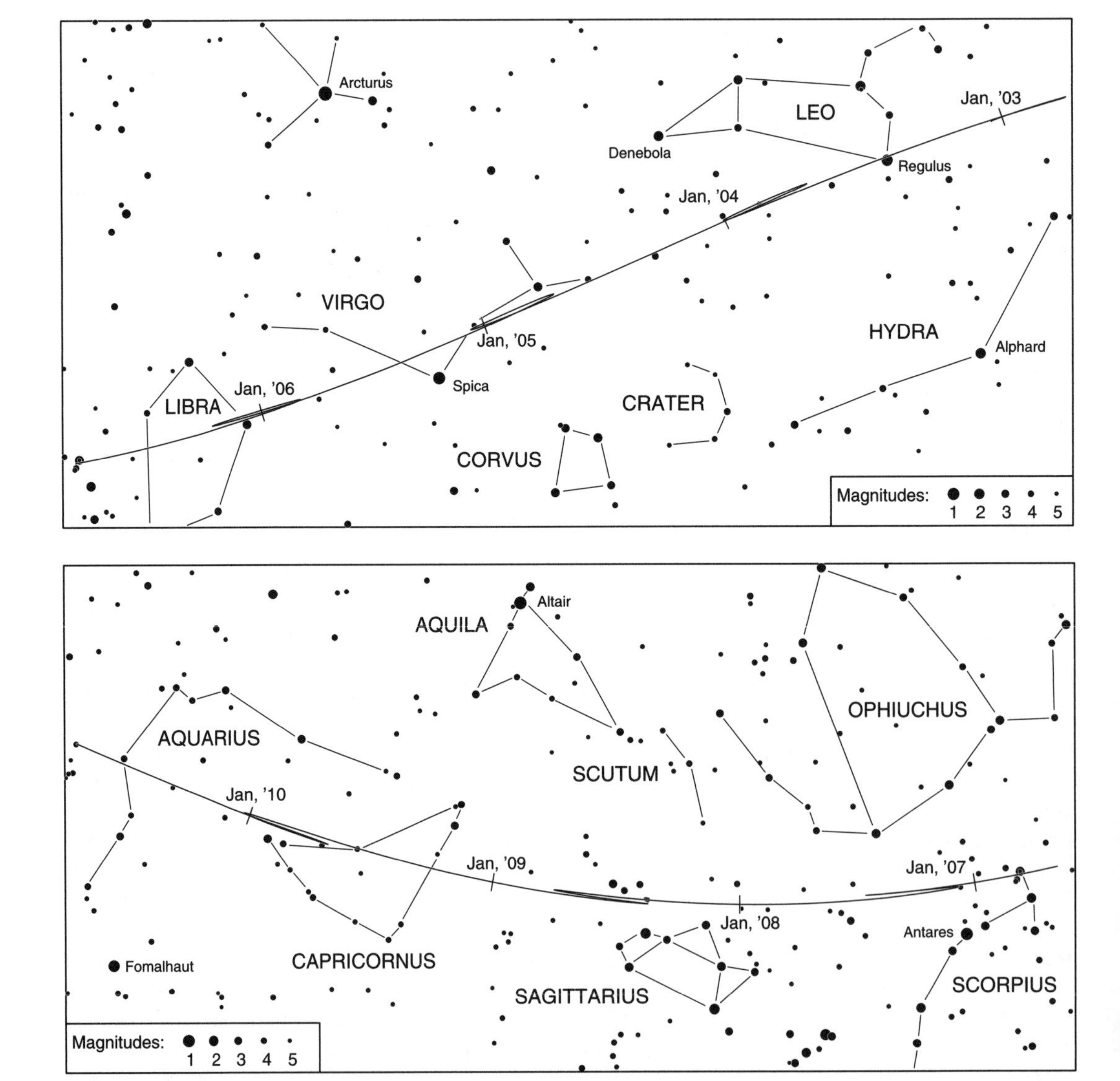

Figure 6-3. Top: Jupiter drifts through a constellation a year, cruising through two-thirds of the sky and passing through seven of the twelve constellations of the zodiac through 2010. The tick marks represent the planet's position at the start of each year from 2003 through 2006. Bottom: Jupiter's path from 2007 through 2010. (Drawings by Robert Miller)

there are large blocks embedded in the rings, fragments of a captured comet or asteroid or a moon that approached the planet too closely. Their impacts with ring particles will erode them and liberate many smaller fragments, fuel that could maintain the ring system for eons. Or perhaps resonances with satellites help to sustain the rings longer than we might expect. The origin and evolution of ring systems, particularly Saturn's, remain lively areas of investigation.

Still another prize orbits Saturn—Titan, the solar system's second-largest moon. Slightly larger than Mercury, its visual appearance through the telescope—and even in Voyager images—is singularly bland: a reddish ball completely covered by a thick haze. But Titan has one feature we can find nowhere in the solar system but Earth—a dense nitrogen atmosphere. In 1925, the English physicist James Jeans (1877–1946) showed that even the feeble gravity of a Mercury-sized moon can retain an atmosphere of relatively heavy molecules if the temperature is cold enough. Receiving only about 1 percent of the solar energy that bathes the Earth, Titan is indeed cold, about –290°F (–180°C). Its atmosphere consists mostly of molecular nitrogen, but methane, traces of hydrogen, and possibly argon are mixed in as well. The pressure at the surface is almost 50 percent higher than sea-level pressure on Earth.

A haze of ethane and other organic molecules hides Titan from our view. Recent observations suggest that a few hurricane-sized weather systems may occur, but the overall cloud cover is extremely low. Under the conditions expected on Titan's surface, it's possible for liquid methane and ethane to exist in pools or shallow seas. Infrared observations, which can penetrate the haze, have provided crude maps that reveal an Australia-sized area of rough terrain. Even through Titan's dense and hazy atmosphere, the distant sun illuminates the landscape with an orange glow about a thousand times brighter than earthly scenes under a full moon.

What *Galileo* did for Jupiter, *Cassini* will do for Saturn. The joint NASA/ESA mission enters orbit in July 2004 and will first make two flybys of Titan before releasing *Huygens,* a sophisticated probe that will explore the moon's atmosphere and surface in early 2005. The *Cassini* orbiter carries a radar experiment to map the surface through the cloud layers—just a small fraction of the volumes of information the probe will return in its four-year-long primary mission to study the rings, moons, and magnetic environment of Saturn.

Dance of the Giants

As we said earlier in the chapter, Jupiter and Saturn are much more sedate than Mars in their

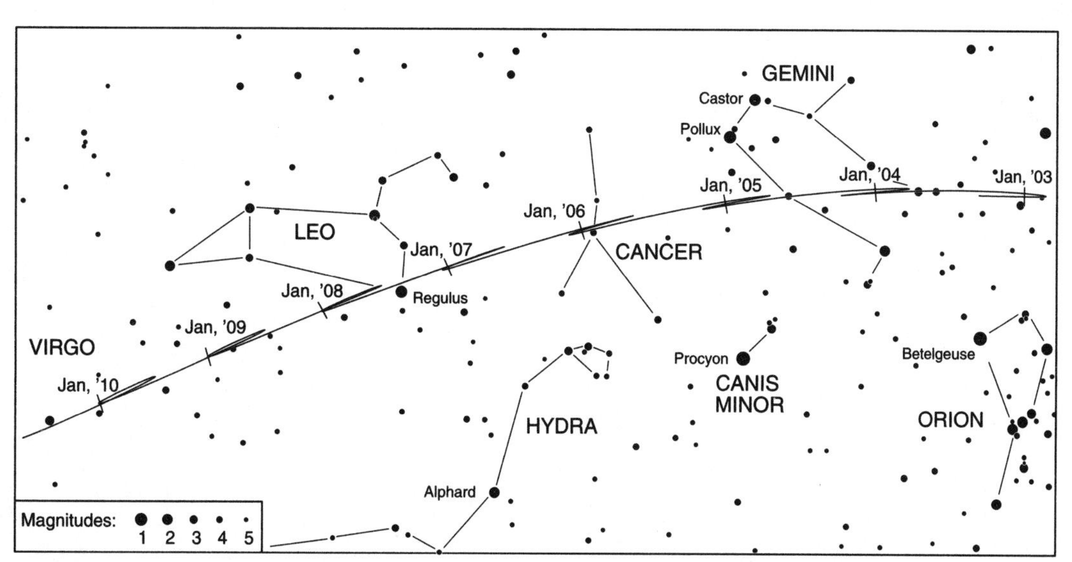

Figure 6-4. Saturn, a much more leisurely wanderer, travels at a little less than half of Jupiter's pace. The tick marks represent the planet's position at the start of each year from 2003 through 2010. (Drawing by Robert Miller)

travels through the sky. This makes it easier for even casual stargazers to become acquainted with them and anticipate their annual appearances. There are twelve constellations in the zodiac, and Jupiter completes an orbit every twelve years, so Jupiter's travels can be summed up in the rule of thumb "a constellation a year." Jupiter lies in the constellation Cancer in 2003, and so appears in the east after sunset in late January and early February. Each successive year it makes its evening appearance about a month later. By the year 2010, observers will have to wait until September for an early evening glimpse of the planet. Saturn, on the other hand, is a late winter/early spring object for the balance of the decade. It begins 2003 in the constellation Gemini and can be seen in the early evening sky by the end of January; by 2010 Saturn rises at opposition in mid-March.

The conjunction of Jupiter and Saturn that occurred in 2000 doesn't happen very often, and it's easy to see why. Dividing Saturn's orbital

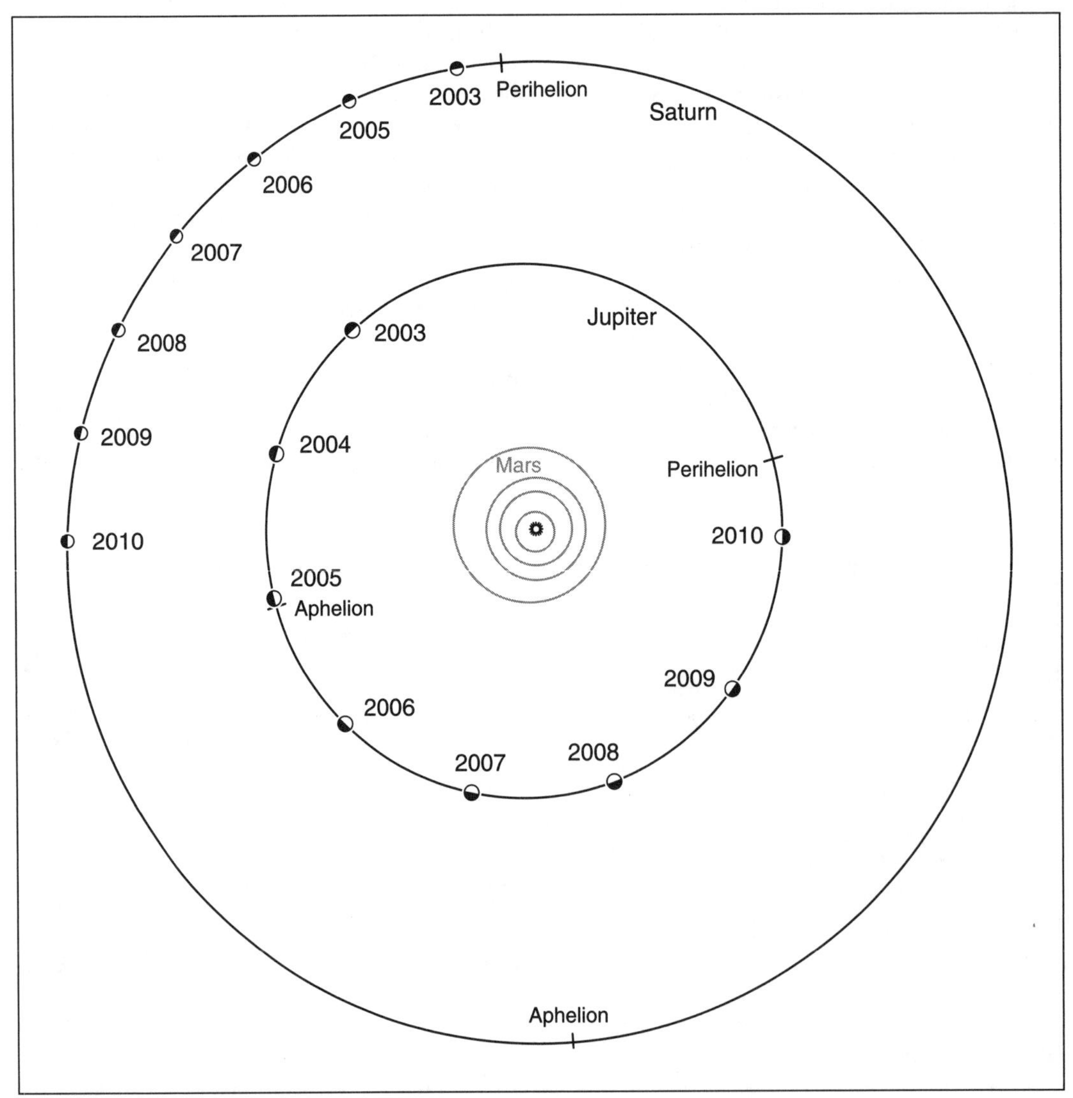

Figure 6-5. The relative positions of Jupiter and Saturn for each of their forthcoming oppositions. Jupiter pulls farther away from Saturn each year.

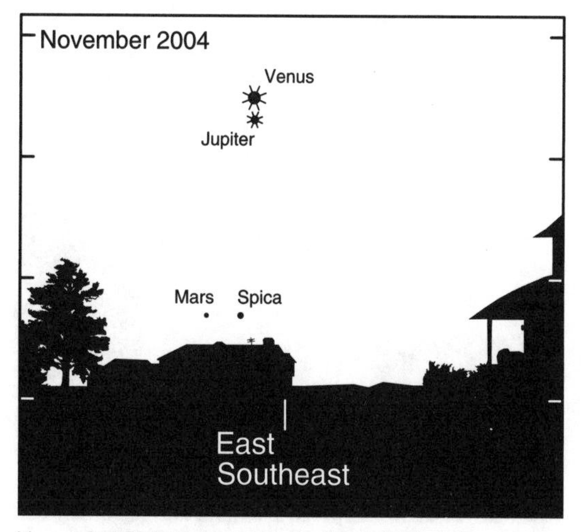

Venus (–4.0) lies closest to Jupiter (–1.7) on the morning of November 3, 2004. Spica (+0.9) and Mars (+1.7) shine faintly near the horizon beneath the brilliant pair. Look east-southeast in the hour before dawn. Saturn (+0.0) is high in the southwest near the waning gibbous moon.

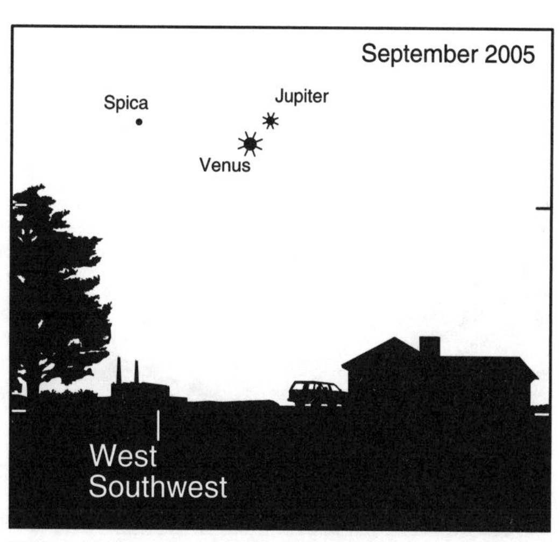

Venus (–4.0) meets Jupiter (–1.7) again on September 1, 2005, this time low in the western sky early in the hour after sunset. The pair forms a triangle with Spica (+0.9), the brightest star in Virgo, to their left. A waxing crescent moon joins the group on September 6.

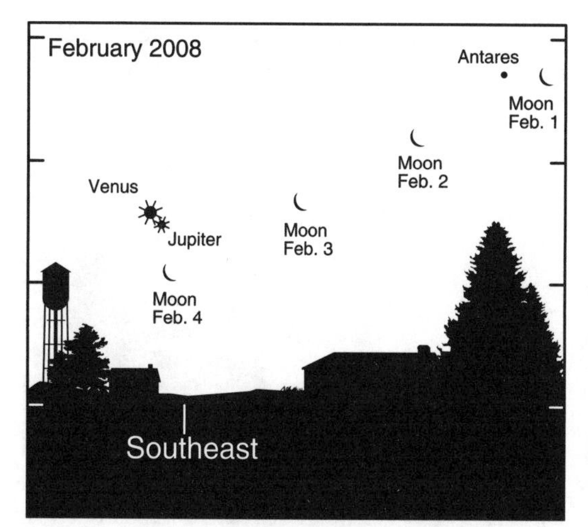

Venus (–4.0) and Jupiter (–1.9) meet in Sagittarius on the morning of February 1, 2008. Look southeast in the hour before sunrise. The waning crescent moon joins the pair on February 4.

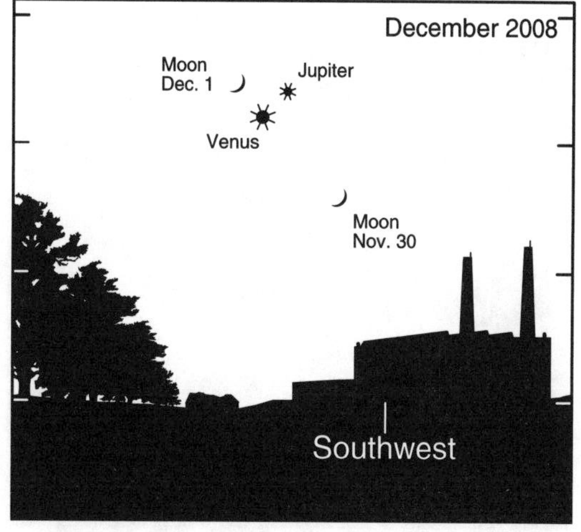

On November 30, 2008, Venus (–4.1) and Jupiter (–2.0) meet again, but this time in the evening sky. Look southwest in the hour after sunset.

Figure 6-6. Jupiter's best gatherings with the other planets through 2010.

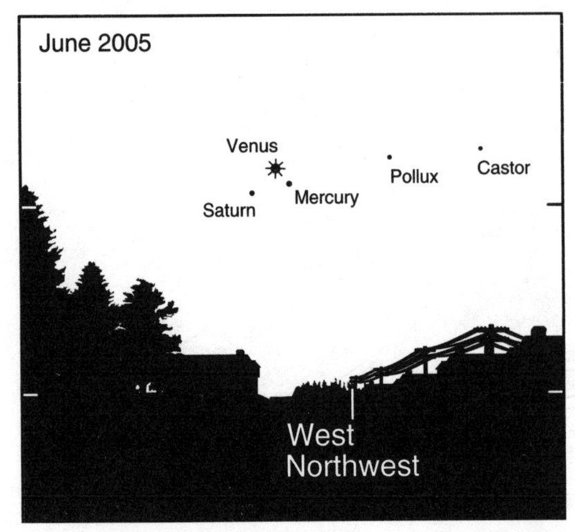

Look for Venus (–3.9) and Saturn (+0.2) low in the west-northwest thirty minutes after sundown on June 25, 2005. Mercury (–0.2), heading for next month's greatest eastern elongation and closing toward a conjunction, can be found below and to the right of Venus. Watch how the pattern created by these three planets changes over the next few evenings.

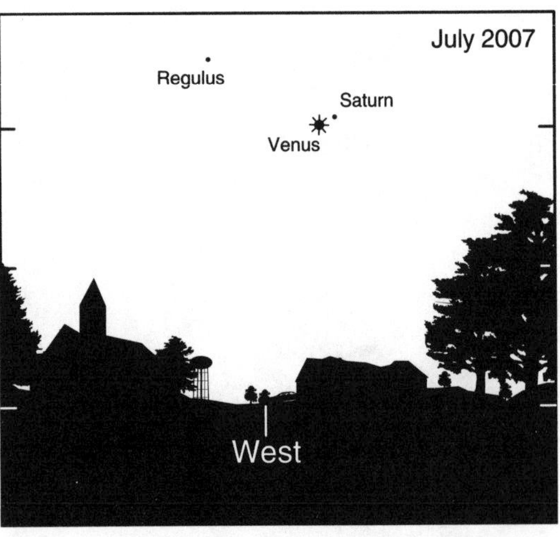

Venus (–4.4) meets Saturn (+0.6) beneath the sickle of Leo. The pair form a triangle with Regulus (+1.3) at the apex in the western sky in the hour after sunset on July 1, 2007. Mars (–0.3) gleams very high above the pair. Look for Jupiter (–2.5) high in the southeast above Antares (+0.9).

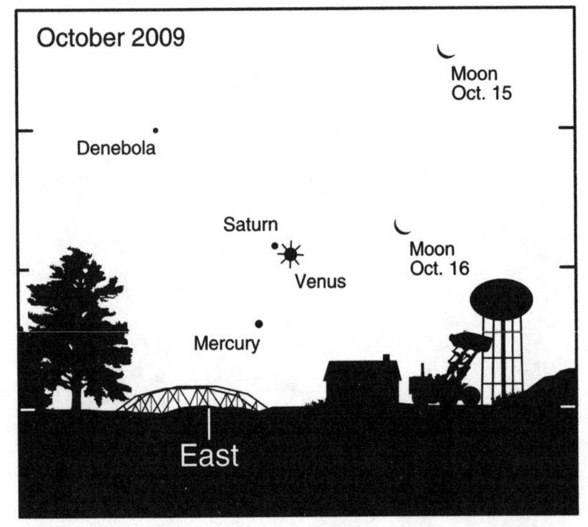

Venus (–3.9) and Saturn (+1.0) are very close to one another low in the eastern sky on the morning of October 13, 2009. Mercury (–1.0) shines below the two. The trio is shown here about thirty minutes before sunrise.

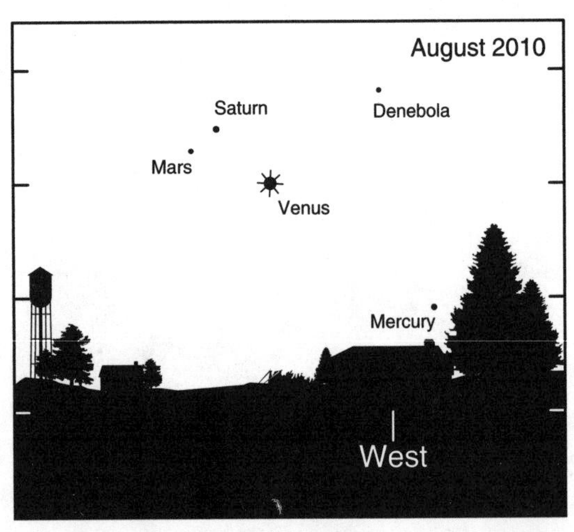

Saturn (+1.1) and Mars (+1.5) are closest tonight, shining in the west in the hour after sunset on August 1, 2010. Venus (–4.2) is far easier to find, below and to the right of Saturn and Mars. Closer to the horizon is Mercury (+0.2), headed toward greatest elongation. Look shortly after sunset to catch Mercury.

Figure 6-7. Saturn's best gatherings with the other planets through 2010.

period of twenty-nine years into 360 degrees, it's clear that Saturn moves eastward through the stars by about twelve degrees each year. Perform the same calculation for Jupiter and the result is an annual eastward motion of about thirty degrees per year. So Jupiter gains about eighteen degrees on Saturn annually, which means that about twenty years must pass before it catches up to Saturn again. This also means that Jupiter and Saturn move ever farther from one another over the course of this decade and lie opposite in the sky in 2010. Refer to figures 6-3 and 6-4 for illustrations showing the tracks of these planets; their best gatherings with the other planets are shown in figures 6-6 and 6-7.

One factor that affects a planet's brightness at opposition is its distance from Earth. Throughout this decade Jupiter improves steadily, but Saturn fades somewhat. Jupiter is farthest from Earth in 2005 but it moves ever closer to Earth at each opposition after that, reaching perihelion in March 2011. Saturn, however, is as close as it will get to us this decade during its 2003 opposition. Each year thereafter its orbit carries it farther from the sun until it reaches its maximum distance in 2018 (fig. 6-5). Saturn's next perihelion is not until 2032.

And it gets worse. The tilt of Saturn's icy rings also affects its apparent brightness. As we discussed earlier, twice during Saturn's twenty-nine-year orbit its rings appear edge-on from Earth. Saturn spins on an axis tilted about twenty-seven degrees to its orbit, and this tilt gives us different perspectives on the ring system as Saturn circles the sun. At Saturn's equinoxes, when neither its north or south pole angles into the sun, we pass through the plane of the rings and they appear edge-on. Because the rings are made of bright, icy material, they reflect sunlight well and contribute significantly to Saturn's overall brightness. Naturally, when these reflective rings are edge-on to us they contribute nothing to the planet's brightness and Saturn appears unusually dim. The southern side of the rings began angling toward us in 1996 and they'll be fully open in March and April 2003, giving Saturn its brightest magnitude at opposition. The rings close throughout this decade and are edge-on to us again in September 2009. Thus, between oppositions occurring ever farther from Earth and the slow closing of its rings, Saturn fades steadily throughout the decade. By its 2010 opposition, Saturn will be less than half as bright as it was in 2003.

7 An Introduction to the Starry Sky

When we are chafed and fretted by small cares, a look at the stars will show us the littleness of our own interests.

—Maria Mitchell, 1866

The seven lights in the sky that we've discussed so far—the sun, the moon, and the five naked-eye-visible planets—move against a starry backdrop. Up until now we've only referred to a few stars and constellations in passing, but here they become the focus. A key to identifying the constellations is to think big, for many of them sprawl across the field of view. The standard way of conveying the extent of star patterns is to give their angular size—for example, the Big Dipper stretches twenty-five degrees from end to end. That doesn't mean much to most people, but fortunately a hand held at arm's length provides a useful measure of celestial distances (fig. 7-1). The Big Dipper's bowl is about the size of the average fist held at arm's length, and the entire Dipper itself spans the distance between your thumb and little finger spread wide.

Our star charts include only the stars we expect to see from a city or suburban location far from glaring lights. Large parks, especially those near a large body of water, offer enough relief from street lights and brilliant billboards to provide a decent view of the starry sky for the urban or suburban stargazer. Some of the constellation lines suggest the locations of stars that complete a standard figure but are only visible in darker locations. Some patterns require a bit of patience to find, but a technique called averted vision can help. Because of the way the human eye is constructed—the center of its field of view is not as sensitive to light as the periphery—observers often spot a faint star by first looking one or two finger-widths away from its true location.

Personal Stars

Most people have known for years the identity of their astrological sign. The signs correspond to the constellations of the zodiac—that band in the sky in which the sun, moon, and planets are always found. This correspondence may actually inspire a few people to go out and look for that special constellation, thereby gaining a new appreciation of the sky. Table 7-1 lists the zodiacal constellations and the figures they represent. The word *zodiac* stems from the Greek *zodiakos kuklos,* "the circle of animals," a kind of celestial

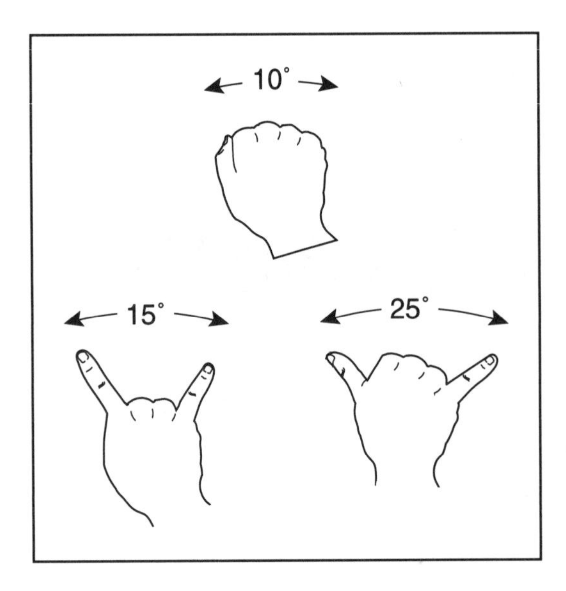

Figure 7-1. A fist at arm's length matches the bowl of the Big Dipper (10°), while the entire Dipper falls within the span of your thumb and little finger spread wide (25°). Stretching the index and little fingers wide forms a measure of the distance across the bottom of the Great Square of Pegasus (15°).

bestiary containing a variety of persons and creatures. Some are mythological, like Gemini the Twins; others are fanciful, like Capricornus—half fish, half goat. The names of the individual characters of the zodiac were largely in place in Babylonian times. As we have noted elsewhere, astrological portents were originally intended only as heavenly messages to the king regarding his management of earthly affairs; only much later was this practice extended to individuals.

While the constellations served as the inspiration for the astrological signs, the two no longer coincide with one another. First, the astrological signs became formalized as twelve equal zones along the ecliptic, but the widths of the zodiacal constellations are by no means equal. It is the sun's motion through these signs that interest astrologers, not its actual position in the constellations. Astronomers often note that the precession of the Earth's spin axis has caused the sun's position among the stars to slide along the ecliptic. For instance, it once stood in both the constellation and sign of Aries on the vernal equinox, but now it rises in the astrological sign of Aries but the astronomical constellation of Pisces. The dates listed for the "sun signs" refer, of course, to the astrological signs, not their astronomical counterparts, so for most flavors of astrology, precession is considered unimportant.

The constellations of the zodiac are not particularly prominent in the night sky; a few are downright invisible to suburban skywatchers. But the planets can serve as guides to the region of sky where that personal constellation resides. The planets Mars, Jupiter, and Saturn are best suited for this, since Mercury and Venus never stray far from the glow of twilight. Table 7-2 lists the zodiacal locations of the three outer planets through 2010. An additional constellation, Ophiuchus, appears in this table. Modern constellation boundaries for Scorpius, Ophiuchus, and Sagittarius were formalized in such a way that the ecliptic makes a short run through a non-zodiac constellation. Finally, don't expect to see a recognizable shape in the stars, even from a very dark site. Most constellations, particularly those of the zodiac, require an almost hallucinogenic imagination to discern anything resembling their namesakes.

We suggest that you turn now to the section in this chapter that matches the current season and start getting acquainted with the rest of the starry sky. Each section is accompanied by a special finder chart that will help guide you to the easiest constellations to spot. You'll find more complete maps covering the sky for the entire year at the end of the chapter.

The Glittering Gems of Winter

Although we typically spend a lot less time outdoors during the cold winter months, the sky at that time of year attracts the attention of many who otherwise don't give the sky a passing

Table 7-1. Constellations of the Zodiac

Aries	Ram
Taurus	Bull
Gemini	Twins
Cancer	Crab
Leo	Lion
Virgo	Virgin
Libra	Scales
Scorpius	Scorpion
Sagittarius	Archer
Capricornus	Sea-Goat
Aquarius	Water Carrier
Pisces	Fishes

thought. Even as we rush from warm car to warm home, we're often compelled to pause and admire the stars that glitter overhead like crystals in a celestial chandelier. The stars seem brighter in winter—and in fact they really are brighter. Table 7-3 lists the brightest stars visible from Earth. Nearly half of them are located in the winter sky. Two of those stars lie in a single constellation, Orion the Hunter, and that's the one we'll use as our guide to the winter constellations. Refer to figure 7-3 as you investigate the crystalline winter sky.

On any clear night at the beginning of the year, we can step outside at about 10:30 P.M., face south, and see a swarm of bright stars. Scan the sky from horizon to zenith (directly overhead) and a distinctive row of three stars becomes apparent. This is the belt of Orion. To the upper left of the belt is a decidedly reddish star—Betelgeuse—and to the lower right is the bright bluish star Rigel. These stars represent the right shoulder and left knee, respectively, of Orion. Scan to the right of Betelgeuse to find Bellatrix, and to the left of Rigel to find Saiph, about where we'd expect the other shoulder and knee (color plate 10). To the right, or west, of Bellatrix is a faint string of stars that just might be visible with averted vision. This is the giant's shield, raised in some renditions to fend off the rush of Taurus, the celestial bull.

Dangling from Orion's belt is a sword of three faint stars. With averted vision, you may notice that the central star in the vertical trio has an odd misty glow, unlike the pinpoints of light adjacent to it. With a pair of binoculars, you can see that

Table 7-2. Planets in the Zodiac, 2003–2010

Near opposition, the planets Mars, Jupiter, and Saturn guide you to all but three of the zodiacal constellations (Pisces, Taurus, and Scorpius). Ophiuchus was not a zodiac sign, but the ecliptic passes through the modern formal boundary of this constellation.

Constellation	Mars	Jupiter	Saturn
Gemini	2007	—	2003–2005
Cancer	2010	2003	2006
Leo	—	2004	2007–2009
Virgo	—	2005	2010
Libra	—	2006	—
Ophiuchus	—	2007	—
Sagittarius	—	2008	—
Capricornus	—	2009	—
Aquarius	2003	2010	—
Aries	2005	—	—

Table 7-3. The Brightest Stars

Name	Magnitude	Constellation
Sirius	–1.46	Canis Major
Canopus	–0.72	Carina*
Arcturus	–0.04	Bootes
Alpha Centauri	–0.01	Centaurus*
Vega	+0.03	Lyra
Capella	+0.08	Auriga
Rigel	+0.12	Orion
Procyon	+0.38	Canis Minor
Achernar	+0.46	Eridanus*
Betelgeuse	+0.50	Orion
Altair	+0.77	Aquila
Aldebaran	+0.85	Taurus
Alpha Crucis	+0.87	Crux*
Antares	+0.96	Scorpius
Spica	+0.98	Virgo

* These constellations are not labeled on the star charts because they are either inconspicuous or not visible from middle northern latitudes.

this is not some optical illusion. This is not a star at all, but the Orion Nebula, a vast cloud of dust and gas within which stars are forming (fig. 7-4). Young, hot stars emerging from this cosmic nursery are what make the nebula's gases glow. The Orion Nebula lies about 1,600 light-years distant—that is, the light we see has taken 1,600 years to reach us—and is about 30 light-years across. Large as that is, it is in fact only the brightest region of a far larger complex that encompasses over half of the entire constellation. One reason the winter stars are so bright is that many are young, and any collection of young stars has a disproportionate number of hot, bright members. Hot stars burn bright but have short lifespans. A star like Rigel may shine for a mere ten million years, whereas our sun has shone for nearly five billion years, about half its expected lifetime. In regions of the sky with a more middle-aged population, such stars have long since disappeared. Regions of star birth such as the Orion Nebula are a characteristic of the plane of the Milky Way, the disk of our galaxy, toward which we look in winter. Outside of this plane there is little gas and dust from which young stars—and their attendant planets—can form today. Astronomers observing the Orion Nebula with the Hubble Space Telescope have found young stars enveloped in protoplanetary disks of gas and dust—called *proplyds* by astronomers. Many of these appear to be in the process of evaporating in the intense ultraviolet radiation and strong stellar winds produced by neighboring hot stars.

Let's turn now to Taurus, a constellation whose stars we might consider adolescent. Taurus is a zodiacal constellation whose main stars are easy to find (color plate 11). Orion's belt points up and to the right (northwest) to the orange star Aldebaran. Aldebaran marks one tip of a *V*-shaped cluster of stars known as the Hyades, which form the face of the Bull. His horns stretch fifteen degrees to the left (east). Roughly the same distance to the upper right you'll find the Pleiades, the lovely little collection of stars that many people mistake for the Little Dipper. The

Figure 7-2. The "signs of the zodiac" originated from twelve constellations that lie along the ecliptic—the path the sun makes around the sky. This map shows the entire celestial sphere, but stars farther south than the tail of Scorpius cannot be seen from the continental United States. The faint band of the Milky Way (shaded) represents the dense population of stars in the plane of our galaxy; intervening clouds of dust give it a ragged appearance. Follow the Milky Way from Cygnus and Aquila to the southern zodiac constellations Sagittarius and Scorpius.

Pleiades are known as the Seven Sisters, after Greek mythology, although few people can spot more than six stars with the naked eye. A pair of binoculars will reveal perhaps more than a dozen or so stars; the cluster totals at least five hundred.

The Pleiades and Hyades are mythological and scientific relatives. The Hyades, daughters of Atlas and Aethra, and the Pleiades, daughters of Atlas and Hesperis, are both open or galactic clusters of stars born of enormous clouds of dust and gas. The Hyades cluster, at a distance of about 150 light-years, is one of the closest to our solar system. The members of this cluster were all born from the same vast cloud of dust over 650 million years ago and are known to be traveling together in space. About 380 light-years distant, the Pleiades is considered a younger star cluster no older than about 100 million years. Photographs reveal wisps of dust and gas still surrounding the young stars of the Pleiades, remnants of the primordial cloud from which the cluster formed.

The Pleiades cluster is such a distinctive pattern that its worldwide prominence in folklore should come as no surprise. Michael Rappenglück has argued that some symbols on the walls of Paleolithic caves in France are intended to

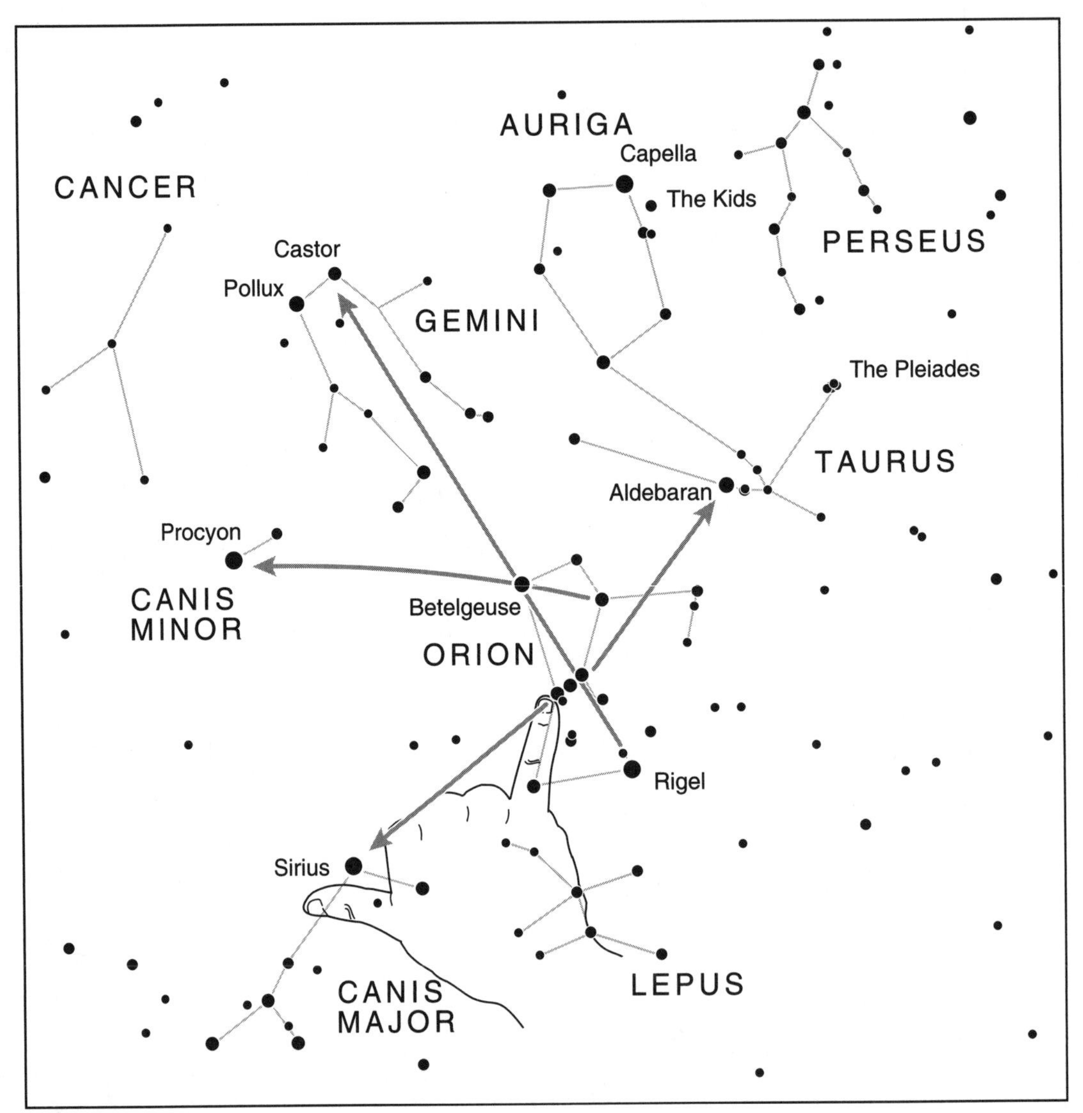

Figure 7-3. Orion will guide you to several of the bright winter constellations. Highlights of the season include Sirius—the brightest star in the sky—and the compact Pleiades star cluster.

Figure 7-4. The second "star" in Orion's sword is a nearby stellar nursery and deserves a look thorough binoculars or a telescope. (Photo by Robert Miller)

represent the Pleiades. Among tribes in the Amazon valley, its appearance marked the start of the rainy season and the migration of birds. The Guaranis of Paraguay begin their year when the Pleiades make their first appearance in the predawn sky. The Navajo and Blackfeet of North America similarly used the cluster as the basis of a stellar calendar. When the Navajo saw Dilyehe (the Pleiades) low in the early morning (late in May), they knew it was too late to plant and still be able to harvest before the first frost; the arrival of these stars in the evening sky (late September) served as a warning that the first frost was near. The principal Navajo deity, Black God, even used the cluster to adorn his forehead. Colonial sources recorded many Inca names for the cluster—Collca, Larilla, Oncoy—and in one case it is described as being the mother of all stars. In Bali and among the Caffres of South Africa, the Pleiades are consulted when the lunar calendar gets out of sync with the growing season. Many aboriginal peoples of Australia associated a rainy period with the appearance of the Pleiades, and cursed the cluster if rain fails to follow it. In Japanese folklore the Pleiades are called Subaru, a name now shared by an automobile company with a stellar logo.

The Aztecs of Mesoamerica believed that the Pleiades would herald the end of the world and began their most important ceremony on a date when the cluster—known to them as Tianquiztli (Marketplace)—crossed overhead at midnight. At the end of their fifty-two-year calendrical cycle, when the dates of their secular and sacred calendars coincided, priests watched anxiously as the cluster approached the zenith. If the Pleiades stopped moving as they passed overhead then the world would come to an end; if not, it would continue on through another fifty-two-year cycle.

Before you turn from Taurus, look for the star that marks the tip of the bull's lower horn, above Orion. A fingertip-width—about one degree—to the upper right lies the remnants of a star that, nearly 950 years ago, shone brightly enough to be seen in the daytime. Now invisible to the naked eye, this debris is the Crab Nebula, an expanding cloud of gas that marks the site of the spectacular supernova of A.D. 1054. We'll return to that famous event in chapter 9.

Our next stop in the winter sky is a pentagon of stars lying above the horns of Taurus—Auriga, the Charioteer. The most obvious member of this constellation is the bright star Capella. To the ancient Greeks, Capella represented Amalthea, a she-goat that suckled the exiled Zeus. We mention this because it's about the only way to make sense of the appellation given to the trio of stars beneath Capella—The Kids. For the beginning observer, Auriga isn't a terribly interesting constellation. A small telescope reveals a number of star clusters like the Pleiades and Hyades, though much more distant and hence smaller and fainter.

Returning now to Orion, we'll trace the line of his belt away from Taurus to the brightest nighttime star visible from Earth. This is Sirius, whose brightness stems largely from its proximity to Earth, a relatively nearby 8.6 light-years. Sirius (the name probably stems from the Greek for hot or scorching) is the Dog Star, the brightest star in Canis Major, the Greater Dog. This star's appearance in the east just before sunrise in early August signals the onset of the hottest days of the year—the Dog Days. To the ancient Egyptians, the first appearance of Sirius (called Serpet or Sothis) in the morning sky was of great importance, for it signaled the start of the vital Nile flood, a coincidence that led them to the discovery of a 365-day year by 2800 B.C. Canis Major is one of the few constellations whose rough outline does suggest the shape of its namesake. Most of these stars will be visible from suburban skies, though the dog's head is made up of fainter stars. The full constellation is about fifteen degrees long.

Animals seem to come in pairs in the heavens, and the Greater Dog has a lesser companion to the north. Trace a line eastward (left) through the shoulders of Orion until you come to the bright star Procyon. This star is Canis Minor's main claim to fame, though beginning stargazers may also appreciate its simplicity: Only one other star is required to complete its standard figure. Canis Minor and Canis Major are often considered one of the hounds Orion took on his hunts. Procyon makes it into the list of the top ten brightest stars and is also one of the nearest stars (see table 7-4).

Our final winter stop is another constellation of the zodiac—Gemini, the Twins. The pair of bright stars that marks the heads of the Twins can be found along a line extended from Rigel through Betelgeuse. The brighter of the two stars is Pollux; his twin Castor lies nearer the Pole Star. The constellation is about equal to Orion in length, extending toward the Hunter from the twin stars. Castor and Pollux would stand out in any other season but they pale before the surrounding stars of winter. Of historical interest: Gemini is the constellation in which Clyde Tombaugh of Lowell Observatory discovered Pluto in 1930.

Before we leave the winter sky, it's interesting to observe a characteristic of stars that is often unnoticed, but fairly obvious when pointed out: their colors. They stand out particularly well when comparing stars of contrasting colors, such as Betelgeuse and Rigel in Orion. Betelgeuse is clearly reddish and Rigel seems to have a bluish tint. Aldebaran in Taurus is another colorful star, running perhaps a bit more toward the orange than Betelgeuse. The color of a star is an important clue to its physical nature since it reveals its surface temperature. The bluest stars are the hottest; Rigel's surface temperature runs about 21,100°F (11,700°C), or a bit more than twice as hot as the solar surface. The cooler the star, the redder it appears—Betelgeuse is about 6,300°F (3,500°C), about two-thirds as hot as the sun. The white and blue-white stars are in the prime of life, but redder stars like Betelgeuse and Aldebaran are nearing the end of their lives. They have reached the so-called "red giant" phase of a star's life, a period marked by a dramatic expansion that spreads the star's energy over a larger surface area and reduces its surface temperature. More massive than our own sun, Betelgeuse actually qualifies as a red supergiant. If placed at the sun's position in the solar system, Betelgeuse would engulf all the planets closer to the sun than Jupiter.

The Stars of Spring

After the bright stars of winter, the spring sky may seem a bit drab, but there are compensations. While the spring stars are generally not as bright as those of winter, the temperatures of spring tend to be more tolerable for those who want to linger outdoors. The major constellations are quite easy to identify since we have a great guiding constellation. Figure 7-5 gives an overview to finding your way around the spring sky.

The key to the spring stars is a constellation that isn't a true constellation. The familiar Big Dipper, also known as the Plow in Europe, is really just part of Ursa Major, the Greater Bear of the north. A prominent grouping of stars that forms only part of a true constellation is known as an *asterism*. The Big Dipper lies relatively close to the north celestial pole, and is one of a handful of circumpolar star groups that never set from middle northern latitudes. For the purpose of finding the spring constellations, the best time to look for the Big Dipper is about 10:30 P.M. local daylight time at the beginning of April, two hours later in May. Face south to locate the Big Dipper, whose stars are visible from all but the most brightly lit urban sites (color plate 12). Hold your hand nearly overhead with your thumb and little finger stretched as far apart as possible; this is the extent of the Dipper. It should be fairly easy to identify the distinctive bowl and curving handle. (Observers in the southern United States and especially Hawaii may find it more easily facing north, since it appears lower in the sky; bear in mind, though, that it will appear upside down when compared with figure 7-5.)

Once you've spotted the Big Dipper, take a good look at the middle star of the handle. This star, Mizar, has a faint companion that can be picked out by those with keen eyesight. The companion, Alcor, is another candidate for the averted vision trick. If you still can't see Alcor with the unaided eye, try a pair of binoculars. This is a double star, two stars that appear close together from our viewpoint on Earth.

Since we mentioned galactic star clusters in the winter section, it's worth noting that most of the stars of the Big Dipper are members of the closest known cluster, lying about seventy-five light-years away. Interestingly, stars in a large volume of space that includes the sun appear to be moving in the same general direction as the stars of the Ursa Major cluster. Perhaps our sun was born in a region of the same vast cloud of gas that gave rise to the stars of the Big Dipper.

Turn north now to find a single star. The two stars of the Dipper's bowl farthest from the handle are known as the pointer stars; they form a line that, if extended about a hand-span northward, passes near a single moderately bright star, Polaris. Polaris, the North Star or Pole Star, lies almost directly above the Earth's north pole and is the pivot around which the celestial vault revolves. The Pawnee of North America called it "the star that does not walk around," and groups in Europe and Asia referred to it as the "nail of the world" or "pillar of heaven." Polaris marks the end of the handle of the Little Dipper in Ursa Minor (the Lesser Bear). Most of this constellation's stars are too faint to see from city sites, though the stars

Table 7-4. The Nearest Stars

Name	Distance (Light-Years)	Magnitude	Constellation
Sun	0.000016	-26.80	—
Alpha Centauri C*	4.2	+10.70	Centaurus
Alpha Centauri A*	4.4	−0.01	Centaurus
Barnard's star	6.0	+ 9.50	Ophiuchus
Wolf 359	7.8	+13.50	Leo
Lalande 21185	8.3	+7.50	Canes Venatici
Sirius	8.6	−1.46	Canis Major
UVCeti	8.7	+12.50	Cetus
Ross 154	9.7	+10.40	Sagittarius
Ross 248	10.3	+12.30	Andromeda
Epsilon Eridani	10.5	+3.70	Eridanus
Lacaille 9352	10.7	+7.30	Sculptor
Ross 128	10.9	+11.10	Virgo
61 Cygni	11.2	+5.20	Cygnus
EZ Aquarii	11.3	+13.30	Aquarius
Procyon	11.4	+0.38	Canis Minor
GJ 725	11.5	+8.90	Draco
GJ 15	11.6	+8.10	Lyra
Epsilon Indi	11.8	+4.70	Indus
DX Cancri	11.8	+14.80	Cancer
Tau Ceti	11.9	+3.50	Cetus

* These two stars—plus a third component not listed—orbit one another as part of a single star system.

corresponding to the Big Dipper's pointers are visible to most observers.

While the North Star seems unmoving in the night sky, it isn't precisely on the north celestial pole. A long-exposure photograph shows a noticeable trail as Polaris moves. The Pole Star is a symbol of steadfastness and reliability, but as we noted earlier, the Earth wobbles slowly and this precession causes the Earth's axis to move across the sky. When the Pyramids were being built in Egypt, the star Thuban in Draco was the pole star; 12,000 years ago, the bright summer star Vega was near, though not at, the north celestial pole. The Earth's axis moves still closer to Polaris until 2102.

Turning back south, we find some constellations we have a better chance of seeing in their entirety. Again we start at the Big Dipper, whose arcing handle also serves as a pointer. Extend an imaginary curve away from the bowl to the southeast—"arc to Arcturus"—until you spot a bright, yellowish star. This is Arcturus, in Bootes the Herdsman, the brightest star in the spring sky. The rather faint stars of Bootes form an elongated kite, about a hand-span high, extending north of Arcturus.

Follow the same arc from the Dipper's handle to Arcturus and then extend it beyond to another star of similar brightness. This is Spica, the brightest star in Virgo. Virgo was associated with the harvest and the name Spica refers to an ear of wheat. Virgo is one of the largest constellations—nearly two hand-spans across—and one of the most conspicuous of the zodiac. It so happens that the spring sky gives us a view out of the plane of our home galaxy, the Milky Way. The dense clouds of gas and dust lying within the Milky Way block our view of the extra-galactic universe. Galaxies are scattered throughout the spring sky. But when we come to Virgo, we find an astounding concentration of over 2,000 galaxies known as the Virgo Cluster of Galaxies. Amateur telescopes can reveal perhaps a hundred of these in the region about a hand-span north of Spica. Although invisible to the naked eye, it's remarkable that they can be seen at all since they lie 60 million light-years away—and it's worth noting that this seemingly empty patch of sky teems with literally trillions of distant suns.

Our final spring target is Leo. If you haven't already made out its distinctive shape, return to the Big Dipper. The side of the bowl near the handle acts as yet another set of pointers, this time south to a bright star halfway between the Big

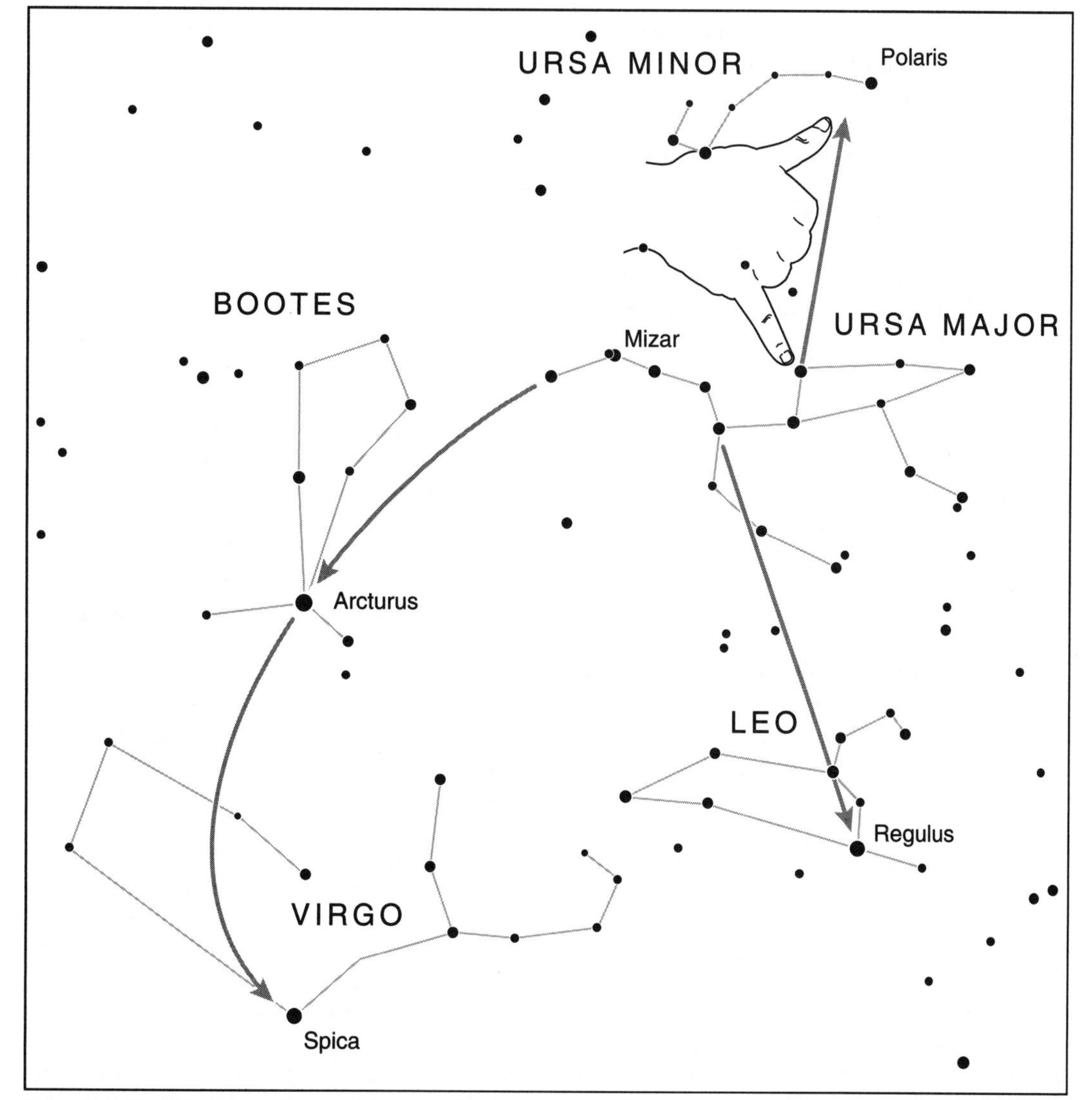

Figure 7-5. The Big Dipper, the most famous of spring star groups, shows the way to several constellations. Mizar and Alcor, in the Dipper's handle, also serve as a test of your vision!

Dipper and the southern horizon. This is Regulus, the "little king" of Leo, the Lion. Leo's most distinctive feature is "the sickle," a backward question mark that rises from Regulus. A right triangle of stars represents the lion's haunches, about a hand-span to the left, or east.

To the right of the sickle is Cancer, one of the least conspicuous constellations of the sky. Outside of the astrologically curious, the only real interest this constellation may hold for the beginning astronomer is the star cluster at its heart. Classical authors referred to it as a cloud or mist, but when Galileo turned his telescope toward the Praesepe cluster in 1610, he noted that it "is not a single star but a mass of more than forty starlets." This object, often called by the whimsical name of Beehive, is a naked-eye object out in the countryside (fig. 7-6). It may be enjoyed with binoculars from a suburban site, but locating it will be a challenge. The cluster itself contains at least 200 stars and lies 577 light-years away. Both its track through the galaxy and the age of its stellar population (400 million years) resemble those of the Hyades cluster in Taurus, and some speculate that the two clusters may have formed from the same stellar nursery.

The Summer Sky

Summer is a bit frustrating for stargazers. The temperatures are congenial, but the nights start late and insects can be a nuisance in many regions. Still, the late hours don't need to be a problem, at least during summer vacation. The summer sky lacks a single constellation that can serve as a guide to the others, but as figure 7-7 shows, there are features that will help you find your way around. Facing east and scanning the sky, we soon spot a bright star nearly overhead. A little lower is another star not nearly as bright, and to the south (right) is a third bright star. Each member of this stellar trio is the brightest star of its own constellation; together they form an asterism known as the Summer Triangle.

The brightest of the three stars is Vega, in the small constellation of Lyra, the Lyre. This is the lyre that the luckless Orpheus used to charm the guardians of Hades so that he could rescue his beautiful wife Eurydice from the realm of the dead. He lost her when, contrary to instructions, he looked back too soon to see if she was still behind him. The Chinese tell a lovely tale in which Vega is Chih-nu, a divine princess who fell in love with a mortal—a poor herdsman, no less. Her father, the sun god, didn't think this a proper match and placed them in the sky, separated by a heavenly river. Once a year, however, a sympathetic flock of magpies forms a bridge between the lovers, who are thus briefly reunited.

Ch'ien-niu, the herdsman of that tale, is known to westerners as Altair, the second brightest star of our stellar triangle and the farthest from Vega. Altair lies at the head of Aquila, the Eagle. This is another one of those rare constellations that bears at least a vague resemblance to its namesake. The eagle flies northeast with broad wings more than a hand-span across.

Deneb, the third star of the Summer Triangle, is also part of an avian constellation. Deneb marks the tail end of Cygnus, the Swan, which is flying in the opposite direction of Aquila. Each of the swan's wings is nearly a hand-span in extent. The neck is equally long, with the head marked by a somewhat faint star not far from the southern end of Lyra. Urban stargazers will have trouble locating the full extent of the constellation, but its brightest stars form the more easily noticed asterism of the Northern Cross (color plate 13).

If in winter we are looking into the plane of the Milky Way and then out of that plane in spring, it stands to reason that summer would give us another view of our galaxy. In fact, summer brings the very best views. Cygnus the Swan is flying right down the Milky Way, the glowing river of stars that represents the stream that separates the mythical Chinese lovers. Tracing the Swan's imaginary flyway southward brings us to the reddish star Antares, the brightest in Scorpius, the Scorpion. The name Antares means "rival of Mars" and the wisdom of the choice is particularly apparent when the Red Planet passes near it. The constellation itself is reasonably bright and distinctive.

Tracing the Scorpion's curving figure to the end of its tail, we come upon a group of stars that resembles a teapot. About the size of an open hand, the teapot asterism is part of the constellation Sagittarius, the Archer. Seen from dark skies this distinctive pattern seems lost within the glow of the Milky Way's star clouds (color plate 14). Since we're looking back into the plane of the galaxy, thick with clouds of gas and dust, we also have a view toward many

Figure 7-6. The Praesepe star cluster in Cancer is also known as the Beehive. It's another target worth a glimpse through binoculars. (Photo by Robert Miller)

regions of star formation. Sagittarius is particularly rich in this regard. Away from the glare of bright city lights, you can use a pair of binoculars to spot dense clouds of stars and nebulas, which appear as faintly milky patches of light, throughout the Sagittarius region.

The summer Milky Way is worth a special trip out to the countryside for a good look. Again, a pair of binoculars is a great help, but not absolutely necessary for a rewarding experience. To truly appreciate the sight, our eyes must have time to adapt to darkness. Two physiological changes take place. The first, which takes only a few minutes, dilates the pupils to their maximum size to allow more light into the eyes. A much slower chemical change takes place among the photoreceptors within the eye, an adaptation to the dark that gradually makes the cells more sensitive to light over a period of about thirty minutes. It's important to stay away from lights, since just a brief glimpse of a dome light or car headlight will partially reverse the process. The eye is less sensitive to red light, though, so a flashlight dimmed by red filters helps preserve night vision.

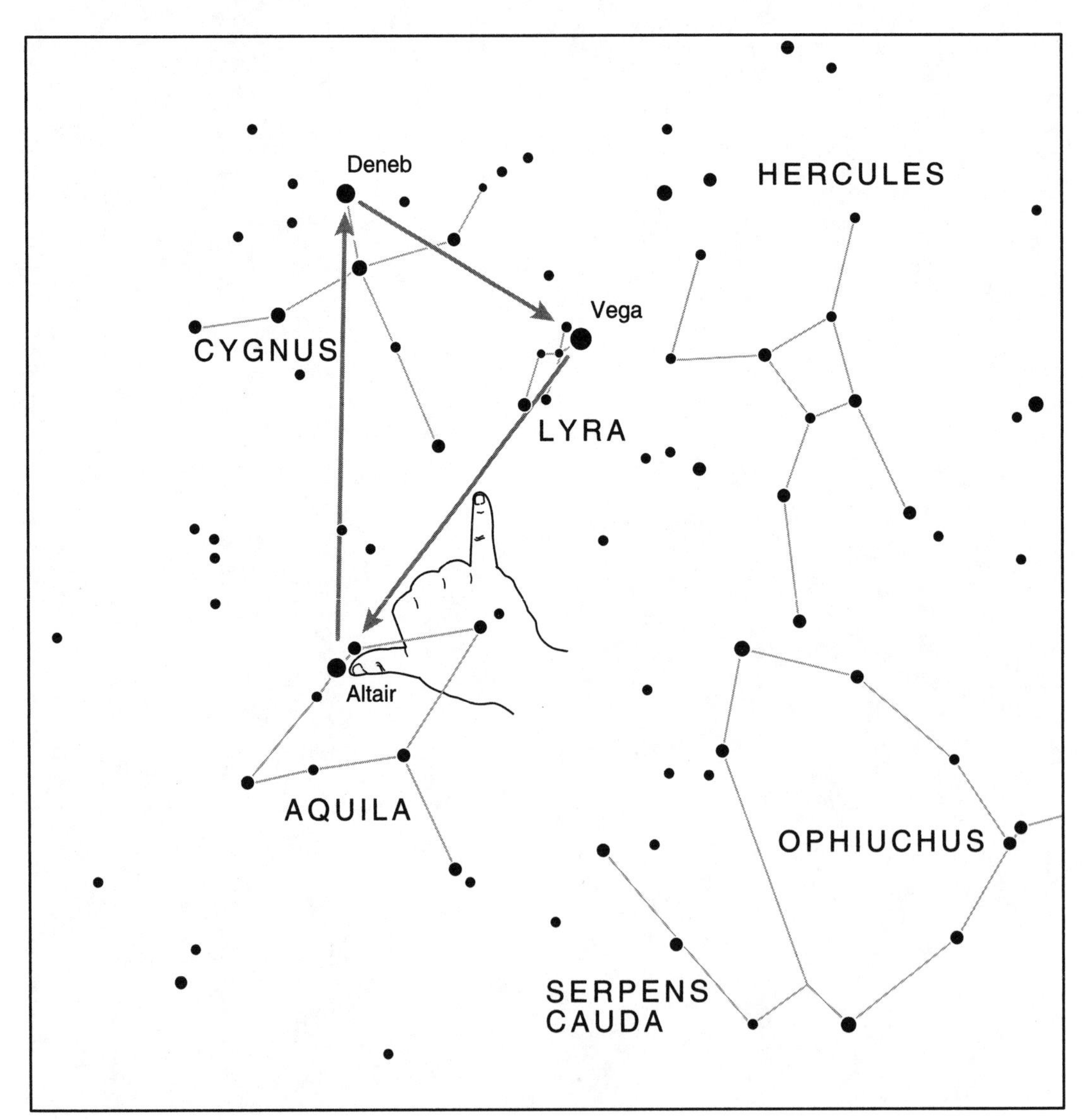

Figure 7-7. Start your explorations of the summer sky with the Summer Triangle of Vega, Altair, and Deneb. Farther south lie two distinctive constellations, Scorpius and Sagittarius.

Once your eyes have adapted to the darkness, surprising variations of light and dark become apparent in the Milky Way. The region near the head of Cygnus is particularly interesting. It is the beginning of the Great Rift, an elongated dark patch that splits the Milky Way down to the horizon. Interestingly, villagers in modern Peru count among their constellations animal shapes formed by dark patches in the southern Milky Way, probably an astronomical relic of the great Inca empire.

As we said earlier, the Milky Way is a sort of celestial flyway for Aquila the Eagle and Cygnus the Swan. It runs from above Cygnus down to Sagittarius. The name Milky Way comes from the Latin *via lactea.* The Greeks called it *galaxias kuklos,* the milky circle, from which we get the generic term galaxy. Many cultures regarded the Milky Way as the river of heaven. Some early natural philosophers speculated that the glow of the Milky Way was the product of innumerable unresolved stars, but it wasn't until Galileo examined the region with his telescope that the matter was settled. "Upon whatever part of it the telescope is directed," he wrote, "a vast crowd of stars is immediately presented to view. Many of them are rather large and quite bright, while the number of the smaller ones is quite beyond calculation." It was over a century, however, before anyone suggested that that glowing circle was actually our home in the cosmos. In the late eighteenth century, William Herschel (1738–1822) attempted to map the galaxy by counting stars, and he correctly guessed the structure of the Milky Way. At the beginning of the twentieth century, Harlow Shapley (1885–1972) charted a particular type of star cluster and recognized that they were distributed in a roughly spherical pattern. He also realized that the center of the sphere was the center of the galaxy.

Today, astronomers reckon that the main disk of the galaxy is about 100,000 light years across, with our solar system lying about 28,000 light years from the center—in the galactic suburbs, as it were. Even at that great distance, the glow of the concentration of stars at the galactic center would be as bright as the full moon, if our view were not blocked by intervening dust and gas. That view is only blocked to human eyes; radio telescopes have been used to study the radio waves that pierce the dusty veil. Such studies indicate that stupendous amounts of energy are being released at the galactic center. One theory holds that enormous stars are being born and exploding in a ferocious "starburst" that produces as much energy as thirty million suns. Others offer a more intriguing idea: a black hole several million times more massive than the sun lies at the galactic center, gobbling up matter. Material spiraling into such a black hole would give off vast amounts of radiation before disappearing for eternity. As we reflect on the silent beauty of the Milky Way, we can try to imagine the incredible energies at work in the invisible heart of our galaxy.

The "Watery" Autumn Sky

As the Earth revolves around the sun, the planet soon turns its night side away from the galactic center toward a region of the sky that seems almost starless by comparison. As in spring, we're largely looking away from the galaxy's disk. The shortening days make the Summer Triangle an obvious feature of the evening sky, its prominence no doubt enhanced by the dearth of bright fall constellations. In particular, the "watery" constellations of the zodiac—Capricornus the Sea-Goat, Aquarius the Water Bearer, and Pisces the Fishes—are as faint as they are famous. Nevertheless, the fall sky does offer some treats, including one of the year's very best. Figure 7-8 illustrates the highlights of fall and the best routes for finding them.

Our first stop is a regal constellation, Cassiopeia. To find this celestial queen, face north at about 10:30 P.M. local time in mid-September. With a clear view to the horizon, we can make out the Big Dipper low in the sky. Using its pointer stars to find Polaris, we keep going until we reach a group of stars that form a rather lopsided numeral *3* nearly overhead. Depending on the time of year and hour, Cassiopeia variously resembles an *M,* a *W,* an *E,* or a *3* (color plate 15). As with many constellations, this one looks small on our maps, but is rather large in the sky, covering roughly the space between the index and little fingers held at arm's length.

Cassiopeia was the matriarch of a legendary family that included Cepheus and Andromeda, two more autumn constellations. Andromeda married Perseus, rider of Pegasus, the winged horse—both also represented in this season's stars. Perseus won Andromeda's hand by rescuing her from Cetus, a sea monster and itself one of the faint water constellations of fall. Cassiopeia, it should be noted, lies embedded in the Milky Way along Aquila's flyway.

In addition to her mythical notoriety, Cassiopeia serves the useful function of guiding us to the Great Square of Pegasus. Facing south now, we lean back to spot Cassiopeia, now a sloppy *E.* From the second-lowest leg of the *E,* extend a line southward to locate the Great Square, which rides high in the sky. The Square is about the width of Cassiopeia, but its stars are bright and it should be an easy target. A square doesn't much suggest a horse, of course, so we must turn to the northeast and view the upper left edge of the Square to see any remotely equestrian features. Extending from the upper right corner is the horse's neck and face; the forelegs are kicking from the lower left corner. Those looking for the wings of Pegasus, however, are on their own.

We turn now to a constellation that holds one of the sky's most splendid naked-eye sights. We begin from a star at the northeast corner of the Great Square, one properly considered a member of the constellation Andromeda. She was the Chained Maiden left out as a sacrifice for monstrous Cetus. In a dark sky we see a *V* of stars extending diagonally from the Square, but in light-fogged city skies only the southerly leg of this *V* can be seen. First we hop two stars along the *V* from the Square's corner, then we look for a star just above that second star. We continue upward along that line and at an equal distance we find a third and fainter star. If you can see this third star, the sky may be dark enough to discern a milky patch of light nearby; if not, try binoculars. That smudge represents light that started its journey to your eyes before modern humans walked the Earth. It is the Great Galaxy in Andromeda, 2.9 million light-years from our own galaxy. From dark country skies, it's quite noticeable as a small glowing cloud of light, making it easily the most distant object that can be seen with the naked eye.

The Andromeda Galaxy lets us see from the outside in the fall what we were seeing from the inside when gazing at the summer Milky Way: a system of hundreds of billions of stars forming an "island universe" in the vastness of intergalactic space. The Andromeda Galaxy was, of course, known to ancient stargazers who had little notion of its true nature. The first record of it is from A.D. 905. For centuries it was known as the Andromeda Nebula and placed in roughly the same class as the Orion Nebula. With telescopes, astronomers eventually saw that the Andromeda Nebula was a member of a class of spiral nebulas. One view fairly popular in the nineteenth century held that the swirling spiral nebulas were solar systems at the earliest stage of formation. In 1912 Henrietta Leavitt (1868–1921) of Harvard College Observatory made an important discovery about a class of stars called Cepheid variables. These stars change brightness in cycles that revealed their true luminosity. The longer they take to run through their cycle, the brighter they are. By comparing a star's intrinsic luminosity to its apparent brightness, astronomers can of course determine the star's true distance. In 1924, Edwin Hubble (1889–1953) discovered Cepheid variables in the Andromeda Nebula and used them to prove that it is a galaxy in its own right, far beyond our own. Hubble thus took the Copernican revolution a step further, showing that our galaxy was just one of many spiral galaxies sprinkled throughout the cosmos. New research has placed the Andromeda galaxy a little farther away than Hubble calculated, and recent estimates of its mass suggest that our Milky Way is a larger galaxy.

With a little effort, anyone can spot the handful of constellations we've briefly discussed. In time they will become familiar companions anticipated with the change of seasons. On the following pages we provide more detailed star maps with additional constellations to be explored. We've included just the stars you can expect to see from a reasonably dark urban site, such as a large park. However, we've also included all of the lines used in standard constellation figures, which means that there may be no star symbol where constellation lines imply that one exists.

To use the charts, simply hold them overhead so the direction on the map matches the direction in which you're facing. Be sure to cover the lens of your flashlight with several layers of red paper or brown grocery-bag paper. This will help preserve your night vision when reading the maps. Do your initial stargazing from the backyard or a suburban park, where the glow of lights washes out the faintest stars and simplifies the sky. Once you've mastered locating a few constellations, look for darker skies to test your skills and appreciate the more subtle wonders we've mentioned.

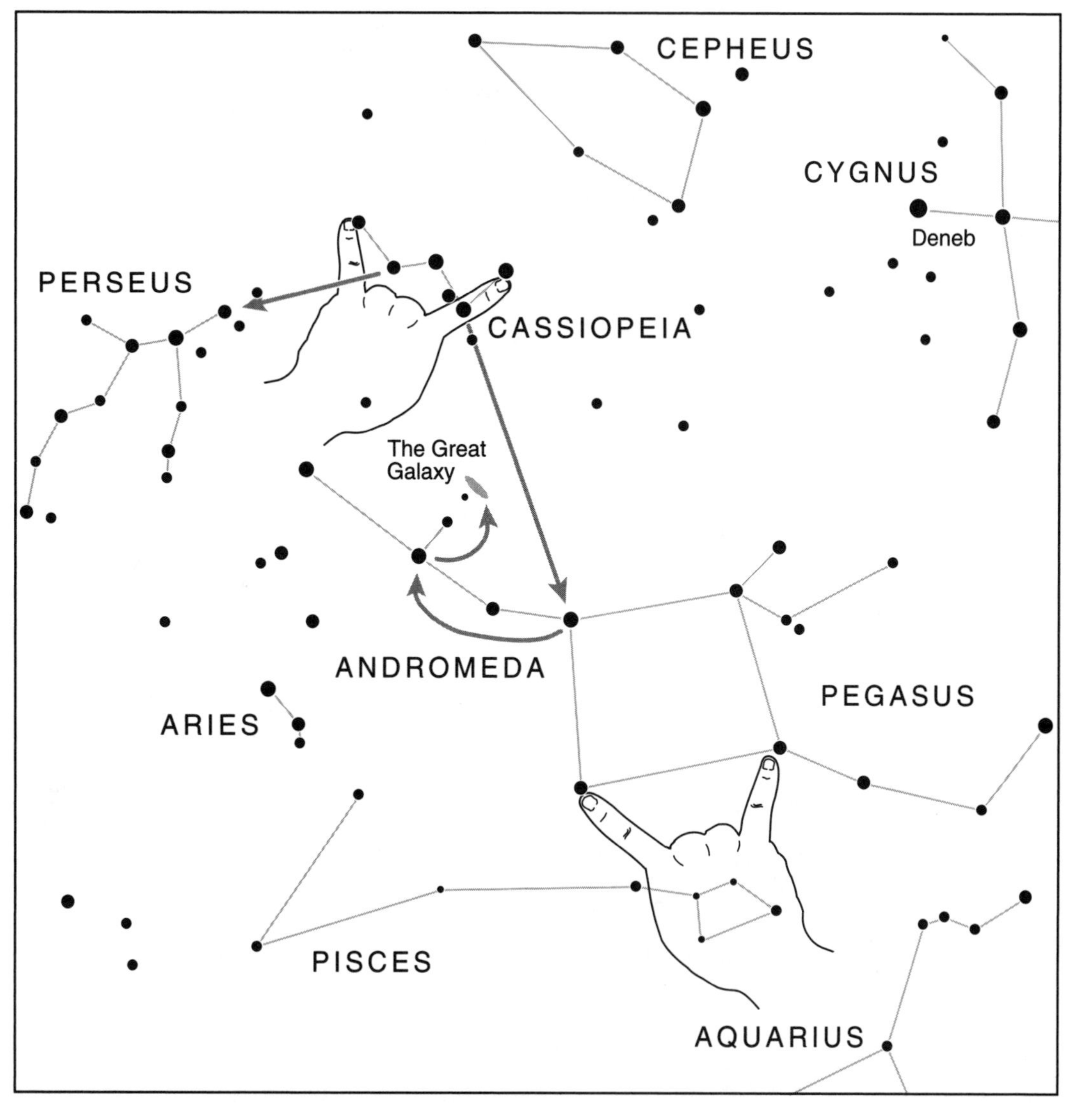

Figure 7-8. The Great Square of Pegasus is the keystone of the autumn sky, though you may need Cassiopeia's assistance to find it. Hop along Andromeda's chains to locate the jewel of the fall sky: The Great Galaxy.

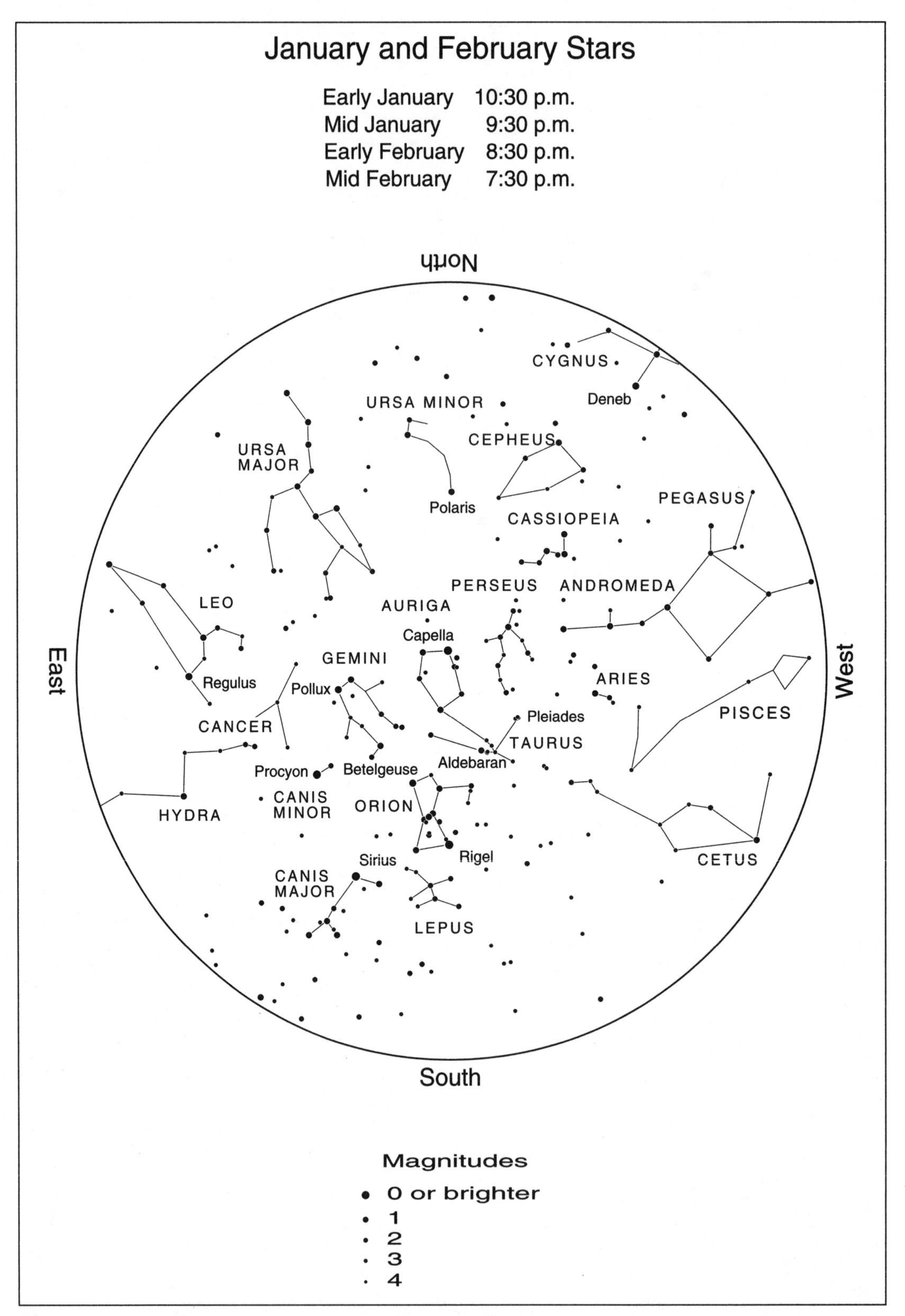

Figure 7-9. These charts illustrate the entire sky as seen from middle northern latitudes. At the center is the zenith, the point directly overhead, and the bounding circle represents an idealized horizon. Late winter evenings gleam with brilliant stars; refer to figure 7-3 for a roadmap to the most prominent constellations.

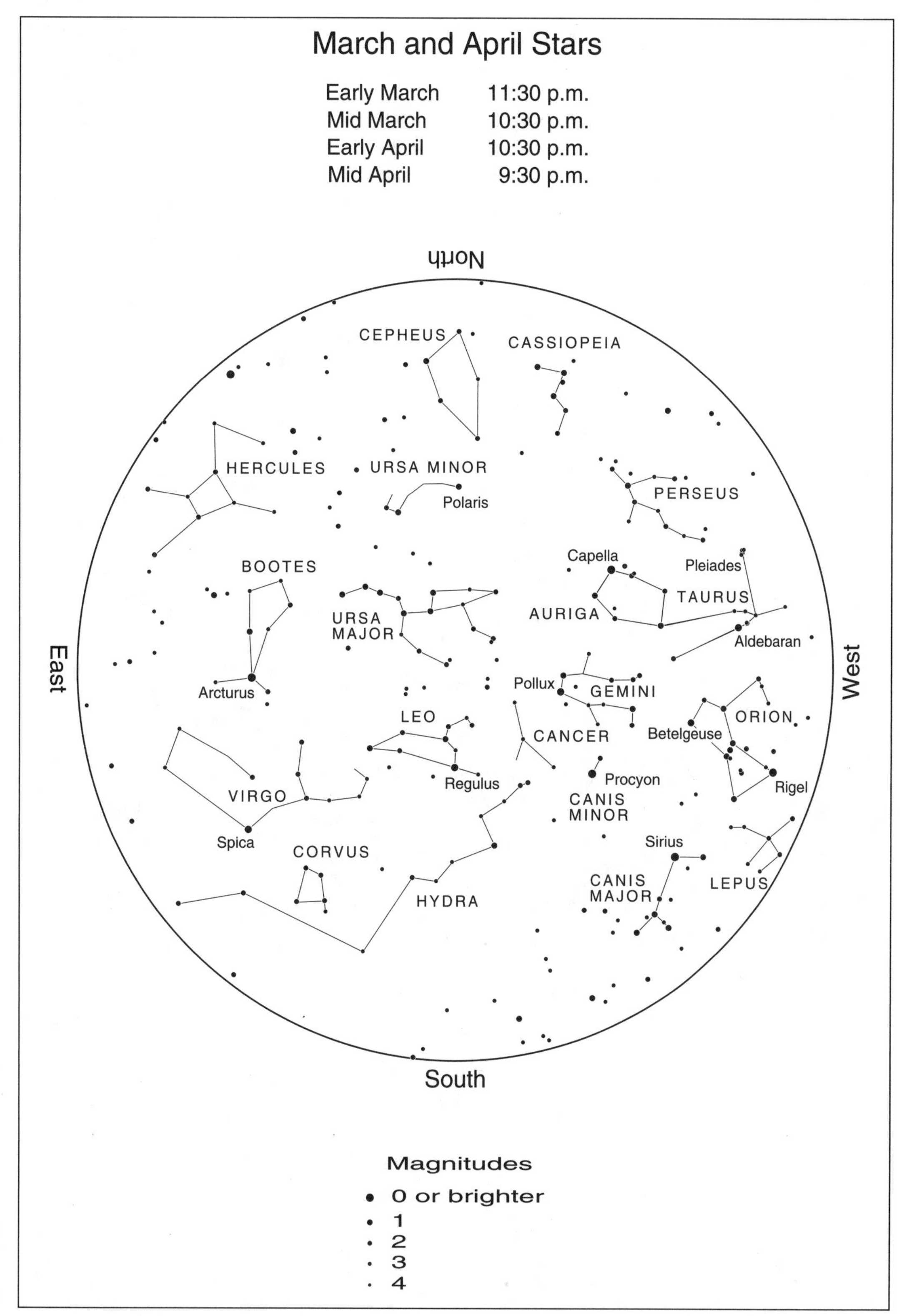

Figure 7-10. The bright stars of winter can still be seen in the western sky as spring arrives, but they drift ever closer to the glow of evening twilight. Ursa Major's Big Dipper is prominent now and serves as a guide for locating Polaris, Arcturus, Spica, and Regulus (fig. 7-5).

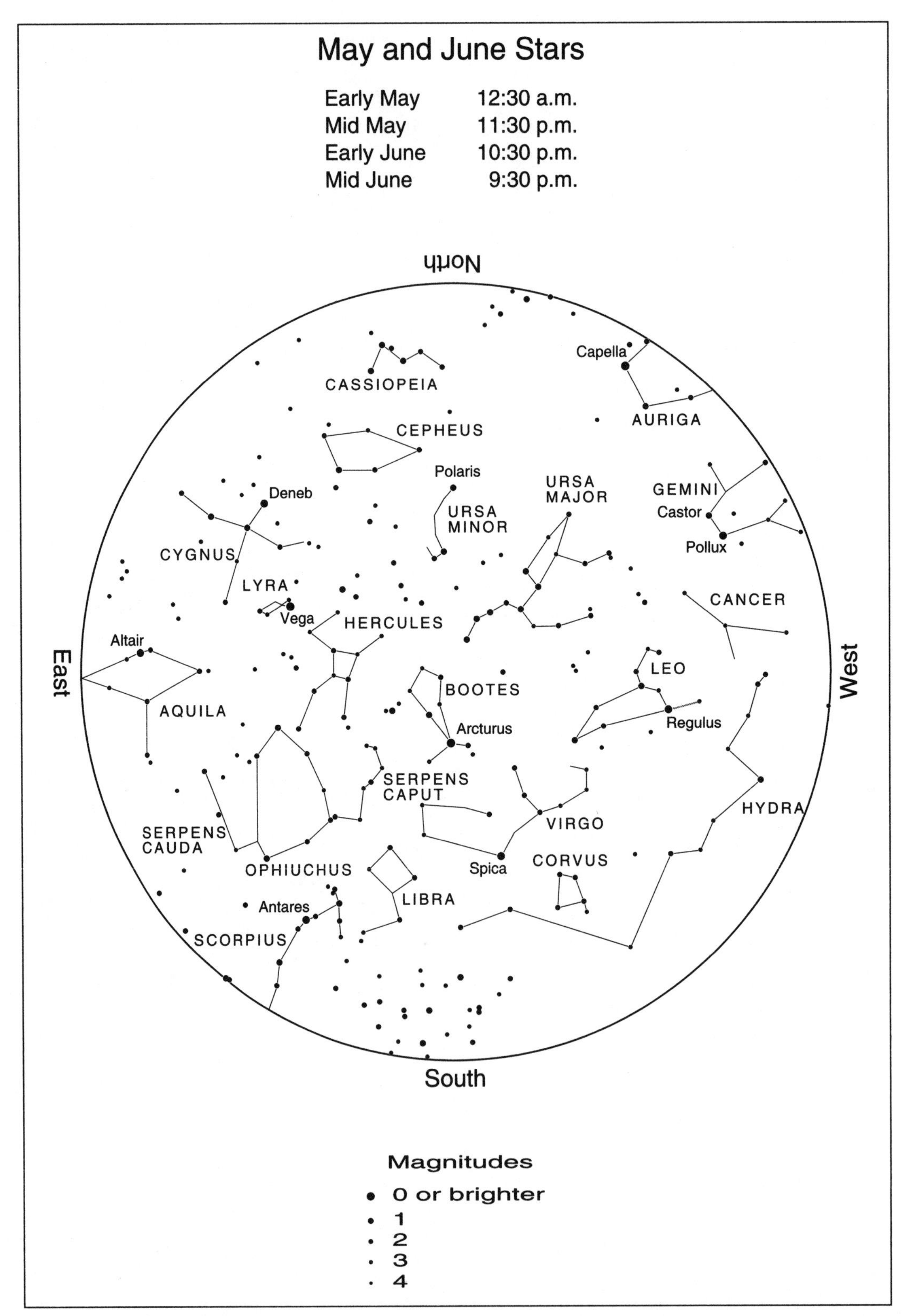

Figure 7-11. Let the Big Dipper in Ursa Major guide you to the prominent spring constellations (fig. 7-5). As spring turns to summer, the last of the winter constellations drift into evening twilight and a new group of bright stars—Deneb, Altair, Vega, and Antares—gleams in the east. The first three form the asterism known as the Summer Triangle (fig. 7-7); all lie in or near the dimly glowing band of the Milky Way (fig. 7-2).

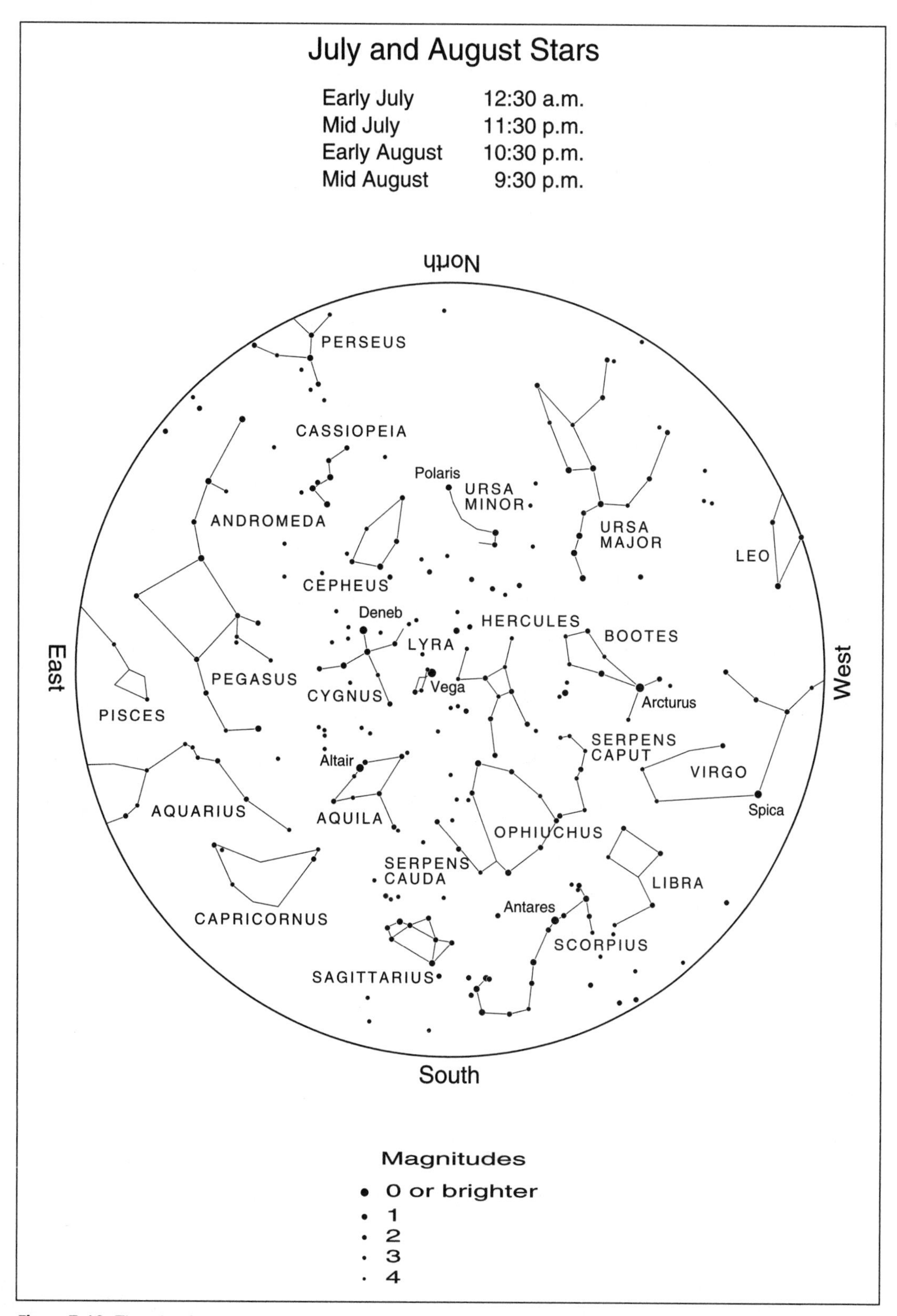

Figure 7-12. The trio of stars in the Summer Triangle (fig. 7-7) are most visible now. From a reasonably dark location, the Milky Way can be seen arcing from Cygnus to Scorpius (fig. 7-2). Rich star clouds occupy the region near Sagittarius, whose stars lie closest to our line of sight with the shrouded heart of our home galaxy. Figure 7-5 still serves as a guide to the spring constellations, which now reside in the western sky.

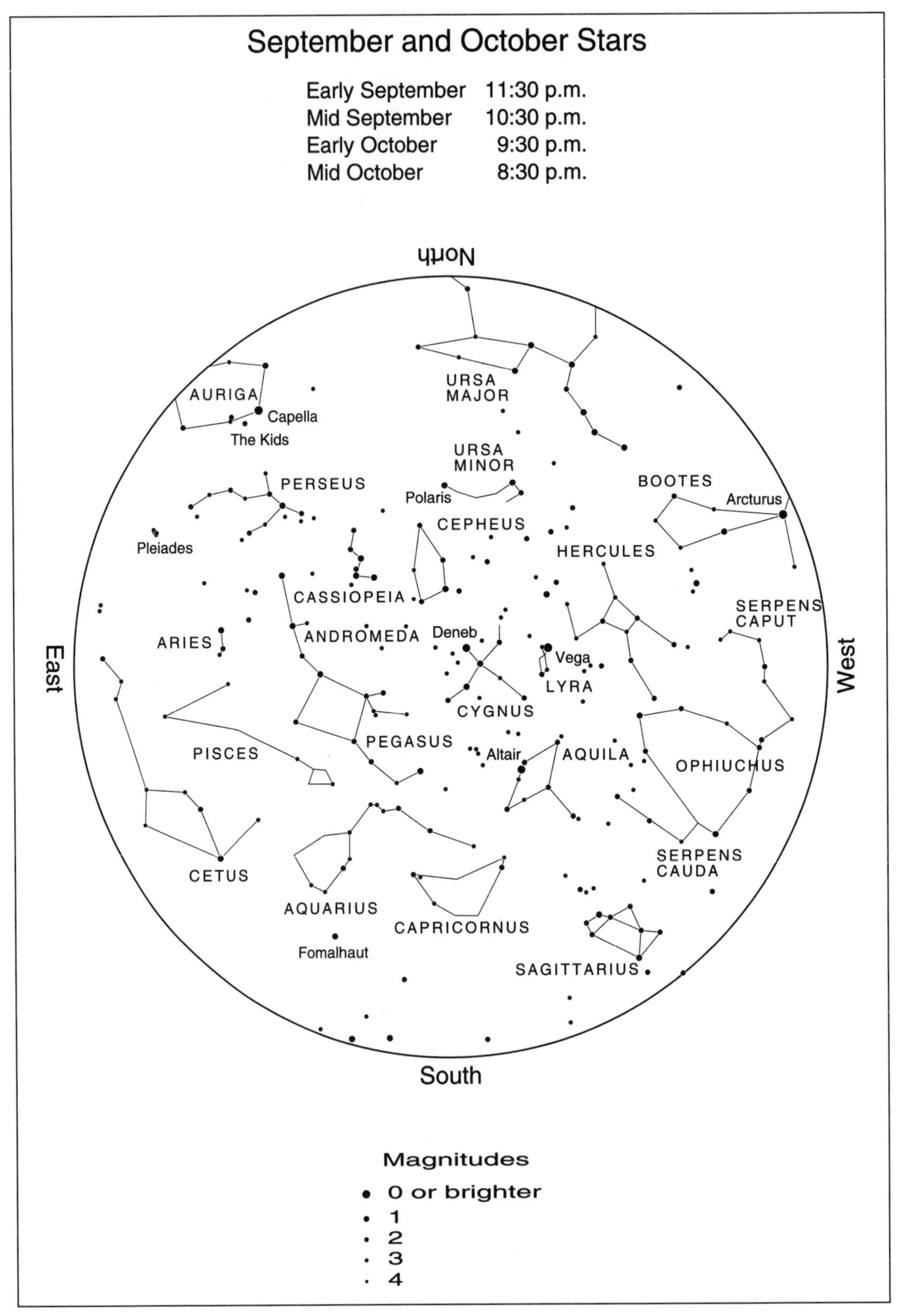

Figure 7-13. The Summer Triangle stars (fig. 7-7) gleam high in the western sky even as the faint constellations of fall emerge in the east. The distinctive shape of Cassiopeia is easy to spot and serves as a guide to the Great Square asterism in Pegasus (fig. 7-8).

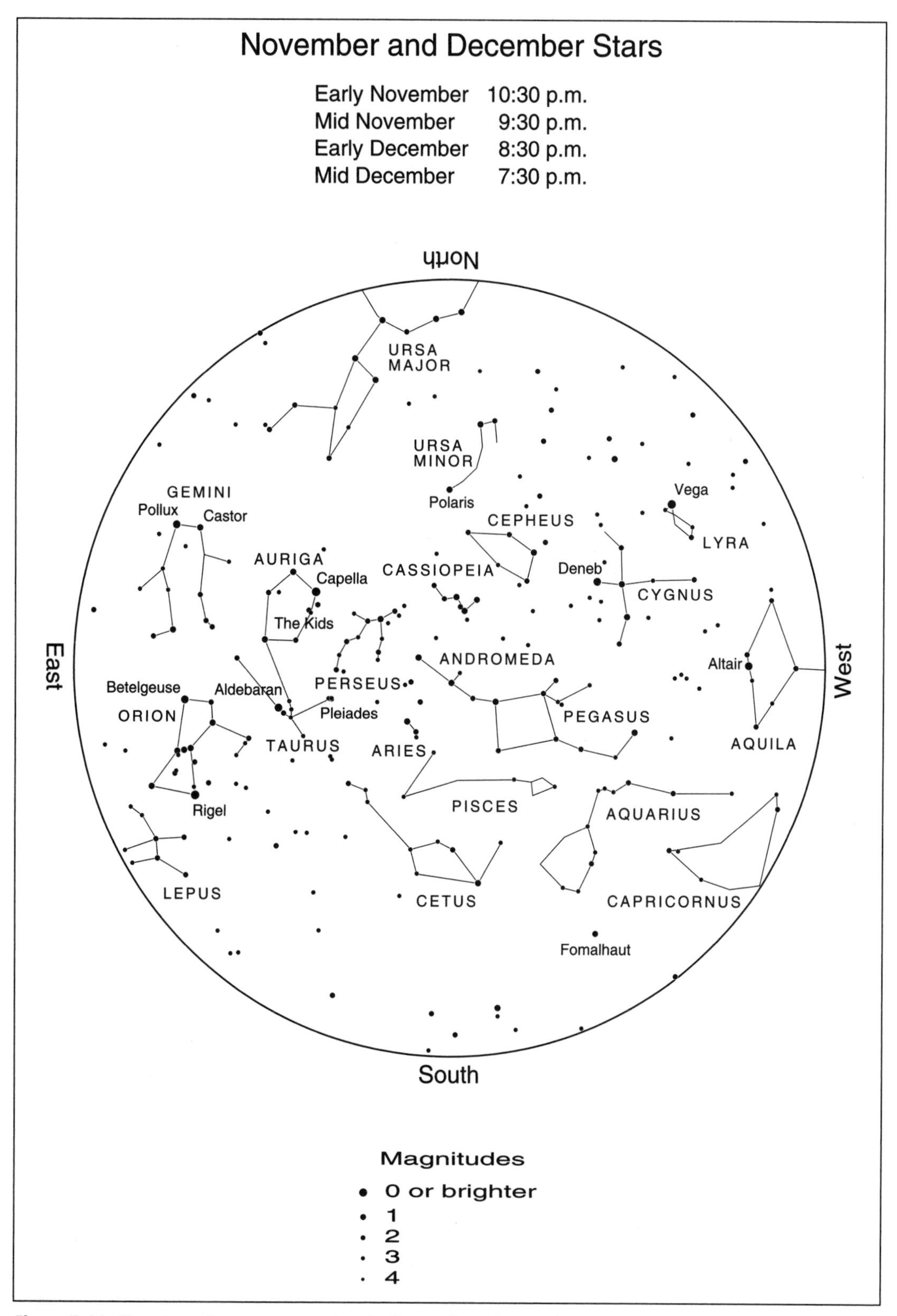

Figure 7-14. The stars of summer, now low in the western sky, gradually yield to the stars of fall and winter. Cassiopeia, Pegasus, and Andromeda ride highest in the sky now (fig. 7-8). The bright winter constellations of Orion, Taurus, and Auriga emerge in the eastern sky (fig. 7-3).

8 Meteors and Meteor Showers

The flashes of light, though less intense than lightning, were so bright as to waken people in their beds.

—Denison Olmsted, 1833

Those spending enough time under the night sky will eventually see a "shooting star," a streak of light that flashes across the sky in less than a second. This is a meteor, a trail caused by the incineration of a piece of celestial debris as it enters our atmosphere. Many meteors are quick flashes, but some last long enough to track their brief course across the sky. Now and then a meteor will truly light up the night, blazing brighter than Venus—and rarely, even brighter than the moon—and leaving in its wake a dimly glowing train that may persist for minutes. Under a dark sky, any observer can expect to see between two and seven meteors each hour any night of the year. These are sporadic meteors, their source bodies—meteoroids—part of the dusty background of the inner solar system.

But several times during the year the Earth encounters swarms of small particles that greatly enhance the number of meteors. The result is a meteor shower, during which observers may see dozens of meteors every hour. Concentrations of material within the swarms may produce better-than-average displays in some years, with rates of hundreds per hour. And every now and then we're treated to a truly spectacular display that produces thousands of visible meteors for a brief period. The science of meteor astronomy began with just such a meteor storm, so we'll start with a look at the usually unimpressive meteor shower that spawned it—the Leonids of November.

The Story of the Leonids

As table 8-1 reveals, the Leonids rank among the year's least impressive showers, producing a dozen or so meteors each hour for a couple of nights in mid-November. Backtracking along each meteor's visible trail shows that they all seem to radiate from a point in the constellation Leo, within the "sickle" or "backward question mark" that rises from the bright star Regulus. This radiant is an effect of perspective. The particles that become meteors travel in roughly parallel paths as the Earth plows into them and, just as parallel highway lines or railroad tracks seem to converge on a distant vanishing point, so too do the meteors (fig. 8-2). Meteor showers are usually named

Table 8-1. Best Meteor Showers

Dates of maximum activity vary from year to year; check the Sky Almanac in appendix A for the correct date in any given year. The Typical Hourly Rates reflect the average number of meteors expected for an observer under ideal conditions (clear, dark, moonless sky) with the radiant overhead; actual rates will be lower. Shower rates may also fluctuate from year to year; outbursts do not necessarily coincide with the date of the annual shower.

Shower	Date of Maximum (UT)	Typical Hourly Rate	Typical Appearance	Source Body	Outburst or Storm Potential
Quadrantids	Jan. 3–4	40–100+	Average mag. +2.8; blue; medium speed.	—	
Lyrids	April 21–22	10–15	Average mag +2.4; swift.	C/1861 G1 (Thatcher)	2042?
	Outburst (~50 per hour) in 1982, weak evidence for a sixty-year periodicity.				
Eta Aquarids	May 5–6	10–20	Average mag. +2.9; often yellowish; very swift; often leave trains.	1P/Halley	
Southern Delta Aquarids	July 27–28	15–20	Average mag. +3.0; often yellowish; medium speed. Dual radiant, but the southern one is strongest.	—	
Perseids	Aug. 11–12	50–100+	Average mag. +2.3; white, yellow, orange; swift.	109P/Swift-Tuttle	2004
	Outburst in 1993, related to the return of its parent comet in late 1992. Greater than normal activity expected for some years ahead, peaking with a strong outburst in 2004 (up to 500 per hour, 21h UT on August 11) and declining slowly thereafter.				
Draconids	Oct. 8–9	Variable	Occurs in years when its parent body is near perihelion. Average mag. +3.5; notable for their slow speed.	21P/Giacobini-Zinner	2005 2018
	An outburst, possibly reaching storm level (over 1,000 per hour), is predicted at 17h UT in 2005. A full-fledged storm is considered likely in 2018.				
Orionids	Oct. 21–22	25	Average mag. +3.1; very swift; often leave trains.	1P/Halley	
Southern Taurids	Nov. 3–5	< 15	Average mag. +2.8; slow. Dual radaint, but the southern one is strongest.	2P/Encke	
Leonids	Nov. 17–18	10–15	Average mag. +3.0; very swift; often leave trains, some very long-lasting.	55P/Tempel-Tuttle	2002 2006? 2007?
	Return of parent comet in 1998, outburst in 1998, storm in 1999, outburst in 2000, storm in 2001. Predicted storms at 4h UT (over 2,000 per hour) and 10h to 11h UT (over 5,000 per hour) on Nov. 19, 2002—moon interferes. Some predict an outburst (100 to 120 per hour) between 4h and 5h UT on Nov. 19, 2006, and another in 2007 (Nov. 18, 22h to 23h UT, up to 200 per hour).				
Geminids	Dec. 13–14	80–100+	Average mag. +2.5; yellowish; medium speed.	3200 Phaethon	

Figure 8-1. The great Leonid meteor storm of 1833 lights up the sky. The cluster of debris that caused it created similar storms in 1866, 1966, 1999, and 2001. This engraving, without doubt the most famous image of the 1833 Leonids, was actually produced decades after the event, although it was based on an eyewitness account. It was used by religious organizations at the close of the nineteenth century as an illustration of events on the Day of Judgment. (Courtesy of Armagh Observatory)

either for the constellation in which their radiant is located or for a nearby bright star.

It's a tricky business to determine the peak hourly rate of a meteor shower from visual observations, even more so when dealing with sometimes very sparse historical records. The goal is to find a number called the Zenithal Hourly Rate, or ZHR, which represents the greatest number of meteors seen every hour under ideal conditions—clear dark sky, moonless night—when the radiant is directly overhead. Observed rates are always lower than this value because every location differs from the ideal in one way or another, but with this number in hand we can compare the activity of different meteor showers or track the changing activity of a single shower from year to year. The estimates of historical Leonid activity given here are drawn from a 1998 review of available original records by Peter Brown of the University of Western Ontario in Canada.

Our tale of the Leonids begins early on November 12, 1799, at the Venezuelan encampment of German naturalist and explorer Alexander von Humboldt and his French companion Aimé Bonpland. "Towards the morning," Humboldt wrote,

> from half after two, the most extraordinary luminous meteors were seen towards the east. Mr. Bonpland, who had risen to enjoy the freshness of the air in the gallery, perceived them first. Thousands of bolides and falling stars succeeded each other for four hours. . . . Mr. Bonpland relates that, from

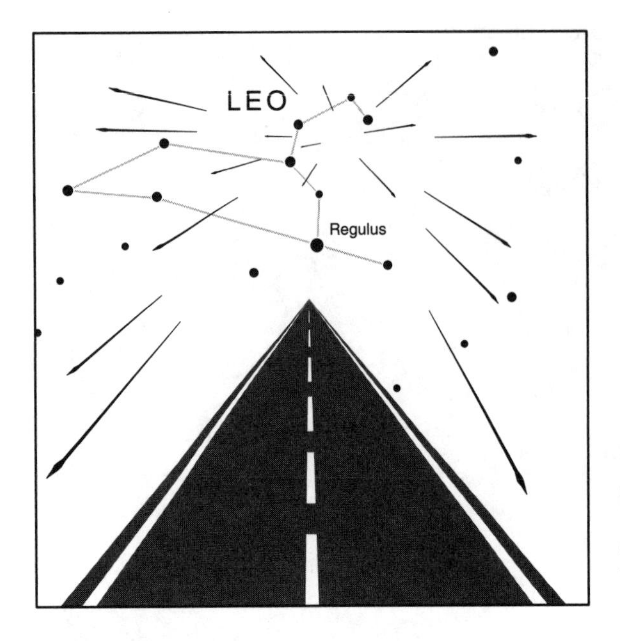

Figure 8-2. A straight road converges to a vanishing point in the distance. The paths of meteors seen on November 17 converge on a point within the constellation Leo—the radiant of the Leonid meteor shower.

> the beginning of the phenomenon, there was not a space in the firmament equal in extent to three diameters of the full moon that was not filled at every instant with bolides and falling stars. . . . All of these meteors left luminous traces from five to ten degrees in length. . . . The phosphorescence of these traces . . . lasted seven or eight seconds. . . .

Andrew Ellicott, a New Orleans-bound American government official, described his view from a ship in the Gulf of Mexico:

> The phenomenon was grand and awful; the whole heavens appeared as if illuminated with sky-rockets, which disappeared only by the light of the sun after daybreak. The meteors, which at any one instant were as numerous as stars, flew in all possible directions . . . .

As vivid as these accounts are, though, they attracted little attention until decades later. There is not enough information in them to determine a reliable number for the storm's peak rate, but it must have been a truly spectacular show, since light from a nearly full moon interfered.

The Leonids then lapsed back to their usual trickle of meteors until 1831, when a few observers in Spain, France, and the eastern United States counted a meteor every minute on the morning of November 13. But the best was yet to come. In 1832 meteors rained through the predawn sky from the Ural Mountains to the eastern shore of Brazil. The display was intense, in spite of a waxing gibbous moon near the shower radiant, and observers reported many bright fireballs, a wonderful display that peaked at 2,000 Leonids per hour.

And then, in 1833, the Leonids outdid themselves. Along the east coast of North America, from Canada to Mexico, anyone under a clear sky in the hours before dawn saw hundreds of meteors every minute with a peak rate of around 60,000 per hour. Native Americans referred to the event as "the night the stars fell." An Annapolis observer described the meteors as falling "like snowflakes." An observer near Augusta, Georgia, reported that "the stars descended like a snowfall to the Earth" and that the brightest meteors left trains that "would remain visible . . . for nearly fifteen minutes."

"The scene was truly awful," wrote a cotton planter in South Carolina, "for never did rain fall much thicker than the meteors fell towards the Earth; east, west, north, and south, it was the same." The display was again rich in bright fireballs and meteors were seen even after sunrise. Some accounts of the storm describe a black cloud overhead from which the meteors seemed to shoot—an illusion caused by the greatly foreshortened meteors closest to the radiant. Others noticed that the meteors seemed to stream from the constellation Leo and that this radiant rose through the night with the stars.

In the days that followed, wild theories involving electrified air or flammable gases filled the popular press. Accounts of the storm witnessed by Humboldt in 1799 and of the 1832 storm drew attention, and many newspapers commented on the coincidence that all three meteor showers had occurred near the same date. Yale College mathematics professor Denison Olmsted (1791–1859) caught the last hour of the 1833 storm and analyzed observations from around the country. He established the shower's geographic extent and estimated that over 207,000 meteors were seen that night. Olmsted determined that the meteors had originated beyond Earth and that they entered the atmosphere traveling in parallel paths. He concluded that the meteors were part of a nebulous body of unknown nature orbiting the sun and that the shower was caused by the Earth's passage through this object.

Astronomers watched the 1834, 1835, and 1836 displays with heightened interest, and while the Leonids showed outbursts that would be considered unusually good most years—with ZHRs between 60 and 150—they were an anticlimax after the great storm of 1833. In 1837 the German physician and astronomer Heinrich Olbers looked at the available information and concluded that the main swarm of the Leonids returned every thirty-three or thirty-four years. "Perhaps we shall have to wait until 1867 before seeing this magnificent spectacle return," he wrote. The Leonids fell back to their usual modest numbers.

In the 1860s interest in the Leonids was renewed with the historical research of Yale professor Hubert Newton (1830–1896), who combed Chinese, Arab, and European accounts of meteor showers looking for previous Leonid returns. He found records of eleven great meteor showers dating from A.D. 902. An account of the Leonids in 934 associated the meteors with another traumatic event: "There was an earthquake in Egypt . . . and flaming stars struck against one another violently." The Leonids made quite an impression in 1366:

> Afterward [the stars] fell from the sky in such numbers, and so thickly together, that as they descended low in the air, they seemed large and fiery, and the sky and the air seemed to be in flames, and even the Earth appeared as if ready to take fire . . . . Those who saw it were filled with such great fear and dismay, that they were astounded, imagining they were all dead men, and that the end of the world had come.

It's worth noting here that modern orbital calculations of comet Tempel-Tuttle, source of the Leonid meteoroids, reveal that it passed within 2.13 million miles (3.42 million kilometers) of Earth—less than nine times the distance to the moon—on October 26, 1366. This is the second-closest known approach of any comet to Earth, bested only by comet Lexell on July 1, 1770, which passed 66 percent closer. The nodes of the comet's orbit advance, which is why the dates of the historical showers differ from the one we experience.

Newton determined that the interval between Leonid storms was 33.25 years and predicted the next return on the night of November 13–14, 1866. After a "warm-up" outburst of one meteor a minute in 1865, a small Leonid blizzard returned on schedule, delighting observers from England to India with a peak hourly rate of about 8,000. Careful meteor counts from the United Kingdom enabled astronomers to determine the moment of peak activity and estimate the width of the cloud of material responsible for the storm. A modern reduction of that data gives the Leonid peak at 1:12 UT on November 14, with the shower above half its peak value for fifty minutes, indicating that the swarm of particles responsible for the shower spread across some 55,000 miles (89,000 kilometers) of space. Another fine display occurred the next year, with rates around 1,200 per hour despite interference from a nearly full moon. The 1868 return occurred under a new moon and was widely observed in Europe and North America. It was an unusual outburst with a broad period of heightened activity—about 400 per hour—that lasted many hours but showed no clear peak.

The 1860s also brought a solution to the mystery surrounding the origin of the Leonids and the other meteor showers then being recognized. Orbital calculations of the Perseid meteor stream by Giovanni Schiaparelli, better known for his later work on Mars, revealed a very strong resemblance to the orbit of a bright comet discovered in

1862; he argued that all meteor showers were caused by the disintegration of comets. The idea was quickly accepted, thanks to additional associations between comet orbits and meteor streams. Using information from the 1866 Leonid shower, Urbain Le Verrier published its orbital characteristics in 1867—and immediately astronomers pointed out the similarity between the Leonid orbit and that of newly discovered comet Tempel-Tuttle.

Comets are now considered "dirty snowballs" containing a mixture of dust and frozen gases. They only become visible near their closest approach to the sun, at which point areas on the comet's icy surface can become warm enough to evaporate. The resulting jets of evaporating gases carry with them any solid matter mixed in with the original ice (fig. 8-3). At each pass near the sun the comet ejects a stream of material. Stream particles receive small accelerations from forces other than gravity and, over time, their orbits are slightly modified. The ejection streams become more diffuse with age, losing density and their individual identities. Initially concentrated near the comet, the debris diffuses along each stream's orbit and eventually forms a thin band of material that we encounter every year. A meteor shower occurs on the date in the year when the Earth passes nearest to the band of material associated with a comet's orbit. The clumpiness evident in the Leonid swarm is an indication of its youth—the clouds of particles simply haven't had time to become uniformly distributed along Tempel-Tuttle's orbit.

This new understanding of the origin of meteor showers, coupled with the terrific track record of the Leonids, gave astronomers confidence that another meteor storm would fill the November skies in 1899. Newspapers in Europe and America spread the word. In 1898 a Leonid outburst of 100 meteors an hour splashed through the sky as an apparent prelude. But the well-advertised spectacle predicted for 1899 simply failed to materialize. This was "the worst blow ever suffered by astronomy in the eyes of the public," wrote astronomer Charles Olivier, "and has indirectly done immense harm to the spread of science among our citizens." In fact, some astronomers had calculated that the Leonid swarm's close encounters with Jupiter and Saturn after 1869 had slightly altered its course, bringing it well inside the Earth's orbit and making a meteor storm unlikely. Astronomers observed another strong outburst of 250 meteors per hour in 1901 and a slightly weaker outburst in 1903, after which the Leonids again settled down.

The shower perked up in the early 1930s, producing outbursts with peak rates usually under 100 per hour, and waned again after 1934. It looked as though the once-great Leonids had finally begun to fizzle out. Judging by the 1899 return, a close approach to the Leonid stream no longer seemed very likely and astronomers held out little hope for a meteor storm in 1966. D. W. R. McKinley, in a book on meteor science published in 1961, stated "it is highly improbable that we shall ever again witness the full fury of the Leonid storm."

Enhanced activity was detected annually beginning in 1961 but never exceeded 130 per hour. In fact, that is a good approximation of what most of the world witnessed on the morning of November 17, 1966. But die-hard observers in the central and western United States were treated to one of the strongest Leonid storms in recorded history under almost ideal conditions. The five-day-old moon had set well before midnight. At 2:30 A.M. the meteor count was 33 per hour, but by 4:00 it had increased to almost 200 and continued to rise. By 5:00, Leonids poured out of the sky at the rate of thirty per minute, and near 6:00 the count peaked at an incredible thirty meteors per *second*—a maximum ZHR of about 100,000. The Leonids were *back!*

The last two years of the twentieth century and the first year of the twenty-first also saw strong Leonid activity. In 1998, relatively chunky material ejected by the comet in the 1300s produced a brilliant display of fireballs. A full-blown meteor storm, with rates as high as 3,700 per hour, materialized briefly over the eastern Mediterranean on November 18, 1999. The bright moon hampered viewing of the Leonid display in the year 2000, which made it about halfway to storm level, but the 2001 shower was the real show-stopper. The Earth passed through several Leonid streams comprised of material ejected in the seventeenth and nineteenth centuries. The result was a period of storm activity lasting several hours, with the best display—about 3,000 per hour—occurring over China and Mongolia. However, the sky show over North America did not disappoint, as observers from Florida to Hawaii were treated to spectacular celestial fireworks, with many mete-

Figure 8-3. The dust-laden jets of Halley's comet were viewed close up by the European Space Agency's *Giotto* probe in 1986. This picture, a composite of sixty-eight separate images, shows bright jets of gas and dust streaming away from the comet's sunward side. The night side of the nucleus is silhouetted against a background of dust. The bright spot on the night side is believed to be a hill or mountain about 1,600 feet (500 meters) high whose peak is just catching the sun. Debris from Halley creates two of the year's best meteor showers—the Eta Aquarids of May and the Orionids of October. (Courtesy of Max Planck Institut für Aeronomie)

ors sporting long trails and red, blue, and green colors.

Astronaut Frank Culbertson watched the show from the vantage point of the *International Space Station.* "It looked like we were seeing UFOs approaching the Earth flying in formation, three or four at a time," he said. "There were hundreds per minute going beneath us, really spectacular. It's like being in the middle of a hailstorm."

Just as the Leonid displays of the 1830s gave birth to meteor astronomy, the last Leonid showers of the twentieth century saw the beginning of a new era in that field. The increased power of desktop computers in the mid-1990s had finally enabled astronomers to implement an idea first proposed by Irish astronomers a century before—computing the orbits of "fictitious" Leonid meteoroids ejected from comet Tempel-Tuttle on each of its passages through the inner solar system. The computational task is impressive: track up to one million imaginary particles as they orbit the sun over hundreds to thousands of years. The orbits are then checked to see if they intersect that of Earth, and the relative numbers of those that do provide information used to develop a meteor activity forecast. Much like weather predictions, these forecasts are a mixed bag—the times of the 1999, 2000, and 2001 Leonid activity peaks were predicted to within a few minutes, but the intensities of the displays were either underestimated (1999) or overestimated (2001).

"Obviously, the meteor forecast models still need a bit of work," says Bill Cooke of NASA's Marshall Space Flight Center, "but the present state of the art is sufficient for NASA and spacecraft operators to determine times and strategies for safeguarding their orbiting vehicles."

Concern for the safety of satellites represents another hallmark of this new era of meteor science. During past Leonid storms, few if any spacecraft were in Earth orbit; now there are hundreds, some of which perform functions vital to our way of life. The material that creates meteor showers is a fluffy conglomerate of dust, too insubstantial to survive passage through the atmosphere and reach the ground. But the enormous speeds of the meteoroids more than make up for their fragility, and satellites above the atmosphere are quite vulnerable to them. Investigators now say it's likely that the demise of one communications satellite was caused by a single strike by a meteor shower particle.

Satellite operators use the forecasts to minimize the exposed surface area of their vehicles and to orient the least-sensitive parts of their spacecraft into the oncoming stream of particles. It's the orbital equivalent of battening down the hatches.

A more rugged satellite, our moon, has been repeatedly struck by Leonids. Between 1970 and 1977, seismic stations deployed on the moon by Apollo astronauts detected impacts during several annual meteor showers, including the Leonids. And something never before recorded took place during the 1999 storm. Independent observers monitoring the moon's night side videotaped six brief flashes no brighter than a fourth-magnitude star. The flashes were caused by the impact of relatively large Leonid fragments.

"We occasionally see kilogram-sized fragments burning up in Earth's atmosphere," says Bill Cooke, "and they appear as very bright fireballs that disintegrate completely before hitting the ground." Although a Leonid particle is composed of very fragile material, it hits the lunar surface at speeds one hundred times faster than a rifle bullet. The strike vaporizes the meteoroid—as well as some of the lunar surface within a few feet of the impact point—and creates a brief flash detectable from Earth. At least two other impacts were confirmed during the 2001 Leonids.

Observing Meteor Showers

A first-time meteor watcher, age nine, described his experience to us as "kind of like fishing"—and that's a pretty fair description. The best way to enjoy a meteor shower is to dress warmly, set down a blanket or lawn chair at a dark site, get comfortable, and watch the stars. Meteors will appear in virtually any part of the sky. Naturally, interference from streetlights or the moon will reduce the count, so the darker the site, the better.

On any night of the year, meteors appear faster, brighter, and more numerous after midnight. That's when your location has turned into the Earth's direction of motion around the sun and plows into meteor particles nearly head-on, rather than having them catch up from behind. The peak activity of a meteor shower occurs in the hours when the Earth passes closest to the orbit of the shower particles. The ideal circumstance for any observer is for the shower to peak at a time when its radiant is highest in the sky during the morning hours; most of the year's best showers have the potential to meet these criteria. Table 8-1 lists information on the major meteor showers, including the approximate date of maximum activity, typical hourly rates at peak, and the general appearance of the meteors. The calendar date for a given shower's peak varies a day or so due to leap years; refer to appendix A for the correct date in a given year. Most meteor streams are spread out enough that looking at the actual hour of peak activity will make little difference in what you see. However, that's not true of the Draconids, Quadrantids, and of course the Leonids, all of whose streams remain quite clumpy; for these showers, appendix A also lists the estimated hour of their peaks.

Most of the meteors seen during one of the annual showers arise from fluffy particles not much larger than sand grains. As the particle enters the atmosphere, it collides with gas atoms and molecules and becomes wrapped in a glowing sheath of heated air and vaporized material boiled off its own surface. Meteors become visible at altitudes between 50 and 75 miles (80 and 120 kilometers), with the faster particles typically shining at greater heights. Many of the faster, brighter meteors may leave behind a train: a dimly glowing trail that persists for many seconds or, more rarely, minutes. Larger debris may create a fireball—a spectacular meteor bright enough to outshine even Venus. Occasionally a fireball will fragment; this event is accompanied by bright flares and even "sparks" thrown a short distance from the meteor's main trail. Such a fireball is called a bolide.

In the following section we provide some background on the meteor showers listed in table 8-1 to get you more acquainted with them.

Quadrantids: Generally visible between December 28 and January 6, the Quadrantids have a sharp activity peak around January 3. As few as 40 and as many as 200 Quadrantids have been seen during the shower's maximum, so although the stream is compact it's also apparently clumpy. This is the only major meteor shower whose parent comet remains unknown. Typical rates vary between 40 and 100 per hour; about 5 percent leave trains. The speed of the meteors—26 miles (42 kilometers) per second—is moderate because the stream intersects the Earth's orbit quite steeply (fig. 8-4). When the shower was first recognized as annual in 1839, the radiant occurred in a constellation now no longer recognized—Quadrans Muralis (Wall Quadrant). It's now divided between Hercules, Bootes, and Draco. The cold nights of northern winters and typically faint meteors keep the shower from being truly popular.

Lyrids: The Lyrids appear from April 16 to 25 and peak (at ten to fifteen per hour) around April 21; the radiant lies between Hercules and Lyra. Although the Lyrids were not recognized as an annual shower until 1839, Chinese observations of the display date back to 687 B.C.—making it the earliest recorded meteor shower. Despite the low annual rate, the Lyrids have the capacity for impressive displays—over fifty per hour. This happened in 1803, 1922, and 1982, weakly suggesting a sixty-year period for Lyrid outbursts. In 1867 the shower was linked to its parent comet (C/1861 G1). The Lyrid meteors are bright and rather fast (30 miles or 48 kilometers per second), and about 15 percent leave persistent trains.

Eta Aquarids: The first of the year's two showers that derive from Halley's comet, the Eta Aquarids occur from April 19 to May 28, with a peak (ten to twenty per hour) around May 6. This shower is best for observers in the southern hemisphere, where the hourly rate climbs to fifty. The radiant is located near the *Y*-shaped asterism in Aquarius and named for one of those stars. The shower was discovered in 1870 and linked to Halley in 1868. The meteors are among the fastest (42 miles or 67 kilometers a second), faint on average, but the brighter ones have a yellowish color; about 30 percent leave trains.

Southern Delta Aquarids: This is the most active of a diffuse group of streams and, as the name suggests, is best seen in the southern hemisphere. They may be seen between July 12 and August 19 and peak (fifteen to twenty per hour) near July 28. The meteors are medium speed (27 miles or 43 kilometers per second); they tend to be faint, and few leave trains.

Perseids: The best-known of all meteor showers, the Perseids never fail to put on a good show and, thanks to a late-summer peak, are usually widely observed. The earliest record comes from China in A.D. 36. Generally visible from July 17 to August 24, their speed (37 miles or 60 kilometers per second), brightness, and high proportion of trains (45 percent) distinguish the Perseids from other showers active at this time (see figure 8-4). The shower peaks around August 12 with observed hourly rates usually around fifty—however, the rate climbed from sixty-five between 1966 and 1975 to ninety between 1976 and 1983. The first meteor shower linked to a comet, the Perseids derive from comet 109P/Swift-Tuttle, which was last seen in 1862. The comet had been expected to return in the early 1980s—an idea bolstered by enhanced Persied activity—but it failed to make an appearance.

Astronomers held out faint hope for a 1992 return, based on the possibility that a comet seen in 1737 represented an earlier apparition of Swift-Tuttle. Perseid outbursts in 1991 and 1992 again heightened expectations for a return of the comet, and astronomers finally recovered Swift-Tuttle on the inbound leg of its orbit in late 1992. The possibility of a large outburst in August 1993

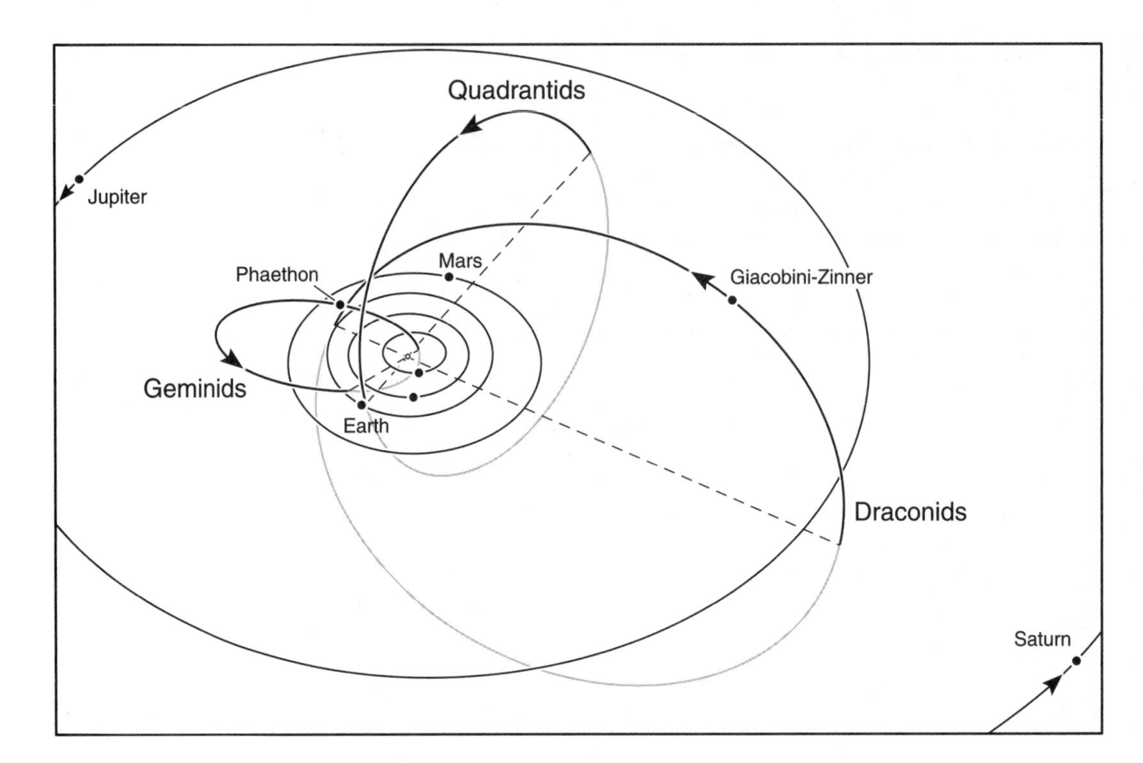

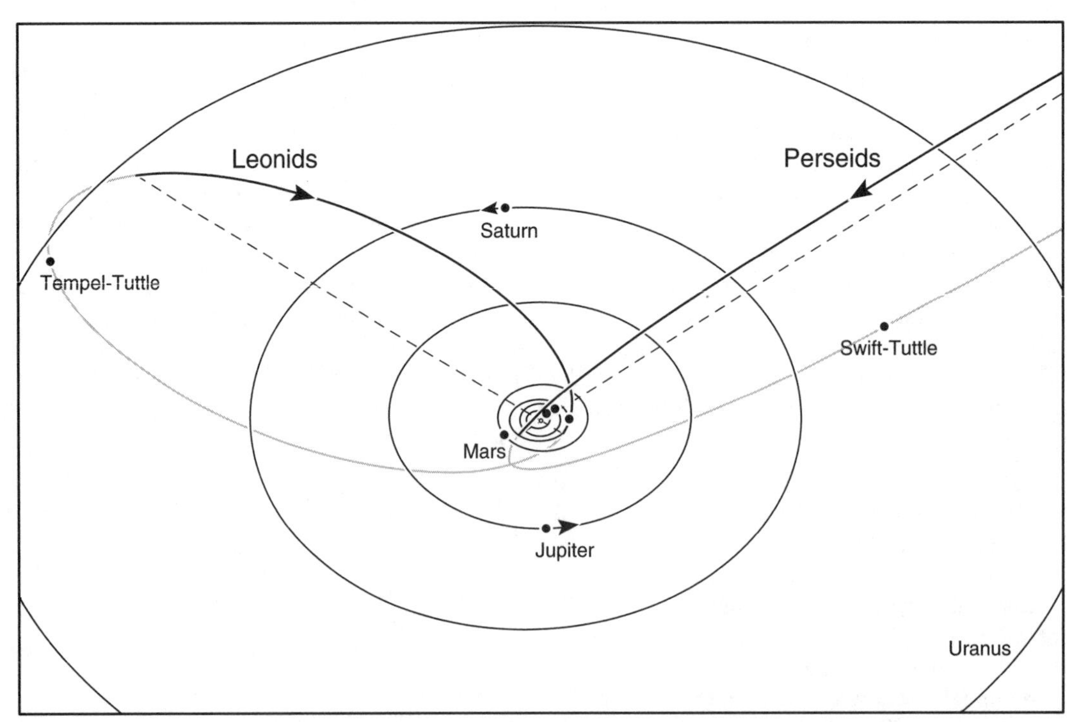

Figure 8-4. The orbits of meteor shower particles. Gray indicates where the orbits pass beneath the plane of the ecliptic. Object positions are correct for December 31, 2010. Top: Particles in the Geminid meteor stream hit the Earth near the midnight side, making it one of the few showers best seen in the late evening. Similarly, the Quadrantid meteors plunge steeply downward into the Earth's orbit. The meteors of both showers are of moderate speed because they're neither catching up to the Earth nor being plowed into by it. The Draconid swarm actually catches us from behind, making its meteors even slower. Bottom: Earth runs nearly head-on into particles of the Perseid and Leonid swarms, making their meteors among the swiftest.

led NASA to postpone a scheduled launch of the space shuttle *Discovery* to avoid the main shower activity and so minimize the risk to both astronauts and vehicle—the first time a space mission was rescheduled due to a meteor shower. The Perseids did not disappoint, reaching a peak about three times the normal rate (300 per hour). Russian cosmonauts aboard the orbiting *Mir* space station, who could watch the fireworks in the atmosphere below them, took precautions. For the peak of shower activity they took refuge in the Soyuz spacecraft (docked to the station); they closed the hatches, ready for a quick getaway in the event that *Mir* became heavily damaged. As many as sixty particles reportedly hit *Mir*, many audible to the cosmonauts, but the most serious damage turned out to be a few holes in the station's numerous and easily damaged solar panels.

The 1993 Perseids hold the dubious distinction of causing the first probable "kill" of a functioning satellite by a meteoroid. *OLYMPUS*, operated by the European Space Agency, was the largest civilian telecommunications satellite at the time of its launch in 1989. While leaving work on August 11, the program's spacecraft manager, Doug Caswell, heard a colleague joke "*OLYMPUS* dies at midnight!" And just before midnight, when the Perseid rate was over 100 per hour and climbing, the satellite unexpectedly shut down its roll gyro, began to spin twice per minute around its roll axis, and subsequently broke contact with Earth. The satellite carried enough fuel for normal operations, but early orientation problems had left it with no margin for anything unusual. To stop the spin, controllers rapidly depleted the remaining attitude-control fuel. Once control was reestablished, so little gas remained that ground control was left with no choice but to declare the satellite dead, place it in a graveyard orbit, and shut it down.

Investigators concluded that one of the satellite's solar panels had probably sustained a hit from a Perseid meteoroid. "It was not absolutely confirmed," says Caswell, "but there is no better explanation." The impact vaporized the meteoroid into a plasma. Seconds before the gyro shut down, a planned firing of the roll axis thrusters was executed. The thruster exhaust gases augmented the plasma produced by the impact, and together they provided a conduit that permitted electrical charges on the surface of the spacecraft to penetrate inside, where they damaged sensitive attitude-control electronics. The space environment is extremely hostile to electronics and, as the example of *OLYMPUS* shows, a meteoroid need not create major structural damage to render a satellite inoperable.

At this writing, only the Perseid and Leonid showers have been modeled with enough detail for scientists to develop credible forecasts. Models of the Perseids predict a rise in activity each year, from the current 100 per hour to a peak in 2004, after which activity begins a gradual decline. The Perseids have never been observed to produce a meteor storm along the lines of the Leonids, but a strong outburst is likely and it's possible that the rates will top 500 per hour at 21h UT on August 11, 2004.

Draconids: The Draconids are also sometimes called the Giacobinids; in a break with convention, this name honors the shower's parent comet, 21P/Giacobini-Zinner. Draconid activity occurs between October 6 and 10, with a peak (when it occurs at all) on October 8. In 1933 and 1946 the shower produced brief but intense (over 5,000 per hour) meteor storms; in 1998 it reached a rate of about 500 per hour over eastern Europe. The occurrence of the shower is intimately tied to the proximity of its parent comet. According to Donald Yeomans, a comet expert at the Jet Propulsion Laboratory, the most intense showers occur when we arrive at the node of the comet orbit within a few months of Giacobini-Zinner's passage: in 1933 we arrived eighty days after the comet, in 1946 we reached the node fifteen days after it, and in 1998 we brushed the orbit fifty days before the comet got there. At the next return, in 2005, we slip past the node ninety-two days after the comet passes through, so it is likely that a Draconid shower will occur, with a peak around 17h UT and possible storm levels of over 1,000 an hour. Most researchers agree that a shower is unlikely with the return of 2012—we pass the node over four months before the comet does—but that a full-fledged storm is likely in 2018, when we follow the comet's node crossing by twenty-three days. Draconids are slow-moving meteors, with encounter speeds of less than 12 miles (20 kilometers) per second, and they are typically faint.

Orionids: This is the sister stream of the Eta Aquarids, both of which arise from the debris of Halley's comet. Discovered in 1864, the Orionids were not linked to Halley until 1911. Orionid meteors can be found between October 2 and November 7, with a peak of about twenty-five per hour around October 21. Orionid meteors are among the fastest (42 miles or 67 kilometers per second); they are generally faint, and about 20 percent leave trains that persist one or two seconds.

Southern Taurids: Visible between October 1 and November 25, this is the strongest of several streams originating from comet Encke. A broad maximum occurs between November 3 and 5, but usually brings an hourly rate of less than fifteen. The shower was first recognized in 1869 and was associated with Encke in 1940. Its meteors are generally faint and quite slow (19 miles or 30 kilometers a second) because they approach the Earth from behind and must catch up.

Leonids: Generally seen from November 14 to 21, with a peak hourly rate on November 17 of between ten and fifteen per hour; about half leave trains that can persist for several minutes. Because Earth runs into the orbiting particles almost directly head-on, Leonid meteors travel faster than those of any other shower—45 miles (72 kilometers) per second (fig. 8-4). The shower's most notable feature, of course, is its habit of producing periodic dramatic outbursts as we intercept streams of dense material ejected at previous returns of comet Tempel-Tuttle.

Our planet passed through such streams annually from 1998 to 2001 and is expected to do so again in 2002, although moonlight will interfere with the display. A peak rate of about 3,000 per hour is expected over Europe at around 4h UT on November 19 and another larger peak over North America at around 11h UT (possibly over 5,000 per hour). Current forecasts predict a return to normal Leonid rates after 2002, with two exceptions associated with debris ejected in 1933. A small outburst of up to 120 meteors per hour is predicted by some researchers for 2006 and at least one forecast predicts another in 2007 that may top 200 per hour. These rates, similar to good Perseid and Geminid displays, are faint echoes of the Leonids at their best. The stream of material responsible for these outbursts is very young and only the smallest particles are likely to have had time to drift far enough into a path Earth will intersect. This means that the outbursts, if they occur at all, will likely be rich in faint meteors. After 2002, though, computer models show that Jupiter's tug on the Leonid stream causes it to miss the Earth, making full-fledged meteor storms impossible until at least 2098.

Geminids: The Geminids are active between December 7 and 17 and peak near December 13, with typical hourly rates just over 80 but ranging to over 100. Because the Geminids intersect Earth's orbit near the midnight side, this shower is one of the few that are good before midnight (fig. 8-4). Its meteors are medium speed (22 miles or 36 kilometers per second) and bright (13 percent magnitude 0 or brighter), and they appear white or yellowish. The parent body of the Geminids, discovered only in 1983, makes it so far unique among meteor showers. The body, named 3200 Phaethon, is classed as an asteroid—one of thousands of rocky objects whose orbits generally keep them between Mars and Jupiter. Eventually all the icy substance of a comet will evaporate, perhaps leaving behind a rocky core that places it in an "extinct comet" class of asteroids. Planetary scientists suggest that perhaps as many as one-third of the asteroids whose orbits cross the Earth's orbit are in fact defunct comets.

Look and Listen

Rarely, something truly surprising will accompany the streak of a meteor: sound. Sonic booms can be associated with fireballs or bolides that penetrate very low into the atmosphere and that may fragment into recoverable meteorites. As with sonic booms created by jet aircraft, these are acoustic waves that move toward observers at the speed of sound. Traveling from the altitude of the meteor, the sound waves take several minutes to reach the ground and observers hear them only after the meteor has disappeared.

Less well understood, though, are seemingly impossible sounds heard simultaneously with the passage of a meteor. A Chinese record from A.D. 817 described a meteor "which made a noise like a flock of cranes in flight." Edmond Halley noted the phenomenon among the eyewitness accounts he studied to reconstruct the path and altitude of a fireball seen over England in March of 1719. He found that its height "exceeded sixty English miles" with a speed of "above 300 such miles in a minute"; he reached this conclusion:

Figure 8-5. The 1998 Leonid "attack of the fireballs" as seen by an all-sky camera at the Astronomical Observatory Modra at Comenius University in Bratislava, Slovakia. About 150 bolides brighter than magnitude –2 can be seen, with the brightest fireball at about –8. The constellation Leo can be seen at the left—just follow the converging trails to find it. At least three bright meteors pass through Orion's torso. The exposure began on November 16, 23:33 UT, and lasted more than four hours, ending November 17, 3:37 UT. (Courtesy Astronomical Observatory Modra)

> Of several Accidents that were reported to have attended its Passage, many were the Effect of Fancy, such as the hearing it hiss as it went along, as if it had been very near at hand . . . .

Although witnesses continued to tell of sounds from bright meteors—and also from the aurora, better known as the northern lights—such observations gradually disappeared from the scientific literature because they were considered psychological rather than physical. And indeed, any investigator looking to explain these anomalous sounds through physical causes has had to contend with several serious problems. First, the sounds are very rare and their occurrence is inherently unpredictable. Very few people hear them, and the sounds themselves were not recorded until the 1990s. Second, witnesses standing next to one another sometimes disagree on whether or not there even *was* a noise. Third, sounds heard at the same time as the meteor is seen imply some sort of electromagnetic radiation moving at the speed of light—but no known method by which this might produce audible noise could work at the distances involved. Fourth, the portion of the electromagnetic spectrum considered most likely to be responsible was the radio regime, but until quite recently it had never been demonstrated that meteors emitted radio waves.

Then, on April 7, 1978, a bolide some forty times brighter than a full moon streaked above the cities of Sydney and Newcastle in New South Wales, Australia. There were numerous reports of sounds from the meteor: "like an express train or bus traveling at high speed," "an electrical crackling sound," "a loud swishing noise," "like steam hissing out of a railway engine." Colin Keay, a physicist at the University of Newcastle, heard of these reports and became convinced there was some physical explanation. He found that meteors had been observed in all but the Very Low Frequency (VLF) portion of the electromagnetic spectrum, a band that contains frequencies from 3 to 30,000 hertz. Keay showed in laboratory experiments that VLF radio waves could set ordinary objects like hair or eyeglasses into motion, vibrating them at audio frequencies and creating a noise very close to the observer. This would explain how adjacent observers could disagree on whether or not a meteor had made a sound. He argued that the source of the VLF radio waves lay in the highly ionized wake of the bolide, which briefly entraps a portion of the Earth's magnetic field. As the wake cools, this "magnetic spaghetti" disentangles itself and in the process releases a burst of radio energy. Keay applies the term "electrophonic" to describe sounds generated in this way. His ideas gained ground in the 1980s with theoretical studies of the wakes of bright bolides and with the first detection of VLF radiation from a meteor in 1990.

In his study of the 1833 Leonids, Denison Olmsted noted reports of "slight explosions, which usually resembled the noise of a child's pop-gun" but didn't know what to make of them. During the 1998 Leonid outburst, researchers in Mongolia obtained the first instrumental detection of electrophonic sounds from meteors. Two Leonid fireballs of magnitude –6.5 and –12 produced short, low-frequency sounds—described by observers as "deep pops"—that were simultaneously recorded by microphones in a special set-up.

In conclusion, while meteor sounds remain a poorly understood phenomenon, they are unquestionably real—and meteor-watchers would do well to keep both their eyes and ears open.

Rocks from the Sky

Most meteors arise from debris no larger than pebbles. For example, a one-ounce (thirty-three-gram) rock traveling at the cosmically slow pace of 19 miles (30 kilometers) per second will create a meteor bright enough to outshine all first-magnitude stars. Yet even objects this small may not be completely destroyed by their fiery passage through our atmosphere; some reach the Earth's surface as meteorites. Astronomers estimate that each day the Earth sweeps up more than 500 objects weighing at least three ounces (100 grams), and about 350 of these fall onto an area the size of the continental United States every year.

Vague stories about rocks falling from the sky occur in many ancient writings, and it is evident that some scribes held meteorites in high regard. The iron Casa Grande meteorite was found wrapped in linen and buried under the floor of a Montezuma Indian temple in Chihuahua, Mexico. A meteorite that fell on Nagota, Japan, in 861 has been preserved as part of a Shinto shrine ever since. The sacred black stone built into the Ka`ba in Mecca—a structure that is the chief object of Muslim pilgrimages—may also be a meteorite. Iron meteorites—which are most easily distinguished from terrestrial rocks—played a role in the development of tool-making in some areas. In China, the iron blade of an axe found in a Shang Dynasty (ca. 1400 B.C.) tomb was clearly forged from a meteorite. Polar explorers in the nineteenth century found that West Greenland Inuits used a trio of meteorites for the nickel-iron tips of their weapons and tools. One of these irons, the fifty-nine-ton Ahnighito (Tent), is the largest ever displayed in a museum; it can be seen today in New York City's American Museum of Natural History. Only one larger meteorite has so far been found—the sixty-six-ton Hoba iron, which still rests where it fell in Namibia.

Modern science resisted any extraterrestrial explanation of meteorites until proof literally fell from the sky. At midday on April 26, 1803, before hundreds of witnesses, a meteorite streaked over the French town of L'Aigle and exploded in a shower of 3,000 stones. In 1807, when small stones fell on Weston, Connecticut, investigators from Yale College concluded that they had fallen from the sky. President Thomas Jefferson appears openly critical in a well-known but probably apocryphal quote: "I would sooner believe that those two Yankee professors would lie than believe that stones would fall from heaven."

The total number of meteorites either recovered from observed falls or found outside of Antarctica currently numbers about 2,900. Antarctica, long known as a meteorite treasure trove, is a special case. The large surface area of its ice sheets acts as a meteorite collector; the cold, dry climate keeps the rocks well preserved; and the underlying topography alters the movement of the ice in such a way that it leads to the transport and concentration of the embedded meteorites. Over 17,000 meteorite fragments have been found to date, probably representing about 4,000 different strikes. None of these samples bears any resemblance to the fragile, low-density material from which comets and their meteor showers are made, and it's clear that meteor shower peaks present no greater chance of a meteorite fall. With the notable exceptions of the moon and Mars, which together have supplied over fifty meteorites, it's the asteroids that provide the main source of rocks from space. Astronomers have determined the orbits of six meteorites whose blazing trails were photographed from widely separated locations, and these orbits share many characteristics with the orbits of asteroids that cross the Earth's path. Mineralogical evidence shows that most meteorites formed in low-pressure environments and at depths no greater than the dimensions of the largest asteroids. Studies of how the reflectivity of asteroids and meteorites changes over a range of wavelengths have revealed a close correspondence between, for example, meteorites classified as eucrites (composed essentially of the minerals anorthite and pigeonite) and the asteroid Vesta.

With all of this material falling from the sky, one might imagine that sooner or later someone would be hit. Chinese records from 616 and 1915 report human casualties, and a fragment of the Nakhla meteorite—one of the Mars rocks—reportedly killed a dog when it landed near Alexandria, Egypt, in 1911. Two authenticated cases of meteorite injury do exist. On November 30, 1954, a stony meteorite weighing in at 8.6 pounds (3.9 kilograms) penetrated the roof and ceiling of a house in Sylacauga, Alabama, bounced off a large radio and struck the thigh of a woman asleep on a couch, inflicting painful bruises. Another incident occurred August 14, 1992, when a 0.13-ounce (3.6-gram) stony fragment bounced off the leaves of a banana tree near Mbale, Uganda, and hit a boy on the head. One estimate of meteor impacts on humans determined that in an area the size of North America there should be one victim every 180 years. Extrapolated to the entire world, this suggests an average of one meteorite-related injury every nine years.

In the early 1990s the U.S. Department of Defense declassified satellite data collected between 1975 and 1992 that revealed over 130 randomly located kiloton-scale explosions in the Earth's atmosphere, airbursts caused by the sudden catastrophic breakup of large stony meteoroids. On average, about nine of these explosions occur each year. One particularly dramatic example of this type of event occurred at 7:14 A.M. on June 30, 1908, when a bolide a hundred times brighter than the sun streaked across the clear skies of central Siberia and exploded 6 miles (10 kilometers) above the unpopulated taiga near the Stony Tunguska river. It detonated with the energy equivalent of ten million tons of TNT, scorching and flattening millions of trees within an area of about 810 square miles (2,100 square kilometers), but of course left no crater. The object that exploded over Siberia was a large stony meteoroid probably less than 600 feet (190 meters) across.

Meteoroids far larger than any recorded in historical times have struck the Earth in the past. Scars from such impacts are quickly eroded on Earth, yet about 130 craters are known and many more are suspected. The famous Meteor Crater in northern Arizona was formed 50,000 years ago by an iron meteoroid less than 275 feet (86 meters) across. Much further back in time, an impact 35 million years ago struck the continental shelf near present-day Cape Charles, Virginia, carving out a crater 53 miles (85 kilometers) across and nearly as deep as the Grand Canyon. The Chesapeake Bay crater is three times larger than any other U.S. crater and the sixth largest on the planet.

An even greater impact occurred 65 million years ago in the floor of a shallow sea that now lies beneath Mexico's Yucatán Peninsula. The blast was felt the world over through its atmospheric and climatic effects—changes that most experts now generally agree resulted in the final curtain for dinosaurs and many other species but brought about a tremendous ecological opportunity for mammals. Impacts this large are expected about every 100 million years.

Astronomers are now attempting to survey all objects in Earth-crossing orbits capable of producing large impacts, in order to locate significant future threats. The International Astronomical Union's Minor Planet Center in Cambridge, Massachusetts, now lists over 400 objects as "potentially hazardous asteroids." Examining future close approaches of the bodies we do know about reveals that, through the year 2178, the asteroid designated 2000 WO107 comes closest to us. It passes within 50,000 miles—less than a fifth of the moon's distance—on December 1, 2140. Every few months, search programs detect objects of similar size to the one thought responsible for the Tunguska event passing within the moon's orbit.

A recent study of the orbit of one half-mile-wide object, asteroid 1950 DA, revealed a twenty-minute interval in March 2880 in which there could be, in the understated words of the study's authors, "a nonnegligible probability" of a collision with Earth. The odds of a collision work out to about 1 chance in 300. The asteroid is large enough that its impact would have global consequences on the Earth. Decades of radar and optical observations make the orbit of 1950 DA one of the best-determined orbits of an asteroid or comet, and the specifics of that orbit happen to minimize many sources of uncertainty in the trajectory even hundreds of years into the future. Ultimately, what determines whether 1950 DA hits or misses Earth is uncertainty about accelerations that arise from the way the asteroid reradiates heat from the sun. Those accelerations depend on the spin axis, chemical makeup, and surface properties of the asteroid. Refining the collision probability may well require direct inspection of the asteroid by spacecraft.

In ancient China meteors were viewed as heavenly messengers. The messages they carry—whether a flash of light, a burst of radio waves, or even the rare rock from space—are now eagerly deciphered by planetary scientists and have revealed volumes about the history of the Earth and the violent past of the solar system. With the exception of lunar samples returned during the 1960s and 1970s, meteorites represent the only samples of extraterrestrial material available for direct study, a kind of "poor man's space probe." This state of affairs will come to an end sometime in the next two decades, when new space missions pluck samples from several other solar-system bodies and return them to Earth.

9 Unpredictable Sky Events

Some say that the Northern Lights are the glare of the Arctic ice and snow;
And some that it's electricity, and nobody seems to know.

—Robert W. Service, "The Ballad of the Northern Lights," 1909

Throughout this book we've emphasized the motions of the moon and planets, listed the best opportunities for seeing them, and pointed out some of their more interesting gatherings. This may give the impression that every sky event worth viewing has already been predicted. Fortunately for those of us who look forward to surprises, there are three types of naked-eye sky events no one can predict yet. We discuss them below in order of the likelihood of their appearance by 2010.

The Northern Lights

The aurora is a sporadic, generally faint atmospheric phenomenon usually seen in the night sky from locations at high latitudes. More commonly known as the northern lights (and in the southern hemisphere as the southern lights), it may first appear as a faint milky glow low in the north, too dim for the human eye to detect any color but bright enough to silhouette any clouds near the horizon. It may develop into steady greenish arcs or form scintillating, swirling curtains of yellow-green light. During the most dramatic displays visible from middle latitudes, a crimson glow fills much of the sky. It was this form that inspired European scientists of the 1600s to name the phenomenon aurora borealis, literally "northern dawn." (The southern lights are called aurora australis.) The patterns and forms of the aurora include quiescent arcs, rapidly moving rays, and curtains, patches, and veils. Since this light show takes place high in the atmosphere, it isn't really an astronomical event. But, as we'll see, the aurora represents the visible manifestation of complex interactions between Earth and the sun.

The lively, colorful forms of the aurora naturally appear in much American and European folklore. A Scottish legend connects the lights with supernatural creatures called Merry Dancers, who fight in the sky for the favor of a beautiful woman. A Danish story explains the lights as reflections from flocks of geese trapped in the northern icepack and flapping to free themselves. The Lapps in Sweden believed that the aurora could scorch the hair of those foolish enough to leave the house without a cap. In Alaska and eastern Norway, children were believed to be at special risk from the northern lights. Greenland Inuits thought the aurora represented signals from dead friends who were trying to contact the living. The Fox Indians of Michigan believed that they could conjure up spirits by whistling to the light. To the Tlingit Indians of southeastern Alaska, the flickering glow was caused by battles between the spirits of fallen warriors; its appearance foretold catastrophes and bloodshed.

There are many historical accounts of the northern lights from areas far south of its usual location, such as southern Europe. The Greek philosopher Aristotle is often credited as the first in Western culture to attempt to discuss the aurora scientifically. He gives several names for the northern lights in his *Meteorologica,* written in the third century B.C. These include burning flames, chasms, trenches—and goats, apparently an allusion to a very active form.

The predominant color of bright auroras seen at the latitudes of the Mediterranean—and the continental United States—is a deep red. An early Chinese record describes it as a "red cloud spreading all over the sky." According to the Roman philosopher Seneca, in A.D. 37 troops moved during an aurora to assist the seaport of Ostia "as if it were in flames, when the glowing of the sky lasted through a great part of the night, shining dimly like a vast and smoking fire." Similar "fires in the air" in 1583 mobilized thousands of French pilgrims, who prayed to avert the wrath of God. On September 15, 1839, an intense aurora dispatched fire departments throughout London. More recently, during the great auroral display of March 13, 1989, police departments and newspapers across the United States fielded telephone calls about "funny red clouds" and a firelike glow in the sky.

The aurora occurs in two great luminous ovals centered on the Earth's north and south magnetic poles. Their glow results from collisions between atmospheric gases and showers of electrons and protons guided by the Earth's magnetic field. Each gas gives out its own particular color when bombarded, and atmospheric composition varies with altitude. The auroral glow can originate 50 to 620 miles (80 to 1,000 kilometers) above us, but typically occurs between 62 and 155 miles (100 to 250 kilometers) above the ground. Excited oxygen atoms provide the yellow-green color most commonly seen in auroras. Ionized molecular nitrogen produces blue and violet emissions, colors to which the human eye is much less sensitive. Excited molecules of nitrogen and oxygen at lower altitudes provide red light. These three primary colors together produce the myriad hues of a typical aurora.

What causes the showers of charged particles that create the northern lights? Ultimately the source lies in the solar wind, a fast-moving stream of particles constantly flowing from the sun that carries the sun's magnetic field out into space. The solar wind, typically moving at 250 miles (400 kilometers) per second, molds the Earth's magnetic field into an elongated bubble or cavity, compressing its sunward side and stretching its night side far beyond the moon's orbit. Under certain conditions the solar wind magnetic field can merge with the Earth's, creating electrical currents that drive electrons into the polar atmosphere. Auroral activity also intensifies in the spring and fall, largely because the Earth's magnetic field is then more favorably oriented for coupling with the solar wind.

A current focus of much solar and space research is a better characterization and forecasting of the response of the space environment near the Earth, changes referred to as "space weather," to gusts and gales hurled at us by the sun. We are increasingly dependent on space technologies that are extremely sensitive to the changing space environment. For example, at 22:00 UT on May 19, 1998, *Galaxy 4,* a heavily used communication satellite in geostationary orbit above the central United States, lost its primary attitude control system and its backup failed. At the time, *Galaxy 4* was handling about 80 percent of all U.S. pager traffic. Controllers could no longer maintain a stable link between *Galaxy 4* and Earth, resulting in a loss of pager service to forty-five million customers. Researchers believe that the failure was caused by an extremely energetic cloud of electrons built up by a sequence of solar events about two weeks prior to the failure.

Transient events occurring on the sun can generate fast-moving clouds of particles that greatly intensify the solar wind's impact on the Earth, buffeting our planet's magnetic cocoon. Solar flares may blast material from the sun's surface for hours. Areas called coronal holes generate broad torrents of solar wind and may last for many months. The most dramatic space-weather effects, however, occur as a result of enormous clouds of material that erupt from the solar atmosphere and race through interplanetary space. These eruptions are known as coronal mass ejections, or CMEs. Somehow a portion of the sun's magnetic field undergoes a sudden disruption, stretching and twisting like a rubber band until it snaps. When it does, as much as a billion tons of matter races away from the sun at speeds up to 1,250 miles (2,000 kilometers) a second. When a CME slams into the Earth's magnetic bubble, it must adjust to the sudden change. The result is a blast of particles into the Earth's atmosphere and a geomagnetic storm. Sometimes a fast CME will overtake and merge with one or more CMEs already on their way, resulting in a "cannibal" CME that can have an especially dramatic effect. The ghostly apparition of the aurora is the visible manifestation of these violent space events. Particularly powerful storms cause the auroral ovals to expand and move southward from their normal locations, bringing the northern lights to skywatchers at far lower latitudes than normal (fig. 9-1).

One of the most important spacecraft in the fleet now dedicated to monitoring the sun is the *Solar and Heliospheric Observatory (SOHO)*, a joint mission between NASA and ESA. Launched in December 1995, it was placed in an orbit around a dynamically stable point 932,000 miles (1.5 million kilometers) sunward of the Earth. From there it has an uninterrupted view of the sun.

"Two instruments on *SOHO* have proved to be especially valuable for continuous real-time monitoring of solar storms that affect space weather," says Paal Brekke, a *SOHO* project scientist. These are the Extreme ultraviolet Imaging Telescope (EIT), which provides images of the solar surface at far ultraviolet wavelengths that are blocked by Earth's atmosphere, and the Large Angle and Spectrometric Coronagraph (LASCO), which looks for the enormous bubbles of charged particles and entrained magnetic field that represent a CME (fig. 9-2). Before *SOHO* was operational, only 27 percent of major magnetic storms were correctly forecast and most forecasts were false alarms. Between 1996 and 1997, *SOHO* detected more than two dozen CMEs. "Over 85 percent caused major magnetic storms," Brekke says, "and only 15 percent of such storms were not predicted." Geomagnetic storms can affect radio communications and navigation signals and can introduce errors in positions determined by the Global Positioning Satellite network, so advance notice is increasingly important.

Coronal mass ejections, solar flares, and coronal holes tend to be more frequent on the active side of the sun's eleven-year sunspot cycle. This peaked in 2000, with a secondary maximum in 2002, so solar activity is now on the downswing and will continue to decline until sometime between 2005 and 2006, when the next solar cycle begins. Activity will then slowly rise as the sun powers up for its next maximum early in or after 2010. Observers in the northern United States and southern Canada may expect to see between one and five auroras every few months until 2004. Those at lower latitudes will continue to see displays associated with powerful solar events, but with decreasing frequency—perhaps one or two each year.

Overall, the chances of seeing an aurora are not all that bad—especially in Canada and the United States. Since the north magnetic pole lies in North America, the auroral oval generally reaches farther south there. This means that observers at a given latitude in North America have a better chance of seeing an aurora than those at the same latitude in Europe or Asia. Both Rome and Chicago lie at forty-two degrees north latitude, for example, but Rome averages one aurora per decade while Chicago sees about ten each year. Figure 9-3 shows the frequency of auroral displays in the northern hemisphere averaged over many years; the number in each curve indicates the number of nights per year in which an aurora can be seen.

Perhaps the strangest question connected with the northern lights is whether or not they produce sounds that humans can hear. Among the names the Sámi people of northern Scandinavia gave the northern lights was *guovssahas*, which means "audible light." Reports of rustling, hissing, and crackling noises associated with strong auroral displays have persisted for centuries. William Ogilvie, an explorer and surveyor in the Yukon, wrote of one incident in November 1882:

> I have often met people who said they could hear a slight rustling noise whenever the Aurora made a sudden rush. One man, a member of my party . . . was so positive of this that . . . when there was an unusually brilliant and extensive display, I took him

Figure 9-1. On November 4, 2001, a fast-moving coronal mass ejection erupted from the sun. It swept past our planet the next night, triggering a geomagnetic storm and expanding the auroral oval southward into the continental United States. Skywatchers as far south as Florida were treated to vivid displays of the northern lights. The satellites of the U.S. Air Force Defense Meteorological Satellite Program have a low-light imaging system that can see faint phenomena like city lights and aurora. This image, which shows a bright arc of aurora cutting across Lake Michigan, was captured by the DMSP *F-15* satellite at 9:45 P.M. EST on November 5, nearly an hour after the storm commenced. The auroral band illuminates clouds in eastern Canada. (Photo courtesy of the Meteorological Satellite Applications Branch, Air Force Weather Agency)

> beyond all noise of the camp, blindfolded him and told him to let me know when he heard anything, while I watched the play of the streamers. At nearly every brilliant rush of the auroral light, he exclaimed: "Don't you hear it?" All the time I was unconscious of any sound.

Noise produced in the rarefied air in which auroras occur simply cannot reach the ground. But according to physicist Colin Keay, who developed a physical theory to explain similar sounds from meteors, the aurora too can create electrophonic sound.

The atmospheric activity responsible for the northern lights occasionally has a profound effect on everyday life. "During the aurora of September 2, 1859," wrote the American researcher Elias Loomis (1811–1889), "the currents of electricity on the telegraph wires were so steady and powerful that, on several lines, the operators succeeded in using them for telegraphic purposes as a substitute for the battery." For a time, messages were transmitted solely on currents generated by the aurora.

A rapidly shifting and expanding auroral oval can induce electrical currents in other long conductors as well. An example that has become legend in the space-weather community occurred in March 1989, when an extremely active solar region broke records held for over thirty years. Auroral activity was seen as far south as Jamaica. In Quebec, Canada, induced currents in seven one-hundred-ton Static Volt-Ampere Reactive

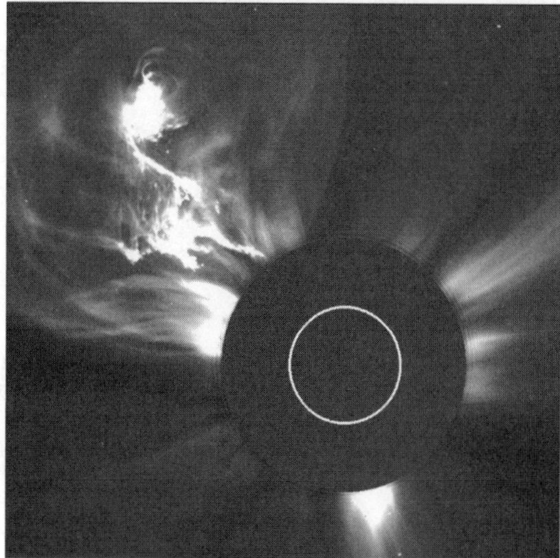

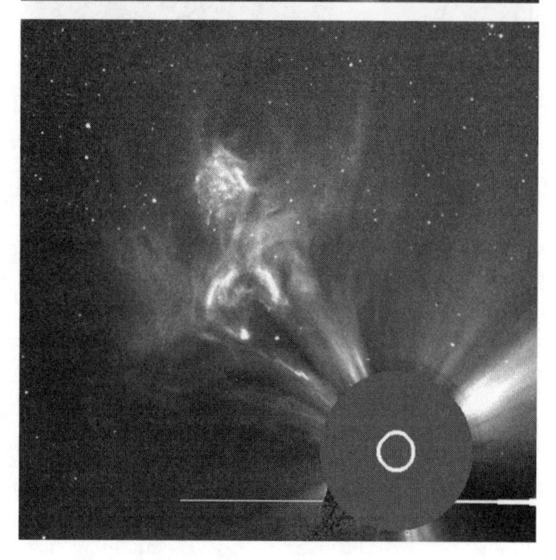

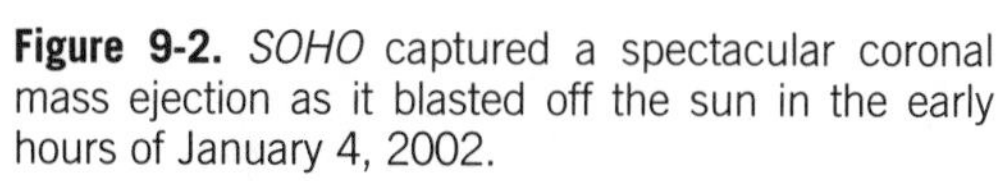

Figure 9-2. *SOHO* captured a spectacular coronal mass ejection as it blasted off the sun in the early hours of January 4, 2002.

Top: It began as a filament eruption seen by the satellite's Extreme ultraviolet Imaging Telescope (EIT).

Middle and bottom: The complexity and structure of the event amazed even experienced solar physicists at the *SOHO* operations center. These views through the spacecraft's Large Angle and Spectrometric Coronagraph (LASCO) instrument show the ejection's expansion in progressively wider views. When these events are Earth-directed they take on the appearance of an expanding halo in *SOHO* images. The circular dark zone is the shield that protects the instrument from the bright light of the sun and inner corona; the white circle within it shows the location and size of the sun's visible disk. (SOHO, ESA/NASA images) capacitors operated by the Hydro-Quebec Power Authority caused their protective relays to detect an overload condition. The relays kicked in and, over the course of about one minute, took the devices offline. With them went about half of Quebec's electrical power generation. Within another minute the entire power distribution system collapsed and 21,500 megawatts of power were no longer available. More than six million people were left without electricity for over nine hours. "The power pools that served the entire northeastern United States were uncomfortably close to a cascading system collapse," says Paal Brekke. Induced currents can also weaken welds in oil pipelines and create damaging electrical surges in telecommunications cables.

Something to keep in mind when an aurora next paints the sky.

Bright Comets

In the previous chapter we discussed comets only in the context of their relationship with meteor showers, but of course comets can be impressive

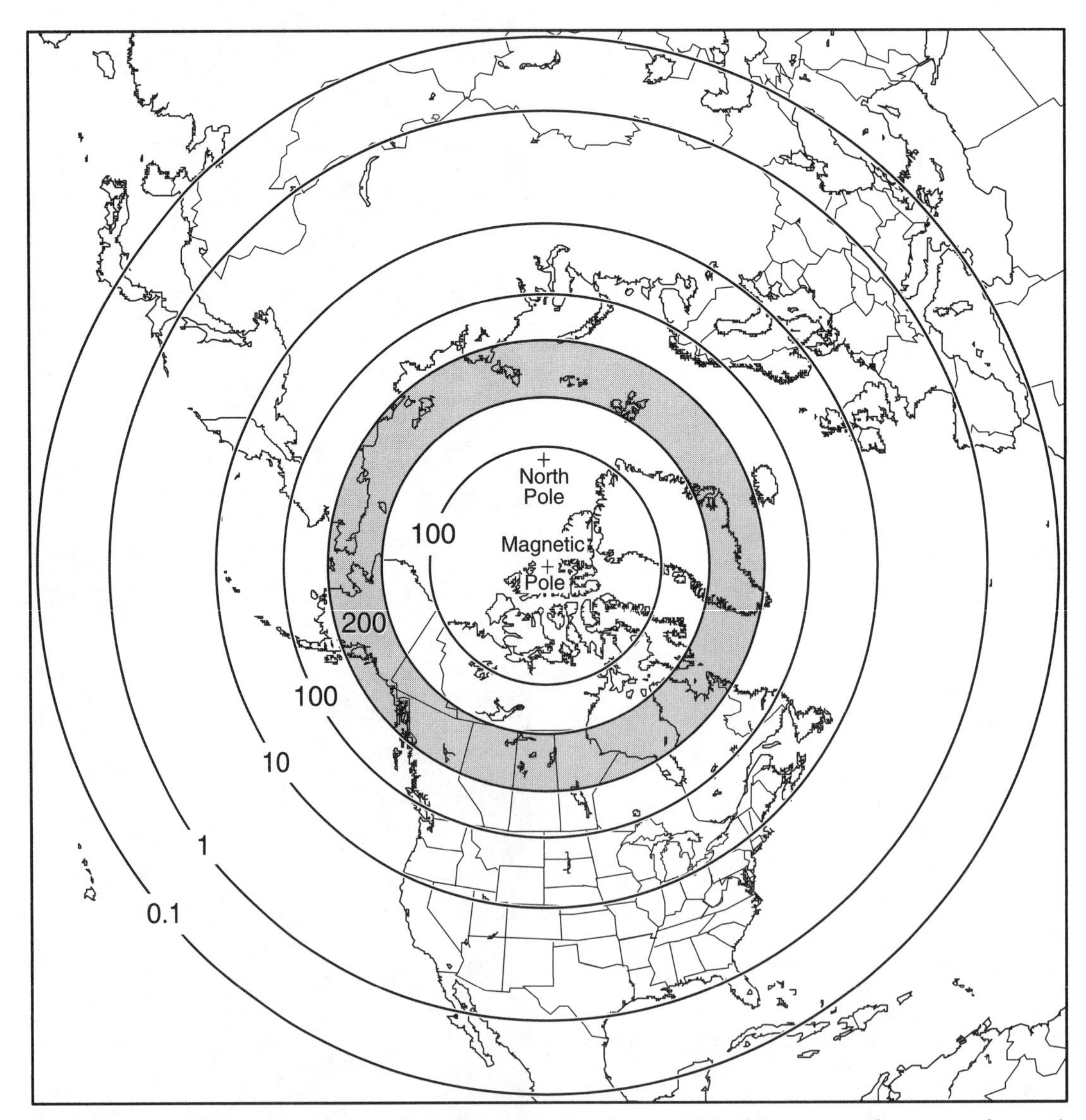

Figure 9-3. This map, centered on the north magnetic pole, gives an idea of the average frequency of auroral displays for different locations in the northern hemisphere. Numbers correspond to the number of nights per year in which an aurora can be seen. The shaded region shows the zone in which auroral displays are most common.

sights on their own. In recent years, amateur and professional astronomers together have discovered an average of more than thirty comets annually. Most of these remain diffuse fuzz balls detectable only with telescopes or, at best, binoculars. A truly bright comet, one that may be easily seen by the unaided eye, appears only about once each decade. In the late 1990s we emerged from a two-decade-long drought of bright comets with not one but two respectable apparitions within one year of each other.

Comets are dark, solid bodies a few kilometers across that orbit the sun in very eccentric paths. Comets can be fairly described as "dirty snowballs" containing a mixture of dust and frozen gases. Some of the icy material—perhaps less than 1 percent—evaporates as the comet nears the sun, creating an envelope of gas and dust that enshrouds the solid body. This envelope, called the coma, may be up to 620,000 miles (1,000,000 kilometers) across. Swept back by the solar wind and the radiation pressure of sunlight, this material forms the comet's tail. Comet tails can span a distance greater than that separating the Earth from the sun. That such a small amount of material could create visible features so large has led some to describe comets as "the closest thing to nothing anything can be and still be something."

To the naked eye, the coma of a bright comet looks almost star-like, a tiny ball of light set within a milky glow. The comet's tail or tails fan out from the coma. If present, a broad dust tail may be the most striking visual feature, arcing across ten degrees of sky or more. The glowing gas tail is straighter, narrower, and fainter than the dust tail. Within the coma, and invisible to both the naked eye and the most powerful telescopes, lies the small icy body responsible for this grand apparition—the comet's nucleus.

The ancient Chinese names for comets reflect their visual appearance. A comet with a prominent tail was called a broom star *(huixing)*, while one with no obvious tail was a bushy star *(poxing)*. The Greeks likewise recognized a comet with an extended tail as a bearded star *(aster pogonias)* and one without a tail was a long-haired star *(aster kometes)*, from which our modern word is derived. Until the mid-1400s, the most detailed and complete observations of comets were made by the Chinese, who as early as 200 B.C. employed official skywatchers to record and interpret any new omens in the heavens. They recognized, some nine centuries before their European counterparts, that comet tails always point away from the sun. The Chinese interest in comets, however, was for their astrological importance as signs of coming change.

Oriental ideas about comets had little influence on the development of Western thought. Aristotle regarded them as a fiery atmospheric phenomenon, to be lumped together with meteors and the aurora. They could not be planets, he reasoned, because comets can appear far from the constellations of the zodiac. Aristotle envisioned comets as being whipped up by the motion of the sun and stars around the Earth, and their appearance as warnings of coming droughts and high winds. As these ideas were extended in the Middle Ages, comets became viewed less as a portent of disaster than as a cause. They were viewed as a fiery corruption of the air, pockets of hot contaminated vapor that could bring earthquakes, disease, and famine.

Some of these ideas were being seriously questioned when the great comet of 1577 attracted the attention of Danish observer Tycho Brahe, recently installed in his observatory on the island of Ven near Copenhagen. Tycho could see no reason why comet tails should always point away from the sun if they were products of the weather. He measured the position of the comet with respect to the stars at different times during the night in an effort to find its parallax—a clue to the object's true distance from Earth. His observations indicated that the comet lay beyond the moon but not as far off as Venus. Tycho's work on the comet of 1577 did not settle the matter—Galileo, for example, dismissed his observations—but it did help break the hold of Aristotle and hasten the scientific study of comets. When Isaac Newton published his monumental *Principia* in 1687, he showed that comets obeyed Kepler's laws of planetary motion and concluded that "comets are a sort of planet revolved in very eccentric orbits around the sun."

Future observations of the comet of 1682 would eventually remove any lingering doubts. Newton's friend Edmond Halley began collecting accurate cometary observations in 1695 with the goal of comparing the orbits of many comets. Looking over his table of orbits, Halley found several comets that seemed very similar and shared roughly the same period, between seventy-five and seventy-six years. "Many considerations

Table 9-1. Notable Comets since 1965

Designations, names, closest approaches to the sun and the Earth, brightest magnitude, and visual ranking of recent bright comets. Entries are ordered by perihelion date.

Designation	Name	Perihelion Distance (AU)	Closest to Earth (AU)	Time to Next Return (Years)	Peak Visual Mag.	Visual Ranking
C/1965 S1	Ikeya-Seki	0.008	0.906	880	> −7.0	Excellent
C/1969 Y1	Bennett	0.538	0.689	1,700	+0.0	Very good
C/1973 E1	Kohoutek	0.142	0.860	80,000	+2.5	Poor
C/1975 V1	West	0.197	0.794	6,400,000	−3.0	Excellent
C/1983 H1	*IRAS*-Araki-Alcock	0.991	0.031	1,000	+1.7	Good
1P/1982 U1	Halley	0.587	0.417	76	+2.4	Poor
C/1995 O1	Hale-Bopp	0.914	1.315	2,520	−0.8	Excellent
C/1996 B2	Hyakutake	0.230	0.102	29,300	+0.0	Excellent
C/2002 C1	Ikeya-Zhang	0.507	0.404	368	+2.9	Poor
C/2001 Q4	NEAT	0.962	0.321	?	>+3.0	?

incline me to believe the comet of 1531 observed by Apianus to have been the same as that described by Kepler . . . in 1607 and which I again observed in 1682," Halley wrote. "Whence I would venture confidently to predict its return, namely in the year 1758. And if this occurs, there will be no further cause for doubt that the other comets ought to return also." Halley's confidence proved well founded—the first comet ever predicted to return was again spotted on December 25, 1758, and has been known as Halley's comet ever since.

Comets are more commonly named for their discoverers, and up to three independent co-discoverers may share the credit. Increasingly, those discoverers are not individuals, but dedicated small-body discovery programs or solar-observing satellites. The 2001 edition of the *Catalogue of Cometary Orbits* lists fifty-one comets named for the Massachusetts Institute of Technology's Lincoln Near Earth Asteroid Research (LINEAR) project, twenty-one found by the Near Earth Asteroid Tracking (NEAT) program of the Jet Propulsion Laboratory, and another five discovered by the Lowell Observatory Near-Earth Object Search (LONEOS). The pace of comet discovery has more than doubled in recent decades, up from an average of about a dozen per year in the late 1980s to about thirty per year in the opening years of the twenty-first century. This does not include the 350 comets found by the *SOHO* satellite, which represents almost one-fourth of the *Catalogue*'s total. The satellite's tally increases by an average of eighty per year, making it the most prolific, if unintended, comet-finder in history.

Since the names of discoverers don't allow for a unique identification, comets receive a more prosaic official designation. This consists of a one-letter prefix, usually a *C* for "comet" or a *P* for "periodic," followed by the year of discovery and an uppercase letter that indicates the half-month in which the discovery occurred. For example, an *A* represents January 1 though 15, *B* is January 16 through 31, and so on, with the letter *I* not being used (to avoid confusion with earlier nomenclature that used Roman numerals) and the letter *Z* being unnecessary. After the letter comes a number that represents the order of discovery during the half-month. Halley's comet, which was the first comet discovered or recovered in the second half of October 1982, therefore receives the designation P/1982 U1. When the return of a comet is well established, either through a recovery or by observing a second passage through perihelion, a number can be added to the prefix. Since Halley was the first comet whose return was identified, its full designation becomes 1P/1982 U1.

According to the 2001 edition of the *Catalogue of Cometary Orbits*, astronomers have detailed orbital information on 1,416 individual comets. Only 151 of these are short-period comets that complete an orbit in less than 200 years. The average short-period comet travels once around the sun every seven years in an orbit inclined to the Earth's by thirteen degrees and comes no closer to the sun than about 1.5 AU, just within the mean distance of Mars. Halley's comet is the brightest and most active member of this group. The remaining population consists of long-period comets, which take 200 years or more to return to the inner solar system. "No spectacular comets are anticipated during the next eight years," said Daniel Green, an astronomer at the Harvard-Smithsonian Center for Astrophysics in Cambridge, Massachusetts, speaking in May 2002. Comet aficionados instead pin their hopes to the unpredictable arrival of an as-yet-unknown long-period comet.

Table 9-1 lists information on the best comet appearances since 1965, including a simple ranking of their visual displays. The two most important considerations in assessing the visibility of a comet are its distance from the sun at perihelion, which controls the comet's activity, and its distance from Earth, preferably after the intense heating of perihelion. Halley, for example, was an impressive sight in 1910, but its anemic 1986 appearance was disappointing even for those who traveled far from city lights. The main difference between those apparitions was the comet's distance from Earth. Halley reached perihelion at a time when the Earth was on the opposite side of the sun, and the comet never came closer to Earth than 0.417 AU (38.7 million miles or 62.4 million kilometers), which is about three times the distance of its 1910 approach.

Another example of the importance of proximity was the 1983 display of comet *IRAS*-Araki-Alcock (C/1983 H1). A small and relatively inactive comet, it was discovered first by the *Infrared Astronomical Satellite (IRAS)* in late April and originally identified as an asteroid. In early May, amateur astronomers Genichi Araki of Japan and George Alcock of England independently discovered the object. It soon became an obvious sight to the unaided eye, high in the northern sky, and on May 12 the comet brushed past the Earth at 0.0312 AU (2.9 million miles or 4.7 million kilometers), closer than any comet since 1770. A typical comet might move across the sky by a degree or so a day, too slowly for the eye to notice. *IRAS*-Araki-Alcock was so close that its motion was clearly evident to observers, who compared its movement to that of the minute hand on a clock. At its best, the comet was about twice the apparent diameter of the moon and looked like a star nestled within a puff of smoke. It showed no evidence of a tail—instead, it presented a fine example of a "bushy star"—and faded from view by the third week of May.

Intrinsically larger or more active comets can produce a spectacle without getting quite so close. Any list of "great comets" must include both West (C/1975 V1) and Ikeya-Seki (C/1965 S1). Comet West improved dramatically within a week of its very close approach to the sun, aided in large part by the break-up of its nucleus into four fragments. West dominated the morning sky of early March 1976 with complex gas and dust tails extending twenty-five degrees or more. A decade earlier, the even more spectacular Ikeya-Seki could be seen even during the daylight as it raced past the sun, skimming its surface by less than one solar diameter. The intense heating led to the break-up of the nucleus into at least two fragments and a corresponding increase in brightness. During the days around perihelion, one could see Ikeya-Seki as a star-like object in broad daylight by simply blocking the sun with a hand—and as a grand finale, the comet emerged from the sun's glare in the last week of October 1965 sporting a bright tail about twenty-five degrees long. Indeed, Ikeya-Seki proved to be the brightest comet of the twentieth century.

Ikeya-Seki's punishing orbit places it in a category of comets known as the sungrazers. Heinrich Kreutz (1854–1907) extensively examined the orbits of sungrazing comets and argued that they shared a common ancestry. Kreutz suggested that the comets he studied were possibly fragments of some much larger comet that fell apart at a particularly close approach to the sun. Sungrazers have a perihelion distance of less than 0.02 AU, an orbital period of a few centuries, and other distinguishing orbital characteristics, and they appeared to be rare. Brian Marsden of the

Harvard-Smithsonian Center for Astrophysics conducted studies of the Kreutz group in 1965 and 1989; he identified eight members and suspected that three others qualified. By the time of his second study, fifteen apparent sungrazing comets had been discovered by the *SOLWIND* and *Solar Maximum Mission* satellites, and Marsden noted these "discoveries suggest that members may in fact be coming back to the sun more or less continuously." Like these fragments, most of the comets so far discovered by comet-scouting champion *SOHO* do not survive their passage, and Marsden says "there is good reason to believe that some 94 percent of these comets are members of the Kreutz group" even though there are too few observations to uniquely determine their orbits. The *SOHO* sungrazers probably measure just a few meters across. Marsden speculates that a historical sungrazer, one the Greek Ephorus reported to have split in two pieces in the winter of 372 B.C., might even be the granddaddy of them all.

Even when orbital geometry promises a good display, the comet itself may simply fail to cooperate. Comet Kohoutek (C/1973 E1), which was widely predicted to be the "comet of the century" in 1973, did manage to become a naked-eye object but never lived up to its publicity. Another example is Comet Austin (C/1989 X1), discovered in December 1989 by New Zealand amateur Rodney Austin. The comet's orbit was very favorable, taking Austin 0.34 AU from the sun on April 9, 1990, and 0.15 AU from the Earth on May 25. Astronomers noted in January that Austin was already more active than Halley at the same distance from the sun, and in February astronomical hobby magazines proclaimed "Monster Comet Coming!" But as Austin closed on the sun, it failed to maintain its rapid brightening and, in the end, proved a bigger dud than Kohoutek.

Both Austin and Kohoutek appear to have been new comets—that is, making their first close pass by the sun. Astronomers believe that comets originate from two "cold storage" zones that sur-

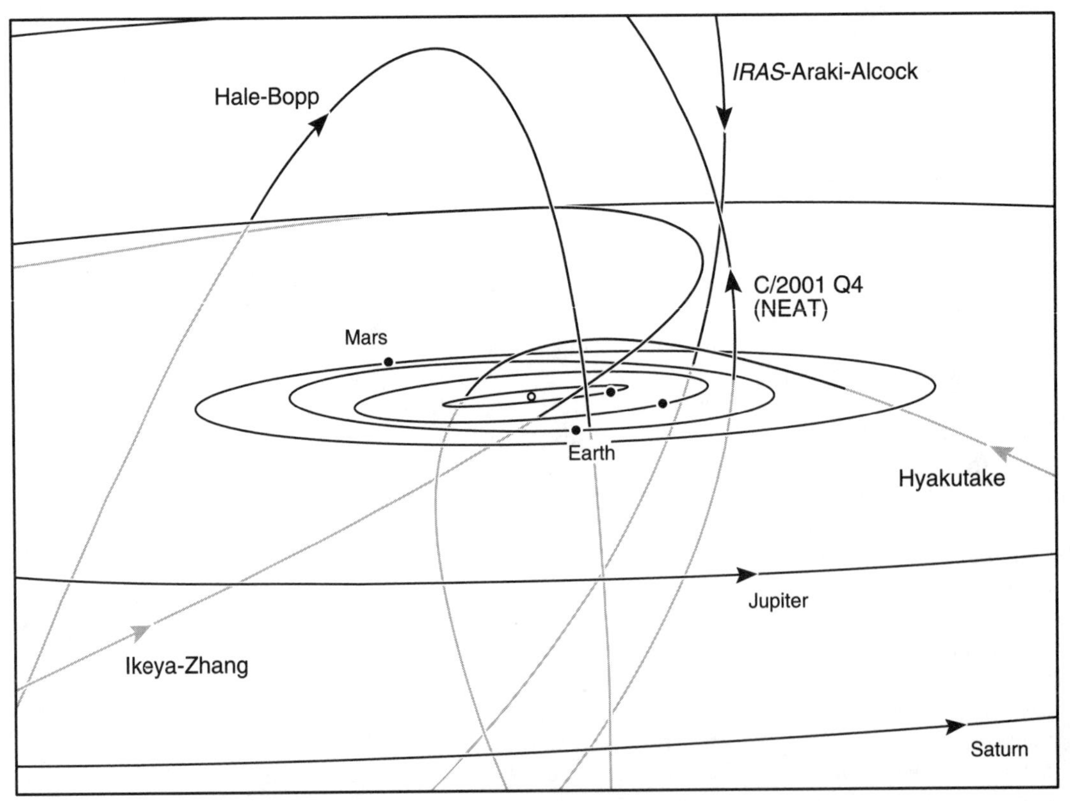

Figure 9-4. The eccentric paths followed by comets differ greatly from those of the planets. This illustration shows the orbits of selected comets listed in table 9-1, a shaded line indicating where the orbit passes below the plane of the ecliptic. The positions of the planets are correct for December 31, 2010.

round the planetary system. The inner portion of this comet cloud is a thick disk centered on the ecliptic that begins near the orbit of Neptune (about 30 AU) and extends beyond the orbit of Pluto to 50 AU. Often called the *Kuiper belt*, it contains at least a few tens of thousands of icy objects larger than about a half-mile across. A much larger and more diffuse component, called the *Oort cloud* and containing perhaps a trillion comets, forms a sun-centered spherical shell extending from the outer Kuiper belt to about one-third of a light-year or more into space. Many astronomers believe that the Kuiper belt is the source for the short-period comets and that the Oort cloud, from which comets are more easily dislodged, is the source for the long-period comets. Feeble gravitational disturbances from passing stars and interstellar gas clouds remove enough orbital energy from Oort cloud comets that they begin their million-year-long fall toward the sun. Long-period comets may arrive from any direction, their elongated orbits randomly oriented to the orbits of the planets, while the short-period comets are confined closer to the ecliptic (fig. 9-4). New arrivals from the comet cloud probably retain a coating of highly volatile ices, such as frozen carbon dioxide, that begins to evaporate at much lower temperatures than frozen water. Such comets "turn on" at relatively large distances from the sun, but brighten only until the coating evaporates.

In the previous edition of this book, after noting the long drought of bright comets that followed the appearance of West in 1976, we concluded this section with the words, "Sooner or later, the 'monster comet' skygazers have hoped for will hover in the morning or evening twilight." It turned out to be sooner, with two objects so impressive that they easily placed in the "great comet" category.

Comet Hyakutake (C/1996 B2) was, in the words of Brooks Observatory comet expert John Bortle, "one of the grandest of the millennium." It was discovered visually by Japanese amateur Yuji Hyakutake when it was at a distance of 2.0 AU—and only fifty-five days before its closest approach to Earth (March 25, 1996, 0.102 AU). By late March, mid-northern observers could see it directly overhead before dawn with a tail at least thirty degrees long. In the days around closest approach it was an easy object to spot even from cities, and its motion against the stars, like that of *IRAS*-Araki-Alcock, was evident in minutes. On March 27, as it moved near Polaris, Hyakutake was visible all night long and could be easily seen from the suburbs (fig. 9-5). In a reasonably dark sky the comet was truly something special, showing a tail that spanned some seventy degrees or longer—all the more impressive because it seemed to contain relatively little dust. Hyakutake took us completely by surprise, upstaging the appearance of another comet that was already widely anticipated.

That comet was Hale-Bopp (C/1995 O1). What made Hyakutake a great comet was its unusually close pass, which turned an intrinsically faint and relatively inactive comet into an apparently bright one. But Hale-Bopp was another matter. It was the brightest and most active comet to pass inside the Earth's orbit since the one Tycho examined in 1577. Hale-Bopp showed unusually high activity even at great distance from the sun and was widely expected to be the one that would end the bright comet drought. It was discovered on July 23, 1995, by Alan Hale in New Mexico and Thomas Bopp in Arizona within minutes of one another. After perihelion on April 1, 1997, Hale-Bopp became a striking object in the northwestern sky, cruising through Cassiopeia and Perseus with a pair of tails. The straight, faint gaseous tail was easy to see from a moderately dark site, but the comet's most striking aspect was its dramatically curved 25-degree-long dust tail. Observers in the northern hemisphere could see Hale-Bopp with the naked eye, even from urban sites, and it remained well placed for viewing throughout April and into May (fig. 9-6). As an indication of the comet's unusual activity, consider that it was never closer to Earth than 122 million miles (197 million kilometers) and passed no closer to the sun than 91 percent of Earth's distance.

Another comet, Ikeya-Zhang (C/2002 C1), became a marginal naked-eye object in the spring of 2002. As its name suggests, it was discovered visually, by veteran comet hunter Kaoru Ikeya of Japan and Daqing Zhang of China. It was only faintly visible to the naked eye from dark-sky sites in March, April, and even May, but was a nice object for binoculars. Ikeya-Zhang is especially interesting because it appears to be a return of a fairly bright comet seen by Johannes Hevelius in February and March 1661. Hevelius was the premier comet observer in the mid-seventeenth

Figure 9-5. Discovered less than two months before its closest approach, comet Hyakutake slipped past the Earth on March 25, 1996. Here it cruises through the constellation Bootes two days before its closet approach. (Photo by Robert Miller)

century; his measurements have allowed astronomers to show that the comet designated C/1661 C1 and Ikeya-Zhang are most likely one and the same.

And the comets keep coming. "C/2001 Q4 appears to be headed for a nice apparition in April and May 2004," says Daniel Green, "at which time it is expected to be at least a faint naked-eye comet for some weeks." Its closest approach to the Earth occurs May 6, 2004, when mid-northern observers will find it low in the southwest, above and to the left of Sirius, in the hour after sunset. Climbing ever higher into the evening sky, the comet lies to the left of Procyon on May 9 and 10. Venus, Mars, Saturn, and Jupiter conveniently guide observers to the comet from May 12 to 15, when it lies along an arc formed by these planets roughly midway between Jupiter and Saturn. On May 14 and 15 comet NEAT lies near the Beehive cluster in Cancer—a treat one can enjoy through binoculars—and reaches perihelion on May 16. Thereafter it will climb higher into the evening sky and gradually fade out. As July opens it will lie beneath the pointer stars of the Big Dipper.

Astronomers anticipate that comet NEAT will be at least as bright as Ikeya-Zhang for a few weeks, and they hold out the possibility of an even brighter showing. However, as of this writing the comet's orbital period is still not clear. "Within the errors of uncertainty at this stage," Green says, "it appears quite possible that this comet is entering the inner solar system for the first time, coming from the Oort cloud." That would place it in the class of recent comets that includes the disappointing Kohoutek and Austin comets—and make a great increase in brightness less likely.

Comets are thought to be remnants of the cloud of dust and gas from which the sun and planets formed. In the deep-freeze of the outermost solar system, these fossils have remained largely unchanged in the four billion years since the birth of the solar system. For this reason, they are intensely studied by planetary scientists, who see in them a chance to glimpse our most ancient past. In 2001 the experimental *Deep Space 1* probe made a distant pass by the nucleus of comet 19P/Borrelly and returned images of its pockmarked and relatively inactive surface. Over the coming decade European and American space agencies are planning numerous missions to comets. The *Comet Nucleus Tour (CONTOUR)* was expected to fly within 60 miles of three comet nuclei: 2P/Encke in 2003, 73P/Schwassmann-Wachmann in 2006, and 6P/d'Arrest in 2008. But this mission ended before it could really begin—contact with *CONTOUR* was lost shortly after the launch in 2002. On July 4, 2005, a projectile released from *Deep Impact* will strike the sunlit side of comet 9P/Tempel's nucleus, an event expected to create a blast that leaves a football-field-sized crater—and exposes fresh ice to the sun—while ground-based observatories and the *Deep Impact* spacecraft watch. In 2006, *Stardust* will return to Earth the first direct samples of cometary material, collected during its pass through the coma of 81P/Wild two years before. The ESA plans an ambitious mission for *Rosetta*, which will rendezvous with and orbit comet 46P/Wirtanen as it approaches the sun in 2012. It will also place a small lander on the comet's surface.

For the rest of us, a bright comet is simply one of the most spectacular sights in the celestial pageant.

New Stars

On February 23, 1987, astronomer Ian Shelton at Las Campanas Observatory, Chile, became the first person in nearly four centuries to spot an exploding star with his own eyes. Located 160,000 light-years from us in the Large Magellanic Cloud, one of the small satellite galaxies that orbit our Milky Way, the star brightened slowly over eleven weeks and reached a visual magnitude of +2.9. At maximum brightness it radiated 200 million times as much energy as the sun. This stellar explosion, called a supernova, marked the cataclysmic death of a star. A list maintained by the International Astronomical Union's Central Bureau for Astronomical Telegrams contains over 2,250 records of supernovas in distant galaxies, with just over 100 discovered in the first half of 2002 alone. The event dubbed SN 1987a—the first supernova, bright or faint, to occur that year—is by far the brightest seen in modern times.

Astronomers had long known that some otherwise faint stars suddenly flare up, usually brightening by thousands of times and then, over a period of weeks, fading back into obscurity. Such a star was termed a nova, short for the Latin *nova stella* (new star). Ordinary novas are now known to occur in close binary star systems containing a normal star and a white dwarf—the

Figure 9-6. Comet Hale-Bopp gave skygazers a grand show on the evening of March 26, 1997, as it passed through the stars of Andromeda. Its straight gas tail and broad, downward-curving dust tail were the best since 1976. (Photo by Robert Miller)

compact, aged remnant of a star like our sun. Hydrogen-rich gas from the normal star streams onto the white dwarf's surface, where it accumulates and eventually explodes. Although the outburst appears quite violent, in fact only the surface material is thrown into space and the white dwarf remains intact. In 1934, before the physical details of the nova process were clear, astronomers Fritz Zwicky (1898–1974) and Walter Baade (1893–1960) recognized that some novas were far more energetic than others—powerful enough to disrupt an entire star—and argued convincingly that these "super novas" were a distinctly different phenomenon.

Astronomers classify supernovas into two broad groups. Type I supernovas occur under similar circumstances as typical novas, in close binary systems containing a white dwarf star. Gas from the companion floods onto the dense dwarf and steadily accumulates rather than erupting in periodic explosions. Eventually the added mass triggers an explosive nuclear reaction that sweeps through the star. Only one second passes before the explosive wave dies out, but in that time the white dwarf has been incinerated and transformed into a rapidly expanding fireball.

Supernovas classified as Type II, such as SN 1987a, originate in stars much more massive than our sun. All stars maintain a balance between the tendency of gravity to collapse them and the pressure generated through the nuclear reactions that occur in their cores. But stars have only a limited supply of hydrogen fuel, and massive stars burn much brighter—and consequently much faster—than the sun. Every second the nuclear fusion reactions in the sun's core convert hundreds of million of tons of hydrogen into a slightly smaller mass of helium plus energy. The sun, for example, has been doing this for about 4.6 billion years and is expected to continue until its fuel supply runs low, some five billion years hence. A star ten times the mass of the sun, in contrast, will run through its supply of hydrogen in just ten million years. As their energy crisis looms, these massive stars contract until their central fires ignite again, using the products of previous nuclear reactions as the fuel. Once one set of reactions runs dry, the star's core collapses and its temperature rises until the next set of reactions can ignite. This extends the star's battle against its own gravity, but it proceeds with diminishing returns. Helium fusion in the core lasts but a million years; neon fusion can continue for only a dozen years, and the fusion of oxygen nuclei lasts a third as long, after which the star's core contracts again to ignite its reserve of silicon fuel. Silicon fusion lasts only a week and the core, now full of iron nuclei, contracts—but no further energy can be extracted and the battle is lost. The core collapses for the last time, triggering a blast wave that may—or may not—rip the star apart. If it succeeds, then a supernova is born, the inner core forming a super-dense stellar remnant called a neutron star. If it doesn't, then the star's collapse inexorably continues and forms a black hole.

It takes about two weeks for the supernova to reach maximum brightness, by which time its expanding cloud of stellar debris has reached a diameter about equal to that of Pluto's orbit. The cloud will continue its rapid expansion, slamming into the interstellar environment for millennia and possibly affecting a bubble of space over a thousand light-years across before it becomes indistinguishable from the ordinary gusts and gales that stir the thin matter between the stars.

The supernova is one of nature's greatest spectacles. Its explosion releases up to ten billion times the annual energy output of the sun, and for a few weeks a supernova may even outshine its parent galaxy—a fact that makes them useful probes of the very distant universe. Long before our solar system was born, most of the chemical elements heavier than helium—including the iron and carbon in our bodies and the oxygen we breathe—were forged inside the cauldron of massive stars and then dispersed into the galaxy by their explosions. It's even possible that the blast wave of an exploding star initiated the processes that gave birth to our own solar system.

Supernovas are rare. In a spiral galaxy such as ours, containing over a hundred billion stars, astronomers expect only three or four supernovas to explode each century. But we witness far fewer than this, since our galaxy is filled with clouds of dust and gas that obscure our view. We usually notice only those supernovas occurring within a few thousand light-years of Earth. SN 1987a, positioned in a part of the sky with very little obscuring dust, was an exception.

Despite its importance to astronomers, SN 1987a was hardly an impressive sight. It could be viewed well only in the southern hemisphere, and even at peak brightness it remained fainter than

Figure 9-7. The Crab Nebula, wreckage of the A.D. 1054 supernova, can be seen with small telescopes. (European Southern Observatory photo)

the brightest stars in the Big Dipper. It was, after all, located in another galaxy. The last supernova in our own galaxy was seen in 1604, just a few years before the invention of the telescope. In truth, though, 1604 was only the year that earthbound observers learned of it; since the star lay about 9,500 light-years from Earth, its light had to travel for 9,500 years before human eyes could see it.

Surveys of reliable historical records have turned up at least seven earlier supernova candidates. Table 8-2 summarizes information on all visible supernovas since A.D. 1000. No one knows when the next Milky Way supernova will blaze forth, but we can get a good idea of what to expect by examining historical descriptions of the past few stellar explosions that attracted notice.

Because the intellectual climate in Europe before the Renaissance did not lend itself to such discoveries, the first supernova to attract wide attention was not recorded until November 7, 1572. A few astronomers dismissed reports of the new star as idle talk—Cornelius Gemma, for instance, waited two weeks before bothering to observe it, despite the fact that it was as bright as Venus. The chief reason for this was a deeply held belief in the immutability of the heavens, an Aristotelian notion that nothing beyond the plan-

Table 9-2. Visible Supernovas Since A.D. 1000

Year	Name	Constellation	Magnitude	Distance (Light-Years)
1006	_____	Lupus	–9.5	5,900
1054	Crab Nebula	Taurus	–4.0+	6,500
1181	_____	Cassiopeia	+0.0	10,500
1572	Tycho's star	Cassiopeia	–4.0	16,300
1604	Kepler's star	Ophiuchus	–3.0	9,500
1987	SN 1987a	Mensa	+2.9	160,000

ets ever changed. Among the first Europeans to begin serious study of the star was Tycho Brahe, whose candid account of his own discovery of the star gives us a sense of how radical an event it was for European astronomers. Poor weather kept it from him until November 11, when, during a walk before dinner, he noticed "directly overhead, a certain strange star . . . flashing its light with a radiant gleam and it struck my eyes."

> Amazed, and as if astonished and stupefied, I stood still, gazing for a certain length of time with my eyes fixed intently upon it and noticing that same star placed close to the stars which antiquity attributed to Cassiopeia. When I had satisfied myself that no star of that kind had ever shone forth before, I was led into such perplexity by the unbelievability of the thing that I began to doubt the faith of my own eyes, and so, turning to the servants who were accompanying me, I asked them whether they too could see a certain extremely bright star. . . . They immediately replied with one voice that they saw it completely and that it was extremely bright. . . . I enquired of some country people who by chance were traveling past in carriages. . . . Indeed these people shouted out that they saw that huge star. . . . And at length, having confirmed that my vision was not deceiving me, but in fact that an unusual star existed there . . . and marveling that the sky had brought forth a certain new phenomenon to be compared with the other stars, immediately I got ready my instrument. I began to measure its situation and distance from the neighboring stars in Cassiopeia. . . .

The star remained visible for fifteen months and did not show any movement, indicating that it was much farther away from Earth than the planets. "Hence this new star is located neither in the region of the Element, below the moon, nor in the orbits of the seven wandering stars [including the sun and moon], but in the eighth sphere, among the other fixed stars," Tycho concluded. His better-known protégé, Johannes Kepler, would also make detailed observations of a supernova—the last seen in the Milky Way galaxy—just thirty-two years later.

Imperial astronomers of China's Ming Dynasty (1368–1644) also noticed the new star, although their measurements of its position were far less accurate than Tycho's. "It was seen before sunset," they reported. "At the time, the Emperor noticed it from his palace. He was alarmed and at night he prayed in the open air on the Vermillion Steps." Their name for such an unusual star-like object was *k'oxing* (guest star).

A supernova of similar brightness appeared on July 4, 1054. In 1928, the American astronomer Edwin Hubble (1889–1953) correctly suggested that an expanding gas cloud called the Crab Nebula represented the debris of this explosion (fig. 9-7). The supernova was first noticed by observers in Constantinople, where it was associated with an outbreak of the plague. It's possible that Native American groups throughout western North America recorded the supernova's explosion—more than a dozen rock carvings and paintings from that era show a crescent moon near a large star-like symbol. Observers in western North America would in fact have seen the supernova two degrees from the waning crescent moon just before sunrise. In the early 1990s, a study of pottery made by the Mimbres people, who lived in New Mexico about 1,000 years ago, provided support for the supernova interpretation of the Indian rock art. Many earthenware bowls and plates made by the Mimbres display geometric designs of astronomical significance. Some markings appear to correspond to the number of days in the moon's sidereal and synodic periods, but one bowl features a stylized rabbit—a common lunar symbol—clutching a circular object from which twenty-three rays emerge. Chinese records indicate that the supernova could be seen in daylight for twenty-three days, suggesting that it was at least as bright as Venus. It remained visible for twenty-one months.

But the best supernova in recorded history occurred in 1006. It was first seen by astronomers in Egypt, one of whom tells us: "The sky was shining because of its light. The intensity of its light was a little more than a quarter of that of moonlight." The following night, observers in Japan, China, and parts of Europe became aware of the new star. A Baghdad observer wrote that its "rays on the Earth were like the rays of the moon." From European latitudes the star skimmed the southern horizon, yet an observer in Switzerland wrote: "A new star of unusual size appeared, glittering in aspect, and dazzling the eyes, causing alarm.... It was seen likewise for three months in the inmost limits of the south, beyond all the constellations which are seen in the sky." In China, too, the strange star's appearance caused widespread alarm. No one could agree on its astrological significance, but there was a growing concern that it portended "warfare and ill-fortune." An astute astrologer named Chou K'o-ming offered an alternative interpretation:

> The country where it is visible will prosper greatly, for it is an auspicious star. . . . I heard that people inside and outside the court were quite disturbed about it. I humbly suggest that the civil and military officials be permitted to celebrate in order to set the Empire's mind at rest.

The emperor not only approved K'o-ming's suggestion—he gave him a promotion as well.

Chinese records indicate that the 1006 supernova remained visible for at least two years, although for observers in the far north it was seen for just a few months. The reports suggest that the supernova was extremely bright, comparable to a first quarter moon. It is difficult to imagine a single point of light so bright; while Venus at its best can give us some idea, it's a poor comparison since the planet's light comes from a relatively large area of its disk. Satellites provide a better example. As sunlight glints off of its more reflective surfaces, a satellite can briefly but brilliantly "flare" to a magnitude that approaches the appearance of the 1006 supernova.

Satellite flares are usually capricious, requiring a unique geometry between the sun, the observer, and some piece of shiny hardware on the spacecraft. As it happens, though, Iridium Satellite's numerous spacecraft flare predictably to magnitudes of –8. Each flare is visible over only a limited area, but many Web sites specializing in satellite observation offer Iridium flare predictions for specific geographical locations. Anyone pondering what the next bright supernova will look like should see at least one Iridium flare.

How will the next stellar outburst in our galaxy stack up to these historical events we've discussed? Only time will tell, for the light of the next supernova is already heading our way.

PENDIX

A

Celestial Events, 2003–2010

The following pages contain an astronomical almanac for the years 2003 through 2010—think of it as a "program guide" to the sky. It lists all important celestial happenings in the order of their occurrence and includes the moon's phases, lunar and solar eclipses, information on the brightness and visibility of the planets, and much more. Since this book focuses only on the most observable events, this is not intended to be an exhaustive list of planetary activity.

To find out what's in store for a given year, read the brief Sky Summary of events for that year. To find out what's happening on a given day, just turn to the nearest date in the almanac. For eclipses and other events that can be seen only over a limited area, we've listed the time as well. Events discussed or illustrated within the book contain a reference to the page number where you will find more detailed information.

Throughout the book we indicate the brightness of the planets and stars by referring to the standard astronomical magnitude scale. We usually give an object's magnitude parenthetically after the object's name—for example, Mars (+1.2) or Saturn (–0.3). Remember that the smaller the number, the brighter the object. Venus, the third brightest object in the sky, has a negative magnitude around –4.0, while stars near the limit of human visibility, magnitude +6.0, are 10,000 times fainter.

A Note on Time and Accuracy

We refer to time in several different ways throughout this book. Our horizon scenes illustrate the positions of the moon and planets as they'll be seen by observers in the United States and southern Canada at the times and dates noted in the captions. This is also true of notes in this almanac that instruct you to look some time before or after sunset.

Our star maps illustrate the constellations as they appear at the times on your clock—your local time—even including the annual "spring ahead/fall back" changes of Daylight Savings Time. If your area does not recognize these changes—and Arizona, Hawaii, and most of Indiana do not—then times on these charts

Universal Time Conversion

To Convert UT to:	For Standard Time, Subtract:	For Daylight Time, Subtract:
Atlantic	4 hours	3 hours
Eastern	5 hours	4 hours
Central	6 hours	5 hours
Mountain	7 hours	6 hours
Pacific	8 hours	7 hours
Most of Alaska	9 hours	8 hours
Hawaii	10 hours	No DST

between April and October are one hour ahead of the stars, so just look an hour earlier than indicated.

Some celestial events, such as eclipses or meteor showers, occur at specific times whether or not North America is angled to witness them. We list the occurrences of such events in Universal Time (UT), which for our purposes is identical to Greenwich Mean Time (GMT)—the clock time on the meridian that runs through Greenwich, England. To convert UT to time in the United States and Canada, use the conversion table above. After you convert from UT to local time, remember that the time is still in a twenty-four hour format in which 0h equals midnight, 12h is noon, and 18h is 6:00 P.M. And remember to keep track of the date! For example, observers in the Eastern time zone interested in an event that occurs at 4h UT on December 15 should expect the event at 23h or 11 P.M. Eastern Time not on December 15, but on December 14. (Everyone makes this mistake at least once!)

One other caveat about time: while in many ways astronomy has served as the science of time, many events cannot be predicted with great precision. Also, most events visible to the naked eye don't require great precision—the unaided human eye simply isn't that precise an instrument. Times for some events, such as Earth's arrival at perihelion or the peaks of some meteor showers, are quoted only to the nearest hour. For any special considerations regarding time, be sure to refer to the chapter in which the event is discussed.

2003 Sky Summary

The year begins with Jupiter and Saturn in the southeast in early evening, and Mercury near the western horizon shortly after sunset. The morning sky belongs to Mars and Venus.

Mercury makes three evening appearances and three morning appearances. The best are the morning apparitions of early February and late September. The mid-April evening appearance is the best of the year. For observers with telescopes, Mercury also has a transit in May.

Brilliant **Venus** is high in the southeast in the morning sky as the year begins, then descends to the north before disappearing in the twilight glow by midsummer. It reemerges from sunlight late in the year, making it an unusually poor appearance for Earth's sister planet.

Mars has something of a mixed year. On the one hand, it reaches its greatest brilliance for the period covered in this book at its August opposition. On the other, it spends the year in the most southerly part of the ecliptic and so never reaches a great altitude in the sky. One nice aspect of its early morning appearance at the beginning of the year is the planet's proximity to the reddish star Antares, whose name—meaning Mars's rival—comes from the Greek name for the planet: Ares. The planet will drift eastward through the stars until late July when it begins its retrograde loop (see the chart on page 123.)

Jupiter is a nighttime planet at the beginning of the year, reaching opposition in early February. The King of the Planets lies near Leo, the zodiac's King of the Beasts.

Saturn, in a winter constellation, is best seen at the beginning and end of the year. The highlights of the planet's 2003 appearance are telescopic. In March and April its rings are fully open to us. Between April 8 and 10 Saturn can be found near the Crab Nebula, a faint but well-known supernova remnant in Taurus.

Meteor showers: The Quadrantid meteor shower peaks in the early evening hours of January 3, when there is little moonlight to interfere with the view. Quadrantid meteoroids—as well as those of the December Geminid shower—don't arrive in a head-on collision with Earth but instead drift down from above the plane of our orbit. The Geminids get some lunar interference but can be enjoyed in the early evening. Both showers are better bets than this year's moonlight-washed Perseids of August.

Eclipses: Of the year's four eclipses, only the two total lunar eclipses are of interest to North Americans. During the May eclipse, totality is visible throughout all but the extreme northwestern portion of the contiguous United States and Canada. In November the entire total phase of the eclipse is visible to all of North America except western Alaska.

2003 Sky Almanac

January	2	New moon, 20:24 UT.
	3	Quadrantid meteor shower peaks (1h UT on January 4).
	4	Earth closest to the sun, 0.983320 AU.
	10	First quarter moon, 13:15 UT.
	11	Mercury at inferior conjunction (not visible).
		Venus (–4.4) at greatest western elongation (46° 58').
	18	Full moon, 10:48 UT.
	25	Last quarter moon, 8:34 UT.
February	1	New moon, 10:49 UT.
		Jupiter (–2.6) nearest to Earth, 4.32714 AU.
	2	Jupiter (–2.6) at opposition. It rises in the east at sunset and is visible all night long.
	4	Mercury (–0.1) at greatest western elongation (25° 21').
		Venus (–4.3) gleams in the predawn light between Mercury (–0.1) and Mars (+1.2), now above and fainter than its stellar rival Antares (+0.9). See page 45.
	9	First quarter moon, 11:12 UT.
	16	Full moon, 23:52 UT.
	23	Last quarter moon, 16:47 UT.
March	3	New moon, 2:36 UT. Saturn's rings are fully open throughout April and at their best for the decade.
	10	First quarter moon, 7:16 UT.
	18	Full moon, 10:35 UT.
	21	Mercury at superior conjunction (not visible).
		Vernal equinox, 1:01 UT.
	25	Last quarter moon, 1:52 UT.

April

1 New moon, 19:19 UT.

9 First quarter moon, 23:40 UT.

16 Full moon, 19:36 UT.

Mercury (+0.1) at greatest eastern elongation (19° 46').

Mercury shines beneath Aldebaran (+0.8) and the Pleiades cluster this evening (see page 45).

22 Lyrid meteor shower peaks. Moon interferes.

23 Last quarter moon, 12:19 UT.

May

1 New moon, 12:15 UT.

5 Eta Aquarid meteor shower peaks.

7 Mercury at inferior conjunction. Normally this would mean that it is not visible, but beginning at 5:13 UT Mercury transits the sun. Mid-transit is at 7:52 UT and last contact is at 10:32 UT. This is a telescopic event and *requires eye protection.*

9 First quarter moon, 11:53 UT.

16 Full moon, 3:36 UT.

Total lunar eclipse; greatest eclipse occurs at 3:40 UT. Totality is visible throughout all but the extreme northwestern portion of the contiguous United States. See page 97 for details.

23 Last quarter moon, 0:31 UT.

31 Annular solar eclipse favoring Greenland, Iceland, and Scotland; partial phases visible in Alaska and northern Canada. Greatest eclipse occurs 4:08 UT. See page 86 for details.

New moon, 4:20 UT.

June

3 Mercury (+0.6) at greatest western elongation (24° 26').

7 First quarter moon, 20:28 UT.

14 Full moon, 11:16 UT.

21 Last quarter moon, 14:46 UT.

Summer solstice, 19:12 UT.

24 Saturn in conjunction with the sun (not visible).

29 New moon, 18:39 UT.

July

4 Earth farthest from the sun, 1.016728 AU.

5 Mercury at superior conjunction (not visible).

7 First quarter moon, 2:33 UT.

13 Full moon, 19:22 UT.

21 Last quarter moon, 7:02 UT.

26 Saturn closest to the sun, 9.03090 AU.

28 Southern Delta Aquarid meteor shower peaks.

29 New moon, 6:54 UT.

August

5 First quarter moon, 7:28 UT.

12 Full moon, 4:49 UT.

Perseid meteor shower peaks. Moon interferes.

14 Mercury (+0.3) at greatest eastern elongation (27° 26').

18 Venus at superior conjunction (not visible).

20 Last quarter moon, 0:49 UT.

22 Jupiter in conjunction with the sun (not visible).

27 New moon, 17:27 UT.

Mars (–2.9) nearest Earth, 0.37274 AU. This is the closest Mars has come to Earth in several thousand years.

28 Mars (–2.9) at opposition. It rises in the east at sunset and is visible all night long.

30 Mars closest to the sun, 1.38115 AU.

September

3 First quarter moon, 12:35 UT.

10 Full moon, 16:37 UT.

11 Mercury at inferior conjunction (not visible).

18 Last quarter moon, 19:04 UT.

23 Autumnal equinox, 10:48 UT.

Over the next few mornings, watch the waning moon slide toward the dawn, first passing Jupiter (–0.9) and then Mercury (–0.1). Look east thirty minutes before dawn. See page 45.

26 New moon, 3:10 UT.

Mercury (–0.3) at greatest western elongation (17° 52').

October

2 First quarter moon, 19:10 UT.

10 Full moon, 7:28 UT.

18 Last quarter moon, 12:32 UT.

21 Orionid meteor shower peaks.

25 New moon, 12:51 UT.

Mercury at superior conjunction (not visible).

November 1 First quarter moon, 4:25 UT.

5 Southern Taurid meteor shower peaks. Moon interferes.

9 Full moon, 1:14 UT.

Total lunar eclipse; greatest eclipse occurs at 1:19 UT. The entire total phase of the eclipse is visible to all of North America except western Alaska. See page 98 for details.

17 Last quarter moon, 4:16 UT.

Leonid meteor shower peaks (3h UT on the 18th). Moon interferes.

23 Total solar eclipse; greatest eclipse occurs at 22:49 UT. Totality visible only in Antarctica, but Australia, New Zealand, and the southern tip of South America see partial phases.

New moon, 23:00 UT.

30 First quarter moon, 17:17 UT.

December 8 Full moon, 20:38 UT.

9 Mercury (–0.4) at greatest eastern elongation (20° 56').

14 Geminid meteor shower peaks, 11h UT. Moon interferes.

16 Last quarter moon, 17:43 UT.

22 Winter solstice, 7:05 UT.

23 New moon, 9:44 UT.

27 Mercury at inferior conjunction (not visible).

30 First quarter moon, 10:04 UT.

31 Saturn (–0.5) at opposition and nearest to Earth, 8.05013 AU. It rises in the east at sunset and is visible all night long.

2004 Sky Summary

This is a banner year for those who dislike waking early to do their planet watching—four of the five classical planets begin the year visible in the evening sky. We are treated to a few other unusual events as well.

Mercury, the morning holdout, makes a respectable appearance in the southeast in mid-January, but in keeping with the theme of the year it makes its best appearance in the evening sky, at the end of March. The evening apparition of late July is also satisfactory. The morning appearances around September 10—enhanced with a close pass of Regulus in Leo—and at year's end are nearly as good, with the chilly December 29 apparition being the best of the morning views.

Venus puts in fine evening and morning appearances this year. The bright planet is our evening star for the first half of the year, then makes a mid-summer dive toward the sun and a switch to the morning sky. Just as it makes that switch, on June 8, Venus transits the sun for the first time in over a century. Those in the eastern portion of North America will be able to watch (with eye protection, of course) the silhouetted planet exit the sun shortly after sunrise.

Mars makes its classic post-opposition eastward flight through the constellations, seemingly determined to avoid the glare of the sun. It finally succumbs in July. Before that, Mars forms a striking trio with Venus and the moon on April 23 and makes a similar grouping with Saturn and the moon a month later. Its return to the morning sky will be tough to spot until the last few weeks of the year.

Jupiter's pace is more stately. It appears in the eastern sky on January evenings and drifts westward with the stars of Leo, coming to opposition in early March. By August it nears the sun with Mars.

Saturn, which reached opposition on the last day of 2003, begins the year low in the east at sunset. The year's highlight is the pairing with Mars around May 22. In the two weeks before that, Saturn and the other planets serve as guides to **comet NEAT** (C/2001 Q4), which will be an interesting binocular—and possibly naked-eye—object on mid-May evenings in the hours after sunset.

Meteor showers: Both the Perseids of August and the Geminids of December are largely without interference from the moon this year. The Perseids in particular bear watching, since there is a possibility of greatly enhanced activity from them this year.

Eclipses: Of the four eclipses in 2004, only the total lunar eclipse of October 28 is of interest to North Americans. The entire total phase is visible throughout Canada and the continental United States, except for a portion of western Alaska. See page 98 for more on this lunar eclipse.

2004 Sky Almanac

January	4	Quadrantid meteor shower peaks, 7h UT. Moon interferes.
		Earth closest to the sun, 0.983265 AU.
	7	Full moon, 15:41 UT.
	15	Last quarter moon, 4:47 UT.
	17	Mercury (–0.2) at greatest western elongation (23° 55').
	18	Moon near Antares (+0.9) this morning. See page 46.
	19	Moon near Mercury (–0.2) this morning. See page 46.
	21	New moon, 21:06 UT.
	29	First quarter moon, 6:04 UT.
February	6	Full moon, 8:48 UT.
	13	Last quarter moon, 13:41 UT.
	20	New moon, 9:19 UT.
	28	First quarter moon, 3:25 UT.
March	4	Jupiter (–2.5) at opposition and nearest to Earth, 4.42567 AU. It rises in the east at sunset and is visible all night long.
		Mercury at superior conjunction (not visible).
	6	Full moon, 23:15 UT.
	13	Last quarter moon, 21:02 UT.
	20	New moon, 22:42 UT.
		Vernal equinox, 6:50 UT.
	22	Moon near Mercury (–0.9) this evening—and it conveniently guides you to each of the other planets over the rest of the month. Look west thirty minutes after sunset. See page 46.
	24	Moon near Venus (–4.3) this evening. See page 46.

25 Moon near Mars (+1.3) this evening. See page 46.

28 First quarter moon, 23:49 UT.

Moon near Saturn (–0.0) tonight. See page 46.

29 Mercury (–0.1) at greatest eastern elongation (18° 53').

Venus (–4.4) at greatest eastern elongation (46° 00').

April

2 Moon near Jupiter (–2.4) tonight. See page 46.

5 Full moon, 11:03 UT.

12 Last quarter moon, 3:47 UT.

17 Mercury at inferior conjunction (not visible).

19 New moon, 13:22 UT.

Partial solar eclipse for the South Atlantic and southern Africa; greatest eclipse at 13:34 UT.

21 Lyrid meteor shower peaks.

23 Moon near Venus (–4.5) and Mars (+1.6) tonight. Look west in the hour after dusk

27 First quarter moon, 17:33 UT.

May

4 Full moon, 20:34 UT.

Eta Aquarid meteor shower peaks. Moon interferes.

Total lunar eclipse favoring Europe, Africa, and Asia; greatest eclipse at 20:30 UT. See page 99 for details.

6 Comet NEAT (C/2001 Q4) is closest to Earth, 0.321 AU. Best appreciated with binoculars, it lies low in the southwest—left of and above Sirius—in the hour after sunset.

9 Comet NEAT, now moving away from Earth and closer to the sun, climbs higher into the evening sky. It is left of Procyon tonight and tomorrow night. Look for it in the southwestern sky in the hours after sunset.

11 Last quarter moon, 11:05 UT.

12 For the next few nights, use an arc of planets to guide you to comet NEAT: Venus (–4.5), Saturn (+0.1), and faint Mars (+1.7) point the way to NEAT, which lies roughly along the arc between Jupiter and Saturn. Look west in the hour after sunset.

14 Mercury at greatest western elongation (26° 55').

Tonight and tomorrow night, use binoculars to view comet NEAT near the Beehive cluster in Cancer.

16 Comet NEAT is closest to the sun, 0.962 AU.

19 New moon, 4:53 UT.

20 A slim crescent moon sits below Venus (–4.4) tonight. Saturn (+0.1) and faint Mars (+1.7) shine above them, closing together over the next few days. The moon is above the pair on May 22. Look west thirty minutes after sunset.

27 First quarter moon, 7:58 UT.

June

3 Full moon, 4:20 UT.

8 Venus at inferior conjunction. Normally this would mean that Venus cannot be seen, but starting at 5:13 UT the planet's black disk will be seen silhouetted on the sun. Mid-transit occurs at 8:20 UT and last contact occurs at 11:26 UT. North Americans east of a line from eastern Texas through northern British Columbia will see Venus exit the sun shortly after sunrise. This is a naked-eye event but *requires eye protection.* See page 54 for details.

9 Last quarter moon, 20:04 UT.

17 New moon, 20:28 UT.

18 Mercury at superior conjunction (not visible).

21 Summer solstice, 0:58 UT.

25 First quarter moon, 19:09 UT.

July

2 Full moon, 11:10 UT.

5 Earth farthest from the sun, 1.016694 AU.

8 Saturn in conjunction with the sun (not visible).

9 Last quarter moon, 7:35 UT.

17 New moon, 11:25 UT.

25 First quarter moon, 3:38 UT.

27 Mercury (+0.4) at greatest eastern elongation (27° 07').

Southern Delta Aquarid meteor shower peaks. Moon interferes.

31 Full moon, 18:06 UT. As the second full moon in a calendar month, this is a "blue moon."

August

7 Last quarter moon, 22:03 UT.
Mars farthest from the sun, 1.66614 AU.

11 Perseid meteor shower peaks. An outburst of up to 500 meteors per hour has been predicted for this shower at 21h UT. This is still daylight for North America, but look during the evening and in the hours after midnight, when the traditional peak occurs, for possible enhanced activity.

16 New moon, 1:25 UT.

17 Venus (–4.3) at greatest western elongation (45° 49').

23 First quarter moon, 10:13 UT.
Mercury at inferior conjunction (not visible).

30 Full moon, 2:23 UT.

September

1 Venus (–4.2) and Saturn (+0.2) are well placed in the predawn sky. The pair shines below the stars Castor (+1.9) and Pollux (+1.1) in Gemini. Look east in the hour before dawn.

6 Last quarter moon, 15:12 UT.

9 Mercury (–0.2) at greatest western elongation (17° 58').

10 Mercury (–0.3) shines just below the star Regulus (+1.3), a temporary double star in the predawn sky. The waning moon lies above, between gleaming Venus (–4.1) and Saturn (+0.2). See page 46. Look east thirty minutes before sunrise.

14 New moon, 14:30 UT.

15 Mars in conjunction with the sun (not visible).

21 First quarter moon, 15:54 UT.
Jupiter in conjunction with the sun (not visible).

22 Autumnal equinox, 16:31 UT.

28 Full moon, 13:10 UT.

October

5 Mercury at superior conjunction (not visible).

6 Last quarter moon, 10:13 UT.

14 New moon, 2:49 UT.
Partial solar eclipse for Japan, Alaska, and Micronesia; greatest eclipse at 2:59 UT. See page 85 for details.

20 First quarter moon, 21:59 UT.

21 Orionid meteor shower peaks.

28 Total lunar eclipse; entire total phase visible to all of North America except western Alaska; greatest eclipse at 3:04 UT. See page 100.
Full moon, 3:08 UT.

November

3 Venus (–4.0) above Jupiter (–1.7) this morning. Mars (+1.7) shines faintly near the horizon beneath the brilliant pair. Look east-southeast thirty minutes before dawn. See page 143.

4 Southern Taurid meteor shower peaks. Moon interferes.

5 Last quarter moon, 5:54 UT.

12 New moon, 14:27 UT.

17 Leonid meteor shower peaks, 9h UT.

19 First quarter moon, 5:51 UT.

21 Mercury (–0.3) at greatest eastern elongation (22° 11').

26 Full moon, 20:08 UT.

December

5 Last quarter moon, 0:53 UT.
Venus (–4.0) and Mars (+1.7) gleam together in the morning sky. Look east-southeast in the hour before sunrise; binoculars help for Mars. Jupiter (–1.8) shines high above the pair. See page 121.

7 Moon near Jupiter (–1.8) tonight.

10 Mercury at inferior conjunction (not visible).

12 New moon, 1:29 UT.

13 Geminid meteor shower peaks, 18h UT.

18 First quarter moon, 16:40 UT.

21 Winter solstice, 12:43 UT.

26 Full moon, 15:07 UT.

29 Mercury at greatest western elongation (22° 27').
Mercury (–0.3) and Venus (–3.9) close the year with a morning meeting; look east in the hour before sunrise. Mars (+1.2), above the star Antares (+0.9), chaperones. See page 46.

2005 Sky Summary

Last year began by favoring evening observers; this year, the planets favor early risers. The year opens with a nice showing by Mercury and Venus, which are joined by the moon on January 8. Mars, in Scorpius, lies above and to the right of the trio.

Mercury's January appearance, while good, is not really the year's best, being the conclusion of the December 2004 apparition. The best evening appearances are around March 12 and July 9. An equally fine morning apparition around August 24 has the virtue of occurring during the warmest month of the year.

Venus descends toward the sun as the year begins. It reappears low in the west after sunset and reappears in early June, but never gains the prominence we're accustomed to in the brilliant planet. Its evening appearance is a low-slung drift toward the south along the western horizon.

Mars puts in another classic appearance, culminating in an early November opposition. It starts the year in the morning sky near its rival Antares, then speeds eastward through the zodiac until it reaches Taurus, where it begins its retrograde loop on October 1 (see page 123). It resumes its direct motion on December 10.

Jupiter begins its more modest retrograde loop on February 2 and reaches opposition in April. As it approaches the bright star Spica in Virgo, it also heads into the evening twilight glow in September and is lost from view by October.

Saturn continues its tour of the heavens and spends its last year in Gemini. It reaches opposition in mid-January and is a prominent evening planet well into spring. In early April it's high overhead in the hour after sunset as Jupiter rises in the eastern sky.

Meteor showers: The circumstances are nearly ideal for the Perseids—the nearly first quarter moon sets well before midnight. The Quadrantids and Geminids are spoiled by moonlight. The moon sets early for the Draconids, a meteor shower that does not usually rate a listing here. However, astronomers predict an outburst—possibly reaching storm level—this year owing to the proximity of the shower's parent comet, 21P/Giacobini-Zinner. Be on the lookout for enhanced activity from this shower.

Eclipses: A partial eclipse of the sun will be visible in the southern United States on April 8, and a partial lunar eclipse is visible for all but extreme eastern North America on October 17.

2005 Sky Almanac

January	2	Earth closest to the sun, 0.983297 AU.
	3	Last quarter moon, 17:46 UT.
		Quadrantid meteor shower peaks, 13h UT. Moon interferes.
	4	Moon near Jupiter (–2.0) tonight.
	7	The waning moon passes Mars (+1.5) this morning. Look for Antares (+0.9) beneath the pair, low in the southeast in the hour before dawn. See page 47.
	8	The waning moon passes Mercury (–0.3) and Venus (–3.9), a close pair of planets, this morning. Look southeast in the hour before dawn. See page 47.
	10	New moon, 12:03 UT.
	13	Saturn (–0.4) at opposition and nearest to Earth, 8.07562 AU. It rises in the east at sunset and is visible all night long.
	17	First quarter moon, 6:58 UT.
	25	Full moon, 10:32 UT.
February	2	Last quarter moon, 7:28 UT.
	8	New moon, 22:28 UT.
	14	Mercury at superior conjunction (not visible).
	16	First quarter moon, 0:16 UT.
	24	Full moon, 4:54 UT.
March	3	Last quarter moon, 17:37 UT.
	10	New moon, 9:11 UT.
	11	The waxing moon is your guide to Mercury (–0.4) tonight and tomorrow night. Look west half an hour after sunset. See page 47.
	12	Mercury (–0.4) at greatest eastern elongation (18° 20').
	17	First quarter moon, 19:20 UT.
	19	Moon near Saturn (–0.0) tonight. See page 47.
	20	Vernal equinox, 12:34 UT.
	25	Full moon, 21:00 UT.
	29	Mercury at inferior conjunction (not visible).
	31	Venus at superior conjunction (not visible).

April

2 Last quarter moon, 0:51 UT.

3 Jupiter (–2.5) at opposition. It rises in the east at sunset and is visible all night long.

4 Jupiter nearest to Earth, 4.45665 AU.

8 New moon, 20:33 UT.

Hybrid (annular/total) solar eclipse, visible as a partial eclipse in the southern United States, greatest eclipse at 20:36 UT. The northern limit of the eclipse runs south of a line roughly from extreme southern California, through central Oklahoma, to central Pennsylvania. See page 86 for details.

14 Jupiter farthest from the sun, 5.45652 AU.

16 First quarter moon, 14:38 UT.

21 Lyrid meteor shower peaks. Moon interferes.

24 Penumbral lunar eclipse, favoring eastern Asia, Australia, and the Pacific, greatest eclipse at 9:55 UT.

Full moon, 10:07 UT.

26 Mercury (+0.5) at greatest western elongation (27° 10').

May

1 Last quarter moon, 6:25 UT.

4 Eta Aquarid meteor shower peaks.

8 New moon, 8:46 UT.

16 First quarter moon, 8:58 UT.

23 Full moon, 20:19 UT.

30 Last quarter moon, 11:49 UT.

June

3 Mercury at superior conjunction (not visible).

6 New moon, 21:56 UT.

15 First quarter moon, 1:23 UT.

21 Summer solstice, 6:47 UT.

Venus (–3.9), Saturn (+0.2), and Mercury (–0.5) form up near Gemini's brightest stars Castor (+1.9) and Pollux (+1.1), low in the west-northwest thirty minutes after sundown. Watch how the pattern created by these three planets changes over the next few evenings. See page 47.

22 Full moon, 4:15 UT.

25 Look for Venus (–3.9) and Saturn (+0.2) low in the west-northwest thirty minutes after sundown. Mercury (–0.5), heading for next month's greatest eastern elongation and closing toward a conjunction, can be found below and to the right of Venus. See pages 47 and 142

27 Venus (–3.9) and Mercury (–0.1) lie within four degrees of one another. See page 47.

28 Last quarter moon, 18:25 UT.

July

5 Earth farthest from the sun, 1.016742 AU.

6 New moon, 12:04 UT.

8 Moon near Venus (–3.9) and Mercury (+0.5) tonight. See page 47.

9 Mercury (+0.5) at greatest eastern elongation (26° 15').

14 First quarter moon, 15:21 UT.

17 Mars closest to the sun, 1.38130 AU.

21 Full moon, 11:01 UT.

23 Saturn in conjunction with the sun (not visible).

27 Southern Delta Aquarid meteor shower peaks. Moon interferes.

28 Last quarter moon, 3:21 UT.

August

5 New moon, 3:06 UT.

Mercury at inferior conjunction (not visible).

12 Perseid meteor shower peaks.

13 First quarter moon, 2:39 UT.

19 Full moon, 17:54 UT.

23 Mercury (+0.1) at greatest western elongation (18° 24').

26 Last quarter moon, 15:20 UT.

September

1 Venus (–4.0) meets Jupiter (–1.7) in the western sky thirty minutes after sunset. The pair forms a triangle with Spica (+0.9), the brightest star in Virgo, to their left. The waxing crescent moon joins the group on September 6. See page 143.

3 New moon, 18:47 UT.

6 Moon near Venus (–4.0) and Jupiter (–1.7) tonight.

11 First quarter moon, 11:37 UT.

18 Full moon, 2:02 UT.

Mercury at superior conjunction (not visible).

22 Autumnal equinox, 22:24 UT.

25 Last quarter moon, 6:42 UT.

October

3 New moon, 10:29 UT.

Annular solar eclipse favoring Africa and Europe; greatest eclipse occurs at 10:32 UT. See page 85.

8 Draconid meteor shower outburst, possibly reaching storm level, predicted for 17h UT. This is in daylight for North America, but the time of the peak is by no means certain; enhanced activity may be visible this morning or evening as well.

10 First quarter moon, 19:01 UT.

17 Partial lunar eclipse, greatest at 12:03 UT. Some part of the umbral portion of the eclipse is visible to all but extreme eastern North America. See page 99.

Full moon, 12:14 UT.

21 Orionid meteor shower peaks. Moon interferes.

22 Jupiter in conjunction with the sun (not visible).

25 Last quarter moon, 1:18 UT.

30 Mars nearest the Earth, 0.46405 AU.

November

2 New moon, 1:25 UT.

3 Mercury (–0.2) at greatest eastern elongation (23° 31').

Venus (–4.4) at greatest eastern elongation (47° 06').

5 Southern Taurid meteor shower peaks.

7 Mars (–2.3) at opposition. It rises in the east at sunset and is visible all night long.

9 First quarter moon, 1:57 UT.

16 Full moon, 0:58 UT.

17 Leonid meteor shower peaks. Moon interferes.

23 Last quarter moon, 22:12 UT.

24 Mercury at inferior conjunction (not visible).

December

1 New moon, 15:01 UT.

8 First quarter moon, 9:37 UT.

12 Mercury (–0.4) at greatest western elongation (21° 05').

13 Geminid meteor shower peaks (0h UT on the 14th).

15 Full moon, 16:16 UT.

21 Winter solstice, 21:19 UT.

23 Last quarter moon, 19:37 UT.

31 New moon, 3:12 UT.

2006 Sky Summary

Mercury has four good appearances this year: two in the evening sky—in late February and mid-June—and two more in the mornings of early August and late November. On August 7, it lies just below Venus in the morning sky; on December 5 it takes part in a predawn gathering with Jupiter and Mars.

Venus is the main attraction of the morning sky in early 2006, but it never gains the prominence we usually expect of it. Even at its best, in late February, Venus rises less than three hours ahead of the sun. The main event happens the morning of August 27, when it is joined by the much fainter Saturn. You'll probably need binoculars to actually detect Saturn in the glow of twilight.

Mars, between oppositions this year, can be found almost stationary against the stars in the evening sky while the constellations pass behind it. On June 17 it meets with Saturn at about the best time to see Mercury during its pop-up in the evening sky—a nice planetary trio.

Jupiter has made its way to the stars of Libra, a fairly nondescript part of the sky. It's a morning object the first third of the year, reaches its first stationary point on March 5, swirls into opposition in early May, and concludes its loop on July 6.

Saturn reaches opposition in late January and begins the year with a completion of its retrograde loop. In the last week of January and the first week of February it lies near the Beehive star cluster in Cancer. Saturn switches to the morning sky in August.

Meteor showers: It's a good year for the January Quadrantids, but early-morning viewing of the August Perseids and the December Geminids is partly spoiled by the moon. Moonlight will not be a problem for any surprise the November Leonids may still try to throw our way—a small outburst has been predicted to occur at the normal peak.

Eclipses: This year's four solar and lunar eclipses all favor the eastern hemisphere. The March total solar eclipse favors Africa, Europe, and Asia, with the moon's shadow crossing the Mediterranean coast of Africa and the eastern Black Sea.

2006 Sky Almanac

January	3	Quadrantid meteor shower peaks, 19h UT.
	4	Earth closest to the sun, 0.983327 AU.
	6	First quarter moon, 18:57 UT.
	13	Venus at inferior conjunction (not visible).
	14	Full moon, 9:49 UT.
	22	Last quarter moon, 15:15 UT.
	26	Mercury at superior conjunction (not visible).
	27	Saturn (–0.3) at opposition and nearest to Earth, 8.12683 AU.
	29	New moon, 14:15 UT.
	31	Over the next week use binoculars to watch Saturn slip past the Beehive star cluster in Cancer.
February	5	First quarter moon, 6:29 UT.
	13	Full moon, 4:45 UT.
	21	Last quarter moon, 7:18 UT.
	24	Mercury (–0.4) at greatest eastern elongation (18° 08').
	28	New moon, 0:31 UT.
March	6	First quarter moon, 20:16 UT.
	12	Mercury at inferior conjunction (not visible).
	14	Full moon, 23:36 UT.
		Penumbral lunar eclipse favoring Africa, Europe, and Asia; greatest eclipse occurs at 23:47 UT.
	20	Vernal equinox, 18:27 UT.
	22	Last quarter moon, 19:11 UT.
	25	Venus (–4.4) at greatest western elongation (46° 32').
	29	Total solar eclipse favoring Africa, Europe, and Asia. The path of totality crosses the eastern Mediterranean and the Black Sea. Greatest eclipse occurs at 10:11 UT. See page 88 for details.
		New moon, 10:16 UT.
April	5	First quarter moon, 12:01 UT.
	8	Mercury (+0.4) at greatest western elongation (27° 46').
	13	Full moon, 16:41 UT.
	21	Last quarter moon, 3:29 UT.
	22	Lyrid meteor shower peaks. Moon interferes.
	27	New moon, 19:45 UT.

May

4 Jupiter (–2.4) at opposition. It rises in the east at sunset and is visible all night long.

5 First quarter moon, 5:13 UT.

Jupiter nearest to Earth, 4.41271 AU.

Eta Aquarid meteor shower peaks. Moon interferes.

13 Full moon, 6:51 UT.

18 Mercury at superior conjunction (not visible).

20 Last quarter moon, 9:21 UT.

27 New moon, 5:26 UT.

June

3 First quarter moon, 23:06 UT.

11 Full moon, 18:03 UT.

17 Saturn (+0.3) and faint Mars (+1.8) gleam close together in the evening sky. Below them shines Mercury (+0.3). Can you find the stellar twins, Castor (+1.2) and Pollux (+1.9) in Gemini, above and to the right of Mercury? See page 48.

18 Last quarter moon, 14:09 UT.

20 Mercury (+0.5) at greatest eastern elongation (24° 56').

21 Summer solstice, 12:27 UT.

25 New moon, 16:06 UT.

26 Mars farthest from the sun, 1.66603 AU.

Follow the waxing moon: it's near Mercury (+1.0) on June 26, between Mercury and Saturn (+0.3) on the 27th, and above Mars (+1.8) on the 28th. See page 48.

July

3 First quarter moon, 16:37 UT.

Earth farthest from the sun, 1.016697 AU.

11 Full moon, 3:02 UT.

17 Last quarter moon, 19:13 UT.

18 Mercury at inferior conjunction (not visible).

25 New moon, 4:32 UT.

28 Southern Delta Aquarid meteor shower peaks.

August

2 First quarter moon, 8:46 UT.

3 As Venus (–3.9) descends slowly into twilight on early August mornings, Mercury (–0.4) jumps up to meet it. On August 3, Venus far outshines the stars Castor (+1.9) and Pollux (+1.1) to its left, but has dropped below them by August 10, when Mercury is closest. See page 48.

7 Mercury (+0.1) at greatest western elongation (19° 11').

Saturn in conjunction with the sun (not visible).

9 Full moon, 10:55 UT.

10 Venus (–3.9) and Mercury (–0.3) closest this morning. See page 48.

12 Perseid meteor shower peaks. Moon interferes.

16 Last quarter moon, 1:52 UT.

23 New moon, 19:10 UT.

27 Venus (–3.9) and Saturn (+0.4) gleam together low in the east-northeast this morning in the hour before dawn. Binoculars help.

31 First quarter moon, 22:57 UT.

September

1 Mercury at superior conjunction (not visible).

7 Full moon, 18:43 UT.

Partial lunar eclipse favoring Asia and central and eastern Africa and Europe; greatest eclipse occurs at 18:51 UT. See page 102 for details.

14 Last quarter moon, 11:16 UT.

22 Annular solar eclipse; greatest eclipse at 11:40 UT. The path of annularity arcs through the South Atlantic and makes landfall only on Guyana, Suriname, and French Guiana. See page 89 for details.

New moon, 11:46 UT.

23 Autumnal equinox, 4:04 UT.

30 First quarter moon, 11:04 UT.

October

7 Full moon, 3:13 UT.

14 Last quarter moon, 0:27 UT.

17 Mercury (–0.0) at greatest eastern elongation (24° 49').

21 Orionid meteor shower peaks.

22 New moon, 5:15 UT.

23 Mars in conjunction with the sun (not visible).

27 Venus at superior conjunction (not visible).

29 First quarter moon, 21:26 UT.

November 5 Full moon, 12:59 UT.

Southern Taurid meteor shower peaks. Moon interferes.

8 Mercury at inferior conjunction. Normally this means that Mercury is not visible, but beginning at 19:13 UT the planet can be seen transiting the sun. Mid-transit occurs at 21:42 UT and the transit ends at 0:11 UT. This is a telescopic event and *requires eye protection.* See page 55 for details.

12 Last quarter moon, 17:46 UT.

17 Leonid meteor shower peaks, 21h UT.

19 Leonid meteor shower outburst predicted, 100 to 120 per hour, from 4h to 5h UT.

20 New moon, 22:19 UT.

21 Jupiter in conjunction with the sun (not visible).

25 Mercury (–0.5) at greatest western elongation (19° 54').

28 First quarter moon, 6:29 UT.

December 5 Full moon, 0:26 UT.

Mercury (–0.6) stands out amid the faint stars of Libra this morning. Try locating dim, ruddy Mars (+1.6) and bright Jupiter (–1.7) below it in the hour before dawn. See page 48.

12 Last quarter moon, 14:33 UT.

14 Geminid meteor shower peaks, 6h UT. Moon interferes.

20 New moon, 14:01 UT.

22 Winter solstice, 0:23 UT.

27 First quarter moon, 14:48 UT.

2007 Sky Summary

The year begins quietly, with most of the planets clustered near the sun. Lone Saturn brightens the late evening sky in the east.

Mercury joins Venus for a couple of good evening apparitions in February and June. In the morning sky, its November apparition is better than its more comfortably viewed appearance in July.

Venus emerges from the sun's glare in the west in mid-January. Best in mid-May, when it sets more than three hours after the sun, Venus is a fixture of the evening sky until July, when it starts to plummet back toward the sun. It's gone by August, only to reappear in a fine morning apparition beginning in September.

Mars reaches opposition at the end of the year and so is a morning sight early in 2007. It begins the year low in the southeast, paired with Jupiter and ruddy Antares, in the hour before sunrise. By year's end it will gleam at its brightest all night long.

Jupiter spends much of the year in the southern summer constellations, Scorpius and Ophiuchus. It whirls in its retrograde loop near Antares before heading on to its next constellation destination, Sagittarius.

Saturn, which is in Leo this year, reaches opposition in mid-February. It receives two visits from Venus: in the evening sky in July, and in the morning sky in mid-October. Each time the planets form a nice triangle with the star Regulus.

Meteor showers: Both of the most reliable showers, the August Perseids and the December Geminids, are largely unaffected by interference from moonlight. The moon is setting at about the time the November Leonids are expected to erupt with an outburst of possibly 200 meteors an hour. This is expected to be the shower's last gasp of enhanced activity until the end of the century.

Eclipses: On March 3 the eastern third of North America will see an eclipsed moon rise into the sky; the moon rises partially eclipsed for the central third of the United States. On August 28 another total lunar eclipse favors the Pacific Rim, but the western two-thirds of North America will see the entire total phase; the rest will see the moon enter the Earth's shadow before moonset.

2007 Sky Almanac

January
- 3 — Full moon, 13:58 UT.
  Earth closest to the sun, 0.983260 AU.
  Quadrantid meteor shower peaks (1h UT on the 4th). Moon interferes.
- 7 — Mercury at superior conjunction (not visible).
- 11 — Last quarter moon, 12:46 UT.
- 19 — New moon, 4:01 UT.
- 25 — First quarter moon, 23:02 UT.

February
- 2 — Full moon, 5:46 UT.
- 7 — Mercury (–0.6) at greatest eastern elongation (18° 14').
- 10 — Last quarter moon, 9:52 UT.
  Saturn (–0.1) at opposition and nearest to Earth, 8.20037 AU. It rises in the east at sunset and is visible all night long.
- 17 — New moon, 16:15 UT.
- 23 — Mercury at inferior conjunction (not visible).
- 24 — First quarter moon, 7:56 UT.

March
- 3 — Full moon, 23:18 UT.
  Total lunar eclipse favors Africa, Europe, and Asia, but the eastern third of North America sees the moon rise in total eclipse; the central third of the United States and Canada will see it rise emerging after the total phase is complete. Greatest eclipse occurs at 23:21 UT. See page 103 for details.
- 12 — Last quarter moon, 3:55 UT.
- 19 — Partial solar eclipse favors eastern Asia and western Alaska. Greatest eclipse occurs at 2:32 UT; see page 90 for details.
  New moon, 2:43 UT.
- 21 — Vernal equinox, 0:09 UT.
- 22 — Mercury (+0.2) at greatest western elongation (27° 44').
- 25 — First quarter moon, 18:17 UT.

April
- 2 — Full moon, 17:16 UT.
- 10 — Last quarter moon, 18:05 UT.
- 17 — New moon, 11:37 UT.
- 22 — Lyrid meteor shower peaks.
- 24 — First quarter moon, 6:36 UT.

May

2 Full moon, 10:10 UT.

3 Mercury at superior conjunction (not visible).

5 Eta Aquarid meteor shower peaks.

10 Last quarter moon, 4:28 UT.

16 New moon, 19:28 UT.

17 Moon near Mercury (–0.9) tonight. See page 49.

19 Moon near dazzling Venus (–4.2) tonight. See page 49.

22 Moon near Saturn (+0.5) tonight. See page 49.

23 First quarter moon, 21:03 UT.

June

1 Full moon, 1:04 UT.

Moon near Jupiter (–2.3) tonight.

2 Mercury (+0.7) at greatest eastern elongation (23° 22').

4 Mars closest to the sun, 1.38148 AU.

5 Jupiter (–2.6) at opposition. It rises in the east at sunset and is visible all night long.

7 Jupiter nearest to Earth, 4.30442 AU.

8 Last quarter moon, 11:44 UT.

9 Venus (–4.3) at greatest eastern elongation (45° 23').

15 New moon, 3:14 UT.

21 Summer solstice, 18:08 UT.

22 First quarter moon, 13:16 UT.

28 Mercury at inferior conjunction (not visible).

30 Full moon, 13:49 UT. As the second full moon to occur in a calendar month, tonight's full moon is a "blue moon."

July

1 Venus (–4.4) meets Saturn (+0.6) in the western sky in the hour after sunset. Both planets are well placed. Can you spot Regulus (+1.3) in Leo above and to the left of the pair? See page 144.

6 Earth farthest from the sun, 1.016706 AU.

7 Last quarter moon, 16:54 UT.

14 New moon, 12:04 UT.

20 Mercury (+0.4) at greatest western elongation (20° 19').

22 First quarter moon, 6:29 UT.

25 Mercury (–0.2) briefly pops into the predawn sky, shining near Castor (+1.9) and Pollux (+1.1) of Gemini; look east-northeast in the hour before dawn. Mars (+0.6) shines high in the east as well.

28 Southern Delta Aquarid meteor shower. Moon interferes.

30 Full moon, 0:48 UT.

August

5 Last quarter moon, 21:21 UT.

12 New moon, 23:03 UT.

13 Perseid meteor shower peaks.

15 Mercury at superior conjunction (not visible).

18 Venus at inferior conjunction (not visible).

20 First quarter moon, 23:55 UT.

21 Saturn in conjunction with the sun (not visible).

28 Full moon, 10:36 UT.

Total lunar eclipse favors the Pacific Rim, but the western two-thirds of North America—on a band roughly from Wisconsin to central Alabama—will see the entire total phase. All but the eastern half of Maine will see the moon enter the total phase before moonset. Greatest eclipse occurs at 10:37 UT. See page 104 for details.

September

4 Last quarter moon, 2:33 UT.

11 New moon, 12:45 UT.

Partial solar eclipse favors central and southern South America and Antarctica; greatest eclipse occurs at 12:32 UT.

19 First quarter moon, 16:49 UT.

23 Autumnal equinox, 9:52 UT.

26 Full moon, 19:46 UT.

29 Mercury (+0.1) at greatest eastern elongation (25° 59').

October

3 Last quarter moon, 10:07 UT.

11 New moon, 5:02 UT.

15 Venus (–4.5) and Saturn (+0.7) shine together high in the eastern sky in the hour before dawn. Mars (–0.3) gleams high above the southeastern horizon.

19 First quarter moon, 8:33 UT.

21 Orionid meteor shower peaks. Moon interferes.

23 Mercury at inferior conjunction (not visible).

26 Full moon, 4:53 UT.

28 Venus (–4.4) at greatest western elongation (46° 28').

30 A dwindling moon tours the morning planets at the end of October and early November. A gibbous moon lies near Mars (–0.6) this morning. See page 49.

November 1 Last quarter moon, 21:20 UT.

3 The crescent moon sits above Saturn (+0.8) this morning. See page 49.

5 Southern Taurid meteor shower peaks.

Moon near Venus (–4.3) this morning. Look east in the hour before dawn. See page 49.

7 Moon near Mercury (–0.3) this morning. Also look for the star Spica (+0.9), the brightest star of the constellation Virgo, to Mercury's right. Look east in the hour before dawn. See page 49.

8 Mercury (–0.5) at greatest western elongation (18° 59').

9 New moon, 23:04 UT.

17 First quarter moon, 22:33 UT.

Leonid meteor shower peaks (4h UT on the 18th). An outburst of up to 200 per hour is predicted between 4 and 5 UT.

24 Full moon, 14:31 UT.

December 1 Last quarter moon, 12:45 UT.

9 New moon, 17:41 UT.

14 Geminid meteor shower peaks, 12h UT.

17 First quarter moon, 10:18 UT.

Mercury at superior conjunction (not visible).

18 Mars nearest to Earth, 0.58933 AU.

22 Winter solstice, 6:09 UT.

23 Jupiter in conjunction with the sun (not visible).

24 Full moon, 1:16 UT.

Mars (–1.6) at opposition. It rises in the east at sunset and is visible all night long.

31 Last quarter moon, 7:52 UT.

2008 Sky Summary

Mercury makes a weak evening showing in January and follows with another weak morning appearance. The evening apparition in May, however, is quite a different story, with the elusive planet well placed for observation for a couple of weeks. A slender crescent moon serves as a guide to the planet on May 6; look for Aldebaran in Taurus nearby. Mercury joins Jupiter at year's end for another nice evening pairing.

Venus concludes its morning apparition and, after a nice pairing with Jupiter in February, has a lingering decline, slowly sliding along the horizon until it disappears from view in mid-May. Its reemergence into the evening sky is similarly inauspicious. Its early December appearance with Jupiter will be low in the southwest after sunset.

Mars is the lone classical planet in the evening sky as the year opens and undergoes another of its post-opposition flights from the sun. It can be found in the south and southwest nearly all year as the zodiac parades westward behind it. In early July the Red Planet pays a call on the bright star Regulus and the planet Saturn in the early evening sky.

Jupiter has moved on to the summer constellation Sagittarius and so lies near the sun at the beginning of the year. It reaches opposition in early July and gets the same double-take from Venus that Saturn enjoyed last year. Its more southerly location makes the pairings somewhat less noticeable.

Saturn joins Mars in the evening sky several hours after sunset as the year opens. It reaches opposition in late February and traverses the constellation Leo, serving as our second evening planet for the first half of the year.

Meteor showers: The two best meteor showers of the year—the August Perseids and the Geminids of December—are washed out by moonlight. The January Quadrantids are affected by a waning crescent moon.

Eclipses: February's total lunar eclipse is well placed for North Americans, nearly all of whom can enjoy the entire total phase of the eclipse. A total solar eclipse in August brings a brief glimpse of a partially eclipsed sunrise to the eastern half of Maine and northeastern Canada.

2008 Sky Almanac

January	2	Earth closest to the sun, 0.983280 AU.
	4	Quadrantid meteor shower peaks, 8h UT. Moon interferes.
	8	New moon, 11:38 UT.
	15	First quarter moon, 19:46 UT.
	22	Full moon, 13:35 UT.
		Mercury (–0.6) at greatest eastern elongation (18° 39').
	30	Last quarter moon, 5:03 UT.
February	1	Venus (–4.0) and Jupiter (–1.9) meet in Sagittarius this morning. Look southeast in the hour before dawn. See page 143.
	4	The waning crescent moon joins Venus (–4.0) and Jupiter (–1.9). Look southeast in the hour before dawn. See page 143.
	6	Mercury at inferior conjunction (not visible).
	7	New moon, 3:45 UT.
		Annular solar eclipse favoring Antarctica, with partial phases visible in New Zealand and eastern Australia. Greatest eclipse occurs at 3:55 UT. See page 91 for details.
	14	First quarter moon, 3:33 UT.
	21	Total lunar eclipse favoring the Americas, Africa, and Europe. All of North America but western Alaska sees the entire total phase of the eclipse. Greatest eclipse occurs at 3:26 UT. See page 105 for details.
		Full moon, 3:31 UT.
	24	Saturn (+0.2) at opposition and nearest to Earth, 8.29141 AU. It rises in the east at sunset and is visible all night long.
	29	Last quarter moon, 2:19 UT.
March	3	Mercury (+0.2) at greatest western elongation (27° 09').
	7	New moon, 17:14 UT.
	14	First quarter moon, 10:46 UT.
	20	Vernal equinox, 5:49 UT.
	21	Full moon, 18:40 UT.
	29	Last quarter moon, 21:48 UT.
April	6	New moon, 3:56 UT.
	12	First quarter moon, 18:32 UT.
	16	Mercury at superior conjunction (not visible).

20 Full moon, 10:26 UT.

21 Lyrid meteor shower peaks. Moon interferes.

28 Last quarter moon, 14:12 UT.

May

2 Can you spot the Pleiades below Mercury (–0.8) after sunset tonight? See page 50.

4 Eta Aquarid meteor shower peaks.

5 New moon, 12:19 UT.

6 Moon near Mercury (–0.4) and Aldebaran (+0.8), brightest star of Taurus, tonight. See page 50.

10 Moon near Mars (+1.3) high in the west tonight. See page 50.

12 First quarter moon, 3:47 UT.

Moon near Saturn (+0.6) and Regulus (+1.3), brightest star of the constellation Leo, tonight. See page 50.

13 Mars farthest from the sun, 1.66594 AU.

14 Mercury (+0.4) at greatest eastern elongation (21° 48').

20 Full moon, 2:12 UT.

28 Last quarter moon, 2:57 UT.

June

3 New moon, 19:23 UT.

7 Mercury at inferior conjunction (not visible).

9 Venus at superior conjunction (not visible).

10 First quarter moon, 15:04 UT.

18 Full moon, 17:31 UT.

21 Summer solstice, 0:01 UT.

26 Last quarter moon, 12:11 UT.

July

1 Mercury (+0.6) at greatest western elongation (21° 47').

3 New moon, 2:19 UT.

4 Earth farthest from the sun, 1.016754 AU.

9 Jupiter (–2.7) at opposition. It rises in the east at sunset and is visible all night long.

10 First quarter moon, 4:35 UT.

Jupiter nearest to Earth, 4.16106 AU.

11 Watch Saturn (+0.8) and Mars (+1.7) in the western sky in the hour after sunset. The pair are closest to each other this evening.

18 Full moon, 8:00 UT.

25 Last quarter moon, 18:43 UT.

27 Southern Delta Aquarid meteor shower peaks.

29 Mercury at superior conjunction (not visible).

August

1 New moon, 10:13 UT.

Total solar eclipse. The path of totality runs from extreme northern Canada to northern Greenland, across Russia to central China; partial phases are visible on the rising sun in eastern Canada and even central Maine. Greatest eclipse is at 10:21 UT. See page 92 for details.

8 First quarter moon, 20:21 UT.

12 Perseid meteor shower peaks. Moon interferes.

16 Partial lunar eclipse favoring Africa, Europe, and central Asia. Greatest eclipse occurs at 21:10 UT. See page 106 for details.

Full moon, 21:18 UT.

23 Last quarter moon, 23:51 UT.

30 New moon, 19:59 UT.

September

4 Saturn in conjunction with the sun (not visible).

7 First quarter moon, 14:05 UT.

11 Mercury (+0.2) at greatest eastern elongation (26° 52').

Mars (+1.7) in conjunction with and very close to Venus (–3.9), low in the western sky after sunset. Binoculars help, and you should start looking for Venus twenty minutes after sunset. Mercury, also difficult to spot, lies below and left of the pair. Jupiter (–2.4) gleams high in the south. The waxing moon, approaching full, rises in the southeast. See page 121.

15 Full moon, 9:14 UT.

22 Last quarter moon, 5:05 UT.

Autumnal equinox, 15:46 UT.

29 New moon, 8:13 UT.

October

6 Mercury at inferior conjunction (not visible).

7 First quarter moon, 9:05 UT.

14 Full moon, 20:03 UT.

21 Last quarter moon, 11:56 UT.

Orionid meteor shower peaks. Moon interferes.

22 Mercury (–0.5) at greatest western elongation (18° 19').

25 Moon near Saturn (+1.0) this morning. Look east in the hour before dawn. See page 50.

27 Moon near Mercury (–0.7) this morning. Look east in the hour before dawn. See page 50.

28 New moon, 23:15 UT.

November 5 Southern Taurid meteor shower peaks.

6 First quarter moon, 4:04 UT.

13 Full moon, 6:19 UT.

17 Leonid meteor shower peaks, 10h UT. Moon interferes.

19 Last quarter moon, 21:32 UT.

25 Mercury at superior conjunction (not visible).

27 New moon, 16:56 UT.

30 Venus (–4.1) and Jupiter (–2.0) closest tonight. Look southwest early in the hour after sunset. The moon is below the pair. See page 143.

December 1 The moon is above Venus (–4.1) and Jupiter (–2.0). The two planets meet again as they did in February, but this time in the evening sky. Look southwest in the hour after sunset. See page 143.

5 First quarter moon, 21:26 UT.

Mars in conjunction with the sun (not visible).

12 Full moon, 16:38 UT.

13 Geminid meteor shower peaks, 18h UT. Moon interferes.

19 Last quarter moon, 10:31 UT.

21 Winter solstice, 12:05 UT.

27 New moon, 12:23 UT.

29 Rising Mercury (–0.7) closes out the year with an evening apparition that includes a close pass to Jupiter (–1.9). Tonight the crescent moon lies above the pair while dazzling Venus (–4.1) looks on. Look in the evening sky in the hour after sunset. Mercury remains well placed for observing until January 10, 2009. See page 50.

31 Moon near Venus (–4.1) tonight. See page 50.

2009 Sky Summary

As the year begins, Venus lies high in the southwest half an hour after sunset. Can you spot the pair hiding in twilight below to the right? That's Mercury and Jupiter.

Mercury's best evening apparitions occur in early January—when it rises past descending Jupiter in the first week—and in late April. Its best morning appearance is in early October.

Venus puts in two fine appearances this year. The evening apparition ends in late March; it's our bright morning star from late April through the end of the year. Venus enjoys a celestial *pas de deux* with Mars, with a distant pairing low in the east on mid-April mornings and a much closer and more observable pass in June.

Mars, making its way to a January 2010 opposition, cruises through the summer, fall, and winter constellations, spending most of the year in the morning sky. In early February Mars is in the constellation Capricornus and emerging from the sun's glare, just five degrees above the eastern horizon thirty minutes before sunrise. The planet's eastward motion counteracts the effect of Earth's travels. The Red Planet progresses through Aries in June and cruises through Taurus in July and August, Gemini in September, and Cancer in October. As November opens, Mars passes right through the Beehive, a star cluster in Cancer—worth a look through binoculars or a small telescope. On December 20, 2009, Mars halts its eastward motion and reaches the stationary point at which its motion reverses and the retrograde loop begins. This also marks the start of prime Mars viewing, with the planet at a magnitude of –0.6 and growing brighter until its January opposition.

It's a quiet year for the outermost of our naked-eye planets. **Jupiter,** which has moved into the watery region of the zodiac, lies near the sun as the year begins. It reaches opposition in August and gleams brightly among the faint stars of Capricornus.

Saturn completes its passage through Leo this year and reaches opposition in early March. On September 4 the Earth passes through Saturn's ring plane and the rings are edge-on to us. Since they contribute little to the planet's brightness, Saturn has one of its faintest oppositions of the decade this year.

Meteor showers: Both the Quadrantids of January and the December Geminids have little interference from the moon this year, but the Perseids of August are washed out by moonlight.

Eclipses: There are six lunar and solar eclipses this year. Three of these are penumbral lunar eclipses, all of which are at least partly visible from North America, but the moon's face is only subtly shaded in these events and they are not particularly noteworthy. The two solar eclipses—annular in January and total in July—and the partial lunar eclipse at year's end follow the eclipse pattern that rules this decade, favoring the eastern hemisphere.

2009 Sky Almanac

January	3	Quadrantid meteor shower peaks, 14h UT.
	4	First quarter moon, 11:57 UT.
		Mercury (–0.6) at greatest eastern elongation (19° 21').
		Earth closest to the sun, 0.983273 AU.
	11	Full moon, 3:27 UT.
	14	Venus (–4.4) at greatest eastern elongation (47° 07').
	18	Last quarter moon, 2:47 UT.
	20	Mercury at inferior conjunction (not visible).
	24	Jupiter in conjunction with the sun (not visible).
	26	New moon, 7:56 UT.
		Annular solar eclipse for southern Africa, Antarctica, southern India, and western Australia; greatest eclipse occurs at 7:59 UT. See page 93 for details.
February	2	First quarter moon, 23:13 UT.
	9	Penumbral lunar eclipse visible from eastern Asia, Indonesia, Australia, and western North America; greatest eclipse occurs at 14:38 UT.
		Full moon, 14:50 UT.
	13	Mercury (+0.0) at greatest western elongation (26° 06').
	16	Last quarter moon, 21:38 UT.
	25	New moon, 1:36 UT.
March	4	First quarter moon, 7:46 UT.
	8	Saturn (+0.5) at opposition and nearest to Earth, 8.39445. It rises in the east at sunset and is visible all night long.

	11	Full moon, 2:38 UT.
	18	Last quarter moon, 17:48 UT.
	20	Vernal equinox, 11:45 UT.
	26	New moon, 16:06 UT.
	27	Venus at inferior conjunction (not visible).
	31	Mercury at superior conjunction (not visible).
April	2	First quarter moon, 14:34 UT.
	9	Full moon, 14:56 UT.
	17	Last quarter moon, 13:37 UT.
		Look for Venus (–4.5) and Mars (+1.2) low in the east thirty minutes before sunrise. Jupiter (–2.2) lies above and to the right of the pair; the moon, nearing last quarter, is high in the southeast.
	21	Mars closest to the sun, 1.38133 AU.
	22	Lyrid meteor shower peaks.
	25	New moon, 3:23 UT.
	26	Mercury (+0.2) at greatest eastern elongation (20° 25').
		Moon near Mercury and the Pleiades tonight. See page 51.
May	1	First quarter moon, 20:45 UT.
	4	Eta Aquarid meteor shower peaks. Moon interferes.
	9	Full moon, 4:02 UT.
	17	Last quarter moon, 7:27 UT.
	18	Mercury at inferior conjunction (not visible).
	24	New moon, 12:12 UT.
	31	First quarter moon, 3:23 UT.
June	5	Venus (–4.3) at greatest western elongation (45° 48').
	7	Full moon, 18:12 UT.
	13	Mercury (+0.6) at greatest western elongation (23° 27').
	15	Last quarter moon, 22:15 UT.
	18	Venus (–4.2) and Mars (+1.1) shine together and are well placed in the east forty-five minutes before sunrise. The waning crescent moon lies above the pair; can you glimpse Mercury (+0.1) below them? Jupiter (–2.5) gleams high in the south. See page 122.
	21	Summer solstice, 5:47 UT.
	22	New moon, 19:36 UT.
	29	First quarter moon, 11:29 UT.
July	4	Earth farthest from the sun, 1.016666 AU.
	7	Full moon, 9:23 UT.
		Penumbral lunar eclipse favoring Australia, the Pacific Rim, and the western Americas; greatest eclipse at 9:39 UT.
	14	Mercury at superior conjunction (not visible).
	15	Last quarter moon, 9:54 UT.
	22	New moon, 2:35 UT.
		Total solar eclipse favoring eastern Asia, the central Pacific, and Hawaii; greatest eclipse occurs at 2:35 UT. In the western Pacific, the duration of totality lasts almost 6.7 minutes, the longest of this century. See page 94 for details.
	28	Southern Delta Aquarid meteor shower peaks. Moon interferes.
		First quarter moon, 22:00 UT.
August	6	Full moon, 0:55 UT.
		Penumbral lunar eclipse favoring eastern North America, South America, Africa, and Europe; greatest eclipse occurs at 0:39 UT.
	12	Perseid meteor shower peaks. Moon interferes.
	13	Last quarter moon, 18:56 UT.
	14	Jupiter (–2.9) at opposition. It rises in the east at sunset and is visible all night long.
	15	Jupiter nearest to Earth, 4.02783 AU.
	20	New moon, 10:02 UT.
	24	Mercury (+0.3) at greatest eastern elongation (27° 22').
	27	First quarter moon, 11:42 UT.
September	4	Full moon, 16:03 UT.
		Earth passes through the ring plane of Saturn (+1.1).
	12	Last quarter moon, 2:16 UT.
	17	Saturn in conjunction with the sun (not visible).
	18	New moon, 18:44 UT.
	20	Mercury at inferior conjunction (not visible).
	22	Autumnal equinox, 21:20 UT.
	26	First quarter moon, 4:50 UT.

October	4	Full moon, 6:10 UT.
	6	Mercury (–0.5) at greatest western elongation (17° 57').
		Mercury joins Saturn (+1.0) and Venus (–3.9) in the predawn sky. Look east in the hour before dawn; see page 51.
	11	Last quarter moon, 8:56 UT.
	13	Venus (–3.9) and Saturn (+1.0) are very close to one another low in the eastern sky this morning. Mercury (–1.0) shines below the two. Look for the trio thirty minutes before sunrise. See page 144. Mars (+0.7) lies high in the sky near Castor (+1.9) and Pollux (+1.1) in Gemini. The waning crescent moon shines between Mars and Venus.
	18	New moon, 5:33 UT.
	21	Orionid meteor shower peaks.
	26	First quarter moon, 0:42 UT.
November	1	Mars (+0.4) lies in the midst of the Beehive cluster in Cancer. Take a look with binoculars.
	2	Full moon, 19:14 UT.
	5	Southern Taurid meteor shower peaks. Moon interferes.
		Mercury at superior conjunction (not visible).
	9	Last quarter moon, 15:57 UT.
	16	New moon, 19:14 UT.
	17	Leonid meteor shower peaks, 16h UT.
	24	First quarter moon, 21:40 UT.
December	2	Full moon, 7:31 UT.
	9	Last quarter moon, 0:14 UT.
	13	Geminid meteor shower peaks (0h UT on the 14th).
	16	New moon, 12:03 UT.
	18	Mercury (–0.5) at greatest eastern elongation (20° 18').
	21	Winter solstice, 17:48 UT.
	24	First quarter moon, 17:37 UT.
	31	Full moon, 19:14 UT. As the second full moon in a calendar month, tonight's full moon is a "blue moon."
		Partial lunar eclipse visible from Europe, Africa, Asia, and western Australia. Greatest eclipse occurs at 19:23 UT. See page 107 for details.

2010 Sky Summary

As the year begins, Jupiter and Mars are like bookends in the evening sky. Jupiter gleams in the southwest in the hours after sunset and the Red Planet rises in the southeast before Jupiter sets.

Mercury makes a fine evening appearance in early April, briefly joining the far brighter Venus, just to the south. It ends the year with a fine morning appearance and another pairing with Venus.

Venus spends nearly the entire year in the evening sky but is not particularly prominent until March, when it appears nearly due west after sunset. It twice encounters Mars near the end of its evening apparition—in early August and, less favorably, at the end of September.

Mars reaches opposition in late January, concludes its retrograde loop on March 10, then speeds east through the constellations. In mid-June it lies close to the bright star Regulus in Leo; on August 1, it's near Saturn. It has drifted near Venus by August 23.

Jupiter has moved into western Pisces, a relatively featureless zone of the sky. It becomes lost in the sun's glare in mid-February, exits the evening sky, and emerges as a prominent predawn object by the end of March. Jupiter reaches opposition in September and is the prominent evening planet for the remainder of the year.

Saturn lies amid the stars of Virgo. Its increasing distance from Earth, combined with its nearly edge-on ring system, make its opposition in late March the dimmest of the decade. Saturn is prominent throughout the spring and summer and in early August it takes part in a planetary pileup in the evening sky.

Meteor showers: Moonlight interferes with the January Quadrantid and the December Geminid showers, so the year's best bet for meteor watchers is the "old reliable" Perseid shower of August.

Eclipses: An annular eclipse, the century's longest, occurs in January and tracks through Africa, the Indian Ocean, and China. In July the moon's shadow arcs through the South Pacific during a total solar eclipse. The June partial lunar eclipse gives residents in the western two-thirds of the United States a chance to see the moon enter the Earth's umbra before it sets. At year's end an early-morning total lunar eclipse precedes the winter solstice and North America sees the entire total phase.

2010 Sky Almanac

January	3	Quadrantid meteor shower peaks, 20h UT. Moon interferes.
		Earth closest to the sun, 0.983290 AU.
	4	Mercury at inferior conjunction (not visible).
	7	Last quarter moon, 10:41 UT.
	11	Venus at superior conjunction (not visible).
	15	Annular solar eclipse—at over eleven minutes, the longest of the century—tracks through Africa, the Indian Ocean, and China. Greatest eclipse is at 7:06 UT; see page 95 for details.
		New moon, 7:13 UT.
	23	First quarter moon, 10:54 UT.
		Mercury (–0.3) gleams alone in the southeast in the hour before dawn, but Saturn (+0.7) shines high in the southwest and fiery Mars (–1.2), now just a few days from opposition, glows low in the west. See page 52.
	27	Mercury (–0.1) at greatest western elongation (24° 45').
		Mars nearest to Earth, 0.66403 AU.
	29	Mars (–1.3) at opposition. It rises in the east at sunset and is visible all night long.
	30	Full moon, 6:18 UT.
February	5	Last quarter moon, 23:50 UT.
	14	New moon, 2:53 UT.
	22	First quarter moon, 0:43 UT.
	28	Full moon, 16:38 UT.
		Jupiter in conjunction with the sun (not visible).
March	7	Last quarter moon, 15:43 UT.
	14	Mercury at superior conjunction (not visible).
	15	New moon, 21:02 UT.
	20	Vernal equinox, 17:33 UT.
	21	Saturn nearest to Earth, 8.50382 AU.
	22	Saturn (+0.5) at opposition. It rises in the east at sunset and is visible all night long.
	23	First quarter moon, 11:01 UT.
	30	Full moon, 2:26 UT.
		Mars farthest from the sun, 1.66594 AU.
April	4	Mercury (–0.5) and Venus (–3.9) closest together this evening. Look west in the hour after sunset. See page 52.
	6	Last quarter moon, 9:39 UT.

	8	Mercury (–0.1) at greatest eastern elongation (19° 21').
	14	New moon, 12:30 UT.
	21	First quarter moon, 18:20 UT.
	22	Lyrid meteor shower peaks. Moon interferes.
	28	Full moon, 12:19 UT.
		Mercury at inferior conjunction (not visible).
May	5	Eta Aquarid meteor shower peaks. Moon interferes.
	6	Last quarter moon, 4:16 UT.
	14	New moon, 1:05 UT.
	20	First quarter moon, 23:43 UT.
	26	Mercury (+0.6) at greatest western elongation (25° 08').
	27	Full moon, 23:08 UT.
June	4	Last quarter moon, 22:14 UT.
	12	New moon, 11:15 UT.
	19	First quarter moon, 4:30 UT.
	21	Summer solstice, 11:30 UT.
	26	Full moon, 11:31 UT.
		Partial lunar eclipse. The western two-thirds of the United States see the moon enter the umbra before moonset. Greatest eclipse occurs at 11:38 UT; see page 108 for details.
	28	Mercury at superior conjunction (not visible).
July	4	Last quarter moon, 14:36 UT.
	6	Earth farthest from the sun, 1.016702 AU.
	11	Total solar eclipse. The shadow of the moon arcs across the South Pacific, barely reaching the southwestern shores of Chile. Greatest eclipse occurs at 19:33 UT; see page 96 for details.
		New moon, 19:41 UT.
	18	First quarter moon, 10:11 UT.
	26	Full moon, 1:37 UT.
	28	Southern Delta Aquarid meteor shower peaks. Moon interferes.
August	1	Saturn (+1.1) and Mars (+1.5) are closest together tonight, shining in the west in the hour after sunset. Venus (–4.2) is far easier to find, below and to the right of Saturn and Mars. Closer to the horizon is Mercury (+0.2), headed toward greatest elongation. Look shortly after sunset to catch Mercury. See page 144.
	3	Last quarter moon, 4:59 UT.
	7	Mercury (+0.4) at greatest eastern elongation (27° 22').
	9	Venus (–4.3), Saturn (+1.0), and Mars (+1.5) congregate in the western sky. Look in the hour after sunset. See page 144.
	10	New moon, 3:09 UT.
	12	Perseid meteor shower peaks.
	16	First quarter moon, 18:14 UT.
	19	Venus (–4.4) and Mars (+1.5) closest in the western sky in the hour after sunset. Saturn (+1.0) lies below and to the right of the pair; to the left of them is the bright star Spica (+0.9) in Virgo. See page 122.
	20	Venus (–4.3) at greatest eastern elongation (45° 58').
	24	Full moon, 17:05 UT.
September	1	Last quarter moon, 17:22 UT.
	3	Mercury at inferior conjunction (not visible).
	8	New moon, 10:30 UT.
	15	First quarter moon, 5:50 UT.
	19	Mercury (–0.2) at greatest western elongation (17° 52').
	20	Jupiter nearest to Earth, 3.95393 AU.
	21	Jupiter (–2.9) at opposition. It rises in the east at sunset and is visible all night long.
	23	Autumnal equinox, 3:10 UT.
		Full moon, 9:17 UT.
	28	Venus (–4.5) and Mars (+1.5) are very low in the western sky thirty minutes after sunset. Binoculars help. Can you spot Antares (+0.9) above and to the left of them?
October	1	Last quarter moon, 3:53 UT.
		Saturn in conjunction with the sun (not visible).
	7	New moon, 18:45 UT.
	14	First quarter moon, 21:28 UT.

17 Mercury at superior conjunction (not visible).

21 Orionid meteor shower peaks. Moon interferes.

23 Full moon, 1:37 UT.

29 Venus at inferior conjunction (not visible).

30 Last quarter moon, 12:47 UT.

November 5 Southern Taurid meteor shower peaks.

6 New moon, 4:52 UT.

13 First quarter moon, 16:39 UT.

17 Leonid meteor shower peaks, 22h UT. Moon interferes.

21 Full moon, 17:28 UT.

28 Last quarter moon, 20:37 UT.

December 1 Mercury (–0.4) at greatest eastern elongation (21° 27').

5 New moon, 17:36 UT.

13 First quarter moon, 13:59 UT.

14 Geminid meteor shower peaks, 7h UT. Moon interferes.

20 Mercury at inferior conjunction (not visible).

21 Full moon, 8:14 UT.

Total lunar eclipse. The entire total phase can be seen from North America. Greatest eclipse occurs 8:17 UT; see page 109 for details.

Winter solstice, 23:40 UT.

28 Last quarter moon, 4:20 UT.

Moon near Saturn (+0.9) this morning.

Mercury (+0.3) closes the year with a morning apparition near Antares (+0.9), as dazzling Venus (–4.5) and Saturn look on. Look east in the hour before dawn. See page 52.

31 Moon near Venus (–4.5) this morning. Look east in the hour before dawn. The moon lies near Mercury on January 2, 2011. See page 52.

ENDIX

B Phases of the Moon, 2003–2010

In everyday discussion of lunar phases, the first visible evening crescent is often called the new moon, and what we refer to as the full moon generally covers the full-looking moon we see within a day or two of the actual time it is opposite the sun. Astronomers, not surprisingly, have come to define these terms more precisely. The phases of the moon—new, first quarter, full, and last quarter—occur when the moon's apparent angle along the ecliptic differs from the sun's by 0, 90, 180, and 270 degrees, respectively. This table gives the instants of the phases of the moon for the years 2003 through 2010. The dates and times are given as Universal Time (UT); refer to the conversion table in appendix A to convert to local time—and remember that this conversion can change the calendar date.

Lunar phase cycles: Every two years the moon shows the *preceding* lunar phase on nearly the same calendar date. For example, a full moon occurs on July 13, 2003, a first quarter moon happens on July 14, 2005, and there is a new moon on July 14, 2007. Backing through the moon's phases in this way brings the same phase to nearly the same calendar date after eight years (full moons on July 12, 1995 and July 15, 2011, for instance). And there is the famous Metonic cycle of nineteen years, or 235 synodic months, after which the phases of the moon recur on nearly the same calendar date (full moons on July 13, 1984 and July 13, 2022). See chapter 2 for more details.

Blue moon: The second full moon occurring in a given calendar month has, over the past few decades, come to be known popularly as a blue moon. Blue moons recur every 2.7 years on average, with about 37 typically occurring each century. Through the year 2010, the blue moon months are July 2004, June 2007, and December 2009. Blue moons can occur twice in years in which February, the shortest month, has no full moon; this next happens in 2018.

New Moon		First Quarter		Full Moon		Last Quarter	
2003							
Jan. 2	20:24	Jan. 10	13:15	Jan. 18	10:48	Jan. 25	08:34
Feb.1	10:49	Feb. 9	11:12	Feb. 16	23:52	Feb. 23	16:47
Mar. 3	02:36	Mar. 11	07:16	Mar. 18	10:35	Mar. 25	01:52
Apr. 1	19:19	Apr. 9	23:40	Apr. 16	19:36	Apr. 23	12:19
May 1	12:15	May 9	11:53	May 16	03:36	May 23	00:31
May 31	04:20	Jun. 7	20:28	Jun. 14	11:16	Jun. 21	14:46
Jun. 29	18:39	Jul. 7	02:33	Jul. 13	19:22	Jul. 21	07:02
Jul. 29	06:54	Aug. 5	07:28	Aug. 12	04:49	Aug. 20	00:49
Aug. 27	17:27	Sep. 3	12:35	Sep. 10	16:37	Sep. 18	19:04
Sep. 26	03:10	Oct. 2	19:10	Oct. 10	07:28	Oct. 18	12:32
Oct. 25	12:51	Nov. 1	04:25	Nov. 9	01:14	Nov. 17	04:16
Nov. 23	23:00	Nov. 30	17:17	Dec. 8	20:38	Dec. 16	17:43
Dec. 23	09:44	Dec. 30	10:04				
2004							
				Jan. 7	15:41	Jan. 15	04:47
Jan. 21	21:06	Jan. 29	06:04	Feb. 6	08:48	Feb. 13	13:41
Feb. 20	09:19	Feb. 28	03:25	Mar. 6	23:15	Mar. 13	21:02
Mar. 20	22:42	Mar. 28	23:49	Apr. 5	11:03	Apr. 12	03:47
Apr. 19	13:22	Apr. 27	17:33	May 4	20:34	May 11	11:05
May 19	04:53	May 27	07:58	Jun. 3	04:20	Jun. 9	20:04
Jun. 17	20:28	Jun. 25	19:09	Jul. 2	11:10	Jul. 9	07:35
Jul. 17	11:25	Jul. 25	03:38	Jul. 31	18:06	Aug. 7	22:03
Aug. 16	01:25	Aug. 23	10:13	Aug. 30	02:23	Sep. 6	15:12
Sep. 14	14:30	Sep. 21	15:54	Sep. 28	13:10	Oct. 6	10:13
Oct. 14	02:49	Oct. 20	21:59	Oct. 28	03:08	Nov. 5	05:54
Nov. 12	14:27	Nov. 19	05:51	Nov. 26	20:08	Dec. 5	00:53
Dec. 12	01:29	Dec. 18	16:40	Dec. 26	15:07		

New Moon		First Quarter		Full Moon		Last Quarter	
2005							
						Jan. 3	17:46
Jan. 10	12:03	Jan. 17	06:58	Jan. 25	10:32	Feb. 2	07:28
Feb. 8	22:28	Feb. 16	00:16	Feb. 24	04:54	Mar. 3	17:37
Mar. 10	09:11	Mar. 17	19:20	Mar. 25	21:00	Apr. 2	00:51
Apr. 8	20:33	Apr. 16	14:38	Apr. 24	10:07	May 1	06:25
May 8	08:46	May 16	08:58	May 23	20:19	May 30	11:49
Jun. 6	21:56	Jun. 15	01:23	Jun. 22	04:15	Jun. 28	18:25
Jul. 6	12:04	Jul. 14	15:21	Jul. 21	11:01	Jul. 28	03:21
Aug. 5	03:06	Aug. 13	02:39	Aug. 19	17:54	Aug. 26	15:20
Sep. 3	18:47	Sep. 11	11:37	Sep. 18	02:02	Sep. 25	06:42
Oct. 3	10:29	Oct. 10	19:01	Oct. 17	12:14	Oct. 25	01:18
Nov. 2	01:25	Nov. 9	01:57	Nov. 16	00:58	Nov. 23	22:12
Dec. 1	15:01	Dec. 8	09:37	Dec. 15	16:16	Dec. 23	19:37
Dec. 31	03:12						
2006							
		Jan. 6	18:57	Jan. 14	09:49	Jan. 22	15:15
Jan. 29	14:15	Feb. 5	06:29	Feb. 13	04:45	Feb. 21	07:18
Feb. 28	00:31	Mar. 6	20:16	Mar. 14	23:36	Mar. 22	19:11
Mar. 29	10:16	Apr. 5	12:01	Apr. 13	16:41	Apr. 21	03:29
Apr. 27	19:45	May 5	05:13	May 13	06:51	May 20	09:21
May 27	05:26	Jun. 3	23:06	Jun. 11	18:03	Jun. 18	14:09
Jun. 25	16:06	Jul. 3	16:37	Jul. 11	03:02	Jul. 17	19:13
Jul. 25	04:32	Aug. 2	08:46	Aug. 9	10:55	Aug. 16	01:52
Aug. 23	19:10	Aug. 31	22:57	Sep. 7	18:43	Sep. 14	11:16
Sep. 22	11:46	Sep. 30	11:04	Oct. 7	03:13	Oct. 14	00:27
Oct. 22	05:15	Oct. 29	21:26	Nov. 5	12:59	Nov. 12	17:46
Nov. 20	22:19	Nov. 28	06:29	Dec. 5	00:26	Dec. 12	14:33
Dec. 20	14:01	Dec. 27	14:48				

New Moon		First Quarter		Full Moon		Last Quarter	
2007							
				Jan. 3	13:58	Jan. 11	12:46
Jan. 19	04:01	Jan. 25	23:02	Feb. 2	05:46	Feb. 10	09:52
Feb. 17	16:15	Feb. 24	07:56	Mar. 3	23:18	Mar. 12	03:55
Mar. 19	02:43	Mar. 25	18:17	Apr. 2	17:16	Apr. 10	18:05
Apr. 17	11:37	Apr. 24	06:36	May 2	10:10	May 10	04:28
May 16	19:28	May 23	21:03	Jun. 1	01:04	Jun. 8	11:44
Jun. 15	03:14	Jun. 22	13:16	Jun. 30	13:49	Jul. 7	16:54
Jul. 14	12:04	Jul. 22	06:29	Jul. 30	00:48	Aug. 5	21:21
Aug. 12	23:03	Aug. 20	23:55	Aug. 28	10:36	Sep. 4	02:33
Sep. 11	12:45	Sep. 19	16:49	Sep. 26	19:46	Oct. 3	10:07
Oct. 11	05:02	Oct. 19	08:33	Oct. 26	04:53	Nov. 1	21:20
Nov. 9	23:04	Nov. 17	22:33	Nov. 24	14:31	Dec. 1	12:45
Dec. 9	17:41	Dec. 17	10:18	Dec. 24	01:16	Dec. 31	07:52
2008							
Jan. 8	11:38	Jan. 15	19:46	Jan. 22	13:35	Jan. 30	05:03
Feb. 7	03:45	Feb. 14	03:33	Feb. 21	03:31	Feb. 29	02:19
Mar. 7	17:14	Mar. 14	10:46	Mar. 21	18:40	Mar. 29	21:48
Apr. 6	03:56	Apr. 12	18:32	Apr. 20	10:26	Apr. 28	14:12
May 5	12:19	May 12	03:47	May 20	02:12	May 28	02:57
Jun. 3	19:23	Jun. 10	15:04	Jun. 18	17:31	Jun. 26	12:11
Jul. 3	02:19	Jul. 10	04:35	Jul. 18	08:00	Jul. 25	18:43
Aug. 1	10:13	Aug. 8	20:21	Aug. 16	21:18	Aug. 23	23:51
Aug. 30	19:59	Sep. 7	14:05	Sep. 15	09:14	Sep. 22	05:05
Sep. 29	08:13	Oct. 7	09:05	Oct. 14	20:03	Oct. 21	11:56
Oct. 28	23:15	Nov. 6	04:04	Nov. 13	06:19	Nov. 19	21:32
Nov. 27	16:56	Dec. 5	21:26	Dec. 12	16:38	Dec. 19	10:31
Dec. 27	12:23						

New Moon		First Quarter		Full Moon		Last Quarter	
2009							
		Jan. 4	11:57	Jan. 11	03:27	Jan. 18	02:47
Jan. 26	07:56	Feb. 2	23:13	Feb. 9	14:50	Feb. 16	21:38
Feb. 25	01:36	Mar. 4	07:46	Mar. 11	02:38	Mar. 18	17:48
Mar. 26	16:06	Apr. 2	14:34	Apr. 9	14:56	Apr. 17	13:37
Apr. 25	03:23	May 1	20:45	May 9	04:02	May 17	07:27
May 24	12:12	May 31	03:23	Jun. 7	18:12	Jun. 15	22:15
Jun. 22	19:36	Jun. 29	11:29	Jul. 7	09:23	Jul. 15	09:54
Jul. 22	02:35	Jul. 28	22:00	Aug. 6	00:55	Aug. 13	18:56
Aug. 20	10:02	Aug. 27	11:42	Sep. 4	16:03	Sep. 12	02:16
Sep. 18	18:44	Sep. 26	04:50	Oct. 4	06:10	Oct. 11	08:56
Oct. 18	05:33	Oct. 26	00:42	Nov. 2	19:14	Nov. 9	15:57
Nov. 16	19:14	Nov. 24	21:40	Dec. 2	07:31	Dec. 9	00:14
Dec. 16	12:03	Dec. 24	17:37	Dec. 31	19:14		
2010							
						Jan. 7	10:41
Jan. 15	07:13	Jan. 23	10:54	Jan. 30	06:18	Feb. 5	23:50
Feb. 14	02:53	Feb. 22	00:43	Feb. 28	16:38	Mar. 7	15:43
Mar. 15	21:02	Mar. 23	11:01	Mar. 30	02:26	Apr. 6	09:39
Apr. 14	12:30	Apr. 21	18:20	Apr. 28	12:19	May 6	04:16
May 14	01:05	May 20	23:43	May 27	23:08	Jun. 4	22:14
Jun. 12	11:15	Jun. 19	04:30	Jun. 26	11:31	Jul. 4	14:36
Jul. 11	19:41	Jul. 18	10:11	Jul. 26	01:37	Aug. 3	04:59
Aug. 10	03:09	Aug. 16	18:14	Aug. 24	17:05	Sep. 1	17:22
Sep. 8	10:30	Sep. 15	05:50	Sep. 23	09:17	Oct. 1	03:53
Oct. 7	18:45	Oct. 14	21:28	Oct. 23	01:37	Oct. 30	12:47
Nov. 6	04:52	Nov. 13	16:39	Nov. 21	17:28	Nov. 28	20:37
Dec. 5	17:36	Dec. 13	13:59	Dec. 21	08:14	Dec. 28	04:20

ENDIX

C

Greatest Elongations and Oppositions, 2003–2010

The following tables give the Universal Time dates and angles for the greatest elongations of Mercury and Venus and opposition dates, constellations, magnitudes, and distances for Mars, Jupiter, and Saturn.

Greatest Elongations of Mercury

Year	West		East	
2003	February 4	25.4°	April 16	19.8°
	June 3	24.4°	August 14	27.4°
	September 26	17.9°	December 9	20.9°
2004	January 17	23.9°	March 29	18.9°
	May 14	26.9°	July 27	27.1°
	September 9	17.9°	November 21	22.2°
	December 29	22.4°	—	
2005	—		March 12	18.3°
	April 26	27.2°	July 9	26.3°
	August 23	18.4°	November 3	23.5°
	December 12	21.1°	—	
2006	—		February 24	18.1°
	April 8	27.8°	June 20	24.9°
	August 7	19.2°	October 17	24.8°
	November 25	19.9°	—	
2007	—		February 7	18.2°
	March 22	27.7°	June 2	23.4°
	July 20	20.3°	September 29	26.0°
	November 8	19.0°	—	
2008	—		January 2	18.7°
	March 3	27.2°	May 14	21.8°
	July 1	21.8°	September 11	26.9°
	October 22	18.3°		
2009	—		January 4	19.4°
	February 13	26.1°	April 26	20.4°
	June 13	23.5°	August 24	27.4°
	October 6	18.0°	December 18	20.4°
2010	January 27	24.8°	April 8	19.4°
	May 26	25.1°	August 7	27.4°
	September 19	17.9°	December 1	21.5°

Greatest Elongations of Venus

Year	West		East	
2003	January 11	47.0°	—	
2004	August 17	45.8°	March 29	46.0°
2005	—		November 3	47.1°
2006	March 25	46.5°	—	
2007	October 28	46.5°	June 9	45.4°
2009	June 5	45.8°	January 14	47.1°
2010	—		August 20	46.0°

Oppositions of Mars, Jupiter, and Saturn

Year	Planet	Opposition Date (UT)	Constellation	Mag.	Nearest to Earth (UT)	Distance (AU)*
2003	Mars	August 28	Aquarius	–2.9	August 27	0.37274
	Jupiter	February 2	Cancer	–2.6	February 2	4.32714
	Saturn	December 31	Gemini	–0.5	January 1	8.05013
2004	Mars	—	—	—	—	—
	Jupiter	March 4	Leo	–2.5	March 4	4.42567
	Saturn	—	—	—	—	—
2005	Mars	November 7	Aries	–2.3	October 30	0.46405
	Jupiter	April 3	Virgo	–2.5	April 4	4.45665
	Saturn	January 13	Gemini	–0.4	January 14	8.07562
2006	Mars	—	—	—	—	—
	Jupiter	May 4	Libra	–2.4	May 6	4.41271
	Saturn	January 27	Cancer	–0.3	January 28	8.12683
2007	Mars	December 24	Gemini	–1.6	December 19	0.58933
	Jupiter	June 5	Ophiuchus	–2.6	June 7	4.30442
	Saturn	February 10	Leo	–0.1	February 10	8.20037
2008	Mars	—	—	—	—	—
	Jupiter	July 9	Sagittarius	–2.7	July 10	4.16106
	Saturn	February 24	Leo	+0.2	February 24	8.29141
2009	Mars	—	—	—	—	—
	Jupiter	August 14	Capricornus	–2.9	August 15	4.02783
	Saturn	March 8	Leo	+0.5	March 9	8.39445
2010	Mars	January 29	Cancer	–1.3	January 27	0.66403
	Jupiter	September 21	Pisces	–2.9	September 20	3.95393
	Saturn	March 22	Virgo	+0.5	March 21	8.50382

* 1 AU = 92.96 million miles or 149.60 million kilometers.

ENDIX

D

Recommended World Wide Web Sites

The following table contains astronomy- and space-related Web sites we have found useful, interesting, and fun. All sites listed were operational as of spring 2002.

General Astronomy and Space News

Abrams Planetarium Sky Calendar	http://www.pa.msu.edu/abrams/SkyCalendar
Astronomy magazine	http://www.astronomy.com/home.asp
Sky & Telescope magazine	http://www.skypub.com
Space.com	http://www.space.com
Heavens-Above	http://www.heavens-above.com

Aurora and Space Weather

Canopus—Real-Time Auroral Oval	http://www.dan.sp-agency.ca/www/rtoval.htm
NASA's Spaceweather.com	http://www.spaceweather.com

Eclipse Information

Fred Espenak's Eclipse Home Page	http://sunearth.gsfc.nasa.gov/eclipse/eclipse.html
Eclipse Photography	http://www.mreclipse.com

Space Missions and Planetary Science

Windows to the Universe	http://www.windows.ucar.edu
Views of the Solar System	http://www.solarviews.com/eng/homepage.htm
Planetary Science Research Discoveries	http://www.psrd.hawaii.edu

Earth

IMAGE	http://pluto.space.swri.edu/IMAGE
Polar	http://istp.gsfc.nasa.gov/istp/polar

Moon

Clementine	http://nssdc.gsfc.nasa.gov/planetary/clementine.html
Lunar-A	http://www.isas.ac.jp/e/enterp/missions/lunar-a/cont.html
Lunar Prospector	http://lunar.arc.nasa.gov
Selene	http://www.isas.ac.jp/e/enterp/missions/selene/cont.html

Mercury

BepiColombo	http://www.estec.esa.nl/spdwww/future/colombo/mercury-colombo.html
MESSENGER	http://messenger.jhuapl.edu

Venus

Magellan	http://www.jpl.nasa.gov/magellan

Mars

2003 Mars Exploration Rovers	http://mars.jpl.nasa.gov/missions/future/2003.html
Mars Express	http://mars.jpl.nasa.gov/missions/future/express.html
Mars Global Surveyor	http://mars.jpl.nasa.gov/mgs
2001 Mars Odyssey	http://mars.jpl.nasa.gov/odyssey
Mars Pathfinder	http://mpfwww.jpl.nasa.gov/default.html
Nozomi	http://www.isas.ac.jp/e/enterp/missions/nozomi/cont.html

Asteroids

MUSES-C	http://www.isas.ac.jp/e/enterp/missions/muses-c/cont.html
NEAR	http://near.jhuapl.edu

Jupiter and Saturn

Cassini	http://www.jpl.nasa.gov/cassini
Galileo	http://www.jpl.nasa.gov/galileo
Voyager	http://vraptor.jpl.nasa.gov/voyager/voyager.html

Comets

Deep Impact	http://deepimpact.umd.edu
Deep Space 1	http://nmp.jpl.nasa.gov/ds1
Rosetta	http://sci.esa.int/home/rosetta/index.cfm
Stardust	http://stardust.jpl.nasa.gov

Space Missions and Planetary Science, continued

Space Shuttle, International Space Station, Space Telescopes

Hubble Space Telescope	http://hubble.nasa.gov
NASA Human Spaceflight	http://spaceflight.nasa.gov
Next Generation Space Telescope	http://ngst.gsfc.nasa.gov

Sun

SOHO	http://sohowww.nascom.nasa.gov
TRACE	http://helios.gsfc.nasa.gov/trace_mosaic.html
Yohkoh	http://www.isas.ac.jp/e/enterp/missions/yohkoh/index.html

Organizations

Astronomical League	http://www.astroleague.org
Astronomical Society of the Pacific	http://www.astrosociety.org
International Dark Sky Association	http://www.darksky.org
International Meteor Organization	http://www.imo.net
Students for the Exploration and Development of Space	http://www.seds.org

Further Research

Comet Observation Home Page	http://encke.jpl.nasa.gov
Extrasolar Planets	http://exoplanets.org
Google Search Engine	http://www.google.com
Jet Propulsion Laboratory	http://www.jpl.nasa.gov
JPL's Horizons Ephemeris System	http://ssd.jpl.nasa.gov/horizons.html
NASA's ADS Abstract Service	http://adswww.harvard.edu/ads_abstracts.html
National Space Science Data Center	http://nssdc.gsfc.nasa.gov
Project Pluto (Guide 7.0)	http://www.projectpluto.com
Shinobu Takesako's EmapWin	http://www2c.biglobe.ne.jp/~takesako
United States Naval Observatory	http://www.usno.navy.mil

Glossary

Altitude: The angular distance, usually measured in degrees, of an object above the horizon.

Aphelion: The point at which an object in orbit around the sun is farthest from it.

Apogee: The point at which an object in orbit around the Earth is farthest from it.

Apollo: U.S. space program that included six piloted lunar landings between 1969 and 1972.

Apparition: An appearance; in astronomy, the period of observation of a planet, asteroid or comet.

Asterism: A noticeable pattern of stars, such as the Big Dipper or the Pleiades, that is part of a larger constellation.

Asteroid: A mostly rocky body less than 620 miles (1,000 kilometers) across that orbits the sun; more accurately called a minor planet. Most asteroids orbit the sun between Mars and Jupiter. Asteroids are the source of most meteorites (see *meteor*).

Astrology: An ancient system of beliefs that attempts to explain or predict human actions by the position and interaction of the sun, moon, and planets. It is not a science.

Astronomical twilight: The time when the sun is twelve to eighteen degrees below the horizon.

Astronomical unit: The average Earth-to-sun distance, equal to 92.96 million miles or 149.60 million kilometers, abbreviated AU.

Aurora: Regions of glowing gas in the upper atmosphere whose molecules are stimulated to emit light by collisions with streams of electrons. Known popularly as the northern lights (or southern lights).

Axis: An imaginary line passing through the center of a body, such as a planet, around which that body spins.

Azimuth: The angular distance, usually measured in degrees, of an object's direction along the horizon starting from north (0° or 360°) through east (90°), south (180°), and west (270°).

Binary star: A system containing two or more stars in orbit about one another.

Blue moon: A popular term denoting the second full moon to occur in a calendar month.

Bolide: A fireball that breaks up during its passage through the atmosphere.

Cassini: U.S. mission to Saturn, launched in 1997 and, following successful flybys of Venus (1998, 1999), Earth (1999), and Jupiter (2001), due to arrive at Saturn in 2004. It will drop the *Huygens* atmospheric probe into the atmosphere of Saturn's largest moon, Titan, in early 2005.

Chaos: In its scientific usage, the irregular motion or dynamics of physical systems. Chaotic systems show two defining characteristics—periods of order interspersed with randomness, and evolution that is extremely sensitive to initial conditions. Chaotic behavior is endemic to most, if not all, physical systems, including the atmosphere and solar system.

Clementine: A global mapping mission to the moon launched in 1994 by the U.S. Department of Defense, with science support from NASA.

Comet: A small body made of ice and rock that orbits the sun, usually much less than 62 miles (100 kilometers) across. As it nears the sun, it usually brightens and develops a gaseous halo, or coma, and a tail of gas and dust. Most comets travel in very elongated orbits that keep them far from the inner solar system.

Conjunction: The alignment of two celestial bodies that occurs when they share similar angles from the sun as measured along the ecliptic. This is also roughly when the bodies appear closest together in the sky. **Inferior conjunction:** That point in the motions of the planets Mercury and Venus at which they pass between Earth and the sun. **Superior conjunction:** That point in the motions of Mercury and Venus at which they appear in line with the sun on the far side of their orbits as viewed from Earth. **With the sun:** That point in the motions of the superior planets at which they appear in line with the sun as viewed from Earth.

Constellation: One of eighty-eight regions into which astronomers divide the sky, based mainly on earlier divisions formed by historical and mythological figures of Greek and Roman tradition.

Double star: Two stars that appear close to one another. They can be physically associated (a binary) or simply appear together from the point of view of an observer on Earth.

Earthshine: A blue-gray light seen during the moon's crescent phases on the portion not illuminated by the sun. The sunlit portion of the Earth is the source.

Eclipse, lunar: An event during which the moon enters into the shadow of the Earth as seen from some locations on Earth. **Penumbral lunar eclipse:** A lunar eclipse in which the moon remains entirely in the penumbral shadow of the Earth. **Partial lunar eclipse:** A lunar eclipse in which the moon partially enters the umbra of the Earth's shadow. **Total lunar eclipse:** A lunar eclipse in which the moon passes completely into the umbra of the Earth's shadow.

Eclipse, solar: An event during which the moon passes in front of the sun as seen from some locations on Earth. **Partial solar eclipse:** A solar eclipse in which the umbral shadow of the moon completely misses the Earth, but the penumbral shadow does not. At locations outside of the central track of total, annular, and hybrid eclipses, the eclipse is commonly said to be partial since maximum possible obscuration of the sun never occurs. **Total solar eclipse:** A solar eclipse in which the moon entirely covers the sun. **Annular eclipse:** A solar eclipse in which the moon covers all but a thin ring, or annulus, of the sun. **Hybrid eclipse:** A solar eclipse that would otherwise be classified as annular but for a small region along the eclipse's central track that experiences a short total eclipse.

Ecliptic: The apparent yearly path of the sun through the sky. Since this apparent motion is actually a reflection of Earth's movement, the ecliptic also marks the plane of Earth's orbit. The moon and planets also roughly follow this path.

Electrophonic sounds: Sound produced through the conversion of radio energy at audible wavelengths by the vibration of objects near the observer, such as hair or eyeglasses. Meteors, lightning, and the aurora can produce sound in this way.

Equinox: The date of the year at which the sun's rays illuminate half the Earth, from pole to pole; neither the north pole nor the south pole is angled into the sun. This phenomenon occurs on two days of the year, near March 21 and September 23. On these dates, the hours of daylight equal the hours of night (hence the name, meaning "equal night"). The March equinox is considered the first day of spring in the northern hemisphere; the September equinox the first day of fall.

Farside: The side of the moon always turned away from Earth.

Fireball: An extremely bright meteor, usually one brighter than magnitude –4.

Galaxy: A vast collection of billions of stars, gas, and dust held together by the gravity of its members. The galaxy in which the sun resides is called the Milky Way.

Galileo: U.S. space mission to study Jupiter's atmosphere, moons, and magnetosphere. The *Galileo* spacecraft arrived at Jupiter in 1995, dropped a probe into the planet's atmosphere, monitored jovian weather, and undertook a series of close encounters with the four major moons—Io, Europa, Ganymede, and Callisto—over the next six years, returning a total of over 14,000 images. *Galileo* is being sent into the jovian atmosphere in 2003.

Gas giants: The planets Jupiter, Saturn, Uranus, and Neptune.

Inferior conjunction: See *conjunction.*

Latitude: The angular distance north or south from the Earth's equator measured in degrees. The equator is at zero degrees and the poles are at ninety degrees north and ninety degrees south.

Light-year: The distance traveled through space by a beam of light in one year. Light travels at 186,282 miles (299,792 kilometers) per second, so a light-year is 5.88 trillion miles (9.5 trillion kilometers), or 63,240 times Earth's distance from the sun.

Longitude: The angular distance east or west between the meridian of a particular place on Earth and that of Greenwich, England, expressed in either degrees or time.

Luna: One of two successful series of Soviet lunar missions. There were twenty-four missions to the moon in the Luna series. (The other series, Zond, had five lunar missions.) The first image of the farside of the moon was taken by the Soviet *Luna 3* spacecraft in 1959.

Lunar Prospector: U.S. mission to the moon launched on January 6, 1998. Its instruments were designed to provide global maps and data sets of the moon's composition and magnetic and gravity fields from a low polar orbit. The mission lasted eighteen months and ended July 31, 1999, with a controlled crash landing into a crater at the moon's south pole.

Magnitude: A measure of the relative brightness of stars and other celestial objects: the brighter the object, the lower its assigned magnitude. This logarithmic scale is based on the ancient practice of noting that the brightest stars in the sky were of "first importance" or "first magnitude," the next brightest being "second magnitude," and so on. In 1854 Norman Pogson formalized this scale and defined a difference of five magnitudes to be exactly a factor of 100 in brightness. The faintest naked-eye magnitude visible from a dark site is +6.5, Mars at its brightest is –2.9, Venus at its brightest is –4.7, and the full moon is –12.5.

Mariner 9: U.S. space mission to Mars, launched in 1971, that achieved global imaging of the surface, including the first detailed views of the martian volcanoes, Valles Marineris, the polar caps, and the satellites Phobos and Deimos. The spacecraft gathered data on atmospheric composition, density, pressure, and temperature, as well as the surface composition, gravity, and topography of Mars.

Mars Global Surveyor: U.S. mission to Mars launched in 1996. Its main instruments include a camera, laser altimeter, thermal emission spectrometer, and magnetometer. Image resolution is several times better than that of any of those taken by the *Viking Orbiter* cameras, enabling features just a few meters across to be seen. An extended mission phase began in 2001.

Mars Odyssey: U.S. mission to Mars launched in 2001. Its main instruments include gamma-ray and neutron spectrometers, a neutron detector, and a thermal imaging camera. In February 2002, early results indicated large amounts of hydrogen, implying the presence of frozen water in the martian soil.

Mars Pathfinder: U.S. mission that on July 4, 1997, landed successfully on Mars. A small rover named *Sojourner* explored the area beyond the lander.

Meteor: The streak of light caused by a solid body in orbit about the sun (a meteoroid) passing through the atmosphere; also called a shooting star. A meteorite is a meteoroid that strikes the surface of a planet or moon.

Meteor shower: The appearance of many meteors that seem to radiate from the same region of the sky. They occur when the Earth passes through the dusty debris near a comet's orbit.

Milky Way: A faint band of light across the sky, composed of vast numbers of stars too faint to see individually. Also, the name of the galaxy in which the sun resides.

Moon: A natural satellite orbiting a planet. Also, the name of Earth's natural satellite.

Nautical twilight: The time when the sun is six to twelve degrees below the horizon. Before sunrise, the period in which the sky begins to brighten noticeably; after sunset, the period in which the sky is still noticeably bright.

Near Earth Asteroid Rendezvous (NEAR): U.S. space mission launched on February 17, 1996. Placed into orbit around asteroid 433 Eros on February 14, 2000, *NEAR* returned data on the body's bulk properties, composition, mineralogy, morphology, internal mass distribution, and magnetic field. On February 12, 2001, it became the first spacecraft to land on an asteroid.

Nearside: The side of the moon that always faces Earth.

Nebula: A cloud of gas and dust, sometimes glowing from the light of nearby stars, sometimes a dark patch that blocks starlight. New stars are born within a nebula.

Nova: A star that suddenly erupts, greatly increasing in brightness.

Nucleus: Of a comet, the solid ice-rock mixture at the center of a comet's gaseous head and tail. Of a spiral galaxy, the dense central portion made of older, redder stars. (Plural: nuclei.)

Opposition: The point in a planet's orbit at which it appears opposite the sun in the sky. A planet at opposition is visible all night long. Because Mercury and Venus orbit closer to the sun than Earth, they never reach opposition.

Perigee: The point at which an object in orbit around the Earth is nearest to it.

Perihelion: The point at which an object in orbit around the sun is nearest to it.

Phases: The cycle of varying shape in the sunlit portion of a planet or moon. The moon, Venus, and Mercury all show phases as seen from Earth.

Photosphere: The visible surface of the sun.

Planet: A body of substantial size held in orbit by the gravity of a star. A planet shines by reflecting the star's light.

Radar: Radio signals transmitted to and bounced back from an object. It stands for *RA*dio *D*etection *A*nd *R*anging.

Radiant: The point in the sky from which a meteor shower seems to appear.

Radiation: Energy transmitted through space as waves or particles.

Retrograde motion: The apparent backward (westward) loop in a planet's motion across the sky. All planets display retrograde motion, but that of Mars is most striking.

Satellite: A natural or artificial body in orbit around a planet.

Scintillation: A tremulous effect of starlight—twinkling—caused by the light's passage through our turbulent atmosphere. Planets usually don't exhibit this effect.

Sidereal period: The time taken by a planet to complete one revolution around the sun (or for the moon to complete an orbit around the Earth) as measured by reference to the background stars.

Solar wind: A stream of electrically charged particles (mainly ionized hydrogen) moving outward from the sun with velocities in the range of 180 to 310 miles (300 to 500 kilometers) per second.

Solstice: The date of the year at which either the Earth's north or south pole is angled most directly toward the sun. This occurs on two days of the year, near June 21 and December 21. The June solstice, the longest day of the year in the northern hemisphere, is considered the first day of summer there; the sun then makes its most northerly arc through the sky. The December solstice, the shortest day of the year in the northern hemisphere, marks the start of northern winter; the sun then makes its most southerly arc through the sky.

Star: A hot, glowing sphere of gas, usually one that emits energy from nuclear reactions in its core. The sun is a star.

Sunspot: An area of magnetic disturbance on the sun. It is cooler than the surrounding area and, consequently, appears darker.

Superior conjunction: See *conjunction.*

Supernova: An enormous stellar explosion that increases the brightness of a star by a factor of more than 100,000. Although the star itself is destroyed, a small portion of its central core may survive (as a neutron star).

Synodic period: The average time between successive returns of a planet or the moon to the same apparent position relative to the sun—for example, new moon to new moon, or opposition to opposition.

Terminator: The edge of the sunlit portion of the moon or planets; the line between day and night.

Terawatt: An amount of power equal to 1×10^{12} watts.

Terrestrial planets: Mercury, Venus, Earth, and Mars.

Tides: Periodic changes in the shape of a planet, moon, or star caused by the gravity of a body near it.

Train: A dimly visible path left in the sky by the passage of a meteor.

Transit: The passage of a planet across the face of the sun. From Earth, only the transits of Mercury and Venus can be viewed.

Twinkling: See *scintillation.*

Variable star: A star that exhibits significant brightness changes.

Viking: U.S. mission to Mars, composed of two spacecraft, launched in 1975. *Viking 1* and *Viking 2* both consisted of an orbiter and a lander. Primary mission objectives were to obtain high-resolution images of the Martian surface (55,000 were returned by the orbiters, 1,400 from the landers); characterize the structure and composition of the atmosphere and surface; and search for evidence of life.

Voyager: U.S. mission consisting of two spacecraft launched in 1977 to explore Jupiter, Saturn, their moons, rings, and magnetic environments. *Voyager 2* went on to explore Uranus and Neptune as well. Each spacecraft took two years to reach Jupiter. The last image was taken in 1989 and now both spacecraft are headed out of the solar system.

White dwarf: A collapsed object formed from a star that has exhausted its nuclear fuel. The sun will one day become a white dwarf.

Zenith: The point directly overhead, ninety degrees above the horizon.

Zodiac: The band of twelve constellations straddling the ecliptic.

Bibliography

General References

Ashbrook, Joseph. *The Astronomical Scrapbook: Skywatchers, Pioneers, and Seekers in Astronomy.* Cambridge, Massachusetts: Sky Publishing Corp., 1984.

Aveni, Anthony F. *Conversing with the Planets.* New York: Kodanasha America, Inc., 1994.

———. *Skywatchers.* Austin, Texas: University of Texas Press, 2001.

Drake, Stillman. *Discoveries and Opinions of Galileo.* Garden City, New York: Doubleday and Co., Inc., 1957.

Evans, James. *The History and Practice of Ancient Astronomy.* Oxford, England: Oxford University Press, 1998.

Evelyn-White, Hugh G., ed. and trans. *Hesiod, the Homeric Hymns, and Homerica.* Cambridge, Massachusetts: Harvard University Press, 1914.

Ferris, Timothy. *Coming of Age in the Milky Way.* New York: Doubleday, 1989.

Hartmann, William K. *Astronomy: The Cosmic Journey,* fourth edition. Belmont, California: Wadsworth Publishing Co., 1989.

Healy, John E., trans. *Pliny the Elder: Natural History, a Selection.* London: Penguin Books, 1991.

Hodson, F. R., ed. *The Place of Astronomy in the Ancient World.* London: Oxford University Press, 1974.

Homer. *The Iliad.* Robert Fagles, trans. New York: Viking, 1990.

Koestler, Arthur. *The Sleepwalkers: A History of Man's Changing Vision of the Universe.* New York: Grosset and Dunlap, 1959.

Krupp, E. C. *Beyond the Blue Horizon: Myths and Legends of the Sun, Moon, Stars, and Planets.* New York: Harper and Row, 1991.

———. *Echoes of the Ancient Skies: The Astronomy of Lost Civilizations.* New York: Harper and Row, 1983.

Maran, Stephen P. *The Astronomy and Astrophysics Encyclopedia.* New York: Van Nostrand Reinhold, 1992.

Meeus, Jean. *Astronomical Tables of the Sun, Moon, and Planets.* Richmond, Virginia: Willmann-Bell, 1995.

O'Neil, W. M. *Early Astronomy from Babylonia to Copernicus.* Sydney: Sydney University Press, 1986.

Peterson, Ivars. *Newton's Clock: Chaos in the Solar System.* New York: W. H. Freeman and Co., 1993.

Richards, E. G. *Mapping Time: The Calendar and Its History.* New York: Oxford University Press, 1998.

Schele, Linda, and David Friedel. *A Forest of Kings: The Untold Story of the Ancient Maya.* New York: Quill, 1990.

Seneca. *Natural Questions.* Thomas Corcoran, trans. Cambridge, Massachusetts: Harvard University Press, 1971.

Shapiro, Max S., and Rhonda A. Hendricks. *A Dictionary of Mythologies.* London: Paladin Books, 1981.

Walker, Christopher, ed. *Astronomy before the Telescope.* New York: St. Martin's Press, 1996.

Weissman, Paul R., Lucy-Ann McFadden, and Torrence V. Johnson, eds. *Encyclopedia of the Solar System.* San Diego, California: Academic Press, 1999.

Chapter 1: The Meaning of the Sky

Cinzano, P., F. Falchi, and C. D. Elvidge. "The First World Atlas of the Artificial Night Sky Brightness." *Monthly Notices of the Royal Astronomical Society,* 328: 689–707 (2001). See also http://www.inquinamentoluminoso.it/worldatlas/pages/fig1.htm.

"Czech Republic Enacts World's First National Light Pollution Law," March 18, 2002, http://www.space.com/spacewatch/skies_czech_020318.html.

De Robertis, Michael, and Paul Delaney. "A Second Survey of the Attitudes of University Students to Astrology and Astronomy." *Journal of the Royal Astronomical Society of Canada,* 94: 112–122 (2000).

Newport, Frank, and Maura Strausberg. "Poll Analyses, June 8, 2001: Americans' Belief in Psychic and Paranormal Phenomena Is Up over Last Decade," http://www.gallup.com/poll/releases/pr010608.asp.

Pankenier, David W. "The Mandate of Heaven." *Archaeology,* March/April 1998, 26–34.

Schaefer, Bradley E. "Conjunctions That Changed the World." *Sky and Telescope,* May 2000, 28–34.

Taylor, Humphrey. Harris Poll nos. 41 (Aug. 12, 1998) and 62 (Sept. 13, 2000), http://www.harrisinteractive.com.

Ziegler, Philip. *The Black Death.* London: The Folio Society, 1997.

Chapter 2: Moon Dance

Abell, George O. "Moon Madness." In *Science and the Paranormal: Probing the Existence of the Supernatural,* George O. Abell and Barry Singer, eds. New York: Charles Scribner's Sons, 1981.

Barker, E. S., et al. "Results of the Observational Campaign Carried Out during the Impact of Lunar Prospector into a Permanently Shadowed Crater near the South Pole of the Moon" (abstract). American Astronomical Society Division of Planetary Sciences, meeting #31, paper 59.03, Dec. 1999.

Buratti, Bonnie J., et al. "Lunar Transient Phenomena: What Do the Clementine Images Reveal?" *Icarus,* 146: 98–117 (2000).

Canup, Robin M., and Erik Asphaug. "Origin of the Moon in a Giant Impact near the Earth's Formation." *Nature,* 412: 708–712 (2001). See also http://www.swri.org/press/impact.htm.

Dollfus, Audouin. "Langrenus: Transient Illuminations on the Moon." *Icarus,* 146: 430–443 (2000).

Egbert, G. D., and R. D. Ray. "Significant Dissipation of Tidal Energy in the Deep Ocean Inferred from Satellite Altimeter Data," *Nature,* 405: 775–77 (2000).

French, Bevan M. *The Moon Book: Exploring the Mysteries of the Lunar World.* New York: Penguin Books, 1977.

Goldstein, David B., et al. "Impacting Lunar Prospector in a Cold Trap to Detect Water Ice." *Geophysical Research Letters,* 26: 1653–1656 (1999).

Goode, P. R., et al. "Earthshine Observations of the Earth's Reflectance." *Geophysical Research Letters,* 28: 1671–1674 (2001).

Kaufman, Lloyd, and James H. Kaufman. "Explaining the Moon Illusion." *Proceedings of the National Academy of Sciences,* 97: 500–505 (2000), http://www.pnas.org/cgi/content/full/97/1/500.

Kelly, I. W., James Rotton, and Roger Culver. "The Moon Was Full and Nothing Happened." In *The Outer Edge,* Joe Nickell, Barry Karr, and Tom Genoni, eds. Amherst, New York: Prometheus, 1996.

Korotev, Randy L. "Lunar Meteorites," May 2002, http://epsc.wustl.edu/admin/resources/moon_meteorites.html.

Laskar, J., F. Joutel, and P. Robutel. "Stabilization of the Earth's Obliquity by the Moon." *Nature,* 361: 615–617 (1993).

Lawson, S. L., et al. "Results from the Lunar Prospector Alpha Particle Spectrometer: Detection of Radon-222 over Craters Aristarchus and Kepler" (abstract). American Astronomical Society Division of Planetary Sciences, meeting #33, paper 4.05, Nov. 2001.

Nozette, S., et al. "The Clementine Bistatic Radar Experiment." *Science,* 274: 1495–1498 (1996), http://www.sciencemag.org/cgi/content/full/274/5292/1495.

Palmer, John D. "The Rhythmic Lives of Crabs." *Bioscience,* 40: 352–357 (1990).

———. "Time, Tide and the Living Clocks of Marine Organisms." *American Scientist,* 84: 570–578 (1996).

Palmer, John D., and Judith E. Goodenough. "Mysterious Monthly Rhythms." *Natural History,* 87: 64–69 (1978).

Spudis, Paul. *The Once and Future Moon.* Washington: Smithsonian Institution Press, 1996. See also http://www.lpi.usra.edu/lpi/abspudis.html.

Stooke, Philip J. "Neolithic Lunar Maps at Knowth and Baltinglass, Ireland." *Journal for the History of Astronomy,* 15: 39–55 (1994). See also http://publish.uwo.ca/~pjstooke/knowth.htm.

Vasavada, Ashwin R., David A. Paige, and Stephen E. Wood. "Near-Surface Temperatures on Mercury and the Moon and the Stability of Polar Ice Deposits." *Icarus,* 141: 179–193 (1999).

Vidale, John E., et al. "Absence of Earthquake Correlation with Earth Tides: An Indication of High Preseismic Fault Stress Rate." *Journal of Geophysical Research,* 103: 24567–24572 (1998).

Ward, William R., and Robin M. Canup. "Origin of the Moon's Orbital Inclination from Resonant Disk Interactions." *Nature,* 403: 741–743 (2000). See also http://www.swri.org/9what/releases/incline.htm.

Whitaker, Ewen A. *Mapping and Naming the Moon.* New York: Cambridge University Press, 1999.

Chapter 3: Morning Stars, Evening Stars: Venus and Mercury

Bray, R. J. "Australia and the Transit of Venus." *Proceedings of the Astronomical Society of Australia,* 4: 114–120 (1980).

Fernie, J. Donald. "Transits, Travels and Tribulations, III." *American Scientist,* 86: 123–126 (1998).

Maor, Eli. *June 8, 2004: Venus in Transit.* Princeton, New Jersey: Princeton University Press, 2000.

Rhodes, Richard. *The Making of the Atomic Bomb.* New York: Simon and Schuster, 1986.

Schaefer, B. E. "The Transit of Venus and the Notorious Black Drop" (abstract). American Astronomical Society, meeting #197, paper 01.03 (2000).

"That Experimental Star," *Boston Evening Transcript,* Thursday, April 15, 1897, 4.

Wolkenstein, Diane, and Samuel Noah Kramer. *Inanna, Queen of Heaven and Earth: Her Stories and Hymns from Sumer.* New York: Harper and Row, 1983.

Chapter 4: Eclipses of the Sun and Moon

Brunier, Serge, and Jean-Pierre Luminet. *Glorious Eclipses: Their Past, Present and Future.* Storm Dunlop, trans. New York: Cambridge University Press, 2000.

Clark, Ronald W. *Einstein: The Life and Times.* New York: World Publishing Co., 1971.

Conot, Robert. *Thomas A. Edison: A Streak of Luck.* New York: Da Capo Press, 1979.

Cooper, James Fenimore. "The Eclipse." *Putnam's Monthly Magazine,* 21 (n.s. 4), Sept. 1869, 352–359, http://etext.lib.virginia.edu/toc/modeng/public/CooEcli.html.

Dyer, Frank Lewis, and Thomas Commerford Martin. *Edison, His Life and Inventions, vol. 1.* New York: Harper & Brothers Publishers, 1910, http://etext.lib.virginia.edu/toc/modeng/public/Dye1Edi.html.

Eddy, John A. "The Great Eclipse of 1878." *Sky and Telescope,* June 1973, 340–346.

Espenak, Fred. *Fifty Year Canon of Lunar Eclipses, 1986–2035.* NASA Reference Publication 1216, March 1989. Cambridge, Massachusetts: Sky Publishing Corp., 1989.

———. *Fifty Year Canon of Solar Eclipses, 1986–2035.* NASA Reference Publication 1178 Revised, July 1987. Cambridge, Massachusetts: Sky Publishing Corp., 1987. See also http://sunearth.gsfc.nasa.gov/eclipse/eclipse.html.

———. "Six Millennium Catalog of Lunar Eclipses," August 2002, http://sunearth.gsfc.nasa.gov/eclipse/LEcat/LEcatalog.html.

———. "Five Millennium Catalog of Solar Eclipses," May 2002, http://sunearth.gsfc.nasa.gov/eclipse/SEcat/SEcatalog.html.

———. "Solar Eclipses of Saros 124," May 2002, http://sunearth.gsfc.nasa.gov/eclipse/SEsaros/SEsaros124.html.

———. "Solar Eclipses of Saros 136," May 2002, http://sunearth.gsfc.nasa.gov/eclipse/SEsaros/SEsaros136.html.

Fernie, J. Donald. "Eclipse Vicissitudes: Thomas Edison and the Chickens." *American Scientist,* 88: 120 (2000).

French, A. P., ed. *Einstein: A Centenary Volume.* Cambridge, Massachusetts: Harvard University Press, 1979.

Harrington, Philip S. *Eclipse! The What, Where, When, Why & How Guide to Watching Solar and Lunar Eclipses.* New York: John Wiley & Sons, Inc., 1997.

Littman, Mark, Ken Wilcox, and Fred Espenak. *Totality: Eclipses of the Sun.* New York: Oxford University Press, 1999.

Meeus, Jean. "The Frequency of Total and Annular Solar Eclipses for a Given Place." *Journal of the British Astronomical Association,* 92: 124–126 (1982).

———. "Nearly Zenithal Central Solar Eclipses." *Journal of the British Astronomical Association,* 100: 227–228 (1990).

Kendall, Phebe Mitchell, ed. *Maria Mitchell: Life, Letters and Journals.* Boston: Lee and Shepard, 1896.

Peterson, Scott. "Mania in the Path of an Eclipse; Some Nations Make Aug. 11 a Holiday. Iran Issues 600,000 Eclipse-Safe Glasses." *Christian Science Monitor,* Aug. 11, 1999, 1.

Schaefer, Bradley E. "Lunar Eclipses That Changed the World." *Sky and Telescope,* December 1992, 639–642.

———. "Solar Eclipses That Changed the World." *Sky and Telescope,* May 1994, 36–39.

Stephenson, Richard F. *Historical Eclipses and Earth's Rotation.* Cambridge, England: Cambridge University Press, 1997.

Zirker, J. B. *Total Eclipses of the Sun.* New York: Van Nostrand Reinhold Co., Inc., 1984.

Chapter 5: Mars: The Red Wanderer

Bricker, Harvey M., Anthony Aveni, and Victoria R. Bricker. "Ancient Maya Documents Concerning the Movements of Mars." *Proceedings of the National Academy of Sciences,* 98: 2107–2110 (2001).

Carlson, Darren K. "Poll Analyses, February 27, 2001: Life on Mars?" http://www.gallup.com/poll/releases/pr010227b.asp.

Carr, Michael H. *The Surface of Mars.* New Haven, Connecticut: Yale University Press, 1981.

Dick, Steven J. *Life on Other Worlds: The 20th-Century Extraterrestrial Life Debate.* Cambridge, England: Cambridge University Press, 1998.

Dreyer, J. L. E. *A History of Astronomy from Thales to Kepler.* New York: Dover Publications, Inc., 1953.

Hoyt, William Graves. *Lowell and Mars.* Tucson, Arizona: University of Arizona Press, 1976.

Korotev, Randy L. "Martian Meteorites," May 2002, http://epsc.wustl.edu/admin/resources/mars_meteorites.html.

Lowell, Percival. *Mars.* Boston: Houghton Mifflin Co., 1895.

McKay, David S., et al. "Search for Past Life on Mars: Possible Relic Biogenic Activity in Martian Meteorite ALH 84001." *Science,* 273: 924–930 (1996).

Moore, Martha T. "Mars Mania Invades Earth." *Florida Today,* July 9, 1997, http://www.flatoday.com/space/explore/stories/1997b/070997e.htm.

Touma, Jihad, and Jack Wisdom. "The Chaotic Obliquity of Mars." *Science,* 259: 1294–1297 (1993).

Williamson, Ray A. *Living the Sky: The Cosmos of the American Indian.* Boston: Houghton Mifflin Co., 1984.

Chapter 6: Distant Giants: Jupiter and Saturn

Burrows, William E. *Exploring Space: Voyages in the Solar System and Beyond.* New York: Random House, Inc., 1990.

Central Bureau for Astronomical Telegrams. "List of Jovian Trojans," May 2002, http://cfa-www.harvard.edu/iau/lists/JupiterTrojans.html.

———. "List of Martian Trojans," May 2002, http://cfa-www.harvard.edu/iau/lists/MarsTrojans.html.

Christou, A. "The Trojans of Ceres and Vesta." American Astronomical Society Division of Planetary Sciences, 2001 meeting, abstract #52.05.

Esposito, Larry W. "Understanding Planetary Rings." *Annual Reviews of Earth and Planetary Sciences,* 21: 487–523 (1993).

Hammel, Heidi. "How Astronomers Use *The Astronomical Almanac.*" In *Proceedings of the Nautical Almanac Office Sesquicentennial Symposium,* Alan D. Fiala and Steven J. Dick, eds. Washington: U.S. Naval Observatory, 1999.

Griffith, Caitlan A., Joseph L. Hall, and Thomas R. Geballe. "Detection of Daily Clouds on Titan." *Science,* 290: 509–513 (2000).

Khurana, K. K., and M. G. Kivelson. "Potential for a Subsurface Ocean on Europa and Its Suitability for Life." American Geophysical Union, fall meeting 2001, abstract #P21C-06.

Kohlhase, Charles, ed. *The Voyager Neptune Travel Guide* (Publication 89-24). Pasadena, California: Jet Propulsion Laboratory, 1989.

Molnar, Michael R. *The Star of Bethlehem: The Legacy of the Magi.* Piscataway, New Jersey: Rutgers University Press, 1999. See also http://www.eclipse.net/~molnar.

Morrison, David, and Jane Samz. *Voyage to Jupiter* (SP-439). Washington: National Aeronautics and Space Administration, 1980.

Murray, Bruce. *Journey into Space: The First Three Decades of Space Exploration.* New York: W. W. Norton and Company, Inc., 1989.

Rogers, John. "The Comet Collision with Jupiter. I. What Happened." *Journal of the British Astronomical Association,* 106: 69–80 (1996).

Scholl, H., and F. Marzari. "On the Stability of Saturn, Uranus, and Neptune Trojans." American Astronomical Society Division of Planetary Sciences, 2001 meeting, abstract #52.06.

Chapter 7: An Introduction to the Starry Sky

Bauer, Brian S., and David S. P. Dearborn. *Astronomy and Empire in the Ancient Andes: The Cultural Origins of Inca Sky Watching.* Austin, Texas: University of Texas Press, 1995.

Henry, Todd J. "The One Hundred Nearest Star Systems," May 17, 2002, http://www.chara.gsu.edu/RECONS/TOP100.htm.

Rappenglück, Michael. "Paleolithic Timekeepers Looking at the Golden Gate of the Ecliptic: The Lunar Cycle and the Pleiades in the Cave of La-Tête-Du-Lion (Ardèche, France)—21,000 BP." *Earth, Moon and Planets,* 85–86: 391–404 (2001). See also http://www.infis.org.

Schafer, Edward H. *Facing the Void: T'ang Approaches to the Stars.* Berkeley, California: University of California Press, 1977.

Toulman, Stephen, and June Goodfield. *The Fabric of the Heavens: The Development of Astronomy and Dynamics.* New York: Harper and Row, 1961.

Chapter 8: Meteors and Meteor Showers

"Aftermath of a Meteor Shower." *Science News,* 144: 217 (October 2, 1993).

Brown, Peter. "The Leonid Meteor Shower: Historical Visual Observations." *Icarus,* 138: 287–308 (1999).

Caswell, Doug. "*OLYMPUS* and the 1993 Perseids: Lessons for the Leonids." http://sci2.estec.esa.nl/leonids/leonids98/OLYMPUS_and_the_1993_Perseids/index.htm.

Cook, Allan F. "A Working List of Meteor Streams." *Evolutionary and Physical Properties of Meteor Streams,* NASA SP-319, 183–191 (1973).

Dodd, Robert T. *Thunderstones and Shooting Stars: The Meaning of Meteorites.* Cambridge, Massachusetts: Harvard University Press, 1986.

Federation of American Scientists Space Policy Project. "World Space Guide: 1993—Piloted Space Missions (Russia)," http://www.fas.org/spp/guide/russia/piloted/1993.htm.

Giorgini, J. D., et al. "Asteroid 1950 DA's Encounter with Earth in 2880: Physical Limits of Collision Probability Prediction." *Science,* 296: 132–136 (2002).

Halliday, Ian, Alan T. Blackwell, and Arthur A. Griffin. "The Frequency of Meteorite Falls on the Earth." *Science,* 223: 1405–1407 (1984).

Keay, Colin S. L. "Anomalous Sounds from the Entry of Meteor Fireballs." *Science,* 210: 11–15 (1980). See also http://users.hunterlink.net.au/~ddcsk.

Kronk, Gary. *Meteor Showers: A Descriptive Catalog.* Hillside, New Jersey: Enslow Publishers, 1988. See also http://comets.amsmeteors.org.

Mason, John. "The Leonid Meteors and Comet 55P/Tempel-Tuttle." *Journal of the British Astronomical Association,* 105: 219–235 (1995).

Minor Planet Center. "PHA Close Approaches to the Earth," May 2002, http://cfa-www.harvard.edu/iau/lists/PHACloseApp.html.

Phillips, Tony. "Space Station Meteor Shower," May 17, 2002, http://science.nasa.gov/headlines/y2002/17may_issmeteors.htm?list517796.

Sanderson, Richard. "The Night It Rained Fire." *Griffith Observer,* November 1984, 2–10.

Upton, Edward K. L. "The Leonids Were Dead, They Said." *Griffith Observer,* May 1977, 3–9.

Yeomans, Donald K. "Giacobinid Meteor Shower Circumstances (1926–2031)," March 2002. Private communication.

Zgrablić, Goran, et al. "Instrumental Recording of Electrophonic Sounds from Leonid Fireballs." *Journal of Geophysical Research*, 107, no. 0, 10.102912001JA000310, 2002. See also http://gefs.ccs.uky.edu.

Chapter 9: Unpredictable Sky Events

Aschwanden, Markus J., Arthur I. Poland, and Douglas M. Rabin. "The New Solar Corona." *Annual Reviews of Astronomy and Astrophysics*, 39: 175–210 (2001).

Baker, D. N., et al. "Pager Satellite Failure May Have Been Related to Disturbed Space Environment," http://www.agu.org/sci_soc/articles/eisbaker.html.

Bortle, John E. "The Bright Comet Chronicles," May 2002, http://encke.jpl.nasa.gov/bright_comet.html.

Brekke, A., and A. Egeland. *The Northern Light: From Mythology to Space Research.* Berlin: Springer-Verlag, 1983.

Central Bureau for Astronomical Telegrams. "Closest Approaches to the Earth by Comets," May 2002, http://cfa-www.harvard.edu/iau/lists/ClosestComets.html.

———. "Lists of Supernovae," May 2002, http://cfa-www.harvard.edu/iau/lists/Supernovae.html.

Central Bureau for Astronomical Telegrams and the *International Comet Quarterly.* "Brightest Comets Seen since 1935," May 2002, http://cfa-www.harvard.edu/icq/brightest.html.

Clark, David H., and F. Richard Stephenson. *The Historical Supernovae.* Oxford, England: Pergamon Press, 1977.

Davis, Neil. *The Aurora Watcher's Handbook.* Fairbanks, Alaska: University of Alaska Press, 1992.

Fleck, B., et al. "Four Years of *SOHO* Discoveries: Some Highlights." *ESA Bulletin,* No. 102, May 2000, 69–86.

Green, D. A. "A Catalogue of Galactic Supernova Remnants," December 2001, http://www.mrao.cam.ac.uk/surveys/snrs.

Helfand, David. "Bang: The Supernova of 1987." *Physics Today,* August 1987, 25–32.

Keay, Colin S. L. "C. A. Chant and the Mystery of Auroral Sounds." *Journal of the Royal Astronomical Society of Canada,* 84: 373–382 (1990).

Marsden, Brian G. "The Sungrazing Comet Group. II." *Astronomical Journal,* 98: 2306–2321 (1989).

Marsden, Brian G., and D. W. E. Green. May 2002. Private communication regarding C/2001 Q4.

Marsden, Brian G., and Gareth V. Williams. *Catalogue of Cometary Orbits, 2001,* fourteenth edition. Cambridge, Massachusetts: Smithsonian Astrophysical Observatory, 2001.

Odenwald, Sten. *The Twenty-Third Cycle: Learning to Live with a Stormy Star.* New York: Columbia University Press, 2001.

Reddy, Francis. "Supernovae: Still a Challenge." *Sky and Telescope,* December 1983, 485–490.

Schechner, Sara J. *Comets, Popular Culture, and the Birth of Modern Cosmology.* Princeton, New Jersey: Princeton University Press, 1997.

Stephenson, F. Richard. "Guest Stars Are Always Welcome." *Natural History,* August 1987, 72–76.

Stephenson, Richard, and Kevin Yau. "Oriental Tales of Halley's Comet." *New Scientist,* September 27, 1984, 31–32.

Yeomans, Donald K. *Comets: A Chronological History of Observation, Science, Myth, and Folklore.* New York: John Wiley and Sons, 1991.

———. "Great Comets in History," May 2002, http://ssd.jpl.nasa.gov/great_comets.html.

Recommended Observing Guides

Ottewell, Guy. *The Astronomical Calendar.* Greenville, South Carolina: Furman University (annual).

Victor, Robert C., and Patti Toivonen. *Sky Calendar.* East Lansing, Michigan: Abrams Planetarium, Michigan State University (monthly).

Index

Photos are indicated by page numbers given in ***bold.*** *Color plate numbers are preceded by* ***pl.***

SKY LOG

SKY LOG

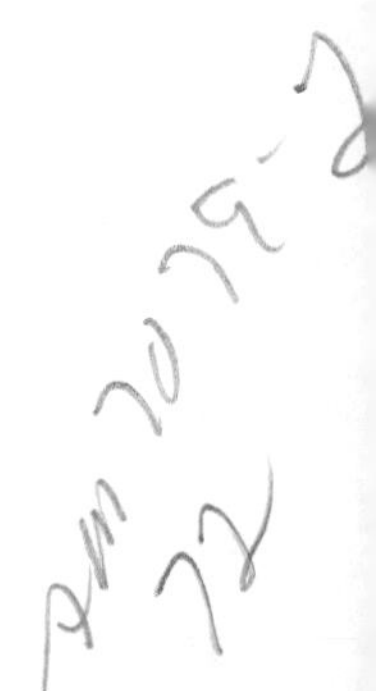

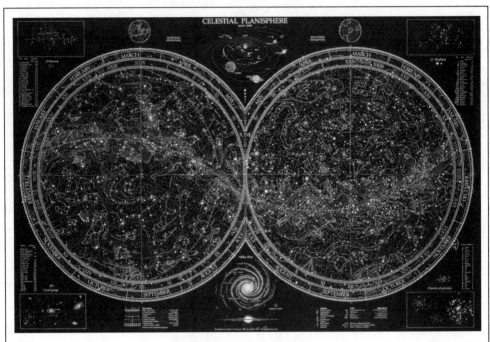